A PLACE

of

TRUTH

An Autobiography

JULIAN W. KING

For Gail, my wife of 67 years,
without who I would not have survived.

A PLACE of TRUTH

How can I face the coming day
when loneliness is on the way?
It's sickly fragrance through the night
captures my soul up in fright.

In fright of living life alone.

Oh! many times have I escaped,
only to be again endraped
by lonely days and lonely nights
by lonely wrongs and lonely rights.

Oh surely someplace there must be
a "Place of Truth" for all like me.

A lovely love filled resting place
where I can wash away my face.

JULIAN WITHROW KING

INTRODUCTION

Having been on this earth for seventy-one years I thought perhaps the story of my life might have something to offer to my children and grandchildren, and possibly to an even wider audience. Thus, during the lull in various cruise ship activities on a twenty-one day trip through the Panama Canal I began this attempt at the following true story. A story that might provide inspiration to others who start out in life somewhat disadvantaged. A tale of determination to achieve more than circumstances would seem to allow. A story of how a less than perfect human being can, despite a myriad of life's roadblocks, still move forward toward a relatively happy and successful life. Each year dozens if not hundreds of books are published describing how famous politicians, sports personalities, movie stars and even notorious criminals rose from obscurity to the heights of their professions.

I do not fall into any of those categories.

It may be true that some, who read books written by famous personalities, will use the authors stunning examples of success as motivation for their own lives. Unfortunately, only a very few will accomplish anything remotely similar. Many readers will admire and enjoy the success of these famous authors yet still have doubts that they can rise that far above their own personal circumstances. Most won't even try. I hope my story will provide inspiration for a much broader spectrum of society. We can't all be sports heroes or superstars but we can all live a life of fulfillment. I do not seek sympathy for what the reader may interpret as a hard start in life. Others have faced far greater adversities and survived to accomplish great things. Still I hope anyone reading this book will see that it is possible to use the lessons learned from adverse circumstances one encounters along the path of life to their advantage in the future. It is my sincere wish that anyone reading this book will understand how determination and the extremely important concept of personal responsibility can lead to a happier life. The words that follow describe a slow, deliberate, eighty-seven year journey, beginning in 1935, from poverty and debilitating insecurity to a life of wealth and happiness.

The author.

PREFACE

How often does a person stop and reflect on who they are and how they came to be the unique and particular person that they are? As a young teenager I occasionally thought about such things. I was aware that I had faults and weaknesses for which of course my parents deserved all the blame. Everything I did wrong was due to them and the way I was raised. Everything I did that was right or good was assuredly to my credit and my ability to overcome a poor upbringing. I gave less and less thought to these matters as the demands of an older and busier life took hold. With the passing of time I slowly began to realize there were faults in the illogical thinking of my early years. Still I have difficulty fully understanding some of things that I do, some of the attitudes I take and my occasional extreme reactions to some events in life. Thus, what experiences and which people influenced me in whatever way to become the cynical, sarcastic, explosive, determined and occasionally crazy S. O. B. that I am, intrigues me to this day.

For several years during occasional quiet moments, these thoughts crept into my consciousness. As I grew older I began thinking more seriously about these things. That inevitably led to wondering about the people and events that played a significant part of my life. They too must have been influenced by experiences they had and the and people they knew. Did that not shape them into who they were as well?

As I thought about the lives of my mother, father, grandparents, uncles, aunts, relatives, family friends and others, I realized how little I knew of their lives prior to my time with them. I know my grandmother was born in St. Andrews, Scotland, my grandfather was from Cornwall, Ontario, Canada and my mother and her brothers were born in Montreal Canada. However, I do not know where my father was born. I don't know how my parents met or how my grandparents met or how, when and why my grandmother immigrated to Canada and eventually wound up in Detroit, Michigan. Basically, I thought of them stereo typically. I did not see them as people with their own weaknesses, strengths, loves, cares and challenges but rather as Mom, Daddy, Grandma, Grandpa and so on. When later in life I began to acquire a great interest in learning about them and possibly understanding them as real people, it was too late. Sadly, anyone who could tell me anything at all about such things is gone and I will never know anything more than I do now, about the great and small happenings of their lives. This then brought to mind my children and especially the children of my children and I thought that they too might only see me as their father or grandfather and not as a real person. That they too, at some point in their lives, would be left wondering and speculating about what their father's, or grandfather's life was like. To a great extent, they would know very little of my life before they were born. Would I remain and be remembered only as a father or grandfather and not as a human being with real cares and problems. From time to time I've related a few stories to one or more of my children but a great many remain untold. Therefore, as I begin this story at the age of seventy-one I have great concern. I wonder what they might think if I reveal the real story of my life. I mean the real story, the good, the not so good and even things they might consider bad. Therefore, I begin to write this memoir with mixed feelings wondering if I should reveal all or hold some things back.

Will they understand?

The following is my story. My recollection of a life's most memorable events. I can only hope to be judged on the totality of my weaknesses and strengths.

CONTENTS

Part Two

PART ONE

Chapter 1

WHAT LITTLE I KNOW
FROM OTHERS

My father was Julian Withrow King. I know very little about him and I know next to nothing about my father's side of the family. My life centered around my mother's side of the family. Grandma was born Wilhemina Gourley in St Andrews, Scotland in 1890. Grandpa (I called him PaPa) was born Charles Edward Cummings in Cornwall, Ontario in 1892. How they met, I know not. I know my mother was born Mary Eva Mildred Cummings in 1915 in Montreal, Canada. Her older brother Murray and her younger brother William were born there as well. My life with them took place in Detroit, Michigan. At some point in time my grandmother had to have first immigrated to Canada and later to the United States. On my mother's birth certificate it lists her father's occupation as a bricklayer. As long as I knew him, he worked for Detroit Edison (an electric utility). I believe he was a lineman. Electricity was a necessary commodity so grandpa's job was secure unlike so many that lived through the "Great Depression". As was the custom in those times grandma was a stay at home housewife. The times I spent with my grandparents were the happiest and most secure times of a chaotic childhood.

All my life I have been called Skip. I remember as a child I asked how I got that nickname. According to my mother, my grandfather had a strong dislike for my father and would not approve of their marriage so in 1932 at the age of 17 she eloped with my father. My father had family in St. Louis. Missouri and so they moved to St. Louis where I was born Julian Withrow King Jr. in 1935 at St. Luke's hospital. On my birth certificate, my father's occupation is listed as clerk for the Great Atlantic & Pacific Tea Company (A&P). He was 22 years of age at that time. According to my mother, my father was a no count, habitual gambler and squandered his paycheck every week on various forms of gambling. (You will note "according to my mother" appears frequently throughout this story. I would learn later in my life that things were not always as she said.)

According to her, his desire for any kind of gambling was so strong that he would even hang around schoolyards and pitch pennies against the wall with the school kids (the one who tosses his penny closest to the wall wins all the other pennies.) Things got so bad between them that they divorced 2 months after I was born. There was little opportunity for women in those days, especially a woman with a baby to raise, so my mother returned to Detroit. With great trepidation, she arrived unexpected at her parent's door and knocked. My grandfather answered the door. Although a word had not passed between them for more than 3 years, he softened a bit when he looked down, saw me in her arms, and asked....

"What did you name him?"

When she told him she named me Julian Withrow King Jr. (after my father), he said,

"I would have named him after a dog before I gave him that name"

Grandpa liked a good joke and as it happened the neighbor's dog was named Skippy. Grandpa refused to call me Julian, Jules, Julie or any other possible variation of my real name so he began calling me Skippy or Skip. It stuck.

I have only vague memories of my very earliest years. Much of what I relate here is based on stories my mother told me when I grew older. However, as I listened to some of the stories she told me I was able to vaguely recall that some of the events had really happened. Other things she told me I am unsure of. There is a photo of me sitting on the front fender of a car. I appear to be about 4 years old. I was told by my mother that the car belonged to the notorious mobster and hit man, Harry Millman. The story as confirmed by my grandparents goes like this….

At that point in time my grandparents were managers of an apartment house where a member of Detroit's "Purple Gang" resided. For some reason Millman had come to Detroit for a meeting with the "Purple Gang" and his car was parked on the street outside the apartment house. Being aware whose car it was my mother quickly sat me on the fender of Millman's car and took a snapshot of me sitting there. I still have this photo. Possibly, this story is even true.

I remember that as a very young child I would occasionally have spells of high energy running through the house with a towel tied around my neck (for a cape) pretending to fly through the air like Superman or Captain Marvel. Suddenly I was collapsed in a chair unable to get up, barely able to lift my arms or turn my head. This condition is with me still today (though I no longer wear a cape.) I didn't know what was wrong nor did my mother or grandparents. I remember being examined and tested in doctor's offices and at Detroit's Children's Hospital repeatedly when these attacks occurred. One of the doctors diagnosed my condition as a mild case of polio, it was called infantile paralysis in those days and there was a great scare across the country at that time regarding this disease. Then President, Franklin D. Roosevelt was a victim of this ailment. They gave me some kind of treatment for this but the attacks of weakness continued along with even more tests and examinations. Another doctor concluded I had been born with rheumatic fever, that I had a weak heart and must be kept from any strenuous activities. That diagnosis, although incorrect, would keep me from participation in school sports for years to come. Much later at the age of thirty-two my condition would be diagnosed correctly.

Music became a solace for me. Sometimes, even as a young child, when I was nowhere to be found my folks would find that I had crawled behind the living room couch singing a favorite song to myself. At a very young age, I had an uncanny knack of remembering the words and melody to a song after hearing it only once or twice. I remember that I always had a favorite song to sing to myself.

Chapter 2

EARLY REMEMBERENCE

Here, I tell of the earliest memories that come back to me unaided by others. I believe that when we try to delve back to our earliest memories we may not come up with a totally accurate recollection. In my case, I certainly hope that is true. What I believe to be my earliest memory may only be a dream and not an actual occurrence yet it is very unsettling to me and might be more than the reader can accept at this stage. Therefore, I choose to reveal it later in this story.

What I relate here comes from fleeting memories. While I can describe certain events that stand out in my mind, I cannot necessarily tell you the details of why I was where I was or other details that both you and I might like to know. I think I must have been about 4 or 5 years old. I remember living on Montgomery St. near Lawton Ave. in Detroit, Michigan for a while. It is a two story brick flat with a huge cement porch. There were a dozen or so cement steps to climb to get up to the porch. Two feet six inch high brick walls enclose the porch. I can barely see over the top of them & when I do the tops of the white and purple lilac bushes block my view of the street. This is home to my grandmother & grandfather (Papa) and their two sons Murray (the oldest) and William (the youngest). My mother was the middle child. I am unsure how long I was there or if my mother is there with me at the time.

Grandma is a short stocky woman (4 foot 9 inches and over 200 pounds) with crystal blue eyes and a touch of gray in her auburn hair. She has a vibrant personality and a quick Scottish wit. When she speaks you can discern a hint of her Scottish brogue which becomes much stronger when she is around any of her former countrymen. Her maiden name was

Wilhemina Gourlay. She claimed to be Presbyterian but I can't remember her ever going to church. My Papa is a tall man. His hair is receedingly gray. I cannot remember the color of his eyes. He has big belly that slopes gently down from his chest. He likes his beer. His name was Charles Edward Cummings. He was an Irish catholic. Grandma calls him Charlie most of the time and he calls her Minnie or sometimes Mina. I also remember hearing Grandma occasionally call grandpa by what sounded like Jock, however she might have been saying Jacques. I have no idea why or how she came to use that name for him but it seemed to me she always had an affectionate tone when calling him by that name. I cannot recall any hint of an accent in my Papa's voice.

My uncle Murray is a big man (six foot and 200 plus pounds) with thinning dark brown hair and hazel eyes. There was something slightly off about his eyes. They weren't crossed but seemed not perfectly aligned. He is built and looks a lot like his father. He works as a bartender at the Detroit Athletic Club. It is 1939 and the economy is struggling but the D.A.C. caters to the well to do & they tip well so Uncle Murray always seems to have a few pennies to give me for candy & gum at the corner candy store. Uncle Murray is unmarried and a rather quiet & reserved man of 25 years.

My uncle William is tall too but with a more lanky build. He is a handsome 20 year old with blue eyes and a full shock of red hair, which earned him the nickname "Red". He has a barely noticeable small circular scar on his right cheek which was a result of running and falling down with a peashooter in his mouth when he was a little boy. He is engaged to Pauline Murray. They are making plans for a soon to be wedding. It is exciting to be around Uncle Red. He is always telling jokes or playing tricks on Grandma. Sometimes he would come in the door unnoticed, sneak up behind Grandma and surprise her with a quick jab in the ribs. I can still see her reaction as she would let out a yelp, turn to see who it was and exclaim …

"Oh! It's you. I'll give you a bat in the eyebrow. You horses hang down!".

(Grandma had several unique phrases and sayings that I never heard from anyone else.)

I do not remember Uncle Red's and Aunt Polly's actual wedding ceremony but I think it was in a Catholic church as my mother and her brothers were raised Catholic. However I can still see the wedding party coming through the front door of the flat on Montgomery Street, the men in their tuxedos, the bridesmaids in gowns, and Aunt Polly in a beautiful white wedding dress. All were happy and laughing, shaking Uncle Red's hand and kissing Aunt Polly on her cheek while I watched from my vantage point between the railing posts at the top of the stairs. My grandma's best friend was there with her husband. Her name was Marie Heimstedt. She was also my godmother and I was to call her Aunt Rie and her husband Uncle Eddie. Aunt Rie was a large rotund woman of with a bowl shaped face and deep raspy voice. She was very fond of me and always had a present or treat of some kind to give me whenever she came to visit. She never failed to bring or send me something for my birthday and Christmas. She was very demonstrative of her affection for me and would often grab me up onto her lap to lavish hugs and kisses. For some reason I was a little afraid of her perhaps because the open display of affection was not the norm for my family. Uncle Eddie was a small skinny man. He wore glasses and a hearing aid as he was almost deaf. He shouted rather than spoke and appeared, to me, to be very cranky all the time. I made it a point to avoid him at all costs. Much later in life as my own hearing declined I would gain some insight into the reasons for his disposition. Aunt Eva and Uncle Harry were there as well. I am unsure whether they were really my relatives. It was a tradition that children called close friends of the family, aunt or uncle. They had come from Canada where they lived. When they spoke I detected a Scottish brogue. Aunt Rie noticed me looking down from the top of the stairs and called out for me to come down whereupon she picked me up and gave me a big hug. Grandma quickly hurried me back upstairs and reminded me that I was not allowed downstairs where the party was going on.

"Children do not belong at a party for grown ups."

I remember summertime in Detroit and, we (like most of our neighbors in those days), spent many evenings out on the front porch. Papa reads the newspaper and he and Uncle Murray are often drinking beer. Grandma makes ice tea for the rest of us and we listen to Walter Winchell on the radio. Sitting on the wide limestone ledge of the front porch I wave hello at neighbors passing by. I am with my Grandma and Grandpa for a while.

I am happy here.

For the most part my grandparents were not prone to outward demonstrations of affection. Greetings with arms wide open, kissing and hugging were reserved for very special occasions. They had lived through some very severe times in the "old country", as they called it, and through America's great depression as well. While the experiences of their lives had imparted them with a conservative nature, they were also fun loving and enjoyed the company of friends and relatives. Rather than the perpetual "I love you" we hear espoused nowadays they demonstrated their love through actions and responsibility. These traits rubbed off on my uncles but not on my mother.

I was privileged to go with my grandparents on a long train trip to Oshawa Ontario, Canada to meet my great-grandparents. Oshawa was a town east of Toronto where my great-grandpa was a shoemaker. His name was Louie. These great-grandparents were my grandfather's mother and stepfather. I was quite young but I remember helping Great Grandpa Louie dig potatoes out of his garden in the backyard. He would turn up & loosen the soil with his hoe. Then I would dig in with my hands and become very excited with each potato I uncovered. It was like finding a buried treasure. I also spent a little time in his shoe repair shop that was attached to their house. I was fascinated to watch, what seemed to my young eyes, a myriad of belts and pulleys running swiftly as he ground down the edges of the new leather heels and soles he had sewn or glued on, to fit the form of the shoe. I recall I liked the smell of leather dust and glue in the air.

One evening, while there, I heard a bell jingling out a musical sound. I excitedly anticipated the "Good Humor Man" coming down the street selling ice cream. I was surprised to see something I had never seen before and have not seen since. A man in a white uniform, driving what looked like an ice cream truck, was ringing his bell to notify he was in the neighborhood. But he wasn't selling ice cream he was selling "chips" out of a truck specially equipped for making and selling what I knew of as french fries. Neighbors were pouring into the street to purchase the tasty treats. Papa gave me a dime to get a small cone shaped paper carton full of "chips". The driver put vinegar on the "chips". They were hot, tangy and delicious. To this day, I still put vinegar on my french fries.

I may have been 5 years old and still with my grandparents when I was sent to Mars. I am not sure if I was attending kindergarten, some kind of preschool or a day care facility but Mars was the name of a school in the same complex as Northwestern High School in Detroit. I made the walk of several blocks from our flat on Montgomery St. to Mars school by myself. The sidewalks were full of other kids walking skipping & frolicking their way to school. It was a simpler time then without all the safety concerns of today's modern world. Or so we thought. One day while walking back home from Mars school I was hopping along from one sidewalk square to the next trying not to step on a crack. "Step on a crack, you'll break your mothers back" was a game we played. Along the way I encountered some kids gathered by the side of a house. They were bending down and looking at something. I was curious and went to see what they were looking at. It was an open lid to a coal bin shaft. At that time, nearly everyone heated their homes with coal. Every house had a coal bin in the basement where the furnace was located. There was an opening from the basement to the outside of the house so that the coal delivery trucks could pull up close enough to run a chute from the back of the truck to the coal bin shaft then lift the gate on the back of the delivery truck so that the coal could slide down the chute and into the coal bin. I squeezed between a couple kids and looked through the opening down into the coal bin. Suddenly (I am not sure how, maybe I was pushed or maybe I tripped) but I was falling through the opening and found myself inside the bin on top of a mound of coal sliding toward the bottom. I looked up at the opening which was now closed (shutting out the light). It was pitch black. As my eyes grew accustomed to the dark I could barely make out the doorway that led from the bin to the rest of the basement. I tried to open it but it was somehow secured from the other side. Next I thought maybe I could climb up on the pile of coal and scramble back out through the opening I had just fell from but as I tried to climb to the top of this mountain of coal it kept sliding down and away under my feet causing me to fall back down to the bottom of the pile. I could not reach the top. Panic set in! I began to cry. I pounded and pounded on the coal bin door screaming and sobbing all the while. No one seemed to hear me. I was terrified thinking I would die in this dark damp terrifying dungeon. I cried & cried until eventually exhausted I feel asleep on the pile of coal. After what seemed an eternity a woman came and opened the door and I was freed. She guided me up the stairs to the door and I ran all the way home crying. Grandma saw me with my entire body and clothes all covered in coal dust.

"What in God's green earth have you been into now?" She asked.

I sobbed all the way through the story....

"Perhaps you'll learn to keep your bloody nose out of places it doesn't belong" "Now go get out of those clothes and hop in the tub you bloody tramp"

As a former resident of the British Isles, she retained many of the colloquialisms of her homeland and "bloody" seemed to be her favorite adjective. Grandma was strict with me most of the time but I knew she loved me. After the bath I went to my room, crawled on the bed and cried myself to sleep still frightened from the experience. I awakened to Grandma calling me. Papa had come home from work and it was suppertime. We were having Scottish meat pies for supper (my favorite). Much later in life I would discover with dismay the ingredients that went into those delicious Scottish meat pies. Sitting at the table with my chin between my hands and my elbows resting on the table I would hear Grandma say….

"Elbows off the table ladie."

After I devoured my meat pie and jumped out of my chair to leave the table I'd hear....

"Mind your manners Skippy"

"Sorry".... I replied"

"Yes Skippy you're excused".

I had forgotten to ask to be excused from the table. Teaching proper manners was considered important in the raising of children during those days. I would also learn to never interrupt an adult, never walk in front of someone without saying "excuse me" and always say "Please and Thank You" when requesting something. Most importantly I was often reminded… "Children are to be seen and not heard!"

Later that evening I found my Papa in his usual spot sitting on a chair in his bedroom smoking a cigarette and enjoying a beer while he looked out the window to see what was going on in the neighborhood. I spent many evenings there with him sitting on his lap watching the neighbors come and go. We would tell each other funny stories that we made up as we went along. We watched across the street as Mrs. Clark an attractive neighbor lady walked through a gate into her yard and up the walk to her door. She opened it and went inside. For some reason I felt disappointed that I could no longer see what she was doing after she went inside. I was curious to know!

"Well what did you do today my little man.?"

Papa listened as I sniffled my way through the saga of the coal bin. He picked me up and sat me on his knee and asked....

"Did I ever tell you about the little boy whose mother gave him a nickel to buy a loaf of pumpernickel bread"?

"Tell me again Papa"

"There was this little boy whose mother gave him a nickel to buy a loaf of pumpernickel bread but on his way to the store he dropped the nickel and it rolled away and fell down through the sewer grate"

At my young age, this story made me laugh. I always found this story funny even though Papa would tell me this same basic story over and over whenever we watched the neighbors from his bedroom window. There were several variations on how the "Little boy" lost the nickel. Sometimes I would tell him this very same story and we always laughed together at the end.

As mentioned before these are fleeting memories. Exactly why I spent so much time with my grandparents instead of being with my mother, I was not sure. I do remember that I spent a lot of time with my grandparents and they both had a profound impact on my childhood. Grandma offered discipline and stability while my Papa indulged me as Grandma pretended not to notice. There was not a lot of outward demonstration of feelings at my grandparent's home. Instead of hugs and kisses, there were polite "How do you dos" I believe it was a cultural thing.

Still I felt loved and secure whenever I was with them.

Around the age of five, my memories begin to become slightly more vivid. I am with my mother and stepfather. We had just moved to the Marianne Apartments on Fourteenth St. and Hudson in Detroit where I would live for a while. My mother calls herself Millie. She goes by her middle name Mildred. She is a slight woman, five foot one about a hundred ten pounds but well proportioned. She has large clear blue eyes which appear even larger when she is wearing her glasses. She calls herself a "dishwater blond". I have a stepfather whose name is George Emerick. I have no recollection of how he came into our lives. I call him Daddy because somehow he had become, in my mind, my daddy and I was unaware of a "real" father. I don't know when my mother married him or how long they were married however, I can't remember a time when I did not think of him as Daddy and I loved my daddy. I remember him as an average built man, a little overweight with balding hair and slightly bulging steely gray eyes. Though I cannot recall any specific experiences that I had with him I had a deep feeling of attachment to him. To this day he remains the only man I ever called Daddy.

I recall we had just moved into the Marianne Apartments and my mom and Daddy were cleaning the old soiled wallpaper that covered the living room and the bedroom. They were using something that resembled modeling clay. They would form a roundish ball of this product and rub it along the wallpaper. It was used to absorb dirty residues from the wallpaper. When eventually it absorbed all that it could it would be discarded and cleaning would continue with a fresh "ball". I soon found that I could play with the soiled "balls" and mold them into various forms like one might do with modeling clay. At a later date Noah and Joseph McVicker would become quite wealthy marketing something similar to this wall paper cleaner as "Playdough"

My daddy is a plumber. My mother works as a sales clerk at Caton Photo located on Fourteenth near Claremont St. For part of the time that I live there I go to kindergarten at Hancock school and for part of the time I attend kindergarten at Goldberg school. Eventually I would change schools 15 times before graduating high school. Although I was only five years of age I walked to and from school every day along with several other boys and girls. There were no school buses to transport us and in those days there was little concern regarding child predators. On the way to and from Hancock school there was an underpass for a railroad track. Whenever we heard the whistle of a train coming we would run up the gravel slope to the railroad tracks to watch the train chug by. If I happened to have a penny in my pocket I would stoop down and lay the penny on the track for the train to run over. When the train finished it's work the penny was nearly the size of a quarter and paper thin.

On one occasion I recall being out on the playground at Hancock school for the recess when a man I didn't know tried to talk to me. I was whisked away by a teacher before any conversation took place. Somehow my mother found out about this and she was very angry and upset. That evening I learned that the man was my real father but at the time my young mind could not grasp the concept. After all wasn't Daddy my real father?

Our apartment on 14th street is small. One bedroom, one bathroom, a small kitchen with a table and two chairs, an ice box and an apartment size four burner gas range. A living room that has a Murphy bed (a bed that hides in a closet during the day, swings around and unfolds down to use as a full size bed at night. The bedroom was for my mother and Daddy. The Murphy bed was for me. There was just one window in the apartment. It looked out on a small grassy area we called a courtyard. There were clothes poles propping up the clotheslines that were strung across the courtyard for tenants to dry their washing on. (Automatic dryers hadn't been invented yet (or if there was such a thing then, they weren't available to the general public).

The following things stand out in my mind from my time on 14th street. I remember sometimes being in the bathtub with my mother. I remember she called her breasts her tillies. She called my male part a "flicker". She would laugh and say things like…

"Hold still while I wash your little flicker" .

She let me play with her "tillies". I think this was all in fun.

Mom & Daddy liked to "drink" and all their friends were "drinkers" too. Mom's best friend was Doris Caton. Doris's father owned Caton Photo where my mother worked. My mother nick-named her DoDo (as in dodo bird). She had a birdlike look and a high pitched voice. I called her Aunt Doris. Doris was divorced. I didn't know her ex- husband but apparently "He was a bastard". She had a son named Burton about my age, everyone called him Butch. I would see Aunt Doris and Butch occasionally at picnics or gatherings of one sort or another. At these gatherings the boys of similar ages would naturally gravitate toward each other, avoiding the girls. We would play games or brag about inconsequential things as young boys are want to do. There were different kids from time to time but it seemed Butch and another kid called Star were usually there. Star seemed different somehow and somewhat condescending to the rest of us. I didn't understand why but I felt uneasy around him. One time I overheard some adults talking about Star. They were discussing something about Star's intelligence. Someone commented he would probably grow up to be a genius or turn out to be a criminal. At a backyard picnic some time later I noticed Star wasn't there. When I asked about him one of the kids said…

"They had to put him in a Home".

I did not know exactly what that meant but it did not sound good. I figured he must have became some kind of criminal. Later that night at home I asked my mother why Star was put in a home and what was a home anyway? She said …

"That's where they put boys who won't behave".

For a few days after that I tried my best not to misbehave. I never saw or heard of Star again.

For some reason I was absolutely terrified of Mom & Daddy's bedroom. I didn't know then, and I still don't know why the fear was so intense I would tremble in terror at the prospect of going in there. I believe now that something happened in there that frightened me but I can't say if it was something that involved me or something that happened to someone else. But the fear was sickeningly real. I was also very afraid of being in the apartment alone and very frightened of being in the dark. I always made sure to be inside before nightfall. The evening routine was for me to be put to bed in their bedroom at 7 pm. then later when they went to bed I would be lifted up and carried to the Murphy bed. At bedtime I would find every possible excuse for not going into their bedroom. When I ran out of excuses I would beg and plead…

"Please don't put me in there. I'll be good, I'll be quiet on the Murphy bed and I won't say a word. Please! Please! Please! "

Most of the time that would work and I would be allowed to fall asleep on the Murphy bed. Although it may seem incongruous, despite my fear of the dark, of the bedroom, and of being alone, I was absolutely mesmerized by weekly radio shows such as "The Inner Sanctum" with it's trademark squeaking door opening sound. The most frightening of all was "The Hermit's Cave " by the Mummers. I did not know what the "Mummers" were but just hearing that word along with the shrill squeaky voice of the "Hermit" croaking out the opening lines.... "Weird stories, ghost stories and murders too! He He He He The Hermit knows of them all".... sent chills through my entire body. Still I would beg to stay up late and listen to these radio shows. There was no television to watch in those times but the radio inspired imaginary monsters far more frightening than T. V. or movies ever could. On most weekends Mom and Dad would go out to a neighborhood bar, and leave me with Marcia, a baby sitter who lived across the hall. Marcia was a young girl, 11 or 12 years old. I liked being with her. When they came home and fetched me from Marcia they would be ready for bed themselves, so I would go directly to the Murphy bed thus avoiding the dreaded bedroom. But some weekends they would have company. Then there was no choice I had to go in their bedroom. Still I would resist pleading again and again not to go in there. Then, out of patience with me, I would be picked up and carried into their room and put in their bed trembling all the way. When they turned out the light my fear increased tenfold.

"Please don't turn out the light"

"You can't sleep with the light on"

I would scream and carry on until one night I heard My mother say the words that frightened me even more.

"If you're going to be a bad boy - I'll have to put you in a *home*."

I lay traumatized with fear under the covers afraid to move. I knew something bad was hiding somewhere in that room. Maybe it was in the closet or under the very bed I was lying on but I knew it was something horribly fearsome and I was sure it wanted to do something terrible to me. Still I had to stay quiet or I might be put in a *"home"*.

Later when the company had gone the door would open and I was rescued at last. It was bedtime for them so back to the Murphy bed for me. Often at that point I was still so traumatized from the "bedroom" I couldn't sleep. I would wait till my mom & dad fell asleep and go exploring through the book rack. There were always a few magazines down at the bottom of the rack with interesting pictures to look at. One was called "Sunbathers Monthly" and there were others of the same genre. They were full of pictures taken at nudist colonies. There were lots of photographs of men and women playing volleyball, shuffleboard and various other activities with no clothes on. I was fascinated. You could see all the girls "tillies" and hairy places too. Without knowing why, I was highly interested in looking at the women and girls in these magazines.

I took every opportunity to do so.

One day I came home from school and found my Uncle Red sitting at the kitchen table talking with my mother .There were tears in his eyes. They were discussing something about a divorce. Uncle Red and my Aunt Polly now had a baby son (William). The story I was told was that while my uncle was performing in some kind of amateur musical show (Uncle Red had a great singing voice) he met a girl. During the many rehearsals and practices they became involved and Uncle Red was considering leaving his wife for this new "woman". My mother and Red were very "close" and she was older so Red often came to her for advice. My mother later told me she had cautioned him,…

"You know how much you love your little boy. If you leave Polly you know she will get custody of the child. Is this new romance really worth losing your son over?"

After a while Uncle Red left. Sometime after that I recall going to a theater and seeing a "show" he was appearing in. A lot of our relatives and friends came to see this "show". My mother and grandmother were talking and pointing at an attractive blond woman. I heard someone say ….

"That's her".

In the end my uncle chose the path that would lead to long lasting happiness. He and my Aunt Polly had four children together and they stayed married until she passed from this world.

There was a corner bar a few blocks down 14th street called 'Jack & Pete's. My mother & dad spent a lot of time in there, especially on weekends. Occasionally Marcia was not available to "sit" with me so they would take me with them. Almost everyone smoked cigarettes in those days so the air in the bar was always thick with smoke. In the "bar" one night I became very curious regarding cigarettes so I asked if I could try one. My mother handed me the one she was smoking and I put it in my mouth. Ugh! The taste was horrible I spit out the cigarette immediately while my mother and daddy looked on laughing. That incident along with another I will relate later are the reasons I never became a smoker while the vast majority of my generation became heavily habituated. There was a band at "Jack & Pete's" that played the popular songs of the day. ""Mairzy Doats," "Pistol Packin' Mama", "The Charleston", "The Band Played On" and others. I was always anxious to go with them because I liked to listen to the band play and see the grownups dancing. Sometimes they even did the jitterbug. Daddy would buy me just one 6 ounce bottle of Coca Cola and a 5 cent bag of potato chips. Then I would search the bag of chips looking for the ones that had air bubbles in them. Next I would gently bite off the top of the bubble, dip it into the glass filling the bubble with Coke, then lift the chip to my lips and slowly sip the Coke from the bubble. What a treat!

The was a surge of patriotism sweeping the country in those days due to what was happening in Europe. Hitler had ordered the German Army to invade France and there was speculation that the United States would soon enter the war against Germany. I didn't understand much about it but those feelings rubbed off on me. I would hear Kate Smith on the radio singing "God Bless America" and it stirred me for some reason. I loved music even then and I had a knack of hearing a song once or twice and immediately I could remember the words and melody. On one of my trips to the bar with my mom and Daddy one of the patrons at "Jack & Pete's" heard me singing "God Bless America" quietly under my breath and he began cajoling me to get up on the bandstand and sing the song out loud. I resisted until he offered to buy me another Coke & chips if I would sing the song with the band. That was too much to turn down so I got up and sang "God Bless America" with the band. Soon I was a regular feature when they took me to "Jack & Pete's" on most weekends.

The possibility of war with Germany was affecting every aspect of life in those days. President Roosevelt had ordered a massive military buildup. The "Draft" was reinstated and fighting age men were nervous about being drafted. Gasoline was rationed. Meat was rationed. Milk and butter were rationed. There were special rationing stamps and little red and green tokens, slightly smaller than a penny, that were distributed every month to the general public. When you wanted to buy gasoline for your car or some meat for dinner you had to present the appropriate stamps or one or more of the tokens. When you ran out you could not purchase anymore of that item until you received the next month's supply of stamps or tokens. The developments in Europe dominated the news. The headlines of the Detroit News, the Free Press and the Detroit Times all featured news of the war in Europe. Every radio station carried the war's latest developments. Even at the "Dump" (a local movie house I went to every Saturday) I watched newsreels of Hitler's aggressions in Europe. The "Palace" was the name above the theater's marquee but we called it the "Dump" due it's run down condition and the mice or occasional rat that scurried below our feet. Come Saturday I would be given a dime for a movie ticket and some candy and sent to "The Dump" where the feature movie, usually a western, was followed by a "serial" featuring various cowboy stars such as Tom Mix, Roy Rogers, Gene Autry, Hopalong Cassidy and others. After the serial came the newsreel and a reminder of the looming war in Europe. Even for children there simply was no way to escape, for long, the world situation. People were saving tin cans and all scrap metal to be recycled for the war effort. The packages that cigarettes came in were enclosed with tinfoil (there was no aluminum foil in those days). Nearly every household had a "tinfoil ball". It would start with a small piece of tinfoil rolled between your fingers into a tiny ball. Then each time you found another piece of tinfoil it would be added on to the ball. When it got to a fairly large size it would be donated for the "war effort" I remember one that we had was about 7 inches in diameter. Even at the age of five the war was significantly impacting my life both emotionally and physically.

In addition to my intense fear of my parent's bedroom I also had a debilitating fear of being alone in our apartment. On school days I would walk back home from school to the apartments. There was a buzzer for each apartment and another for the manager. Normally I would push the one for our apartment and my mother, who I would expect to be home from work at Caton Photos before I came home from school, would buzz me in. At times though there was no responding buzz to let me in when I pushed on the button. This happened frequently and sometimes I would sit on the cement step in front of the leaded glass doors that led to the vestibule and on to the interior of the building and wait. All the little sections of glass in the door were beveled on the edges and I would stare in fascination at the rainbow I could see in them. (I would learn later this was called a prism effect.) Other times I might look for a neighbor boy (Donny) and we would go exploring in the empty field behind the apartment building I lived in. In late fall the wild grassy weeds in the field were turning brown and had grown as high as we were tall. We pretended we were in the jungle and would run down the paths, hide from each other and then jump out trying to scare one another. At one edge of the field there was a large building housing a potato chip plant. Occasionally we would encounter an employee out on the dock and he would give us a bag of potato chips hot and fresh right off the line. Wow! they tasted so good. When darkness was approaching I would hurry back to the Marianne apartments hoping my mother had returned from work to let me in. Unfortunately that was not always the case. So I would wait for another apartment dweller to come in or out of the door and I would then sneak in behind them before the door closed. I would run down the dark, narrow, stained wallpapered hallways to our apartment and walk right in. (People didn't lock their doors in those days) Sometimes I would find my mother asleep or in the bathroom so that she didn't hear the buzzer when I rang. Sometimes however she was quite late coming home from work. With no one there to observe me I would rummage through the magazine rack. Sometimes there would be new "Sunbathers" magazines to look through.

As winter approached the days grew shorter and darkness arrived earlier with each passing day. Occasionally after school when Mom didn't buzz me in, it would start to get dark before someone coming or going would present the opportunity for me to enter the building. Due to my fear of the dark I would hurry down the hall and burst into the apartment only to find no one there. Panic set in! I knew there were bad people in the dark lurking outside the "courtyard window" with knives or guns who would try to kill me. Suddenly realizing I was alone

I would grab my chest, let out a big gasp, as though I'd been shot, throw myself on the overstuffed couch and pretend I had already been killed. I believed if they thought I was dead they would not kill me again. This was terrifyingly real to me and I would not move for as long as 30 minutes to an hour until my mother came home. Then when she arrived I would jump up and act like nothing was wrong but I was mad at her for being late. Other times I would hide in a closet curled up and afraid to stir until she came home. Often, at these times I could smell beer on her breath.

Chapter 3

FINDING STABILITY

One day in the spring, 1941 my mother told me I was going to stay with Grandma and Grandpa again. They had moved to an apartment house on Schoolcraft and Littlefield Streets in Detroit where Grandma had again accepted the position of apartment manager. It was a small apartment building. There were eight apartments upstairs with a front entrance facing Littlefield (the side street), two basement apartments with the entrances at the back of the building and two basement level retail stores facing Schoolcraft (the main thoroughfare). One of the stores was a confectionery shop and the other was a beauty parlor. For collecting the rent from the other tenants as well as the general maintenance of the property they could live there rent free. This would become their permanent home. They would never move again and it would become the only place, as a child, I would feel truly safe and secure. I would have go to another new school called Monnior which was only four or five blocks from their apartment home. I looked forward to staying with my grandparents but I was reluctant to change schools again.

"But ma, I won't know anyone at Monnior school"

"You'll make friends after you get there"

I wasn't given a reason and I had no choice anyway so off I went to my grandparents. I enjoyed having regular meals with my grandparents.

Filling the furnace stoker with coal and removing clinkers from the giant furnace in the basement was one of my Papa's responsibilities. He usually did this after dinner and I liked to watch. The "stoker" was a huge bin that papa would fill with coal from the coal bin. He would take coal shovels full of coal and toss them up and into the bin (which was higher than the top of my young head). At the bottom of the stoker bin was a very large screw like mechanism that turned slowly and continually fed the coal from the bin into the furnace on a slow but deliberate pace. This process allowed for filling the stoker once a day and assuring the fire would not go out due to lack of coal. After filling the stoker Papa would begin removing the clinkers from inside the furnace. Most of the coal that burned would simply become ashes but there would also be solid residue that Papa called clinkers. They formed in various amorphic shapes. Some were quite heavy and as much as a foot in diameter. Many were too big to lift out of the furnace with the set of giant iron tongs specifically designed for that purpose. Papa would take a long iron spike and jam it into the bigger clinkers to break them into manageable sizes. He would then use the set of tongs to grasp the clinkers one at a time, pull them out of the furnace and place them in a metal bushel basket to cool. Many of them were quite heavy. A full bushel basket could easily weigh over fifty pounds. They were red hot in the furnace and I was fascinated with the fire and extreme heat radiating through the furnace's iron entrance door.

I especially liked sitting on Papa's lap again every evening while we exchanged stories about the "little boy and the pumpernickel bread" and spied on the neighbors out of his bedroom window. Oh, how I loved being with my grandparents. It was there I first met and struck up an acquaintance with a boy who would become and remain my best friend as long as he lived. Leonard Antkoviak lived across the alley from my grandparents place. He was my age and quite an exciting kid to be around. We became friends. By then I was attending my fourth school and had not known anyone long enough to call my friend. Leonard was bigger and stronger than me. He had a large but straight nose with close set eyes and light brown hair. Unlike me he was very bold and adventurous. While I was withdrawn and afraid of almost everything, he seemed afraid of nothing except maybe his father (Joe Antkoviak). Mr. Antkoviak was a bus driver for the

Detroit Transit System. He was a heavy drinker and often came home inebriated after work. Occasionally I could hear loud wails from across the alley. Some of the wailing sounded like Leonard. Some did not.

Leonard showed me how to hitch a ride on the "Sheeny Wagons" that plied the alleys for salvageable trash. We would hide around the corner of a garage till the sheeny man passed us by and then sneak up behind the horse driven wagon and grab on to the back of the wagon. Holding on with our hands and lifting our feet from the ground, we went for a short ride before the horse pulling the wagon slowed from the extra weight and we were discovered.

"Ged offa dere crazy kids, goddamn gingalos"

Another favorite pastime was sneaking up unnoticed to the back of ice trucks delivering large blocks of ice for the iceboxes in the many neighborhood homes that didn't yet have an electric refrigerator. We would swipe a small chunk of ice that had broken off the bigger blocks and suck on the ice like it was a special treat.

A somewhat darker story I remember was our encounter with Peggy. Peggy lived in the same apartment house as my grandparents. Peggy was a couple years younger than Leonard and I. About three or four years old I would guess. Somehow we got her into the basement stairwell and pulled down her underpants. We told her we were doctors and needed to examine her. She was unafraid and giggled while we used small sticks to poke around under her arms, her belly button and private areas. I found myself very curious and excited with a vague feeling of naughtiness.

Chapter 4

THE FARM

Just after school was out in the late spring of 1941 my mother came to grandma's apartment to see me She took me to downtown Detroit to see a movie. Snow White and the Seven Dwarfs, I think. Afterwards we went to Sanders Ice Cream store where she treated me to a chocolate milk shake. This was a rare treat. In 1941 a milk shake cost a lot (twenty-five cents). After I was finished with my special treat she asked me how I would like to go on a vacation to a farm where there would be horses, cows, chickens and pigs. I could play on the hay stacks and it would be a lot of fun. She painted an exciting picture for me and I was anxious to go on this vacation. So the following week Grandma packed up all my belongings and my Daddy drove all of us out to a farm located near Clinton, Michigan. (Clinton was a little farm town in the "Irish Hills" area of southern Michigan.) The farm was owned by "The Johnsons" I was introduced to Mrs. Johnson and her two daughters (Betty and Marge). Mrs. Johnson looked to me to be about the age of my grandmother. She was an average looking woman with graying hair, glasses and a friendly smile. Betty, the youngest daughter looked to be in her early twenties. She was a tall, thin girl and I thought quite pretty while Marge who I would guess to be three or four years older was more sturdily built and average looking. Mom suggested I go outside and see what might be in the large, faded red, weather aged barn we had seen as we drove up the gravel drive. The big people had something to discuss. Outside I met another boy about my age. His name was Frank.

"Do you live here?" I asked.

"No I'm just staying here for awhile."

"How long will you be here?"

"I dunno maybe a couple weeks. I'm here on a vacation."

"Me too."… I replied

Frank showed me around the farmyard. There were two horses in the big barn, a bunch of sows and hogs in a pen along with a dozen or so little piglets. Chickens were running around everywhere. I noticed a small wooden shed about four feet square with one door on the front. It didn't look like it could hold more than one person.

I asked Frank what it was.

"That's the outhouse."

"What's an outhouse?"

"That's where you go number one or number two."

"Don't they have a bathroom?"

"Nope that's it."

I would soon to learn there was no running water either. We had to get it from a hand pump at the kitchen sink. Many other modern day conveniences we now take for granted were not at the "Johnson's farm", near Clinton, Michigan. When I went back into the farmhouse my mom & dad were getting ready to leave. I was having second thoughts about staying there and began to whimper that I wanted to go home. My mother said....

"It's just for a few weeks"

I turned to my daddy… "Do I have to stay here?"

"Now be a little man and don't cry. We'll be back to get you in two weeks"

The farmhouse was primitive by today's standards. No electricity! No gas heat!

No hot and cold running water. The house was lit with lamps that burned oil or kerosene (I'm not sure which). Water came from a well in the ground outside or from the pump in the kitchen sink. Heat came from a pot bellied wood stove in the living room. Mrs. Johnson cooked all the meals, and did all her baking on a wood fired cook stove in the kitchen. The pies and cookies she baked in that wood stove were the best I ever tasted. One of my chores was to carry in wood for the stove from the woodpile outside. The downstairs was comprised of a kitchen, living room, one bedroom and a small parlor. The upstairs held two bedrooms one of which was assigned to Frank and me. The other bedroom, across the hall, was for Betty and Marge. Betty was at the farm most of the time but Marge was only there on weekends. I think she had a job and lodged in town during the week.

I spent the next two weeks exploring the farm and meeting all the animals. The piglets were especially fun to watch as they cavorted around squealing all the while. The hogs and sows were mean looking and dirty from rolling around in the slop and mud in their pens. I liked to take a stick and try to poke at their noses through the slats of the fence that kept them contained in their pen. They would make loud high pitched squeals and threatening grunts when I teased them with the stick. Sometimes I would go searching for eggs that the loose hens had laid in hard to find places and take them to Mrs. Johnson. She would reward me with a cookie or piece of pie she had baked that day. They were delicious. I got to know the horses by name. Billy was an aging gray mare. She was a gentle horse and I could stroke her on the legs and along her sides without incident. With Jack it was different. He was temperamental and I was warned not to get to close to him. I saw little of Mr. Johnson. He was up every morning before dawn, off to milk the cows, then back for a quick breakfast and then back to work in the fields. He was a wiry stern looking man with a black beard (no mustache). He spoke very little. In the first two weeks I was there I don't think he uttered more than two words to me. I had no reason to be afraid of him, but I was. I slowly adjusted to farm life. Frank showed me some of the secret places that the loose hens sometimes laid their eggs. They were always trying to outsmart us by laying eggs in new and different places but we would find them under the corn crib, behind the barn, anywhere the hens could find a little hay or straw for a makeshift nest. We gathered them up, still warm from the hen's body and often with a little chicken poop on them, and took them to the farmhouse where Mrs. Johnson would clean them. I explored my way down various paths through the woods spotting the occasional rabbit, and picking wildflowers for Mrs. Johnson. I liked her.

Frank was a sullen sort of kid and didn't seem totally thrilled with being on the farm. Then one day Frank's parents arrived at the farm and Frank went with them in their car. He never returned. I was saddened to see him go because there would be no one else to play with. I began looking forward to going home but after two weeks no one came to take me back. A few weeks later my mom and dad showed up with a brand new bicycle. At first I was excited to see them with this new "two wheeler". Wow! I couldn't wait to try and ride it. The first try I fell off sideways. Next try I fell again. I kept trying with my Daddy holding on to the rear fender and seat to keep me steady but I couldn't make more than three or four feet before tipping over. Finally it was decided the problem was the uneven surface of the gravel drive that was causing the difficulty. After I fell down again and scraped my knees on the stones we decided to put the bike away. I would try again the next day and again and again I would fall off. I would be 10 years of age before I learned to ride a bike. Then came the reason for this special gift. I was going to have to stay on the farm a little while longer.

"Just a few more weeks, Skippy"

It wasn't long before the "dreams" started. I would awake in the middle of the night terrified by a dream that recurred several times a week. The dream was always the same…

"I am inside a house looking out a window. The house is in a small town (the sort of town that you see in old western movies) with only one main street intersected by a couple of side streets. There is a small yard in front of the house. The yard is enclosed by a short

white picket fence. The fence is only about two feet high. Suddenly from around the corner of a side street appears a huge shaggy maned lion. This ferocious animal approaches the house I am in, roaring, snarling and baring his huge white fangs. He is looking for me. All at once I find myself out the door and into the yard where the lion sees me. He nears the two foot high fence that he can easily leap over. I try to get back into the house where I will be safe but the door is closed and I cannot open it. I can clearly see his long, sharp, sparkling white teeth as he snarls and roars at me. I am yelling for someone to let me in to no avail. The lion leaps the fence and just as I am about to be devoured I wake up terrified, screaming and crying."

Mrs. Johnson or sometimes Betty would come to my bedroom to see what the commotion was about. They would remind me it was only a dream. Neither Mr. Johnson nor Marge ever came. Sometimes Betty would hold me and try to calm me down. Betty was a warm, caring person and would attempt to console me. I liked her most, of all the Johnsons. This dream reoccurred often as my stay at the farm kept being extended. This same dream continued long after my stay at the farm ended. The frequency of this dream gradually diminished as I grew older.

Fall was approaching and I was getting anxious to return to life in Detroit. On one of my mother's visits she began asking questions about the farm. What had I been doing? How did I like being on a farm? How was I getting along with the Johnsons?

I told her it was okay there and Mrs. Johnson was nice but I was ready to come home. Later that summer of 1941 as the time for school was drawing near She broached the question…

"How would you like to stay on the farm and go to school there."

"No! I want to come home".

"But I thought you liked it there."

"I do but I want to be with you."

"Your Daddy will likely be drafted into the army and could be called up at any time."

"I don't care. I want to go home."

"I took a job working nights in a defense plant. Who will take care of you?"

"Can I go to Grandma and Grandpas?"

"No you have to stay on the farm."

When I began to cry I heard the magic words that would convince me of anything....

"If you don't want to stay at the farm I'll have no choice but to send you to a home."

She promised they would come and visit me every weekend.

As mentioned at the beginning of this story on rare occasion a very vague and undefined memory would make an attempt to enter my consciousness. Maybe it is not a real memory but rather a memory of a dream I once had. It starts out with me as a very little boy, perhaps just a baby.

"I am lying down next to someone in a narrow bed next to a window. It is a woman, perhaps my mother. Suddenly I notice my grandmother with a group of people standing in a doorway looking at the bed and me. I can tell by the look on their faces something is wrong but I don't know what it is."

Then just as this memory begins to form in my mind for some reason it gets pushed back into my sub consciousness and forgotten. At odd and unpredictable times this elusive memory will attempt to return to my conscious mind sometimes separated by several years. Over a very long time more of this dreamlike experience will, unfortunately, come back to me.

The one room schoolhouse I attended was a mile away on the same road as the farm. It was a small white wooden sided building with a little steeple and bell perched atop. It housed all the students from 1st grade through 8th grade. I was the only child in 1st grade. We memorized the alphabet, colored pictures, and learned some elementary math. We practiced writing in storybooks we were given. These storybooks had a moral saying or proverb at the top of each page followed underneath by several blank lines. Each page had a different moral saying such as ..."I will not tell a lie, Thou shall not steal, The wages of sin are death" and so on. The blank lines were there for us to copy over and over, the heading at the top of each page. We were practicing our writing and learning something about right and wrong simultaneously.

Although I was very shy I eventually made friends with a girl named Alice. She was the only kid in the second grade. During the warmer fall days Alice and I would play in the grassy field behind the schoolhouse. By late autumn the field was overgrown with long dried out grassy weeds that in some areas were taller than we were. I got the idea to pound several sticks into the ground to form a primitive sort of frame then Alice and I would pull up some of the longest grassy weeds we could find and place them between the sticks forming a makeshift wall. All too soon the bell would ring signaling recess was over and we would abandon our project till the next recess. Over a period of a week or so we finished all four walls. We formed a grass roof and had a little opening to crawl in and out of. Our makeshift playhouse wasn't big, probably only two feet high and just large enough to house the two of us. We showed our project to other school kids and some would crawl inside to see what it was like. The older kids laughed. Each recess we would run out to get inside our little playhouse. When I was in there with Alice I felt close to her and safe. It felt good to be close to someone.

After school I would walk the mile back to the farm singing songs to myself along the way. My favorite was "Long Ago and Far Away". Back at the farm I now had chores to do. Gather the eggs from the hen house take out the trash and carry in wood for the cast iron cook stove so Mrs. Johnson could cook supper for the family. After chores I could pass the time playing in the haystack or immersing myself in a silo half full of corn. I remember sitting up to my neck in bins or silos full of grain, (barley, wheat oats and others). I would let the sea of grain flow around and through my fingers like water and breathe in the rich aroma of the freshly harvested grains.

Suppertime was very organized as was breakfast and lunch. First we would all bow our heads and say grace. Then Mr. Johnson would take a portion from each dish of food and pass the dish to Mrs. Johnson who would take her portion and pass it to Marge, if she was there, then Betty and finally to me. The seating arrangement was the same every day. When occasionally there was not enough of one of the dishes being served, Mr. Johnson had priority. After all, I was informed, he was the man of the house and had to work very long and hard out in the fields to keep the farm going. Thus his health and strength were of vital importance to the rest of us. Here too, I could not leave the table without asking to be excused. Life on the farm was rigid. My bedtime was 7 pm. and there was no way around it, 7 pm. was bedtime, *period!*

One night I was in the middle of the "dream" but before the lion appeared something caused me to wake up. There was noise coming from across the hall. I arose and walked to the door. The door of my room was open a crack. I peeked out to see what the noise was and saw the door to Betty's room was half open. Betty was standing by a large basin of water and washing herself. She was completely undressed. I watched in fascination as she used a washcloth to clean her breasts, stomach, legs and all in between. I knew I shouldn't be watching this but I couldn't not look. That warm feeling of naughtiness came over me again. After that I would occasionally try to stay awake until Betty's bedtime, hoping to watch her again. Most of the time I would fall asleep before Betty came to bed and often, even when I was able to remain awake long enough, she did not bathe that night.

Ever so often though, my efforts were successful.

Winter came in early November and it became much more of a challenge to walk that mile to school through the snow that covered that country road. Mostly I would try to follow in the narrow tracks left by a horse and wagon that had gone down the road earlier that morning. Occasionally the neighboring farmer had traversed the road earlier that morning on his "Farmall" tractor and left a nice wide track for me to follow but sometimes the tracks would turn off into a field. Sometimes with a heavy snow on the ground I could barely lift my six year old legs high enough out of the snow to take the next step. Still onward I would trudge as I didn't want to miss school and I looked forward to seeing my friend Alice. Since Frank had left the farm Alice was the only other child, close to my age that I had any regular contact with and we were good friends for the short while I was at that school. I enjoyed going to that country school. The teacher was kind and I liked having lessons to learn. I was able to finish my lessons in short order allowing me to sit and listen to the lessons being taught to the older grades sharing that one room schoolhouse. Besides teaching all the studies from first to eighth grade the teacher also arranged many activities that all grades could partake in. Once or twice we all went to a nearby swamp that had frozen over to go ice skating. A railroad track ran nearby and a towering wooden trestle carried the trains over the swamp. I can still visualize a speeding train rushing across the trestle, timbers trembling and the whistle cracking through the frigid winter air. Once while trying to show off for Alice I went skating across the ice on my twin bladed ice skates as fast as I could. Unable to stop myself as I neared the edge of the ice I slammed headlong into a fallen log and crashed onto the shore while Alice and all the older kids looked on and howled with laughter. I wasn't hurt and got back up relieved to see that the older boys thought I was funny. You see I was somewhat afraid of the older boys as they were much bigger than I was and sometimes they bullied the younger kids. With this simple accident I was learning that I might be able to fend off aggression by doing something funny.

Good news came later that month. Thanksgiving was coming and the Johnsons had received a letter from my mother. I was going back to Detroit for Thanksgiving. I hadn't seen them since they brought me back to the farm in September. On the Wednesday before the Holiday the Johnsons drove me to Clinton in their Model T Ford truck and put me on a Greyhound bus bound for Detroit where I was met by my mom and Daddy. The next day we all went to Uncle Red and Aunt Polly's new house on Hubbell Street for Thanksgiving dinner. They now had two children little William who earned the nickname Butch and their daughter Sue. Grandma and Grandpa and Uncle Murray were there too. I was happy to be back with my family for a while. The following Sunday on the way to the bus station I was told ….

"Your Daddy has been drafted into the army."

I was unsure of the importance of this revelation but knew it wasn't good news. Tears came as I hugged and kissed my Daddy goodbye. I was back on the Greyhound bus headed for Clinton and then on to the farm. That night the "Lion" returned. I woke up screaming! Mrs. Johnson came to my room and assured me everything was alright "It was only a dream". Eventually I calmed down and she left. I thought she had a strange look on her face and I saw her shaking her head as she left the room.

In early December I was in the parlor looking through a magazine (I think it was called Coronet Magazine). This was a small monthly magazine, about the size of a "Readers Digest", and often in the middle there was a page that folded out with a full color illustration of a "Petty Girl" or sometimes a long legged scantily clad (occasionally nude) pin up girl by "Vargas". I enjoyed looking at them but sensed I shouldn't. I would wait till I was alone to view the centerfolds again and again. On one December day I perceived a lot of tension in the air. Mr. and Mrs. Johnson were glued to the radio. Betty and Marge came in the door and we heard Mrs. Johnson announce….

"The Japs have bombed Pearl Harbor. President Roosevelt has declared war."

From that time on all the news on the radio or in the newspapers focused on the war the United States was now in with both Japan and Germany (The Axis). I was quite interested in everything to do with the war as I worried that my Daddy might have to go overseas to fight the Germans or the Japs. Despite her earlier promise to visit me at the farm every weekend the visits became less and less frequent. I resigned myself to life on the farm continuing on as it had been with my frequent dreams of the lion, fighting with the pigs, chasing cows, hiking through the woods and..... occasional peeks at Betty bathing in her room.

CHAPTER 5

HEADING SOUTH

In late spring 1942, at last school was out. My mother promised I could come home when I finished first grade and I was anxious to return home. Grandma and Grandpa drove my mother to the farm to retrieve me. I was deliriously happy to be going home. I said my goodbyes to Mrs. Johnson and Betty. Mr. Johnson was out in the fields and Marge was at work. On the drive back to the city I learned I was not going to be staying back at our apartment on 14th street. My Daddy had been assigned to Camp Sutton near Monroe, South Carolina for training. We were to join him there for the rest of the summer. Again, I would be reunited with my mom and dad. It was decided that we would take a Greyhound bus to meet him there and be with him during his weeks of training. I was excited to go and was awed to see what I thought was unusual red earth as we rode south through the mountains on the bus to Monroe.

Due to my Daddy's experience as a plumber his designation was as an Army Engineer. Camp Sutton was used for the training of thousands of army engineers. At first we lived in housing that was provided on the base. I remember being impressed by all the jeeps, tanks, cannons and other military paraphernalia. There were uniformed soldiers marching back and forth on the grounds. I had a feeling of pride when I would see my Daddy in uniform marching in what I thought were parades but more likely were simply training exercises. We were only there for about eight weeks so there are only a few significant happenings to relate. At times when my daddy had a weekend pass we all went into town I was usually dropped off at a movie theater in downtown Monroe while my parents went to a tavern to have a few beers (this was a frequent happening.) I didn't mind as I loved the movies and usually I was given a nickel or dime for candy or popcorn. On one occasion they were not waiting for me outside the theater when the movie ended so I walked across the street where there was a park with swings and a slide to play on. After some time passed I became thirsty and strolled over to some drinking fountains near the entrance to the park. As I was bending over to take a sip of water I heard my mother's voice yelling

"No Skippy no!"

I straightened up to look and saw her running toward me, waving frantically and yelling....

"Don't drink from there.".

"But I'm thirsty."

She had reached me by then and motioning to another fountain about ten feet away said...

"Okay but you have to take your drink from this other fountain."

"Why"?

She pointed to a sign above the fountain I was about to drink from that read....

"Colored Only.

There was a sign above the fountain she told me I should drink from that read....

"Whites only"

I had never seen anything like that in Detroit and asked why there were signs like that. My mother tried to explain what racial prejudice was and while we didn't believe in discrimination we had to abide by local customs to avoid any problems.

There is another incident that occurs to me. While we were at the Army base there was an entertainment show of some kind that was being put on for the soldiers stationed there. There were posters all around the base promoting the upcoming show and I was anxious to go see what it was all about. On the evening of the show my parents dropped me off at the front door and left me there while they went to the N.C.O. club to drink. I went inside, sat down & watched the show. There were comedians, singers, musicians and dancing girls. It was great fun. My mother had told me to wait inside when the show was over and they would come in and pick me up. The show ended and people began filing out. I waited and waited but no Mother and Daddy. Eventually I became fearful and began to cry, A pretty lady stopped by my chair asking …

"Why are you crying little boy?" "Where are your Mommy and Daddy?"

"I don't know. They went out somewhere and I'm supposed to wait here till they come get me."

"Well you just come with me" … she said, leading me backstage to the ladies dressing room.

"You can stay with us until your folks come to get you"

She was in costume and I realized she was one of the dancing girls I had seen on stage during the show. There were three or four other girls in the dressing room and they made quite a fuss over me giving me candy, chips and coca colas to drink. They were in various stages of changing out of their costumes. Some had no tops on exposing their "tillies". Some were walking around totally undressed. They seemed unbothered by my presence. I assume that as I was only a seven year old boy they had little concern with my seeing them in that manner but I was fascinated by the sight of all the curves and shapes of their naked bodies. Shortly afterward my parents arrived to get me. While I was quite angry with my parents for being late I found this experience with the show girls highly exhilarating.

My Daddy's training was coming to an end and he would soon be sent overseas to join the battle. We had to return to Detroit. I began sobbing heartily as I kissed my Daddy goodbye. I did not know it at that time but I would never lay eyes on him again.

CHAPTER 6

HOME AGAIN

Upon our return to Detroit I found myself once more staying with Grandma and Grandpa. I did not understand the reasons but didn't object because I really liked being with my grandparents. Once again a feeling of safety and security returned while I stayed with them. It was summertime in Detroit. I was anxious to renew my acquaintance with Leonard Antkoviak but was also fearful that he might not still like me. With so little experience at having friends I was unsure of myself however I was unaware at that time that Leonard was not popular with the other kids in the neighborhood and he too had very few friends. He was as glad to see me as I was to see him. One day he showed me his "rubber gun". It was made by cutting a "two by four" into several short pieces that were then nailed together to form the rudimentary shape of a sawed off shotgun. Then an inner tube was cut in strips about an inch wide to form giant rubber bands. These strips of rubber were stretched across the wood frame in such a way that pressing on the wooden trigger mechanism would release the overstretched rubber and send it 15 or 20 feet through the air at the intended target. He warned me that there were several neighborhood kids that had these "rubber guns " and they were planning an attack on him and probably me as I was the new kid. I was chased a few times by kids with "guns" but was never hit by a flying "rubber". I worried about this for a few weeks but before long the fad passed. For the most part it was just boys trying to act tough. As on my previous visits Leonard was frequently getting "the belt" or being grounded. I didn't always know why.

There was an open lot behind my grandparent's apartment house where the men from the neighborhood would gather in spring, summer and fall to play horseshoes in the evening. I would sit on a little green bench my Papa had made and watch him and the other men toss the "shoes" and consume bottles of beer. Sometimes during the day I would play on a swing set that had been placed on this empty lot. I would climb up on the high crossbar and hang by my legs hoping to impress someone. I especially wanted to impress Barbara. Barbara was an older girl (probably ten or twelve years old) who lived in one of the other apartments in Grandma's building. I would wait to see her approaching the building and then quickly climb up and drape the back of my knees across the high bar and hang upside down in hopes she would notice. Not once did she ever acknowledge the tremendous feat that I performed for her. Either she did not notice or more likely pretended not to notice a silly little boy trying to show off.

Even at our early age Leonard and I were curious about girls. One way or another we had both seen pictures of women partially undressed. While we were too young for strong sexual impulses we were still fascinated by women's bodies. Leonard's house had a large porch with an open space beneath it surrounded by lattice. At times we would crawl into the open area under the porch and "hide out". While there we would sometimes tell ghost stories and try to scare one another. Sometimes the stories took a darker track. We would take turns making up fantasies about seeing older girls from school naked. Sometimes these fantasies involved such things as punishing girls by sticking them with needles, burning certain parts of their bodies with hot pokers, applying various tools to their breasts etc. The fantasies became more and more dramatic as we would take turns trying to outdo each other with tales from our depraved imaginations. Then we would laugh and giggle about it.

I have no idea if this is normal for seven year old boys.

Leonard and I met up most every day after school except when he was being punished for something or other. It seemed he was always getting in trouble and being grounded or getting the "belt" His father Joe was a strict disciplinarian. Leonard however was a bold kind of fellow and deserved most of what he got. With him leading the way we had many adventures together as seven year olds. I'll relate a couple of the most memorable ones. One time Leonard took a gallon can of gasoline from his father's garage. We obtained some matches and looked for a place we could experiment with setting the gasoline on fire. On the Schoolcraft end of my grandparent's apartment building there were two basement level shops. Due to being below ground level there were cement steps on each side leading down to the shop's entrance doors. It was a Sunday and both shops were closed. This seemed like the ideal place for our experiment. On the sidewalk at the bottom of the steps we were below eye level and couldn't be easily seen by anyone passing by. In the center of the middle sidewalk square there was a drain for water to go down when it rained. This drain had a second rim in the middle of it that formed a little circular trough about an inch wide. Leonard poured enough gasoline in to the drain to fill the little trough. He told me to stand back as he pulled out a pack of matches. He announced proudly....

"I've done this before and it's dangerous so don't stand too close."

Then standing about 4 feet away he tossed a lit match at the drain. The gasoline flamed up instantly. I was awestruck. At the age of seven I had never seen anything like it. The flames were mesmerizing. Then as I watched, the flames became smaller and smaller. The fire was about to go out.

"Put some more gas on it Leonard, before it goes out"."

"We better not it's dangerous."

I didn't want the fire to go out so I grabbed the can myself and swung it back and forth to slosh some more gas on the fire. To my amazement the fire leaped up from the drain and followed the trail of gasoline in mid air to the can I was holding. The fire singed the hair on my fingers. The can dropped from my hand instantaneously. The flaming gas was now splattered all over the sidewalk and onto the wooden entrance doors to the shops and they were afire. We knew we were in big trouble. We ran and hid in a vacant field a block away. We heard the wail of fire engines coming and saw people running toward Schoolcraft and Littlefield. A while later we summoned up the courage to go back and survey the damage we had done. All the tenants from the apartment building were outside their apartments watching the firemen at work. Grandma was there too. The fire was out but the doors to the shops were badly damaged. As the firemen gathered up their equipment suddenly Leonard's mother appeared, grabbed him by the ear and marched him home. I stalled around avoiding the inevitable as long as I could until Grandma walked over to me. I must have given myself away with a guilty look because she asked….

"Did you have any part in this Skippy?"

"Leonard did it. I just watched while he threw gas on the fire."

Grandma gave me a long look, took both my hands in hers and turned them over to reveal the tiny little hairs on the back of my hands that had been singed by the flames. She knew! Nothing more was said about it but for a few weeks I noticed Grandma being short with me when I had a question or asked for something. I don't know what she told Grandpa but the "Pumpernickel stories" went missing for a while.

Chapter 7

RETURN TO A FARM

The summer soon passed. I saw my mother occasionally when she came to visit. Then one day in late August of 1942, while visiting, she reminded me school would be starting in a few weeks so I would be leaving grandma and grandpas and going back to a farm.

"I don't want to go back to the farm."

"You can't stay with your grand parents forever and I have to work."

"No! I won't go."

"Then I'll have to put you in a ***home.***"

Once again I am helpless to control my situation so I must give in. At least I already knew the Johnson's and I would see my only other friend (Alice) at school. But that was not about to happen as my mother informed me I was going to a different farm and a different school.

"But why can't I go back to the Johnson's."

"They said they aren't taking any more boarders."

"Can't you ask them to please take me back? "

"I did they said no."

I was sure it was my fault that they refused to accept me back. Most likely the nightmares and my screams in the night did not help.

Right after Labor Day grandpa drove us out to the new farm and I met the Pences. Edith Pence was a sharp featured woman with close set piercing blue eyes and a thin sharply pointed nose that ended with a small brown mole. Her husband was a short thin man with a black plain mustache. He like Mr. Johnson was a man of very few words. As far as I know they had no children. Mrs. Pence was a very stern woman with exact ideas on how everything should be. She was highly disciplined and expected the same from me. Although I was used to the loving discipline from my grandmother, Mrs. Pence's discipline seemed not to give me the same secure feeling. I continued to wake up in the middle of the night screaming with fear over the dreams. Mrs. Pence came to my room to see what was wrong. When I told her about the lion she said….

"You had a nightmare. It's not real. You have nothing to be afraid of. Go to sleep."

After a few more night time awakenings she stopped coming. Alone, I laid in bed trembling. I did not like being at the Pence farm. I have only a few vivid memories of being there perhaps because I don't want to remember. I also cannot remember any one from that school. I didn't try to establish any friendships. They never lasted anyway. I do recall one winter day we had a bad snowstorm and as I started down the driveway to school I had great difficulty climbing through the snow that was above my knees. I turned around and went back into the farmhouse.

"What are you doing back here young man?"

"I can't make it. The snow is too deep."

"Nonsense! You are going to school today. No excuses! Now go!"

So out I went again trudging my way to school. The snow was so deep that no farmer with a horse and wagon or tractor had ventured out on the road that morning. There was no trail that I could walk in. Each step took extreme effort as the snow was almost up to my knees. Thirty minutes was the normal time it took to walk to school but on this day it took more than an hour and a half. The wind was blowing the falling snow directly into my face. My feet felt like they were frozen and my nose and ears were paining so that I began to cry. I finally arrived at the school with feet that I could no longer feel. The teacher looked at me and exclaimed, "My god! What happened to you?" We didn't think you would come on a day like this. She hurried me over to a pot bellied wood stove, yanked off my boots, shoes, and socks then began rubbing my feet to try to get some feeling back in them. Eventually the senses returned to my feet. This was one of the worst days at the Pence farm. I can't remember how I got home from school that day. From that day forward I had a strong dislike for Mrs. Pence and the entire situation I was in at the Pence farm.

I decided to keep to myself as much as possible. After school I would retreat to my room and pass the time doing homework and listening to the serials on the radio. "Jack Armstrong" the "All American Boy" was my favorite. The "war" was still going on and the letters from my Daddy had grown less frequent. Still I took solace in his letters. Reading and re reading them over and over reassured me that he hadn't been killed. On one of my mother's infrequent visit to the Pence farm I told her about the incident with the snowstorm and school. Whether connected or not, within a few weeks in early spring 1943 Mr. Pence drove me to the Greyhound bus station In downtown Clinton were I was put on the bus for Detroit. My Papa was there with my mother to pick me up. On the drive to my grandparents apartment I learn that I am once again to spend some time with my grandparents and I would finish out the last month of second grade at Monnior school. If I was given a reason for staying again with my grandparents it escapes my memory. The reason probably was not important to me at the time as I was relieved to be far away from the Pence farm and felt secure and loved whenever I was with my grandparents. I thought…

"My life will once again be somewhat normal".

I wondered would my friend Leonard still live across the alley. No sooner had I arrived at my grandparents apartment when Leonard came knocking. I still had a friend.

While at Monnior school one day during recess while climbing on the "Monkey Bars" on the playground something strange happened. I was at an upper level of the "Monkey Bars" looking down at a few other kids climbing around below me. One of them was a little girl. All I can remember of her was that she had dark curly hair and was much smaller and younger than I was. For some reason for which I have absolutely no explanation I simply looked at her for the first time and became overwhelmed with an intense feeling of hatred directed solely at her. As she neared my position on the "bars" I slowly moved my feet in proximity of her fingers that were wrapped around one of the bars below me. I then quietly ground my foot on her fingers exerting as much pressure as I could muster. She let out a scream and fell to the bottom of the "bars" whereupon one of the teachers overseeing recess rushed over to see what happened. The little girl was rushed away and I was taken to an office inside the school and questioned as to the reason for my actions. I had none to offer and was severely reprimanded.

"If you ever do anything like this again you will be expelled from this school."

"I'm sorry I won't ever do it again."

At this very young age I was learning that it was possible (for me at least) to immediately have a strong feeling of like or dislike at first sight of another person without any reason or knowing anything at all about them.

While I had been away at the farm my uncle Red was drafted into the army infantry. He was serving somewhere in Europe and Grandma seemed worried about his safety. There was an 8 x 12 framed photo of Uncle Red on the desk in my grandparent's living room. He looked very strong and handsome in his uniform. Almost every day I would stop and stare at his photo and then get out the small photograph I had of my Daddy that I had learned was on Guadalcanal in the Pacific Ocean. Both Uncle Red and my Daddy were then serving overseas in the United States Army. My mother and Aunt Polly agreed they could save on expenses if my mother and I moved in to the house on Hubbell. We moved in with Aunt Polly and my cousins William (who was nicknamed Butch) and Sue.

Chapter 8

LIFE ON HUBBELL ST.

Uncle Red and Aunt Polly owned a small 2 bedroom bungalow on Hubbell St. near Plymouth Ave. in Detroit. I would guess it was no more than 1000 square feet. My mother and Aunt shared one bedroom while I shared the other bedroom with my cousins. Our room was furnished with bunk beds and a crib. I was assigned the top bunk and Cousin Butch the bottom bunk. Sue slept in the crib. I thought it was great to be living in this new house. It seemed quite modern to me with an electric refrigerator, a gas stove and a basement I could play in. My mother and aunt placed 8½" by 11" photos, of Uncle Red and of my Daddy on the dresser in their room that I could look at while reading the letters from my Daddy. I was content to be living here with people I knew and I was happy to learn that when school started again I would be attending Ford Elementary, a nearby school. I would not have to go back to the Pence's or any other farm and be away from my family.

My aunt worked in an office and left early each morning for work returning home around 4 pm. My mother worked in a defense plant and left for work around 3pm. Even though I am only eight years old I was put in charge of myself and my cousins during this hour or so lapse of an adult presence. Usually my cousins would be down for naps during this time. Left alone, my old fears would sometimes overtake me and often I would hide in a closet thinking I would be safe there till my aunt arrived home. Sometimes, crouched and trembling in a corner of the closet, I would eventually fall asleep. Once while asleep in the closet of the bedroom shared by my mother and aunt I was awakened by a noise. I thought it was my aunt coming home from work. I did not want anyone to know of my fear and discover me hiding in a closet. Immediately I burst out of the closet. To my dismay I found my aunt already home and sitting on the edge of her bed. She apparently was changing out of her work clothes and was bare from the waist up. Totally embarrassed I quickly turned and ran out of the room. I avoided my aunt's eyes for a few days after this unsettling experience.

At that time the area around Hubbell street was undergoing a tremendous boom in new housing construction. Many of the lots on Hubble had new unoccupied bungalow style houses on them but there were several empty lots as well. The next block west of Hubbell and for several blocks further to the west there many more lots where new bungalow style houses were being erected. The houses were in various stages of completion. Many of them were only framed out with wooden stud walls to delineate the rooms. Several of these were without roofs, plumbing or electricity. Some had doors that were locked to keep intruders out as the electric and plumbing had been installed. The houses that were completed looked almost exactly like my aunt and uncle's house. In retrospect I am puzzled as to the reasoning behind a housing boom at the time that World War ll was still being waged. However when the war ended these homes were quickly filled by the returning servicemen and their families. So I guess someone knew something?

While at the house on Hubbell I gradually made a couple of friends (Kenny Hedricks and Kenny Harper). The two Kennys and I liked to play tag, hide and seek, or cops and robbers, and generally horse around inside the newly framed out houses. If a house we were playing in one day was occupied the following day by workers busy completing construction we would simply move on to another one where no work was going on. Sometimes we would have to venture several blocks away from Hubbell Street to find an unfinished house to play in. Occasionally we would run into kids from nearby neighborhoods and join in playing friendly games but sometimes it developed into a challenging confrontation. At those times whichever was the largest group would run off the smaller group. There was never any actual physical contact. Verbal threats and posturing usually determined the winners. These activities were great fun and continued most of the summer until there was an accident at one of the new construction sites. A girl from a nearby neighborhood had slipped between the 2 x 4 cross beams and fell through to the cement basement floor breaking her leg. When word of this accident got back to our parents we were forbidden from playing in the framed out homes.

There were a lot of open grassy fields around the area at that time, awaiting clearing for new house development. After being banned from the new house construction we turned to exploring these fields and soon discovered something we called "The Plastic Mines". The "plastic mines" were located in a field adjacent to a factory where "Kelvinator" refrigerators were manufactured and they were really nothing more than piles of discarded plastic scrap that had been dumped by someone from the factory. Plastic was a relatively new product in 1943 so we were very excited to search through the piles of plastic shavings and dust to occasionally find a solid piece of plastic that we could take home to our "toy boxes". These pieces were of no practical use except as a trophy to show off to our friends but we went often to the plastic mine site hoping to find a new dumping of scrap to explore.

As fall approached it was soon time to start school again. I was supposed to be entering the third grade however on the first day of school I was assigned to the second grade classroom. I informed the teacher that I had already finished second grade and was supposed to be in third grade but she told me I had to repeat second grade because I had come from a non sanctioned one room country school and would not be able to keep up with the other third graders. Upon learning of this development my mother went to the school to protest. She convinced the principle to agree to put me in third grade (where I belonged) but it would only be on a trial basis for eight weeks. If I couldn't keep up I would still have to go back to second grade. After eight weeks there was a new discussion about advancing me to fourth grade as I was way ahead of the other third grade students.

Apparently while sitting in the one room country school house I had inadvertently picked up a lot of the lessons being taught to the older grades. My mother decided it would be best to keep me in the third grade as I was very small for my age and might be intimidated by older and bigger kids.

Around the end of September as the days grew shorter and temperatures gradually grew colder my mother bought me a new warm suede jacket. She cautioned me that the jacket was expensive and I was to wear it to school but after school I was to put on an old jacket to go out and play in. I believe it was one or two days after this admonishment that I forgot to change and went out after school with the new jacket on. I met up with the two Kennys and some other boys and we went to one of the empty fields to play. Someone had brought some matches (maybe it was me). We decided to pull up some of the tall dead weeds that dried out after summer ended and light them on fire. We made a clearing where we thought this would be safe to do and started a small fire. We watched mesmerized as glowing sparks from the fire rose in the air. One of the sparks ignited some nearby grassy brush and suddenly more grassy spots began to burn. Knowing we could get in trouble for this we tried to stamp out the flames with our shoes. When I saw the small fires were gaining ground, without thinking, I took off my new jacket and began using it to beat out the fire. This, also, did not work. Due to all the dry grass and brush the fire was quickly out of hand and soon the entire field was aflame. When we heard the fire engines in the distance we ran. In what seemed like mere moments the entire field was ablaze. There were four fire engines at the site and crowds had gathered to watch the firemen fight the blaze. We quickly skedaddled home hoping to avoid discovery by the authorities. When my mother saw me covered with dirt and soot and my brand new jacket ruined with more than a few charred spots she gave me the first spanking I can remember. She was extremely upset and screamed at me …

"I knew I should have put you in a HOME".

For some reason I could sense a tension building between my mother and my aunt. Likely, due to my mother's lack of sharing the burden of oversight for me and my cousins. All too often my mother would return from work very late. Frequently on weekends she would leave Aunt Polly to watch us while she left the house in the evening and didn't return till the wee hours of the morning.

Chapter 9

SUSSEX ST.

In the early summer of 1944 after school was ended we moved from my aunt's house to a small basement apartment on Sussex one block south of Joy Road. I was greatly saddened to once again be separated from relatives I knew and loved. The furnished apartment consisted of a living room, kitchen, one bathroom and one bedroom with a full size bed that I shared with my mother. The apartment was quite small and the bedroom was separated from the living room by a set of folding leaded glass doors. One set of doors folded open to the left and one folded open to the right. During the day both sets of doors were left open. My Daddy's photo was placed on a small end table in the living room. The few odds and ends of furniture we owned were stored along with the two wheel bike (I still hadn't learned to ride) in a locker room that was commonly provided to apartment dwellers. Not anxious to go to the trouble to meet new friends I spent most of the summer in the apartment reading Batman, Captain Marvel and other comic books or listening to "serials" on the radio). I was still getting letters from Daddy which I would read and reread again and again. Once he sent me a box with various sea shells from Guadalcanal where he was stationed. The newspapers frequently covered the battle for Guadalcanal and the great loss of life there. I prayed over and over that my Daddy would be safe.

A neighbor boy I had occasionally seen, on my rare excursions outside approached me one afternoon. He was friendly and told me his name was Edward. I reluctantly revealed my name was Skip.

"What school do you go to?"

"I dunno, what school do you go to?

"I go to Parkman."

Our conversation revealed he was starting fourth grade at Parkman School in the fall. I remembered my mother mentioning Parkman and was happy that I now would know someone there when school started. Thus began a friendship of sorts and I began to crawl back from my retreat of the world.

My mother continued working in a defense plant. She was on the afternoon shift (3pm to 11pm) thus after school I would return to an empty apartment. For my dinner she might leave a casserole of macaroni and cheese (my favorite) or a can of Franco American spaghetti which I could barely choke down. Sometimes she just left a note telling me to make myself peanut butter and jelly sandwiches for dinner. In the morning she seldom got up to make breakfast. At the age of eight I learned to fry eggs, make toast, and a cup of tea for myself before leaving for school. Often alone at dinner time I occasionally ventured outdoors and meandered down Sussex street observing the comings and goings of other people in the neighborhood. I wondered what their lives were like. Sometimes looking through their windows I saw families sitting down to have dinner together. They were talking, smiling, sometimes laughing and occasionally, from the looks on their faces, they appeared to be arguing. I wondered if this was normal life?

I rarely experienced this normality when I was with my mother. I longed for my life to be like other normal families. My friend Edward's mother became aware that I was usually alone at dinner time. Occasionally, she invited me to have dinner with them. While I appreciated the opportunity to sit at a dinner table with other people and enjoy a regular meal, I found this to be a rather strange family. Edward's father sat down at the dinner table usually wearing some kind of uniform trousers and only an undershirt. He was a brusque man and seemed to shout every time he spoke. Edward's mother was a slight woman and had an offish "air" about her. Although she seemed to cower when her husband started shouting she continually nagged on about something or other. One of the times I was there for dinner they began arguing. He was shouting at her more ferociously than usual and she jumped up from the table and threw herself on the sofa wailing and screaming....

"Oh God, why are you doing this to me? What sin have I committed to deserve this man? I know he's going to kill me someday. Why are you letting him kill me? Mother of God take me away from all this."

She continued this demonstration for several minutes and I was growing uncomfortable. All the while she was carrying on Edward's father kept shouting even louder than before in an attempt to drown her out. I looked at Edward, who seemed unmoved by either of his parent's screaming. He said to me....

"Don't pay her any mind. She's crazy as a bedbug.!"

After that I saw very little of Edward and never went to his place for dinner again.

It was winter and Christmas would be here soon. Grandma had taken me to J.L. Hudson's department store in downtown Detroit. They had extravagant displays of toys and Christmas decorations. A street side display window was filled with magnificent Lionel electric train sets complete with little toy train stations, tunnels and bridges for the trains to run around on and over. My young mind was filled with all sorts of fantasies about the coming holiday. I couldn't wait for Christmas to arrive even though I knew I would not be getting all those magnificent toys. On Christmas Eve., as was our custom, we put up the Christmas tree. With each bulb I hung on the tree my anticipation grew stronger. Finally I fell asleep around midnight. I awoke at daybreak and ran out of our bedroom to see the largest display of gifts I had ever seen under our Christmas tree. I quickly tore open all the presents with my name on them. They were all from my mother. There was a "Copyfun", a "Lincoln Logs" set, "Tinker Toys", a set of army men, a "Flexible Flyer" sled, a baseball mitt, bat, ball and more . But the one thing stands out in my mind that I so dearly wanted was something called a Carom Board. A Carom board was approximately 36 inches square with net like pockets at each corner. It came with little black and red circular hollowed out discs and two short wooden cue sticks that were used to shoot the discs into the netted hole on each corner. There was a checkerboard on one side and a backgammon board on the other side along with many other parts and designs. The instructions stated there were a hundred different games to be played however I only played the ones I mentioned. When my mother awoke she pointed out that I hadn't looked to see what was in my Christmas stocking. It was full of lots more treats such as candy bars, peanuts, and little toy items. There was even and an apple, and an orange which was a rare treat to receive in the winter months in those days. I was delirious with joy. After I tired of playing games on my new Carom board I put on my snowsuit to go outside and try my new sled. When I opened the door I was surprised to see a huge box with a big red ribbon and bow sitting at the bottom of the cement stairwell that led to our apartment. The box had Skippy King written on it. I brought it in to open it and found even more toys, fruit and candy. Who was *this* from? My mother was as surprised as I was to find out it was a gift from "The Goodfellows" (a charitable organization of men that once a year around Christmastime stood on street corners all over town and sold an special edition of their so called newspaper to raise funds. They used the funds to buy gifts for underprivileged children at Christmas. Apparently someone who knew my dad was in the army overseas perceived that I was an underprivileged kid and turned my name into the "Goodfellows". So here was I on the most generous Christmas of my life receiving charity as a deprived child. I kept it. I would remember in the future no matter how well intentioned the motives, where people are involved, results did not always come about as planned. To this day I remain highly dubious of the claims of good works by many so called charities.

Chapter 10

LOSS

A few weeks after New Years I learned the probable reason for the lavishness of that Christmas. I came home from school one day to find the 8½ x 11 photo of my Daddy, that sat on one of the end tables was missing from it's frame. I was filled with panic! What happened? Where was his picture? I looked everywhere but it was nowhere to be found. I stayed up late that night waiting for my mother to come home from work or wherever else she was. When she came in with the smell of beer on her breath, I shouted….

"Where's my daddy's picture?"

"Skippy I have something to tell you. I am no longer married to George Emerick."

I divorced him so I don't want his picture sitting around anymore. I threw it out!"

"But he's my Daddy"…. I began to cry…. "Why did you get divorced?"

"Because he was a bad man. He used to beat me and I don't love him anymore."

I carried on sobbing for some time but what was done was done. I was powerless to change anything.

"Can't I keep his picture?"

"No I don't want that S.O.B's picture in the house."

That night and for many nights to follow I cried myself to sleep.

The following day while my mother was at work I searched through the trash and found my Daddy's picture. My mother had inserted a baby picture of myself in the frame that had previously held my Daddy's photograph. I took apart the picture frame and placed my daddy's photo behind my own. For a very long time when I was alone I would retrieve my Daddy's picture, trying not to lose my memory of him. I believed that someday he would return from war and make our family whole again. After each viewing I carefully hid it behind my baby photo and prayed my mother would not discover it. With the passage of time serious doubts arose regarding her reason for divorcing my daddy while he was overseas fighting in World War II. On many nights while asleep "The lion" made his return to my dreams.

A week or so after being told my mom & dad were divorced I received another blow to my dream of a normal family. Since we had moved to Sussex St. my mother and I had shared the only bed in the apartment. After all the moving and long separations from family I had experienced, it was very comforting to feel so close to someone I loved. With her in bed beside me I need not fear the evil demons I was sure still lurked in the dark. Late one night while alone and asleep in bed I was awakened by my mother returning home. It was quite late and the strong smell of alcohol had once more accompanied her. She was telling me I had to get up and go sleep on the couch.

"But why?"

"Don' ask why. Jus' do as I shay."

Reluctantly I got up to go to the living room a few steps away. There I saw a rather large man with dark brown hair, a sharply receding hairline and a mustache like Clark Gables. He smiled at me and said ....

"Hi, I'm Lester".

My mother placed a pillow and some blankets on the couch and as I situated myself I saw Lester enter the bedroom where my mother was tidying up the bed. Then the folding glass doors closed behind him. Through the glass doors I could see him get undressed and get into *my* bed. As I watched my mother join him I had a feeling of abandonment and betrayal. Who was this man? Why was he replacing me in my bed? What had I done wrong? I sobbed myself to sleep.

The next morning it was explained to me that Lester would be living with us for a while. I didn't like or understand why this was happening and objected profusely to this strange man coming between my mother and I. My resentment grew with each passing day and I made it known at every opportunity. It wasn't long before I was informed that I was going to stay at Grandma and Grandpa's once again. Most likely this was due to my continual obstinate state of mind. Once more I would have to change schools. I would be going back to Monnior again. Disappointment and relief were companions in my mind. Disappointment to be separated from my mother and relief to return to my grandparents where life was normal. I would also be removed from the presence of this unwelcome hulk of a man. By now changing schools did not seem that unusual to me and besides my friend Leonard attended Monnior school and I had that to look forward to.

I stayed with my grandparents for several weeks during the late winter and spring of 1945. Leonard and I quickly renewed our friendship and I found he was still the bold adventurer while I was still the cautious introvert. Our most significant adventure that spring took place at Monnior School. One Sunday afternoon Leonard suggested we go to the playground at Monnior. After we arrived there and horsed around for a while Leonard said….

"Follow me. I want to show you something."

I followed him to the other side of the school where he began shinnying up a large drainpipe attached to the outside wall of the school. Halfway up to the rooftop he looked down.

"What are you waiting for? Come on up."

"It's too dangerous."

"What's the matter, you too chicken?"

Not wanting to lose face with my only friend, I followed him. When he reached the rooftop level he scrambled onto the roof. With great trepidation I followed. Leonard led me to a 3 foot square cover which he lifted off revealing an opening to a steel ladder that extended straight downward ending six feet from the floor.

"We better not go in there Leonard. What if someone's there?"

"No one's there. It's Sunday. The janitors don't work on Sundays."

I followed him down the ladder. We hung from the bottom rung then dropped the rest of the way to the floor below. We found ourselves in some sort of storage room. Quickly we were out the door and into the school hallway. Down the hall we ran, then through the gymnasium doors. We found some basketballs and began tossing them around the gym and at each other. We attempted shooting baskets with little success. As nine year olds we hadn't quite the strength to reach the hoop. We shinnied up the climbing ropes that hung from the high gymnasium ceiling and swung back and forth. Next we had a great idea … There was a cinder block partition wall about eight feet high separating the locker rooms from the gym proper. One of us would climb to the top of the wall and the other threw the end of the climbing rope up to the one on top who would then grab hold of the rope and jump off swinging almost all the way across the gym letting out a Tarzan like "ahoooah" all the way. When we tired of these shenanigans we started back down the hall to leave. On the way we encountered the girl's lavatory. We looked at each other with a big grin and went in to look around. There was nothing special about the girl's lavatory except the absence of urinals but we giggled a bit enjoying the thrill of doing something we knew was off limits. Later we bragged to other boys that we knew what was in the girls toilet but we wouldn't give them any details. We came close to regretting those boasts as this information mysteriously reached the principal's office and the break-in was reported to the police. An investigation ensued and soon a couple of police detectives came knocking. Leonard and I denied any knowledge and claimed we were only making up the story about the girls lavatory. In all probability we were not believed but we stuck to our story and the cops went away. I got the usual all knowing look from Grandma, and Leonard was grounded for a week.

Another event that spring shook the entire country and my grandparents in particular. I came into the apartment to find Grandma and Grandpa hunched over in front of the Hallicrafters floor model radio, sitting on two kitchen chairs they had dragged into the living room. They were listening intently to the radio broadcast. I asked

"What are you listening to?"

"President Roosevelt is dead."

They looked up at me as they responded and I saw tears in both of my grandparents eyes.

The "tone" in the Littlefield apartment was very solemn for a long long while. Most of the grownups I encountered were similarly sad. Many people credited President Roosevelt for bringing the country out of the "Great Depression" and for the impending end of World War II. Within a few weeks though, Papa was out in the field next door tossing the "shoes" with the neighborhood men. Things began to normalize once more.

With each stay at my grandparent's apartment I was becoming more aware of their habits and the little things they did that were so different from life with my mother. Once in awhile grandma would send me down the street to the corner grocery store with some money and a note for the butcher containing a request for some kind of meat and a few other things she might want. The butcher placed the groceries and the meat, which had been wrapped in brown paper and tied up with string, in a paper bag and gave it to me to take home. When I got back home Grandma would carefully untie the string, unwrap it from the package of meat and then add it onto a large ball of string that always sat on her kitchen counter. On another occasion, while taking a bath, the bar of soap had become so thin and small that I couldn't use it without it crumbling or breaking so I tossed in in the waste can and retrieved a new bar of soap from the bathroom closet. Later that evening Grandma went into the bathroom and when she came out she asked....

"Skippy, what happened to the old bar of soap."

I explained it was too small and had tossed it out. She told me to retrieve the old soap bar from the waste basket and then showed me a mason jar where she put the old soap bars to dry. After she accumulated several of these and they had dried out sufficiently she would use a grater to grate the small old soap bar into tiny chips which then were used to do laundry in the wringer washer. Having survived many periods of deprivation including "The great Depression", no string, no soap or anything else went to waste in my grandparent's home. I was learning many such lessons in thrift and the clues to independent survival whenever I spent time with my grandparents. Alas the school year came to an end all too soon and I was on the move again. My mother and Lester had moved to a new flat and I was to join them.

Chapter 11

THE BRADY YEARS

My new home was a two story brick flat on Carter Street near Lawton Blvd. We occupied the upstairs flat. It was much larger than the other places I had lived in with my mother. I had my own large bedroom with lots of closet space and room for all my toys and my growing collection of comic books. School was out for summer recess and I was home alone most days. On weekday evenings my mother and Lester would meet at a local bar on the way home from work where they would spend several hours. Due to my fear of being alone in the flat at night I was glad that they usually returned home around nine o'clock, before dark arrived. On weekend nights, when they did not have to work the next day, they went out and stayed out drinking till the "bars' closed. The usual routine, then, was to take me to the local confectionery store where I would be given a quarter to buy a new ten cent comic book, a five cent coca cola and a large bag of potato chips to placate me for being left alone all night. After they left I turned on every available light and curled up in bed with my new comic book or sometimes I read one of "The Hardy Boys" mystery novels my Aunt Rea had given me. I was still fearful of this new place and once safely ensconced in my bedroom I did not get out of bed again. The coke and chips were in easy reach on the bedside table.

Other times they would drop me at the movie house while they went to the bar. I liked going to the movies as it was an escape from the reality of my life. The comedy team of Abbot and Costello were one of my favorites. Their movies were very popular in the "1940s". I recall one of their movies featured a scene that had me rolling in the aisles. The movie was "Lost in a Harem" and somehow Costello is sharing a jail cell, in a Middle Eastern country, with a old crazy bedraggled bum. The bum sits quietly in a corner of the cell never saying anything while Costello is pleading for Abbott to get him out of the jail. When one of them utters a certain word (Pokomoko) it supposedly reminds the bum of his arch enemy who has wronged him in some way in the past. Immediately the bum goes into a routine where in a deep gravelly voice he says… *"Slowly I turned step by step inch by inch"* …. All the while he is moving in a hunched over cripple-like gait until he reaches Costello whereupon he begins violently thrashing blows upon his imagined enemy. When Costello lets out a scream the bum comes to his senses and ceases beating on Costello. Then Abbott says "He doesn't like you to say Pokomoko. Upon the sound of the trigger word once more the bum goes into the previous routine repeating *"Slowly I turned step by step inch by inch"* and Costello receives another trouncing. This is repeated several more times during the movie. I mention this movie because at the time I found this so funny that I began practicing the routine when I was alone at home imitating the deep gravelly voice of the bum and trying to approximate his slow turning hunched over limping gait. Eventually I became quite adept at this imitation and would use it to my advantage at a later time. Many times when the movies were over my parents weren't there to pick me up. When the theater manager became aware that I was standing in the lobby long after all the other patrons had left he allowed me to wait inside. He locked the doors and began his nightly accounting of the day's ticket and candy counter sales while I waited. Eventually my mother or Lester would arrive full of various excuses. This scenario often repeated itself. I got to know the theater manager quite well.

During the first few weeks at the Carter flat I spent a lot of time in my room listening to the radio, playing with my toy soldiers and still wondering when I would be reunited with my Daddy (if he was still alive). I became bored but was still reluctant to go outside where I knew no one in this new neighborhood. I asked my mother if I could go to Grandma's for a day. She told me how to get to my grandparent's apartment by riding the bus. My mother was always quite willing to provide me with the bus fare. The bus trip involved walking several blocks to the closest bus stop, paying the bus fare, (ten cents I think) plus two cents more for a "transfer slip". I had to transfer to two other buses before finally being let off on Schoolcraft Ave. As I exited at the bus stop just one block away from the Littlefield apartments the warm feeling of being home comforted me. I was only moments away from seeing Grandma and my Papa. Maybe too I would find Leonard at his house and we could go on more "adventures" together. I spent the day there, became reacquainted with Leonard, enjoyed supper with my grandparents then returned by bus to my present home on Carter Street. I would take many bus trips back to this "safe haven" during the coming years.

One day warm weather and the brightly shining sun finally drew me outside the Carter flat. I sat down on the concrete porch steps. Down the street I noticed other kids playing some kind of game. They were laughing and running back and forth apparently having a lot of fun. I considered trying to join them but rejected the idea out of shyness. Seemingly out of nowhere a girl, I guessed to be about my age, walked right up to me and said...

"What's your name?"

"My name is Skip."

"Do you live here?"

"Yeah. We just moved here a few weeks ago."

"I haven't seen you outside before."

"This is the first time I've been out."

"Too bad you didn't come out yesterday."

"Why?"

"Because we were fucking!"

At that point in my life I'm not sure if I had ever heard that word before and not understanding what she meant I asked....

"What is fucking?"

"Me and my girlfriends went in our garage with some boys and took off our clothes then we rubbed our butts together with the boys."

The thought of this intrigued me even though I had no idea of what sex was. Still, fascinated with the idea of seeing a girl with no clothes on. I asked....

"When you do it again can I come too?"

"We won't ever do it again."

"Why not.?"

"My mother caught us and she said we'll be grounded for life if we do it again."

At that point I regretted hibernating in my room so long. Still I thought maybe they *will* do it again and I'll be around. For whatever reason I cannot remember her name nor can I remember any of the friends she introduced me to. What stands out in my mind was that there was an undercurrent of naughtiness among those kids. I especially remember I was with a group of neighborhood boys one evening when they told me they were going to "fuck" the girls again. This idea appealed to me as I thought I would get to see the girls naked. This time though the plan was different. I was to meet the boys after dark on the corner and bring a short stick with me. The excitement I felt over what I thought was to take place overrode my constant fear of the dark and I showed up at the designated time stick in hand. Following their instructions I unbuttoned my pants and put one end of the stick inside my fly with about 4 inches protruding out. I then fastened the buttons of my fly so that it held the stick somewhat firmly. Next we went looking for the girls. I watched as the other boys chased the girls and wrestled them to the ground, then with one hand holding the sticks (still sticking out of the general area of their groins) they poked the sticks at the girls bellies. I soon followed suit. The girls were giggling and the boys were laughing. After only a few minutes this activity ceased and we all decided to play hide and seek instead.

Brady school was only a few blocks away on Joy Road and Lawton and I would be attending fourth grade there in the fall. The kids from the neighborhood would go there to play. The boys would play baseball, or tag or simply run around burning up the excess energy that young boys are gifted with. Usually they would ride on their bikes so it was time for me to try again to learn how to ride my bike. I retrieved the bike that was stored in the basement and made several unsuccessful attempts at riding. It was no use. I was simply too afraid of falling so at the first wobble I would jump off the bike. I resigned myself to never being able to ride a bicycle. Instead I followed them over there on foot.

One afternoon at Brady School playground I observed some boys playing on the grass with pocket knives. They were playing a game with their knives that involved performing various feats of skill. I learned that there were twelve skill levels to master with each one more dangerous than the one before. The first level involved laying an open Jackknife across the middle of your open palm, then without closing your hand swing your arm upward over your head in a wide arc until gravity pulled the knife from your hand and it fell to the ground behind you. If the knife stuck in the ground you then proceeded to level two. Level two was a similar feat only you started by laying the knife on the back of your hand between two fingers. Again, an arching swing to stick it in the ground. Next time, backwards over your shoulder in hopes it would once again stick. One boy was at level ten. I watched as he placed the point of his knife on the tip of his nose, held the butt end of the knife with his index finger then flipped it forward in an attempt to have it stick in the ground. If it at any skill level your knife failed to stick you had to go back and start at level one. I obtained a Jackknife of my own and began playing this game with the boys. In those days virtually every single boy owned a pocket knife and carried it with him at all times ready to play this game even when school was in session. I never heard of a teacher or school official chastising or taking away a boys knife and I never heard of anyone ever getting hurt playing "mumbletypeg".

At the school playground, I met another boy, Billy, who was not part of the "naughty kids" gang. He was very outgoing and seemed to want to make friends with me. So lacking in confidence was I that I immediately gravitated towards anyone that appeared to accept me. After a few weeks of playing together Billy invited me to go to church with him. Anxious to please my newfound friend I began attending church services with him. As far as I can remember this was the first time I had ever been inside a church. My only knowledge of religion came from an illustrated children's story book of Jesus and a King James Bible that my Aunt Rea had mailed to me as a birthday present while I was still on the "farm". Aunt Rea never forgot my birthday or Christmas. I had little understanding of the bible passages but I loved to read the children's story book. I found looking at the beautiful illustrations, some of Jesus sitting and speaking to a gathering of children and some of Jesus performing his miracles, quite calming. I liked the people at the church. Everyone was pleasant, friendly and compared to my limited experience appeared to be living normal lives, something I greatly longed for. At one of the services the minister announced they were sponsoring a summer camp out near Waterford, Michigan. It would be open for eight weeks during July and August. Outside the church, after the service was over, my new friend Billy said …

"I'm gonna' ask my folks if they'll let me go to the summer camp."

"Me too."…. I said excitedly, hoping against hope that they might actually allow me to go. I was greatly surprised when my mother said yes I could go to summer camp. She contacted the church and arrangements were made. I was elated! Billy and I would be going to "camp" together. When I saw Billy again I exclaimed…

"I can go!"

"Me too."

"How long are you going for?"

"Two weeks."

"I'll tell my mother I want to go for two weeks also."

In early July Lester and my mother drove me out for my two weeks of "Summer Church Camp". The camp was located on the shores of a beautiful lake near Pontiac, Michigan. I was registered at the main administrative building and introduced to the camp director "Captain Smith". Captain Smith was dressed then and always in a soldiers uniform. I was given a slip of paper with a rudimentary map showing the layout of the camp and marked with an "X" indicating the cabin I was assigned to. My excitement was such that I paid little attention as Captain Smith explained the general rules and camp regulations. As soon as my parents left to go back to Detroit I began searching the grounds for Billy. After looking for what seemed like forever, I found a group of boys swinging on some ropes that hung in "Maypole" fashion from a tall metal post. The boys would run around the pole to gather speed then lift their legs off the ground up to their chests allowing the centrifugal force to carry them outward around the circle in midair for several seconds. To my delight one of these boys was Billy.

"Hi Billy, I'm here."

"Hi Skippy, What cabin are you in?"

Looking at the paper map I was given I replied….

"I'm in cabin 4. Where are you?"

"Aw nuts, I'm in cabin twelve."

I was greatly disappointed as I wanted to be in the same cabin as my friend Billy. I knew Billy but I did not know any of the other boys in cabin four. With the continual change of addresses and schools my reluctance to meet new people was becoming more and more a serious problem. Although Billy didn't seem to be bothered by our assignment to different cabins I cajoled him into asking Captain Smith to relocate one of us so we could be together in the same cabin. Billy came back to tell me Captain Smith said "No way". So off to the assigned cabin I went. Entering cautiously I surveyed the surroundings. Eight sets of bunk beds, four on the left, and four on the right with no one in sight. Relieved to find no one there I laid down on one of the bottom bunks. Then a young man (I would guess in his late teens) entered the cabin.

"And just who are you? Why aren't you outside playing with the other boys?"

"I'm Skip."…. I replied then mumbled…. " I dunno"

He looked at a sheet of paper and said…

"I don't think your in the right cabin, there is no Skip on my list."

"My real name is Julian."

(I hated using my real name because I was named after my father who according to my mother was a very bad man.)

"Oh I see I do have a Julian King listed. So that's you and do you like to be called Skip or Skippy?

"Yeah"

He introduced himself as Richard (The Group Leader)" for cabin four and showed me a top bunk where I would sleep at night. Eventually the other "Cabin Four" assignees began showing up and the awkward process of getting to know one another started. That night as I tried to go to sleep in my bunk I found myself sucking my thumb, as I always did and realized the other boys might see this. I knew I would be teased and taunted so I tried to position myself in such a way that the other boys couldn't see me with my thumb in my mouth. My plan didn't work and I was razzed mercilessly by the rest of the cabin four inmates.

During the next few days I slowly adjusted to the routine at the summer camp. Each morning at 7 am. we would awaken to the sound of a trumpet playing Reveille. We then got dressed and hurried to the mess hall for breakfast at 7:30 am. We all bowed our heads as "Grace" was said by the camp chaplain. During that first breakfast Captain Smith's voice came over the loudspeakers ...

"Lunch mess" is promptly at noon and supper is at 6p.m. sharp. Everyone is to be in their cabins with "Lights out" when you hear Taps.

Every evening at dusk we would hear that lone, lonely bugle echoing it's version of "Taps" across the campgrounds each evening.....

> "Day is done,
> Gone the sun,
> From the hills,
> from the lake,
> From the sky.
> All is well,
> safely rest.
> God is nigh.

Each morning at breakfast we would learn of the activities planned for us that day. Sometimes we would all get into huge rowboats and take turns learning to row out on the lake. Other days we might go on long hikes through the woods learning to identify various wildflowers and trees along the way. Once a week it was down to the beach area for swimming lessons. Learning to float in water that was only 3 feet deep was our first lesson but I just couldn't manage to stay up. "Try to relax" I was told but every time I laid back on the water with my arms spread wide and tried to relax I would sink to the bottom. The next lesson was the dog paddle. I attempted this several times during my stay at the camp. Kicking vigorously and pawing the water, like a dog, I would only progress a couple of feet before gradually sinking to the bottom again. One of the group leaders ventured that it was because I was so skinny with no fat on my body and it was fat that helped keep a person buoyant. Another time we would all pile into camp vehicles and be driven to a huge quarry. The sides of the quarry went almost straight down about ten feet where they met with the clearest bluest water I had ever seen. The water was extremely deep yet you could see clear to the bottom. There was a small dock jutting out at one end of the quarry and many of the older boys who knew how to swim would gleefully jump into the water from the dock, hoopin' and hollerin', all the way. I was encouraged to join them but, fearful of my swimming abilities, I declined.

Every Saturday we played "Capture the Flag". The camp attendees were divided into "The Red Group" and "The Blue Group". Each boy was given a colored ribbon to tie to his belt indicating which side he was on. Then each group picked a spot to plant their "flag." Then, to win the game, each side would to try to capture the opposite sides "Flag" and bring it back and plant it next their own flag. If someone was caught trying to steal the other side's flag he could be overpowered and drug off to an area that each side designated as their "Jail" This activity turned out to be quite rough and tumble and often smaller boys got hurt interacting with the older and larger boys. I had previously been cautioned regarding my so called heart condition and I was extremely small for my age. Afraid of getting hurt, I avoided any physical interaction as much as possible. My "Cabin Group Leader" noticed this and later in "Cabin Four" (in front of the other boys) he ridiculed me for my cowardice.

My favorite activity was when we all got in the huge lifeboats and rowed our way across the lake to the other side where we encountered a huge culvert, just large enough to accommodate our life boats but without enough room to extend the oars. To navigate through the culvert we reached out our arms to touch the sides of the culvert and pushed our way through. Once out of the culvert we were in another smaller lake. We crossed that lake and rowed under a concrete bridge. Once past the bridge it was a short distance to shore where we disembarked. At the top of a steep incline we found a highway that went right through Waterford, Michigan. We were in the center of the small business district where we found a confectionery store that sold candy and ice cream. Everyone spent their pennies and or nickels on their favorite treat. With twenty-five cents I had saved I indulged myself with a chocolate soda! This trip to Waterford was a bi-weekly affair that we all looked forward to. All in all the two weeks at camp were quite exciting. Days we spent in the woods reminded me of the more pleasant times on the "Farm". I enjoyed the various field trips we took and leisure time on the beach as well as the boat trips to Waterford. On the last Saturday that Billy and I were to be there we packed up our belongings awaiting the arrival of our parents to retrieve us. Around lunchtime Billy's folks arrived. We said our goodbyes vowing to get together the next day back at home. Later around 4 pm. my mother and Lester showed up. I grabbed my little bag of clothes and ran to meet them, excited to be going home. My mother said lets go up to the "Main building", I have something to tell you.

"What is it?"

"I'll tell you when we get there?"

We proceeded to the "main building" where there was a visitor's area, a sofa, and some tables and chairs.

"What do you have to tell me? Aint I going home?"

"You can't come home right now."

"Why can't I?"

"It's a bad time right now."

"Why? What's so bad."

It was then I noticed the dampness in my mother's eyes as she told me....

"Your Papa is gone."

"Papa's gone! Gone where?"

"He's dead"

"He's what? NO! NO! He can't be, he can't be dead. Not my Papa. It can't be true!"

"I'm so sorry Skippy but it is true He had a stroke and died suddenly without warning."

I began to sob uncontrollably when Captain Smith was passing by. He stopped and turned to me saying...

"Hear hear! This is no way for one of "our boys" to behave."

His comment caused me to cry even more. My mother then informed him regarding my grandfather's death. Although there was a rule that no camper could leave the jurisdiction of the camp during their stay Captain Smith granted my mother permission to leave with me for a while. We got in the car and drove to a tavern a few miles away where they drank a few beers and I sipped on a "Coke" and nipped on a nickel bag of potato chips. I was given money and encouraged to play the "Ski Ball" game but saddened over the loss of my Papa, I had no interest in playing anything. Instead I sat depressed with elbows on the table and my head resting in the palms of my hands. Then making one final plea...

"Can't I please go home with you?"

"No. I'm sorry Skippy but you've just got to stay at camp a few more weeks."

"I will be good. I won't get in the way."

"Sorry! Because of losing Grandpa there's just too many things I have to help Grandma with."

I was totally dismayed with the news of Grandpa's death. In the absence of my Daddy he was my image of a loving male role model. The fact that I was not going home further depressed me. I enjoyed the first two weeks I had spent at "camp" but Billy was gone now and he was my only friend at summer camp. In spite of my pleas to go home I was driven back to "camp". I was crying again as my mother and Lester left for Detroit. I felt terribly alone once more.

The "Lion" visited my bunk that night.

I awoke the next morning determined to struggle through the situation I found myself in. The boys assigned to my cabin had changed. A new group of two week campers had moved in however Richard remained the "Group Leader" for cabin four. I wasn't sure he liked me but having him remain seemed better than having to meet a new "Leader". I needed to find a way to make a new friend. But lacking confidence I shrunk back and waited for a new friend to come my way. One rainy afternoon we were all confined to our cabins waiting for the rain to stop when Richard announced he was able to hypnotize people. He requested a volunteer on which to demonstrate this skill. When no one volunteered he surprised me by calling my name…

"How about you, Skippy? Why not let me hypnotize you? You're not afraid, are you?

Running quickly through my mind were thoughts of….

"This could be my chance to prove myself to the new kids" and *"Maybe if I do this they will like me!"*

Meekly I answered…. "Okay, you can try it on me."

He asked me to lay back on one of the bottom bunks.

"Look directly into my eyes and try to relax. Think of a pleasant place you have been to. Now as you count backward from one hundred you'll begin to feel sleepy."

I felt no change in my mental acuity but anxious to please I pretended to become drowsy. He asked me to raise one arm over my head and wave goodbye (which I did). He asked me to perform a few other stunts (which of course I did as well.) Suddenly one of the other boys spoke up saying....

"He's faking! He's not really hypnotized."

Faced with this challenge Richard revealed the final test. He took out a safety pin from his desk drawer, he unclasped it to expose the needle like point and said....

"Skippy I am going to stick a pin into your arm but you will not cry out as you will not feel anything."

Then turning to the rest of the boys.... "Do you all agree if Skippy doesn't react in any way to the pin prick that he has been hypnotized?"

Everyone agreed. With both myself and the "Cabin Leader facing humiliation as frauds I braced myself for the upcoming pin prick. Then he proceeded to prick my skin with the open safety pin. Despite the pain I remained still. I wanted to yell out but I dared not. After three or four pricks with the pin he asked if everyone was satisfied with the test. All agreed I had been hypnotized.

"When I count to three and snap my fingers, Skippy, you will wake up and not remember anything that happened to you and after you wake up you will never suck your thumb again."

I pretended to wake up at the designated time and acted out the part as I was told. I made a determined effort to stop my thumb sucking and I was successful for a few weeks. The other boys were asking me what it was like to be hypnotized, did I feel anything and what did I remember? I dutifully proclaimed no memory of the entire event. From that point on I was somewhat of a celebrity with the other boys at the camp. Even Richard seemed to take a more favorable attitude toward me. The next day I encountered Captain Smith…

"I understand you were hypnotized the other day *Mister* King."

"Yes sir I was."

With a strange twinkle in his eye he smiled and began walking away saying as he left.…

"That's nice"

I was not happy with the situation I found myself in but I knew I had to make the best of it. All the scheduled events of my second two weeks at camp were a repetition of the first two weeks. The excitement I had felt previously while taking trips to places I had not seen and doing things I had not done before was obviously gone. I soon discovered that I could use my experiences of the first two weeks to my advantage as nearly all the other boys were new and looked to me to "let them in" on what was going to happen the next day.

The last Saturday of second two weeks finally arrived. I packed up my clothes and anxiously awaited the arrival of My mother and Lester to retrieve me. Many cars were driving onto the grounds some picking up those leaving and some dropping off the new "campers". As time passed fewer and fewer cars were arriving. I sat on the wooden step at the front door of the cabin wondering why they were so late. When I heard the bell ringing announcing supper mess I reluctantly headed off to the mess hall. When they came to get me they would surely look for me there. In the mess hall Captain Smith motioned me over to his table and said …

"Julian your mother called me a while ago and asked me to inform you that she can't pick you up this week. You will be staying here two more weeks."

"Why?" I blurted out in anguish…. "Did she say why?"

"She said something had come up. She'll come for you in two more weeks."

I thought to myself ….

"There is nothing I can do. I am at the mercy of these "big people" who control my whole life. I am in a place I no longer want to be and I am powerless to change it. If only my Daddy would come home. He wouldn't let this happen to me"

Circumstances and feelings such as this would become the norm for me. Resigned to my fate once again I tried to make the best of it. I assumed the face of the most experienced camper and won over a friend or two in the new batch of "campers" The camp's scheduled routine was becoming a bore except for the weekly boat trip to Waterford.

Hitler surrendered and the war in Europe ended that spring. In early August rumors began circulating throughout the camp that Japan might also surrender to the allies and the war in the Pacific would come to an end. This rumor had everyone excited. You had to look far and wide to find anyone who didn't have a father, an uncle, a brother or a friend who was in the "service" overseas somewhere in Europe or the South Pacific. I was desperately hoping this rumor was true as it meant my Daddy would be coming home and he would know how to make everything right again. Then during the first week of August my "Group leader" informed us that President Truman had dropped some sort of gigantic bomb on Japan, killing thousands of Japs, and Japan was about to surrender. I and many other campers raced excitedly through the camp confirming that it was true and spreading the news. Now I knew for sure my Daddy was coming home.

When the final Saturday of my third two week assignment to camp arrived my mother and Lester came to visit with the news that I would be spending yet another two weeks with "Captain Smith and the boys".

"Why are you making me stay here so long, I was only supposed to spend two weeks at camp. If I have to stay here again I will have been here eight weeks. Please take me home with you this isn't fair."

"Skippy, you know your Papa died and I had to help Grandma with some things and then other things came up and I've been extremely busy. I just can't handle having you home yet.

"You're never going to take me home. You're going to leave me here for good."

"No, you'll be coming home for good in two weeks, I promise."

"I don't believe you. You told me that before. You're a liar."

"No! It's true You're coming home in two weeks. You have to start school and the camp is closing down for the season."

So I endured my last assignment to the camp and finally at the end of August when I returned to Detroit I found the place I called home had changed once more.

This time it was another basement apartment on the corner of Lawton Ave. and Philadelphia St. only six blocks from the flat on Carter. There were two bedrooms separated by a large living room and a small kitchen. The furniture was old and worn bare in spots exuding a musty odor. The wallpaper was discolored and peeling off the wall. I was sure I was not going to like this place. Another move meant separation once more from the kids I was just getting to know and I began to think it was a waste of time making new friends so back I went to spending my days inside reading and listening to radio serials all day long. With each change of address these retreats from the outside world were growing longer.

The school year began and I was glad to learn I was still in the area served by Brady School. Surely some of the kids I knew would be there. Maybe I could meet up with Billy and resume our friendship. For a few days I roamed the playground at recess looking for him but alas Billy was nowhere to be found. None of the other children had seen him either. Possibly he had moved away. I remember two other fourth grade students, Bobby Snell and Betty Jankowski. I remember Billy because he was the "class cut up" always wise cracking and making the rest of us laugh. I remember Betty because she was the prettiest girl in the fifth grade with long blond hair and big blue eyes. I liked her and tried to be near her whenever the opportunity presented itself. I adjusted to this new school rather quickly. I found being in school preferable to spending time alone in the musty apartment on Philadelphia.

My mother and Lester were spending all their spare time at a bar on Hamilton Ave. Sometimes they took me with them to their new hangout (Benny Kirk's Bar)) where they spent most evenings and weekends. They would sometimes introduce me to other bar patrons According to the custom of the day I was required to shake their hands. Once while shaking hands with one man he felt my weak and limp grip and decided to give me a lesson in the importance of a firm grip. He grabbed my hand a second time and squeezed hard. He squeezed so hard I thought he would crush my hand. Tears began to appear in my eyes. As was true of most of the people in Benny Kirk's bar I detected the strong odor of alcohol when he was up close to me. When he saw I was about to cry he handed me a nickel and told me to go play one of the games that were located throughout the bar. There was a game called Ski Ball, a pool table and a machine that you could look into a small window and watch various short scenes of comic characters or real people actually moving. I have since learned this machine was called a mutoscope. They were manufactured by the "International Mutoscope Reel Company. Television was not yet heard of at that time and to be able to see a moving picture inside this machine was fascinating. There were a number of different choices but it required a nickel for each one. I stumbled upon one scene that I would watch again and again whenever I was sure no one was paying attention to me. It was called "What the Butler Saw". Supposedly a butler was peeping through a keyhole to watch a woman disrobing. Eventually fully undressed she turns and faces the keyhole. *You could see "everything!"* I would beg my mother or Les for nickels so I could watch more. I am not sure if my mother and Les knew I was looking at this naked lady but I am also not sure that it mattered to them as long as I left them alone to consume more of their beloved alcohol. I spent many weekend days and weekday evenings at "Benny Kirks"

Eventually I grew weary of either going with my parents to the "bar" or staying home alone in the Philadelphia apartment reading and rereading my collection of comic books or listening to the radio. One day I gathered enough courage to venture outside. "Joseph's Confectionery Shop" was a few blocks away and neighborhood boys hung around outside on the sidewalk. I approached cautiously and observed their activities. I watched as two boys placed a nickel on the line (crack) that separated two sidewalk squares and then each boy took a stance in opposite directions an equal distance from the nickel. They would alternate tossing a tennis ball at the nickel with the object of hitting the coin in such a way as to flip it over from heads to tails or vice versa. Whoever achieved the "flip" first won a nickel from the other boy. After observing for some time I asked them if I could try.

"Sure" one of them said "If you've got a nickel"

Luckily I had a nickel in my pocket but I soon lost it to the more experienced "gamblers". This was my entryway to yet again a new group of friends. My interaction with this new group would be limited as before long, we would be relocating once again. My time with them was short and remembering their names impossible. It was a diverse group made up of Catholics, Jews, Chaldeans, and Episcopalian Protestants like me. I was always extremely fearful to meet new people but sometimes situations forced me to make new acquaintances. If it turned out they were friendly I integrated quickly. This new gang of friends showed me a new game (roof ball)! Four, five, six or more boys would go to the alley behind a slanted roof garage. Each boy would be assigned a number then one boy would start the game by tossing a tennis ball up on the roof and calling out a number. The boy whose number was called then had to catch the ball before it hit the ground or he was eliminated from the game. Due to our size and the height of the roof we couldn't always see where the ball would exit the roof until the very last minute. With each toss various attempts were made to fool the next player and cause him to miss. Often a ball would get stuck on the roof and someone would climb onto the roof to fetch it. Sometimes we would all climb up to the rooftop to observe how far we could see. The houses and garages in the neighborhood were set rather close together enabling the more daring boys to jump from one garage roof to the next. It became a challenge to see how many roofs one could traverse. It was quite thrilling leaping through the air across the gaps (most of them six feet wide) to the adjacent garages. These jumps required a lot of energy and occasionally I experienced the weakness and lethargy that had dogged me since early childhood so I wasn't always able to follow and some of the boys would go much farther than I could.

One afternoon while I was hanging around Joseph's Confectionery with a couple of my new friends one of the boys asked...

"Hey Skip, you wanna go for a ride in a new car?"

"I guess so. Who's car?".... I hesitantly replied...

"It's some guy we know. He's a nice guy. He comes by once in awhile and drives us around in his car. He'll take us anywhere we want to go."

For some reason I wasn't sure if this was a good idea but then I did not want to appear afraid in front of the other boys and said...

"Well if you guys are goin' I'll go with you."

I followed the other two boys a few blocks down Lawton Ave. Where sure enough, there was a black four door sedan idling at the cross street. A heavy set man was sitting in the driver's seat. As we approached he reached across to swing open the passenger side door and said ....

"Hi guys, get yourselves in here and let's take a spin in my new car."

At this point the other two boys jumped in the back seat. When I attempted to get in the back seat with them they said I should get in the front as it was my first time and I should have the best seat. Although I was apprehensive I complied with their instructions. The man began making small talk as he drove slowly down the street. His voice seemed nervous as he spoke and he was perspiring heavily. After several blocks he reached over and placed his right hand on my leg. I couldn't understand what was going on but I became extremely nervous. Afraid to voice my objection my nervousness turned into fear as he began gently massaging my leg. I knew something was not right and eased my way closer to the passenger side door then when we came to a stop light I quickly opened the door and jumped out. The other boys jumped out of the back seat laughing and pointing fingers at me as the black sedan sped off. I was mad and upset not knowing why I was being laughed at.

"What was that all about?".... I asked.

"Na na na!".... they laughed and derided me. "You got felt up by a Fairy."

"What's a Fairy?"

"A guy who likes boys."

"What is wrong with liking boys?"

"Doncha know a Fairy likes boys a little too much."

Fairy was the word the boys used to describe a homosexual. That was my first encounter with one and I was not even sure what that was all about. I just knew I did not like the position those boys had put me in.

In those times there were few if any stores we now call "supermarkets". Most of the populace purchased groceries at small neighborhood grocery stores operated by an individual owner who ordered supplies, stocked the shelves, cut the meat, bagged the groceries, rang the register and extended credit all by himself. As far as I know there was no such thing as a credit card either. Each time we moved into a new neighborhood my mother would visit one of these local grocery stores and establish a credit account. In this neighborhood the store was named "Solomon's Groceries". Often my mother gave a me a note listing some things she wanted to buy and sent me to the store to get them. Sometimes she gave me money and I would hand the note to the Mr. Solomon along with the money, but sometimes she did not give me any money and the note would say....

"Please charge it".

On October 31st (Halloween) I was with a group of neighborhood boys out "begging" as it was called then. We went from house to house in our costumes chanting "Help the Poor" expecting to be given candy or whatever treats that household might be giving out to the Halloween "beggars". We especially looked forward to "hitting" the local stores as they usually gave out better treats. One of the stores I went into with several other boys was "Solomon's Groceries". Mr. Solomon gave us all a piece of candy then he looked at me intently and firmly uttered these words…

"Tell your mother she needs to come and see me regarding her bill."

Without knowing why, exactly, I felt embarrassed by his remark. From that day forward I refused to go in to "Solomons" for any reason.

One morning I overslept and was late leaving for school. While running down the street in an attempt to get to school before the second bell rang a boy riding by on his bike stopped and asked me if I wanted a ride. I said okay and hopped on the "carrier" on the back of his bike. While he peddled the bike to school he asked…

"Don't you have a bike?"

"Yeah but I can't ride it."

"Why not?"

"Don't know how."

"You're kidding. Want me to teach you how?"

"I've tried before but just can't stay up. I fall over every time."

"Meet me after school and I bet I can teach you. It's easy."

When school was over I met this boy, Dennis, on the playground. We went to the back of the school building to the paved parking area. He gave me a few simple instructions then asked me to try to ride his bike. I threw one leg over the crossbar, gave a push off with my left foot and started peddling. To my utter amazement I did not fall. I just kept peddling and maintained my balance as I rode that bike all the way to the end of the teachers parking area and back to where I started. The elation I felt was overwhelming. I could hardly believe I had finally ridden a bicycle without falling. I thanked Dennis and rushed home from school totally thrilled and excited to get my bike out of the basement locker where it was stored. I ran to the basement area where the lockers were located, found the locker for our apartment and looked inside. I could not see a bicycle in there. I moved a few odds and ends and made a thorough search but still no bike. Puzzled and disappointed I went to our apartment and looked all through the apartment hoping against hope to find my bicycle had been moved there for some unknown reason. It hadn't. I spent the evening and night in my bedroom finding solace in reading. Around midnight my mother and Lester came home. They had been to "Benny Kirk's" again. My mother came to see why my light was still on.

"Why aren't you ashleep?"

"I've been waiting for you! Where is my bike? It's not in the Locker."

"Skippy, lishen to me. We shold it."

"You sold it! You sold it! How could you sell my bike it's not yours!"

"Well, you never ride it anywaysh."

"Your drunk again! I hate you!"

Suddenly she slapped me so hard across the face that I started crying and screaming at the same time.

"I hate you! I hate you! You're drunk. You're always drunk."

She stared at me for a moment then a look of pain filled her face....

"I'm sorry I slapped you, Skippy. We'll geshou another bike."

With that she gathered me in her arms and her strong alcohol breath confirmed my earlier accusation. We cried together till I fell asleep sucking my thumb. I would be fifteen years old before I would get another bike... or stop sucking my thumb.

In early November we moved to a two story brick "flat" on Hazelwood, just east of Lawton Ave. This time we were in the upstairs "flat". Like all the other places my mother rented it was furnished with old worn out furniture. The carpet had worn through in spots exposing the wood floor underneath. The stuffed furniture was threadbare and soiled. Wallpaper was peeling and stained in several spots. I took an immediate dislike to the place. My "parents' resumed their normal routine spending most of their time at Benny Kirk's and charging groceries at the local grocers. My new home was only three blocks from Brady School and I was relieved to find I would not have to change schools.

Up to that point in time I still harbored a strong resentment toward Lester and had little interest in learning anything about him. I was unaware of where he worked, where he was born, how old he was or anything else about him. I believe he sensed my displeasure with him in my life and wisely did not try to assume the role of father where I was concerned. He was gone to work every day and when not working he spent most of his time at the local taverns in whatever neighborhood we currently resided in. Thus my interaction with him was limited. Lester was over six feet tall and while not overly muscular was still a really strong man. He was quiet most of the time and despite his strength he had a gentle disposition. Whenever he and my mother disagreed he was the first to back off. I discovered that he was also quite generous. Whenever he had some money he was more than willing to spend it on his bar friends. Often, when no one was home at suppertime and I found nothing in the old ice box to eat I marched down the street to "Benny Kirk's". There I found my mother and Lester (sitting at the bar drinking) and asked ….

"What am I supposed to have for supper?"

Lester rarely responded to my queries and my mother would come up with some sort of lame excuse such as….

"Oh! Is it suppertime already." - or- " I thought I left you something."

Although I wanted them to come home with me that rarely happened. Instead Lester would give me some money to buy a corn beef sandwich at one of the local delicatessens and tell me to go home. I would object….

"Why won't you come home and make me something to eat."

As a matter of course my pleas would be ignored. Lester would sit with a sheepish grin and my mother would say….

"We'll be home shortly."

Frequently I observed other bar patrons grumbling or snickering at me.

On a Saturday evening my mother and Lester announced that they were going to the apartment of a "couple" they had made acquaintance with at the "bar" and that I was going with them. I wasn't crazy about the idea of going with them. I knew it would result in a lot of "drinking" and didn't want to be someplace where I couldn't make an easy escape.

"Why do I have to go?"

"They have a daughter about your age that you can play with.

"I still don't want to go."

"We're going "out" together and they don't want to leave her alone so you are going with us."

When we arrived at the apartment of my parents friends I was introduced to Sandy. She appeared to be eleven or twelve years old (a year or two older than I was) and physically bigger as well. She had a pleasant face and sandy blond hair that came down to the top of her shoulders. I wondered if "Sandy" was a nickname due to her hair color or just short for Sandra. I took notice of the area of her breasts which were in the early stage of development. The four adults went into the living room to consume a few beers and we began playing the Monopoly game that was already set up on the kitchen table in anticipation that Sandy and I would play. It wasn't long before the adults informed Sandy and that they were going "out" for a while. (I knew "out" meant the nearest "bar".) I was shown a small bedroom where I could sleep if I got tired before they returned. After they left, Sandy and I played "Monopoly" for a while and became better acquainted. Before long I became aware that Sandy liked to be in charge. Whenever there was a dispute about how the game should be played, Sandy had to be right! I always gave in as I was too shy and afraid to argue my side of the argument. As the evening progressed into night we were both becoming sleepy and bored with the game. Sandy said we should go to bed as it was getting late. We went to our respective bedrooms to lie down. I got into the bed and pulled a blanket over me. Before long I heard Sandy calling my name from her bedroom just across the hall. I yelled back…

"What?"

"Are you asleep yet?"

A dumb question (I thought).

"No."

"I'm not either. Why don't you come in my room for a while and we can talk or play or something."

"Okay"

I got up and went into her bedroom. She was sitting up in bed, dressed in her pajamas. Surprisingly she said …

"You can get in the bed with me if you want to."

At this point I started thinking about the description of rubbing butts together "fucking" that I had heard from that girl when we lived on Carter Street. A feeling of excitement began coursing through my body as I thought (maybe I will get to see Sandy naked.) I jumped up on the bed with anticipation of what would come next. She then said…

"We can't let our folks catch us in bed together so if you hear the door you gotta get outa here."

"Okay, what should we do now?"

I was hoping she would say let's take our clothes off or something similar as I was way too shy to say anything like that myself. Instead she told me to stay at the bottom of the bed while she stayed at the head of the bed. I obediently followed her instructions and positioned myself where she directed. We made "small talk" for awhile then Sandy got out a book and started reading it aloud. It was a fairy tale book with pictures. I began inching my way to the head of the bed, pretending I wanted to look at the pictures. Eventually I was close enough to feel her upper arm touching my upper arm. A feeling of warmth came over me as our arms brushed against each other. We sat in bed for several minutes. I could feel my heart racing. Suddenly there was a noise. Someone was at the door.

"Oh my God! Its my parents. You've got to get out of here now!"

I Jumped out of Sandy's bed, dashed across the hall to the bedroom I was assigned, leaped into my bed, pulled up the covers and pretended to be asleep. During this fast maneuver I saw the adults entering through the door. I prayed they had not looked my way. My mother came in the room and called my name. I played the part of just waking up as best I could.

"Come on Skippy we're going home now."

"Alright."

I was unsure if we fooled our parents. As we were leaving I thought Sandy's mother gave me a "funny" look or It could have just been my feeling of guilt. For quite awhile after that I held out the hope that my folks would go back to visit Sandy's mom & dad and take me with them so that I could see Sandy again but for whatever reason that never happened. It would be several years until I saw Sandy again.

Late in November winter weather descended and snow covered the roads. I learned a new "sport" from the neighborhood boys. We would wait till dark and crouch down between the cars parked on nearby neighborhood streets in close proximity to a "stop street". When a car or truck stopped for the stop sign we would scramble from our hiding place and grab on to the back of the vehicle's chrome bumper. When the driver accelerated through the intersection we leaned our weight backward and slid along on our shoes behind the automobile on the snow packed (sometimes icy) road. The ride would end when the auto got going too fast. Then we would let loose of the bumper sliding forward for several feet laughing all the while. This activity would also end when a driver realized something was dragging his vehicle down and hit the brakes. This could be dangerous if the driver slammed the brakes on hard. If the car stopped abruptly the forward momentum of the "hitchers" could carry them forward and under the frame of the vehicle. It was important not to position yourself directly behind the wheels of the vehicle as one could get seriously injured. Some drivers were aware that "hitchers" were on his bumper and deliberately pumped the brakes on and off trying to dislodge us. After a while this activity wore down the soles of my shoes. There was no money for new shoes so Lester showed me how to cut cardboard out in the shape of my shoe and place it inside my shoes to keep my feet from contacting the cold ground. I soon found it necessary to replace the cardboard every few days. It could be a long time waiting in the cold and dark for a car to come by to hitch onto for a thrill ride. Some of the older boys started quietly opening the doors of nearby parked cars and rifling through the glove compartments hoping to find something of value they could confiscate. Soon I was following suit. I never found anything of much value, only a few coins now and then. Then our criminal pursuit advanced to a higher level. There was a more lucrative reward to be found inside "milk chutes" of houses. Most people got their milk from "milkmen" who delivered fresh milk, kept cold with ice, to their homes. Many of the homes had been built with a small compartment that could be opened both from the outside and the inside. This compartment was called a milk chute. It was positioned so a milk man could easily open it and place one, two, three, or four bottles of milk inside the chute. The occupants of the house could open the "chute" from the inside to retrieve the delivered milk. Once a week, the milkman would leave that weeks "bill" in the chute. Often the cash to pay the bill would then be left in the "chute" for the milkman to pick up on his next delivery. The other "criminals" and I decided to proceed to another neighborhood several blocks away, where the "rich" people lived. We expected the "pickings" to be more profitable. We occasionally found one with a couple of dollars but most of the "chutes" were empty. Eventually someone reported money missing and the police cars began patrolling the area. I decided not to continue my association with this group of boys as I seemed to be going in the wrong direction. I resumed my day trips on the bus to Grandma's apartment. She was always seemed glad to see me as was my old friend Leonard.

For reasons, I did not know at the time, shortly after we moved to Hazelwood, Lester had stopped leaving for work every morning. Instead he stayed home all day. He was there when I left for school and when I returned from school he was still there. My mother continued her employment at Caton Photos so I had to endure a few hours alone with Lester every day. I had grown weary of trying to make new friends with each move and made up my mind to stay inside the flat after school. It was during this time that I began my grudging acceptance of Lester and we started conversing occasionally. One afternoon I observed Lester sitting at the kitchen table apparently working on some sort of project. Spread out on the table were small oval pieces of various colored plastic, a can labeled "acetone", some sandpaper, three or four toothbrushes and strips of polishing cloth. As I drew closer I could see he was trying to put a shine on a plastic ring of some sort.

"What're you doing?"

"Making a ring"

"Why?"

"To sell."

"Who's gonna buy them?"

"Dunno."

There were a few completed rings laying on the table. I thought they were quite pretty and became interested. When I inquired how he made the rings he informed me that he was using the handles from old toothbrushes. I watched as he used a coping saw to cut the handles into strips approximately three or four inches long then narrow them down to suit the size and shape of the ring he wanted to make. Next he would place the piece of cut down handle into boiling water until it was pliable enough to bend. Once it was formed into a small ring he would make the ring thinner by cutting in along the sides leaving a wide spot at the top that served as the base supporting more thin, oval plastic strips cut from different colored toothbrush handles. The strips were of different sizes and were placed on the base with the largest on the bottom and the smallest on the top. Each strip was brushed with acetone then pressed together. I assumed the acetone had some kind of effect on the plastic so that the pieces adhered to one another. The next step was to sandpaper the ring until it was smooth and shiny. Lester called them dinner rings. Lester asked me if I wanted to help him with this project. I hesitantly replied okay. He said he needed more different colored toothbrushes and wanted me to go looking in the trash barrels in the neighborhood alleys. I willingly complied and spent several days after school searching through people's trash for old toothbrushes.

Now that Lester wasn't bringing home a paycheck money was scarce. As days passed it was becoming difficult to find anything to eat in our flat. I was too young to understand about finances but I guessed this was due to Lester not working. The local grocer had cut off our credit (again). It was Winter and it was constantly cold in the flat. When I complained that it was cold I was told …

"We can't afford to buy more coal right now. We must conserve the little we have to burn during nighttime when it is the coldest."

Late one Sunday afternoon we all drove to Grandma's apartment in Lester's old pickup truck. On the way there I was happy knowing I would see my Grandma and maybe Leonard would be around as well. I was thrilled to find Grandma had dinner ready for us (at last a normal meal) and quickly took my place at the table. After dinner I went across the alley to Leonard's house only to find he wasn't home. I walked around the neighborhood looking for him for a while without success. It was fast growing dark so I returned to Grandma's and saw Lester carrying some of the metal "clinker" baskets up from the basement. I thought he was helping Grandma by carrying out the clinkers from the furnace but as I watched I became aware that there was more to it than that. He indeed carried up a bushel of clinkers on one trip but on the next trip the metal basket was full of coal. He would dump one bushel of clinkers in the trash pile and the next one, full of coal, would be dumped into the back of his old pickup truck. He made several trips alternating between clinkers and coal. During this process, when I asked Lester why he was putting grandma's coal in his truck, he put his index finger to his lips signaling me to be quiet. Back in Grandma's apartment I inquired of Grandma what Lester was doing she responded…

"Mind your Ps and Qs laddie."

After Lester finished loading his truck we left with my mother carrying a brown paper package. I asked….

"What's in the package?"

"Something for dinner tomorrow."

"How come Lester took the coal from Grandma's coal bin?"

"We don't have any coal at home so Grandma's lending us some."

"But that coal doesn't belong to Grandma it's Mr. Platt's coal."

(Mr. Platt was the owner of the apartment building that Grandma managed.)

"Mr. Platt has a lot of coal, he'll never miss it."

"But that's stealing!"

"Would you rather freeze to death?"

The next day I learned what was in the brown paper package grandma had given my mother, a large ham bone and a container of bacon grease. My mother used the ham bone along with some potatoes, onions and carrots to make a large pot of beans. At first I found the "bean dish" quite tasty. The bacon grease was for toast. I loved toast for breakfast. Although we had no toaster I improvised by sticking a fork through a piece of bread and holding it over the flame from one of the burners on our small apartment -sized stove. The result was something that could pass for toast if one wasn't too particular. When the bread was sufficiently browned I spread the bacon grease on it as there was no money for butter or even oleo margarine. For several weeks following I was sent to the butcher shop to purchase ham bones. Beans became our only meal and after weeks of nothing but beans to eat for supper I could hardly choke them down. When I complained (which was often) my mother's constant response was...

"That's all we can afford."

I wondered to myself ... *"How come they can still could afford to go to the bar?"*

Christmas was approaching and remembering the spectacular array of gifts I received the previous Christmas I was filled with anticipation of another fantastic bounty under the "tree". I was not yet at an age where I could foresee the impact of our destitute financial situation on my expectation of an abundant Christmas. So despite there not being enough money to provide an adequate supply of food to eat or coal to keep the house warm I still looked forward to another great Christmas.

About a week prior to Christmas Eve while outside during the evenings I could see Christmas trees decorated with shiny bulbs and strings of lights glowing through the windows of other neighborhood homes. I began asking if we could get a Christmas tree to decorate too. My interrogations were answered with….

"We'll see" or "Maybe tomorrow"

I kept pestering every day to no avail. On the day before Christmas there was still no "tree". That morning my mother promised we would get one when she came home from work. I waited impatiently for her return around 5 pm that afternoon but 5 o'clock came and she had not yet arrived. At 6 pm she still hadn't shown. Lester had left earlier that afternoon so I was alone and worried where they both might be….

"After all it was Christmas eve and they should be home." …. I thought

As far as I knew all the other kids were spending Christmas Eve at home with their parents. When 7 o'clock came and I was still alone I decided to go to "Benny Kirks" to see if they were there. Sure enough there they sat at the bar laughing and talking with other bar patrons. I was furious.

"What are you doing here? Why aren't you home? Where is the Christmas tree you promised?

"Hi Skippy, don't get upset we'll come home soon and bring a "tree" so go along now and don't be sassy."

As I was reluctantly leaving I noticed some of the ladies at the bar were wearing Lester's "toothbrush rings" on their fingers. Apparently he had sold some of them. Back at home I waited growing more impatient and angry with each passing minute, finally at 9 o'clock I marched down Hazelwood St. to Hamilton Ave. then down Hamilton a few more blocks to "Benny Kirks". There they still sat at the bar.

"Oh! Hi Skippy, you're back."

"Please! Can't we get our "tree. Tomorrow's Christmas and we haven't even put up our tree yet."

"Les, take thish kid and go get him a "tree" will you. He's gonna drive ush nuts ."

"Okay Millie, Come on kid, lets go get the damn "tree.""

As we were leaving Lester turned to the bartender and said….

"Give everyone at the bar a drink on me. I'm buying."

Lester and I left the bar and crossed Hamilton Ave. There was an open lot where someone had placed several Christmas trees for sale but no one was there to sell the "trees"Lester said ….

"Alright, pick one out."

"How are we going to pay for it? No one's here"

"Don't worry about it. They're not gonna sell anymore now anyway. They'll just go to waste and be thrown in the dump."

I was happy to finally be getting a "tree" to decorate and decided to just do what he told me. We put the "tree" in Lester's pick up and he drove back to our flat on Hazelwood where he carried it up the stairs to our flat and said....

"There's your Christmas tree. Go ahead and decorate it I'm gonna go get your mother."

After he left I dragged out all the Christmas tree lights and ornaments and began decorating the tree. It took some time to complete the tree trimming and by the time I finished I had grown quite tired. Still there was no sign of my mother and Lester. I really cannot remember the exact time but I was very depressed at being alone on Christmas Eve and eventually went to bed and cried myself to sleep. I awoke with a start on Christmas morning and immediately scrambled out of bed and went to the Christmas tree expecting all kinds of presents. Under the "tree" was a small solitary package wrapped with plain paper and a tag that read "To Skippy" I opened the package and found one pair of gray anklets. I was dumbfounded. I thought there must be more gifts and started looking through the house, searching all the closets, assuming they had come home "drunk" and forgot to put out the rest of my presents. There was nothing to be found. I went back to my room, lay on my bed and sobbed. When my mother woke up I asked....

"Where are the rest of my presents?"

"I am so sorry, Skip, but that's all there is. You know money's tight these days."

I couldn't accept her explanation and screamed back at her ....

"You say there's no money but I saw Lester buy a drink for everyone in the bar last night! You don't care about anything but drinking and your lousy barfly friends!"

"Please don't be impudent Skippy I'm doing the best I can."

What could I do? Nothing! I was powerless to change the situation. I was mad, sad and totally confused. I just could not believe this all was real. How could this be? I went again to my room and cried some more then I remembered the "Goodfellows" bundle of gifts that were left at my door a year ago. Maybe there was another one waiting for me. I rushed down the stairs hoping to find a package from the "Goodfellows". I opened the door.... nothing was there. More depression followed. I felt somewhat more cheerful when I remembered we were going to Grandma's for Christmas dinner. Surely she would have a present for me.

Later that day we drove to Grandma's for dinner and I was relieved to find she did have a present for me and another present from Uncle Red and Aunt Polly who were there as well along with my cousins Butch and Sue. My Godmother, Aunt Rea had also left a gift for me so I was beginning to feel a little less dejected until my cousins began describing all the wonderful gifts Santa had brought them. As I listened to their excited descriptions of their Christmas bounty, dejection over my own situation slowly overtook me. Then they began asking....

"What did Santa bring you?"

I was too embarrassed and avoided answering. My mood was such that I Just wanted to go home. I didn't want to be around anyone. I just wanted to go to my bedroom and not talk to anybody. The day ended and we returned to our dilapidated flat on Hazelwood. Several days passed before I spoke to my mother or Lester.

When Christmas break was over I returned to school to finish the second half of fourth grade. I was pleased to see Betty Jankowski was still in my class. Betty was the prettiest girl in fourth grade. It was the time in my life when I was becoming acutely aware of the opposite sex. Although I did not know for sure what real sex was I found myself wanting to be near attractive girls. Betty had long blond hair, blue eyes, a pleasant smile and she seemed quite willing to talk to me which I of course found amazing. The extreme shyness and insecurity I suffered from would not allow me to believe a beautiful girl, or any girl for that matter, could possibly be interested in being a friend to someone like me. Despite the fact that I was developing a "schoolboy crush" on Betty, I was still unable to profess my interest to her. Whenever an opportunity for students to work together arose I made every effort to position myself to be on the same team as Betty. She did not appear to find this out of the ordinary and I was beginning to relax around her but any inroads I was making toward making her a friend was soon to come to a halt.

Ringworm!

I started noticing a constant urge to scratch my neck and scalp. During this constant scratching I began feeling raised areas on the skin beneath the short hair on the back of my neck. I positioned myself in front of a mirror and could see the raised areas were circular and scabby. When my mother observed this I was sent to a doctor who diagnosed the condition as ringworm. There were several circular scabs all through my hair and the doctor said it was contagious. The treatment was to have my head shaved and apply mange medicine to the affected areas each day. I had to look in the mirror in order to see where to apply the medicine to the back of my head. It was then I noticed a small thin scar about an inch long on the left side of the back of my head. I could feel it was slightly raised as I ran my finger across the spot. I asked my mother what it was. She explained....

"Skippy, when you were just a little boy you fell off a stool in "Cunningham's Drug Store" and you cracked your head open. We had to take you to the hospital. That spot is from the stitches you had."

I wondered why I was never told about this before but soon forgot about it. Ringworm is contagious so I had to wear a skull cap whenever I was around people. In the past I had observed other kids at school with these skull caps and learned they had ringworm. These children were often teased and ridiculed by the other school kids and unfortunately I too had joined in making fun of them and their funny hats. I was about to find out how it felt to be one of the ridiculed. My embarrassment was significant. I had to wear the "cap" to school and it was obvious to all that my head had been shaved. The mange medicine left deep orange stains that could be seen on the sides of my head and the back of my neck.

I gave up my so called pursuit of Betty. In fact whenever possible I avoided being anywhere near her. I didn't want her to see me. I didn't want anyone to see me so the rest of the winter and spring was spent inside the Hazelwood flat. The ringworm finally cleared up about the same time that school was out for summer vacation. I was now fit to rejoin society. While I was suffering with the ringworm condition I stopped the bus travel to Grandma's apartment. I was mortified to be seen by anyone including my grandmother and my best friend Leonard. Once the ringworm had been conquered and my hair grew out I felt as though I had been released from prison. I was free! I was anxious to visit Grandma and excited to reconnect with Leonard. I resumed my bus trips to Grandma's. Now that school was out I found my day trips to Grandma's often turned into week long visits (or longer). I didn't care how long my mother wanted me to stay there, as far as I was concerned being with Grandma was the next thing to being in heaven. Grandma made breakfast for me every morning and we shared supper together at the same time every day. There was always something to eat and Grandma had an electric refrigerator that didn't require ice from the "iceman" to keep things cold. There were of course rules at Grandma's. Bedtime was set at a certain time and I was awoken each morning at the same time. Life was normal there and I craved normality with a passion.

During one of those visits Grandma taught me to play pinochle and we spent many evenings playing cards together. I got reacquainted with Leonard and learned that he knew how to play pinochle too, so Skippy, Leonard and Grandma spent many evenings playing pinochle, often till midnight, at Grandma's kitchen table that summer. Certain chores were assigned to me. I was required to dry the dishes, carry out the trash, and sometimes grandma sent me to the corner grocery store with a list of things she needed. The grocers got to know me as her grandson. They always seemed happy to see me come in their store and they happily placed all the items on the list into the brown paper grocery bag. Never did anyone frown at the list or say….

"Tell your grandmother I need to speak with her."

I loved my Grandma and for the most part attempted to comply with her rules which were mainly concerned with being polite and respecting my elders. If on occasion I was smarty-alack I would hear Grandma say….

"None of your lip, laddie or I'll give you a bat in the eyebrow"

This was of course, a facetious remark as I never received a (Bat in the Eyebrow). In fact even now, while I understand the implication, I'm not sure exactly where that expression came from.

I had reached eleven years of age during the winter of 1945 - 1946. My Uncle Red had returned from his overseas stint as an infantry man for the United States Army. I was extremely happy to see him reunited with his wife (Aunt Polly) and his two children (Butch and Sue) as it gave me hope that my Daddy would also be coming home soon to rescue me from all this. Now that Uncle Red was back home my mother and Aunt Polly began warming up their relationship which had cooled for some reason back when we were living together on Hubbell. It wasn't long until I found myself being shuffled off for visits with Uncle Red and Aunt Polly. Sometimes, for weeks at a time. I liked these visits because life there was normal and regular much the same as at Grandma's. As far as I could discern my Uncle Red was the same good natured and witty fellow that had left to fight the Germans a few years earlier. One could easily conclude that fighting a war might have a negative effect on a soldier however I never heard him speak of his war adventures. Not then or at any time in the future. The two Kennys still lived in the same houses so I spent a lot of time adventuring with them. There was a large open field nearby where someone had constructed a makeshift baseball diamond complete with slabs of wood marking first, second, third and home. There was even a backstop behind home plate made up of cyclone fence material stretched between two wooden posts that had been dug into the ground. The neighborhood kids would gather there to play baseball. There were no organized sports such as the "Little League" of today's world, instead teams were made up by whoever showed up and wanted to play. In order to have enough players to make up two teams it was necessary to include all age groups so there might have been three or four boys aged 10-12, a few 7-8 year olds some 5-6 and so on. The teams were selected, one player at a time, by two captains who took turns announcing their choices. Occasionally when we were severely short of players we would even allow girls to be included. Once in awhile on weekends we were able to coax some fathers to come and play softball with us. I distinctly remember a day that we coaxed my Uncle Red to come play with us. Before that day was over the initial excitement I felt, at his appearance, turned to dismay. During one of Uncle Red's times at bat one of the wooden posts supporting the backstop suddenly popped loose from the dirt where it had been planted. Before anyone could react the entire backstop swayed to one side immediately pulling lose the second supporting post allowing the entire structure to collapse on my uncle. Some people were screaming and some were dumbstruck at the sight of this tragedy. A few other fathers, who were there, raised the offending backstop that was crushing my uncle and helped him to his feet. He seemed to be in a lot of pain and required assistance from the men to help him back home. I was extremely distraught thinking my Uncle Red might die. Although the injury was serious no bones were broken and no arteries were severed thus this was not in any way life-threatening. I was eleven years old, however, and unable to understand the possible consequences of this accident. I was told it was going to take some time and require some special care for Uncle Red to recover so I was returned to my mother at the Hazelwood flat.

Not much had changed at the "flat". During my winter ringworm hibernation I had lost touch with the few friends I had in the neighborhood and I was not anxious to rekindle these associations. They made it a point to avoid me when the news spread that "Skip has ringworm." My embarrassment remained so another retreat from the world seemed to be in order. My mother and Les were still whiling away all their free time in the "bar". There was seldom any food in the icebox and if there was food, with no ice to keep it cold, it was often spoiled. I made frequent calls to the "bar" in an effort to get them to come home or at least inform me what I was supposed to eat. Most often my pleas were answered with…..

"We'll be home soon" (which seldom happened) or " Come down to "Benny Kirks" and we'll give you some money to buy something to eat."

I did not understand then and I don't understand now how they could afford to give me money to buy a meal at a restaurant when they couldn't pay the local grocer's bill and Lester was still not working. My mother was working at Caton's Photo Shop so there was some money coming in but obviously it was not well spent.

Chapter 12

ALMOST SEX

One Saturday afternoon while I was home alone and quite hungry I called my mother at Benny Kirks and was told to come to the bar for food money. I was standing at the bar collecting fifty cents, which was enough for a corned beef sandwich at the local Jewish delicatessen, when a boy about my age or maybe a year older came through the door and walked up to a man and woman sitting next to Lester. He too was being given money for lunch. My mother addressed this boy….

"Hi Patrick. I want you to meet my son Skippy. Skip this is Pat and that's his mom & dad, sitting next to Les."

"Hi" I replied.

"Hi" … Pat answered.

We both felt awkward and just stared blankly at each other without saying a word.

My mother broke the silence suggesting….

"Why don't you boys go have some lunch together."

We both wanted to get out of there so we left and went to the nearest restaurant where I got my favorite, a hot beef sandwich with mashed potatoes all covered in dark brown gravy. I don't recall what Pat ordered. We left the restaurant and Pat asked ….

"Waddaya want to do now?"

"I dunno."

"I know some cool places, wanna go with me?"

"I guess."

We started walking down Hamilton Avenue for a few blocks then crossed the street, passed through some open lots arriving at one of Pat's "cool places". It was a large two story house in run-down condition. We passed through a rusty gate at the side of the house to discover a dozen or so boys playing in the backyard. Some were playing mumbletypeg, others were tossing basketballs at a net-less hoop over the garage doors. There was a dilapidated automobile complete with four flat tires, dented fenders and several broken windows. Three boys sat inside this wreck of a car with their heads down apparently engrossed in some sort of activity. Pat walked over to the car indicating for me to follow. As I approached I could see they were pounding on something they had in their laps. Curious, I looked in the car window and then I could see exactly what they were doing. They were holding their penises in one hand executing a rapid up and down stroking motion. This seemed, to me, to be a rather stupid thing to be doing so I asked Pat…

"Why are they pounding on themselves like that?"

"Because it's fun. Come on I'll show you."

Pat opened a car door and got inside motioning me to follow. When I got inside Pat unfastened his fly, and told me to do the same. Then he reached in his pants, pulled out his penis and began stroking it just as the other boys were doing. I was surprised to see his penis, twice the size of mine, erect and there was hair.

"Come on Skip, try it."

This all seemed very strange to me and being extremely shy I refused.

"What's the matter, you afraid?"

"I am not afraid. It's just dumb."

"You're just a fraidycat!"

"I am not!"

"Then do it like me."

I really did not want to do it as I had noticed the other boys in the car moaning now and then which caused me to think there was some kind of pain involved but I might lose my new found friend so I made an attempt to comply. I would estimate that at the time my penis was the size of an adult little finger. There was no hair. I gripped it between my thumb and index finger and began the required stroking motion. I observed Pat begin to perspire. He let out a little moan and ceased stroking. He started to fasten his pants so I began fastening mine too and then he said…

"No keep doing it, you haven't come yet."

I had no idea what he was talking about. I continued as he directed for what seemed like forever, but was probably only five minutes, without achieving whatever I was supposed to achieve. Finally I gave up. My penis was sore and I was weary of doing this activity just to please Pat and said…

"This is stupid! You're stupid! All you guys are stupid! I'm going home."

As I left I heard them laughing at me. Wanting to get as much distance as possible between us, I started running. That was the last time I saw Pat.

In the not to distant future I would gain a distinct appreciation for Pat's strange activity.

Chapter 13

WEARING OUT YOUR WELCOME

That summer, as was usual and constant, I was sent for visits to my relatives. My supposition is that my mother didn't want to be deal with my expectations of a normal family life and my repeated requests for her to stay at home instead of going to the "bar" every night. Her problem was solved by simply sending me to Grandma's or Uncle Reds' and even to Uncle Murray's on occasion. Thus most of my days were spent alternating between those places for weeks at a time. They say every action has a reaction and I was to learn the truth of that statement late in the summer of 1946. My grandmother had planned a trip back to the "old country" as she called it. She had paid for a flight to St. Andrews, Scotland, where she was born, to visit with her mother, who was still alive, and some other relatives and old friends. Grandma never learned to drive a car so Uncle Red was to drive her to the airport and pick her up when she returned. I was excited for this event to take place, thinking I would be able to go see her off and have an opportunity to see an actual airplane. Air travel by the public was still in it's infancy in 1946. Not many kids had ever been to an airport or seen a real airplane. On the day she left for Scotland I was greatly disappointed. For some reason that I cannot now recall I was not able to go to the airport to watch her take off. I remember however I was assured that I could go with My Uncle and family to pick her up when she was scheduled to return. During the time Grandma was gone I was pawned off to my uncle Red's once more, this time was to be for one week. As I previously stated I really loved the time I spent at my aunt and uncle's house so when the week was up I asked if I could stay another week. My mother said okay but Aunt Polly informed me I had to go back to my mother. I wondered if I had done something wrong but was afraid to ask. When I returned to my so called home on Hazelwood I asked my mother why I couldn't stay at Uncle Red and Aunt Polly's. She said my aunt and uncle were having friends come for a visit and needed more room at their house. Time flies when you're young and without realizing it the time had come for my grandmother's return from Scotland. I was absolutely sure I was to be included in the trip to pick her up, yet Uncle Red, Aunt Polly, Butch and Sue went to the airport to retrieve my grandmother without me. When I learned my grandma was back home and I had not been included to pick her up at the airport I was devastated. I felt betrayed. *"Why would they go without me? They knew how much I wanted to go! Are they mad at me? Don't they care about me? They don't like me. No one likes me. No one has ever liked me and no one ever will."*.

All these negative and destructive thoughts were running through my young head. I asked my mother why they went to get Grandma without me but she had no answer. I remained "down in the dumps" for days then I decided to take the bus to see my grandmother. During that visit I told her I was sorry I hadn't come to greet her at the airport. I said I was supposed to go with Uncle Red and Aunt Polly to pick her up and did not understand why they went without me. I clearly remember my grandmother saying....

"Maybe you wore out your welcome."

Self consciousness would get in the way of my willingness to visit my relatives on Hubble Street for some time.

September came and it was time to return for the fall semester at Brady school. Although there were no signs remaining of my previous bout with ringworm and my hair had grown back I was apprehensive to return to school.

"How would I be treated. Would my classmates still avoid me as they had before or now that I was cured would they accept me as normal?" and most importantly... "Would Betty accept me as normal?"

My shyness was now more pronounced due to the ringworm episode. Happily, most of the sixth grade students were the same ones that shared the fifth grade classroom with me. Without the visible stigma of the shaved head and the skull cap things returned to normal. Over the summer Betty had developed some bumps in the front which I noticed immediately. In fact she appeared, to me, to be even more attractive than the last time I saw her. At roll call Mrs. Rawleigh called out each of the names of all her students to which we were to respond present and raise our hand. When I heard her call the name Betty Mason I saw Betty Jankowski raise her hand and say present. I was confused by this and later at recess I eased my way slowly in Betty's direction. Summoning up the courage to speak to her I posed the question....

"I thought your last name was Jankowski but you answered to Betty Mason?"

"I know. That's my name now."

"Why did you change it?"

"I have a stepfather and he adopted me so my last name is now the same as his."

I didn't know much about those things then but she was still Betty and I still liked her no matter her last name. As mentioned before Betty was a very attractive eleven year old girl thus it wasn't just me who was interested in her. Several other male classmates also sought favor with Betty Mason. I, of course, backed off whenever another boy competed for her attention. My innate shyness had been exacerbated by the unfortunate bout of ringworm that destroyed any self confidence I might have had. Over the course of the school year my hope of becoming Betty's friend diminished gradually and eventually I gave up.

Nothing of note comes to mind for the rest of the school year. I still had no interest in associating with any of the kids in the neighborhood of Hazelwood and Lawton Ave. Most of my weekends were spent traveling on buses to Grandma's apartment where I could reunite with my friend Leonard. At some point in the last few years Leonard's father (Joe Antkoviak) had experienced a spiritual awakening of some sort. He gave up drinking and smoking. His religious experience required him to eat no meat and he and everyone in his entire household were now vegetarians. Leonard seemed proud that he was now a vegetarian and made several unsuccessful attempts to influence me to join him in this meatless lifestyle. I suspected that he was trying not to be the only "oddball" among our friends. Mr. Antkoviak spent his free time tending to a large vegetable garden he had established in his backyard or reading "The Oahspe" the so called bible of the religious sect he had connected with. The claim was that the "Oahspe" was written by a New York dentist named John Ballou Kimbrough in 1882 while he was in some sort of trance. While in this trance the belief was that he auto-typed it on his typewriter. This all seemed quite unbelievable to me however Joe Antkoviak was apparently now a much nicer and gentler man. I no longer heard wails emanating from the house across the alley. On one occasion Leonard convinced me to attend a lecture given by a "leader" of this strange religious group. I remember little of what was said but I distinctly recall that lecturer state that it would be impossible for mankind to go to the moon due to the fact that the earth was enveloped by a some sort of protective force that could not be penetrated without destroying the world. (It seems all religions have to have their own particular taboos.)

When I was not at my Grandmother's I remained in the flat on Hazelwood alone most of the time, scrounging for something to eat other than the ever present pot of beans and making frequent trips to the bar to beg them to come home. As the holidays neared I held no expectations of a huge Christmas bounty. In fact I cannot recall receiving any specific gift at all. What I remember about Christmas 1947 was going to the bar on Christmas Eve. and being told to "steal" a Christmas Tree from the "lot" across the street and drag it home. Just like the previous year whoever owned the Christmas tree lot had abandoned the few trees that were left. I picked out the nicest one I could find, dragged it back to the flat and proceeded to decorate it by myself. So much for "Merry Christmas."

When the holiday break ended I returned to school. It was January, 1947. I liked going to school as it afforded an opportunity to be somewhere else than home. During my time alone at the Hazelwood flat I practiced my version of the "Slowly I Turned" skit I had seen at the movies. During morning recess while out on the playground I decided to try my performance out on Bobby Snell as he was always attempting to amuse the rest of the class with antics of his own. When he saw me crouched over, turning slowly with a severely contrived limp, legs askew and uttering in a deep raspy voice "Slowly I turned", he busted out laughing and said….

"That's so funny. Where did you get that idea?"

"I saw it at the movies."

Bobby called over some of the other kids on the playground and encouraged me to repeat the act. I hesitantly complied and was pleased to receive another laughing response from all of them. The realization that I had the ability to make others laugh started me thinking perhaps I could cause other kids to like me by acting foolish. Then one day at recess I observed Betty approaching. She walked up to me and said….

"I heard you can do a funny imitation"

All of a sudden I became quite nervous and afraid Betty would think I was silly. I did not want her, of all people, to think I was just another stupid kid showing off. I said….

"It's just a stupid act. You won't think it's funny."

"I won't think it's dumb. Come on do it for me."

Torn between looking stupid or disappointing this pretty girl I had no choice but to go through with my comedy routine.

I was thrilled to see Betty bent over with laughter at my crazy performance. This apparently "broke the ice" and we began talking with one another more often. I of course believed that her only interest in me was for my clownish ability to make her laugh. Still, that was something.

As the end of the school year neared Mrs. Rawleigh informed us we would be going on a class trip. It would be a trip to Rouge Park where we would rent bicycles and explore the park. Every student was excited to go on this adventure especially as we would not have any lessons that day. The day of the trip arrived and we all piled onto the bus that would take us to the park. When we arrived everyone hurried off the bus to the bike rental station. I watched Betty and followed close behind her hoping to stay near her on the bike ride. Some other boys had the same idea and Betty was surrounded. As she rode off on her rented bike three or four boys (including me) were on all sides of her. I hung back a little expecting to see her team up with one of the others. Surprisingly that did not happen. One by one the other boys turned off in a different direction and soon I was the only boy in her vicinity. Still, the timid one, I hung back a few yards. Finally I built up enough courage to slowly ride up next to her. To my surprise she stopped peddling and slowed her pace until I was beside her. She said….

"Why don't we go down this trail on the right."

"Okay"

So down the trail to the right we went together, a boy and a girl, two very young people with little understanding of love or life. I knew I liked her a lot. I was unsure if she liked me. In fact I couldn't believe she could *really* like me. I was sure she just thought I was funny. We rode our bikes down a myriad of paths, just the two of us, exchanging little conversation along the way. I was secretively elated to be spending the afternoon alone with the most attractive girl in school and equally disappointed when I heard the sound of the horn signaling it was time to leave. We hurried back to the bus for the return trip to Brady school. For the next few days I wondered what I should think about my interaction with Betty that day…

"Could she possibly want to be my friend?"

Then I dismissed it as probably only circumstance….

"After all wasn't I the kid with ringworm."

During the week preceding fifth grade graduation most students brought little autograph books to school to collect the signatures and some funny little notes from their fellow classmates. We had to accomplish this before class started and I definitely wanted Betty to sign my autograph book so I asked her the first time I saw her. There were several others after the same thing and many of them asking me to sign theirs at the same time. Everything was hectic, books were getting passed around from student to student and there was little or no opportunity to read what anyone had written. Class was called to order and we were told to put our autograph books away before I could see what had been written. Later that day while at home I read some of the entries in my "book" Bobby Snell (always the comedian wrote….

"When you get old and drink your tea. Burn your lip and think of me"

Betty wrote….

"Thank you for going bike riding with me."

I could not believe what I was reading! She actually thanked me for riding with her. Wow! Maybe she really did want to be my friend. I was exhilarated. The next day at school I asked Betty where she lived. I was disappointed to find she lived in a neighborhood quite far from where I lived. I cannot remember, now, the name of the apartment complex where she lived but approximately a week after school was out I summoned up enough courage to make the walk of several blocks to the apartments Betty had described to me. I did not have an exact address so I began looking at the mail slots in the lobby area. I found no last name of Mason or Jankowski so I thought maybe I was at the wrong apartment complex. As I was about to leave to search other apartment buildings a woman came through the lobby doors, looked suspiciously at me and inquired….

"What are you up to young man?"

"I was trying to find the Betty Mason's apartment.

"Oh."…. she said…. "Betty doesn't live here anymore. They moved out yesterday."

"Where did they move to?"

"They moved out of state somewhere."

That did it for me. If they had moved somewhere reasonably close I could have found her somehow but out of state was out of the question for me. So there I was again, every time I thought I had a friend something came out of nowhere to mess things up. It was back to the flat alone as usual. My regrets over the Betty situation were soon forgotten when a few weeks later I was driven to my grandmother's apartment where I would spend several weeks. This was good news for me. At least I would have a friend in Leonard while I was there and being with Grandma was the best part of my life. At Grandma's there was always something to eat, mealtime was regular as was bedtime, and the rules were always the same. How I loved my Grandmother.

Chapter 14

A REAL FATHER

Later that summer my mother and Lester came to pick me up from Grandma's. We were on the move again. My mother and Lester had rented an apartment on the corner of Morrell St. and Toledo Ave. about 12 blocks from the Detroit River. I hated leaving my Grandma's place and losing contact with my friend Leonard but off I was, regardless. The apartment was on the basement level again. Like the other apartments I experienced it was small but this one had two bedrooms. In the tiny kitchen there was a painted white wooden table attached to the wall. By removing a wooden prop underneath the table, it would lie flat against the wall allowing more room when preparing meals. There was the usual apartment size range and a small icebox, which was seldom filled with ice. I do not know why but the room I was given for my bedroom was one step up from the rest of the apartment. Just like the Sussex apartment the room was partitioned from the rest of the apartment by a set of leaded glass doors. The windows to the outside were approximately twelve inches high and twenty-four inches wide. Standing on my bed I could look out to see the sidewalk leading up to the building's entrance was eye level. Never knowing how long this new abode would last, and not wanting to bother meeting anyone new, much of my time on Morrell St. was spent in my room reading. I saw relatively little of my mother and Lester. When they were not at work they spent most of their time in a local bar a couple blocks over on Junction Street where they were often met by my Aunt Doris (Dodo) and whoever her latest beau happened to be.

I was informed, one morning, that this was the day I was going to meet my real father, Julian Withrow King Sr.. Filled with apprehension I objected, to no avail. Soon, came a knock at the door. My father was a short slightly stocky man about five feet four with a square face. He was a somewhat handsome man with a little dark mustache and dark brown hair. He was dressed in suit and tie. I was immediately fearful of him not because his appearance was frightening rather because he was a stranger to me, an unknown. He did not attempt to hug or hold me right away. Instead, he held out his hand for me to shake, which I did, reluctantly. After a short get acquainted visit, he departed. I retreated to my room and fell onto my bed confused and crying holding my "Daddy's" picture. Thinking ….

"Who is this man that claims he is my father? What do I know of him? What does he want with me? Is he trying to replace my daddy? Where is my daddy? Is he still alive or have the "Japs" killed him? Why doesn't he send me any more letters?"

I fell asleep crying.

After spending a week or so hibernating in my bedroom again, reading books and listening to my favorite serials on the radio I ventured outside into the real world. As I stood outside the apartment building observing my surroundings a boy about my age approached.

"Hi, who are you? Do you live here?"

"Yes."

"What's your name?"

"Skip."

"I'm Donny Dombrowski."

"Hi"

"You don't say much. Did you just move in?"

"Yeah."

" Do you like to play baseball?'

" I guess so."

"Well we're having a game at Clark Park tomorrow. You wanna play?

"Okay."

"We're meeting up at 11 o'clock to practice so be at the park by then if you want to play."

My mother had warned me against playing baseball or any other sports as the diagnosis of Rheumatic fever, when I was young, could mean my heart was damaged. Still here was a chance for me to be part of a team and maybe actually make a friend. I wanted very much to do this so I asked.

"Where is Clark Park?"

Donny Dombrowski gave me directions suggesting I could get there in 5 minutes on my bike. I informed him I did not have a bike. He seemed amazed at the fact I did not own a bicycle....

"How come you don't have a bike."

"I had one but my parents sold it."

"Why'd they sell your bike."

Too embarrassed to provide the real answer to his question I replied....

"It kept breaking down so they ordered me a new bike but it hasn't come in yet."

The next morning I began walking to Clark Park, which was only seven blocks away. When I was about one block from the park Donny Dombrowski pulled up alongside me on his bike and said....

"Hop on. I'll ride you the rest of the way."

I perched myself upon the crossbars of his bicycle and he took off peddling. We arrived at the park and Donny joined the other boys while I held back, unsure of myself. Eventually I was introduced to the other boys and assigned to play center field.

"Where's your glove?" I was asked by one of the boys.

"I forgot it." (Truth was I didn't have one.)

"You can use this one. It's my old one. Kinda beat up but better than nothing."

"Thanks"

I was up to bat four times during the game. I struck out twice, walked once and was hit by a ball. When I was playing outfield I kept praying that no one would hit the ball my way and if they did, I hoped it was way over my head so I would have no chance to catch it. I had never caught a baseball before and was afraid that if one came my way I wouldn't be able to catch it. Every time the opposing team player hit a fly ball, I would run toward it deliberately slowing my pace a little pretending I could not get to it in time and hoping the outfielder on either side of me would get to it before I did. I could sense the other boys on my team were having doubts about my baseball skills. They began ragging on me…

"Come on! Skip."

"Move it! What's the matter? You aren't even trying"

I was mortified….

"Why did I ever come here? I knew I couldn't play. I'm not supposed to participate in sports anyway. I'm getting what I deserve. I can't wait until this is over. Now Donny won't want anymore to do with me."

The ninth inning finally arrived and our side was ahead by two runs. The other team was up to bat. They had the bases loaded with two outs. The boy at bat was one of the bigger guys on their team. I was out in center field still praying, *"Please don't hit it my way."* But wouldn't you know it he smacked the next pitch soaring straight out to center field. It was long, high and way above my head. I had been given so much razing over my slowness at getting to the ball that I decided to make a show of it, knowing it was surely going over the high fence in back of me. I ran as fast as I could to where the ball seemed to be headed then jumped as high as I could reaching up with my glove. Suddenly I felt something slam into the glove. As my feet landed back on the ground I looked at the glove and, to my utter amazement, there was the ball. I could not believe what I was seeing. All at once, I was surrounded by my teammates yelling things like....

"Way to go!"

"What a catch."

"Thanks to you we won!"

I knew it was simply luck and that as long as I lived I probably could never replicate what happened that day but still I enjoyed the feeling of being able to be part of a team and thought well of by others. I would walk to Clark Park many more times to participate in the ball games but never to repeat my previous glory.

During the few weeks we lived at the Morrell apartment I had little interaction with Lester who my mother informed me was my new step dad as they had finally gotten married. Upon hearing this news I strongly stated....

"He's not my daddy! I'm never going to call him daddy!"

"That's okay you can call him Lester but you will have to mind him."

The fact of the matter was that Lester, despite his large size, was an easy going sort and really didn't want any confrontations with me or my mother. I didn't have a lot of contact with him anyway as they both spent much of their free time drinking in the neighborhood bars.

Soon came the time I was to visit my real father's home in River Rouge, Michigan. River Rouge was a small suburb situated between Fort St. and the Detroit River south of Detroit city proper. My father came to pick me up and drove me in his car to his house, He had remarried and he and his second wife, Anna, had four children, Richard, Frank, Joyce and Bobby. Richard was about six years old (I think). He had short dark hair and a stocky build like his father. Frankie was about 3 years old he was thin with very long light blond curly hair almost to his shoulders. That was the first time I had ever seen a boy with hair that long. I thought he was a girl at first sight. Joyce was maybe two years old she had curly light brown hair but not as long as Franks. Bobby was a baby still confined to his crib or playpen. Later I would ask my mother why Frank's hair was so long. She said that it was the original hair he had been born with and they had never cut it. She explained it was a tradition in some families not to cut the baby hair until a certain age. I thought it very strange for a boy to have long hair like a girl. (I still do!)

Now that my mother had established a connection (of sorts) between me and my father she had one more place to shuffle me off to whenever it suited her. So for the summer of "Forty-eight" I found myself being sent to spend time at my father's house. One time I had to walk the five miles from the Morrell apartment to my father's house in River Rouge. I have little remembrance of my stays with my father's second family but I remember that I never felt quite comfortable there. Although I was once again faced with the challenge of meeting and making new friends, I really had no interest in doing so as I never knew how long l would be in this place. Instead, I mostly kept to myself spending my time reading and walking to downtown River Rouge to go to the movies twice a week. My father was at work all day as a welder for a company I cannot name. His wife Anna was a stay at home homemaker, as were the vast majority of women in those days. She seemed nice and I gradually grew less apprehensive of my status in this new household.

Twice during my stay at my fathers home he took me fishing. Once to a spot by the Detroit River and another time it involved a trip quite a way out of the city to a farm of some sort owned by a friend of my fathers. I recall his name was Elmer Droulliard and he was joining us on this fishing adventure. I was very excited about going fishing. For some reason the fishing was to be done at night. We left for the trip after my father got off work and arrived at the farm late evening. The plan was to get some sleep and then go fishing later that night. I was so filled with anticipation that I just could not fall asleep. The appointed time arrived to find me still lying in bed awake and anxious to go. We packed all the fishing boxes and "poles" into the car and were off. During the long drive to the fishing spot, I fell sound asleep and when I finally awoke it was too late. The fishing was over and the others were putting the fishing gear back in the car along with several large fish they had caught.

"Why didn't anyone wake me up?"

"We tried to but you wouldn't wake up"

I did not believe them! This experience left me quite dejected and depressed. I kept to myself and pouted for a few days then announced that I wanted to return to *my* home.

"We'll have to see what your mother has to say about that".... said Anna.

How my mother was contacted I don't know as we didn't have a phone but I was soon greatly relieved to be back at the Morrell Apartment.

I was happy to return to my normal routine. Spending most nights alone, reading my comic books or one of the "Hardy Boys" mystery novels that Aunt Rea sent for my birthday. She always sent a present or money for my birthday and I had been taught by Grandma that I was always supposed to say thank you for gifts I received, either in person or else in a letter. My mother and Les spent their evenings and nights drinking at the neighborhood bars often with Aunt Doris and her latest friend "Van". His last name was Van Brocklin so everyone called him Van but I never learned his first name. He had a look about him that women in that era would describe as wolfish. An average built man with slick little mustache and pomaded black hair combed straight back. He seemed pleasant enough and whenever he came in contact with me, he would smile and make small talk giving me the impression that he liked me. I kind of enjoyed seeing him come around as he always had a joke or humorous story to relate. I often went to Clark Park hoping to get in on a "game". While playing ball one Saturday afternoon it started to rain in the eighth inning and everyone started running for home. There was a Y.M.C.A. across from the park where you could play pool, basketball or go swimming. It was a long way back to the Morrell apartment and I was already soaked from the rain so I ducked inside the Y.M.C.A. to wait it out. When the rain stopped, I headed out again for home. It was about six in the evening. Still plenty of time to get back home before darkness set in. When I got back to the apartment and tried the door, it was locked. I couldn't understand why as we never locked the doors. Hardly anyone locked the doors to their homes in those days. I knocked on the door several times but got no answer. I decided to walk over to the bar on Junction Street where my mother and Lester hung out. I found them there and asked why the door was locked. My mother said she loaned the apartment to Aunt Doris for a while and that I should go play with my friends until she was done. I did not understand this explanation and grew angry.

"Well just give me a key so I can unlock the door."

"No! You're not getting the key. Do as I shay and go play awhile"

Her breath reeked of alcohol and I knew there was no reasoning with her so I left. It was getting late and I was becoming fearful that it would get dark soon. I still had not completely conquered my fear of the dark. I could handle being outside in the dark as long as I was with someone else but alone I would panic. Returning to the apartment, I tried the door again. Still locked! I knocked hard but no answer. I began yelling for Aunt Doris to let me in. After screaming at the top of my lungs, I heard a man's voice.

"Go away Skippy."

It was Van's voice. Dusk was settling and I was growing panicky and very very angry.

"This is my house not theirs. How can they be allowed to keep me out of my own house?"…. I thought.

I decided to try the windows that led to my bedroom and found one unlocked. The window was narrow and being a basement apartment the bottom window sill was only a few inches above the ground so I had to lie on the ground and push with my hands to enter the opening feet first. It was a short fall to my bed below.

I scampered off the bed and triumphantly threw open the leaded glass doors.

"I'll show you." I thought. *"You can't keep me out of my own house"*.

To my surprise, Aunt Doris was lying naked on our sofa and Van, also naked, was lying on top of her.

"What was going on? Why don't they have any clothes on? … I wondered.

Upon seeing my sudden and unexpected entrance through the double doors, they both leaped up and made a dash into my mother's bedroom closing the door behind them. I sat down in the living room chair with my arms crossed, still angry that they wouldn't let me in. After a few minutes Van, now fully dressed, came out of the bedroom smiling.

"Well little man I hope your satisfied with yourself. You scared us half to death".

"Why wouldn't you let me in"?

"We were busy."

"This isn't your house it's mine. You had no right to lock me out."

"Aw, what's the matter Skippy? Did we make you mad? Are you unhappy? "Should I take down my pants and cry?".... Van said tauntingly.

His last remark caused me to chuckle a bit. Then he laughed too and I slowly got over my indignation. Aunt Doris,also dressed, soon came out of the bedroom and quickly said to Van ....

"Let's go."

They left shortly without Aunt Doris saying a word to me or even looking my way. When my mother and Lester returned around 2 am., I was still awake. I told them what happened with Doris and Van and asked my mother what they were doing.

"Jusht taking a 'lil' nappy poo"

I noticed Lester standing in the doorway to the kitchen with the strangest smile on his face. A few months would pass before I would see my Aunt Doris again.

Chapter 15

AWAKENINGS in HIGHLAND PARK

We had not lived at Morrell very long (a few months at most) when I was informed that we were moving yet again. My new home was another basement apartment on the corner of Lincoln and Elmhurst in Highland Park, Michigan. This apartment was furnished with old musty semi dilapidated furniture as were all the other apartments and flats my mother rented. I was to attend seventh grade at Ferris Elementary in the fall. With each of these frequent moves it became more and more difficult for me to gather the courage to go outside and make new friends.

"After all" (I thought) *"what was the point? We would just be moving again"*

With each change of neighborhood I settled inside for longer periods of time. I preferred staying in bed most of the day as opposed to the challenge of confronting the outside world. Books and the radio filled most of my time while I waited for the start of the school year.

Aunt Doris' was a frequent visitor wherever we happened to reside, at the time. On one of her visits she mentioned a neighbor of hers was giving away some puppies. I cannot know for certain but I think my mother sensed my depression and thought a new puppy might help snap me out of it. Off we went to see the puppies that afternoon. There were just two puppies left out of the litter and Doris announced she wanted one. The sight of these cute little black and white spotted puppies lifted my spirits and hoping against hope I asked....

"Can we get one too?"

"If we get one your going to have to look after it."

"I will! I will. Please can we take one home?"

"Alright Skippy."

My heart soared. I would now have a permanent friend to play with. Aunt Doris announced she would name her puppy Pepper due to it's black and white spotting. Lester, who had said nothing so far, suggested that if Doris' puppy was to be named Pepper perhaps we should name ours Salty. Salty and Pepper were purebred English Setters. Salty and I became good friends. I fed him each day, helped to potty train him to go outside and took him for walks. Having Salty was a Godsend. I no longer spent nights alone as Salty kept me company while my mother and Lester were out "drinking".He licked my ears while I brushed his fur, we played fetch the ball and at bedtime he crawled into bed with me.

One day while taking Salty for his morning walk I encountered a boy who lived in the same apartment complex. His name was David. David stopped to talk with me about my dog. I was reluctant to start a conversation but David was very friendly and kept asking questions about Salty. He wanted to know what kind of dog he was, where did I get him, how big will he get and so on. Eventually I decided I liked David and over the next few days we became friends. Gradually my confidence in this new found friendship grew to the point that I revealed my rendition of …, "Slowly I turned" and my imitation of Peter Lorre as done in Spike Jones' version of "My Old Flame". David found my performance of these comedy skits extremely funny. As the days passed David introduced me to other neighborhood kids and he invariably asked me to perform these comedy routines for them. I hoped these talents to make people laugh would help me make new friends. At home alone with Salty I spent many evenings perfecting these imitations and began adding more imitations of other actors and singers. Nat King Cole, Bill Kenny of The Ink Spots, Vaughn Monroe and Billy Eckstein to name a few.

Labor Day 1948 arrived and it was time to go back to school. I was unsure how to get to Ferris Elementary so I arranged to go with David on the first day of school. As we neared our destination we encountered a busy street that we had to cross just before the school property. My recollection is that it was Second Ave. It was a one way street and traffic was quite swift and dangerous for school children to cross. A tunnel like underpass had been constructed that went under the street allowing people to get to the other side without encountering the cars speeding down Second Ave. As David and I went down the steps into the tunnel we noticed a group of five or six boys milling around at the other end of the tunnel. They were all bigger than either of us. As we approached the stairs leading out of the tunnel they quickly positioned themselves on the stairs blocking our exit. One of the boys was bigger than the others and appeared to be the leader of the group. He looked older and stronger than the rest of the boys. He glared at me menacingly and said….

"Where do you think you're going?

Terrified by the situation I found myself in, I answered weakly….

"I'm going to school."

"You think so, huh? Show me your pass."

"What pass? I don't know what you mean."

"You need a pass to get out of this tunnel."

"I don't have a pass. How do I get one?"

"You gotta get a pass from me.

I knew I was in for serious trouble and was on the verge of crying but I was also aware that crying would probably inspire even more aggression from my adversaries. Then David spoke up on my behalf….

"Hey Tony! Leave him alone. He's a nice guy. He doesn't want any trouble."

Despite David's intercession the boy he called Tony slammed me up against the tunnel wall, cocked his arm back and was apparently about to deliver a significant blow when David yelled out....

"Tony wait a minute! Ask Skip to do his "Slowly I turned" impersonation."

"Whadaya talking about? I aint got time for no bullshit."

"No Tony, it's not B.S. it's really funny.

I was shaking with fear when Tony said....

"Okay pal, let's see what David is yappin' about."

Despite being scared out of my wits I managed to go through the comedy routine I had practiced at least a hundred times before. To my amazement some of the boys began laughing and then Tony burst into laughter as well. I continued on with the Peter Lorre imitation eliciting even more laughter from the gang of hooligans. Tony then announced....

"Hey kid, you really *are* funny. I'm gonna let you pass but from now on you gotta do this funny stuff whenever I ask. Okay?"

Greatly relieved I agreed and was allowed to proceed to school. It wasn't long till word spread throughout the school of my performance for Tony and soon other kids began asking me to perform. Realizing that acting the clown was an avenue to making friends helped me overcome my trepidation of being rejected by others. Thus I began using my comedic talents to mask the deep seated insecurity that lay below the surface. I was approaching the start of my teen age years and a natural drive for independence was beginning to emerge. I would soon become acquainted with several other neighborhood boys and girls approximately my age. We all became friends and after school we would sometimes gather on the corner of Richton and Lincoln in front of "Simons" (the local grocery store) where we would play various games such as "roof ball" or "kick the can". Other times we met up at the local drug store on Hamilton Avenue and Richton where we might enjoy a milkshake, hot fudge sundae or banana split if we had any money. Jack White was "Mr. Cool" always dressed in the latest teen age fad. He always ready with a glib word on almost any subject. Dan Mac Cormick was just a nice easy to get along with guy. Joy Wiseman was a pleasant looking girl with one outstanding feature, her breasts. Joy was well developed for a 13 year old and all of the guys were attracted to her for that reason, including me. Judy Dahlby possessed a natural beauty with long dark hair and facial features that were almost perfect, still most of the boys overlooked her as she was not as "developed" as Joy. I was initially attracted to Judy but got caught up in the competition for Joy's attention.

Some of the kids would have parties at their homes with parents supervising . These parties always ended up with kissing games like "spin the bottle" or "Post Office". All was innocent in those days. Although I had to kiss a few girls in the process of playing the "games" there was no emotional feeling or desire for the girl I was kissing. I was anxious for every opportunity to get close to or even to kiss Joy, but it was really just the competition with the other boys that motivated me. It was the time in our early teen age lives when boys and girls began thinking about someone of the opposite sex as a boyfriend or girlfriend. I was no exception and Joy seemed quite impressed with my comedic demonstrations so I began to entertain the notion that I might be her favorite and that she might want me as her boyfriend. However, as the days and weeks passed I gradually realized that Joy was interested in another boy (Jimmy). Then one day I worked up enough courage to ask Joy to go to the movies with me. She replied…..

"No! I'm going to the movie with Jimmy. He's my boyfriend now."

I was devastated. I felt like a fool. My thirteen year old mind filled with negativity. I thought…

"How could I have ever thought that Joy liked me. After all wasn't I the new kid in the neighborhood. Wasn't I simply a silly

*skinny kid with stupid imitations trying desperately to fit in. Of
course Joy didn't like me. No one really liked me. They just tolerate
my presence for their amusement. Well no more!"*

Joy's rejection was a devastating blow to my recent upswing
in self confidence. I decided to stay away from this group for a
while and remained at home playing with Salty or staying in my
room for several weeks. I did not want to see any of these kids
again.

David stopped by my apartment one afternoon and asked
me if I wanted to go with him to a Boy Scout meeting. I was
not sure why but David had not been part of the group of kids
that met on Simon's corner every evening. I decided to renew my
friendship with David and agreed to go with him to the "Scout
meeting at seven o'clock. My Mother and Lester were still not
home from their nightly visit to their favorite local tavern when I
left for the "Scout" meeting. Salty was left alone in the apartment.
At the meeting I met other "Scouts" and the Scoutmaster, Mr.
Taggart. Everyone made me feel welcome and I thought this
could be a good alternative to hanging out with the kids from
the "neighborhood. I decided to join that night and was given the
"The Boy Scout Handbook" to study. I returned to our apartment
to find Salty had chewed a large hole in the living room carpet. I
knew this meant trouble. When my folks came home Salty would
be "in for it". As suspected, Mother and Les arrived home half
drunk, and found the evidence of Salty's transgression. Salty got
a severe whipping with a newspaper from Lester while I watched
terrified. Later in my bedroom I attempted to soothe Salty's
feelings. I stroked his head and asked him….

"Why did you chew a hole in the rug?"

He just looked at me quizzically but did not answer (of
course). I told him…

"I love you Salty."

The next day I returned from school expecting to take
Salty for his usual afternoon walk. Normally when I came home

he would meet me at the door wagging his tail and jumping up on me. He did not meet me at the door that day. I called out for him but no Salty appeared. For a change my mother and Lester were home when I got there. I noticed a strange look on my mother's face. I asked her....

"Where's Salty?"

"Salty's gone."

"Salty's gone? What do you mean Salty's gone?"

"We gave Salty away to a friend who lives on a farm. The city is no place for a big dog like Salty. On a farm he will have lots of fields where he can run free. Salty will be better off there than here with us."

While relaying this devastating story to me she tried to hold me but I broke free screaming.......

"I hate you. You took away the only thing I love. You don't care about me! If you stayed home instead of going to the "bar" every day and night Salty wouldn't have eaten the rug. It's not fair. You're not fair. I'll never forgive you."

I refused to speak to my mother or Lester for a few days. Feelings of disgust filled my thoughts whenever I looked at either of them. I was anxious to get out of the apartment and avoid contact with them as much as possible. I was greatly relieved when my grandmother came to visit one day. I had not seen her for some time and I always felt happy when she was near. During her stay she mentioned that Aunt Rea was disappointed with me. This came as a surprise to me as I could not begin to recall any thing I might have done to disappoint my godmother. I asked what I had done. Grandma said Aunt Rea was displeased that I had not sent her a note of thanks for the last two gifts she had mailed to me for my birthday and Christmas last year. I told my grandma that I had not gotten any presents from Aunt Rea for a long time. Grandma informed me that Aunt Rea had twice mailed me five dollars so I could buy something I wanted. I replied….

"I never got any money in the mail from Aunt Rea."

Grandma looked strangely at my mother who remained silent during this conversation. Then grandma said she would tell Aunt Rea that it was not a good idea to send actual cash in the mail. I went to my room and wrote a letter to Aunt Rea explaining I hadn't received her gifts and that I was sorry she thought I was impolite.

I began to attend regular Scout meetings with David. At one of the meetings Mr. Taggart apparently noticed that something was troubling me and called me to stay after the meeting ended. After some prodding I tearfully revealed to Mr. Taggart the facts regarding the loss of Salty and my extremely negative feelings toward my mother and Lester. I also told him I was sure they had stolen the money my Aunt Rea had sent in the mail. He listened carefully and did not say anything until I was finished. When I was done he tried to console me saying perhaps Salty was better off on a farm even though I missed him terribly. Regarding my feelings toward my parents he reminded me of a few of the things required of a "Scout". Reverence, obedience, cheerfulness, friendliness, courtesy were all required. Mr. Taggart suggested I ponder how those requirements fit with my attitude toward my mother and Lester. His willingness to listen to my problem and his suggestions made me feel better and shortly thereafter I gave up the silent treatment at home. (Note: Upon reflection much later in my adult life with many years of experience to draw upon I became aware that "Salty on a farm" was probably just a story. After all how could they have known anyone with a farm when all their time was spent in a bar in the middle of the city?)

Although I had convinced myself that the gang of kids from "Simon's" corner really did not like me I was totally surprised when

Jack White and Dan Mac Cormick approached me at school one afternoon asking ….

"Where've you been? How come you haven't been meeting up with the rest of us after school anymore."

"I don't know."

"Well why don't you come over to my house after school. Dan and I want to show you something."

"Well okay maybe I will."

After school that day I returned home and found my mother was home for a change. She handed me a slip of paper with some grocery items listed on it and asked me to go to "Simon's" and ask Mr. Simon to put it on her bill. I took the list and started down the street to "Simons". On the way I remembered Jack White asking me to come to his house after school. I so wanted to fit in and have some regular friends that I decided I would go to Jack's house first to see what they wanted to show me. I planned to stop at the store on my way back home. I arrived at Jack's house and proceeded up the three concrete steps to his front porch. The curtains on the three front windows were drawn open and I observed Jack, Dan and Johnny's little sister (Martha) hovered in a circle in the middle of the living room. I was rapping on the window with my face pressed on the glass to get their attention when I heard a rumble behind me. I turned to look and saw it was Jack's mother and step dad coming home from work. I looked back expecting to see Jack coming to let me in but instead I saw the three of them jump up and run out of the room toward the back door. Totally puzzled by this I turned around to see Jack's step dad and mother approaching the front porch. His mother had a strange look on her face and Denny (Jack's step dad) gave me a menacing look. I said hello and asked them to tell Johnny I was there. Denny said gruffly….

"Jack is not home right now."

The tone of his voice frightened me and I thought it best to say no more and leave right away. I began my journey home and stopped at "Simons" store. Joy Wiseman and Judy Dahlby were standing at the counter when I handed the note to Mr. Simon. He looked at the note then looked back at me shaking his head and said....

"Young man I cannot fill this order. You better tell your mother to come herself. I need to speak with her."

My heart sank. I knew what this meant, she had run up another big bill and not paid for it. More disgrace! In my mind everything was going wrong. Joy and Judy now knew my folks were deadbeats and they would surely spread the word. I trudged home totally despondent. My parents were stealing my birthday money, Salty was gone, Jack's parents were obviously put out with me for some reason, Joy had made it clear she had no interest in me. Three years had passed with no word from my Daddy who apparently did not care about me. Once more I began to lose interest in the outside world.

The Christmas season was soon upon us and I recall being home alone again on Christmas Eve..Decorating the Christmas tree by myself that I had confiscated late that night from a Christmas tree lot that had closed down. This routine became an unwelcome Christmas tradition for several more years. On Christmas Day Aunt Doris came to visit along with her boy friend Van. It was obvious they had been drinking, as usual. Aunt Doris joined my mother and Lester in the kitchen who, although already quite inebriated, were pouring themselves yet another drink. I was alone with Van in the living room while everyone else was in the kitchen. He was smoking a cigarette and smiling at me. He said....

"Well little man are you a real man?"

"I guess so."

"Well let's just see."

With that he took his cigarette and pressed it into the palm of his hand for a split second. He did not show any sign that it caused him any pain.

"Can you do that little man?"

"No! I don't want to do that. That's stupid."

"Come here Skippy and I'll show you how to do it so it doesn't hurt."

When I refused he quickly grabbed hold of me and turned my hand palm up and spit on it. When he started moving his cigarette toward my hand I tried to twist loose and the cigarette made contact with the knuckle side of my hand instead of the palm. The extreme pain caused me to scream out whereupon my mother came to the living room to see what was happening. I was crying from the pain. Between sobs I told her what happened. She looked at Van and asked what the hell is wrong with you. She told him to leave immediately. As he was departing he turned toward me and smilingly said....

"Shall I take down my pants and cry?"

Van" never showed up at our apartment again.

School was out for Christmas vacation and the weather was relatively mild that week. Recent events had me down in the dumps but the sunshine lifted my spirits somewhat. I decided I had enough of staying indoors. That morning I went for a walk down by "Simon's corner" and ran into Jack White. I was surprised to find he was very friendly. I still didn't understand why he did not let me in his house that day when his parents saw me looking through their window. He invited me over to his house again. I said I better not come over as I didn't think his parents liked me because of what happened the last time I was there. He explained that his folks had a rule that after school he wasn't supposed to have any friends in the house until they came home from work. To avoid being caught they made a dash for the back door when his folks pulled up in their car. He told me not to worry about it. Dan Mac Cormick was meeting him at noon and I should also come over. Later that day, somewhat apprehensively, I made the walk from Elmhurst St. to Richmond St. then down Richmond to Jack's house. I climbed the three brick stairs, crossed the cement porch and rang the door bell. Jack's ten year old sister, Martha, opened the door and said hello. I asked if Jack was home. Martha giggling replied they're in his bedroom. She led me to the bedroom door. I opened the door and observed Jack and Dan sitting on the edge of a bed grinning sheepishly. I saw that they both had their pants unzipped and their penises were stiff and sticking out a little. I asked what they were doing. Jack gripped his penis and began quickly moving his hand up and down. Dan began doing the same to his penis and said ....

"Pull out you pecker and do what we're doing."

It had been a year or more since I had been encouraged to try this same silly ritual by Pat and those other boys in the abandoned car. I replied....

"That's stupid! I tried it before and nothing happens."

They both seemed very excited by what they were doing and continued to cajole me into giving it a try. I was reluctant to go through what I believed to be a waste of time but wanting very much to fit in I timidly unbuttoned by fly to expose my penis. It was still the size of one of my little fingers with a slight showing of peach fuzz around my genitals . I placed it between my thumb and forefinger and began the back and forth movement. The erection was immediate but otherwise nothing seemed to be happening so I stopped. Jack said....

"Don't stop! Keep going!"

"This is stupid." I replied.

"You've got to do it faster."

I quickened the pace of the back and forth motion for what seemed like a minute or two and then suddenly a swell of warmth swept over me. It seemed to culminate in my groin area. Simultaneously a tiny drop of sticky fluid emerged from the orifice at the end of my penis and an overwhelming feeling of ecstasy emanated from my groin. I felt something akin to an extreme sweetness concentrated in the tip of my penis. After a semi swoon I let out a small moan. I saw the other boys smile and say….

"I told you."

My amazement at this experience left me without speech for a minute or two. Finally all I could say was….

"Wow what happened?

"That's called coming. That's what happens when guys screw girls."

Next Jack reached under his mattress to retrieve a small but thick little book. He gripped it in his palm with his thumb placed on the edge of the book allowing the pages to flip rapidly by. Dan moved to peer over Jack's shoulder and they both began giggling. This aroused my curiosity so I looked over Jack's other shoulder to see what was so funny. What appeared on the pages was a moving cartoon depiction of "Popeye", "Olive Oil", and "Bluto" engaged in various sexual acts. The book was made up of hundreds of pages of cartoon drawings with each page slightly modified. When the pages are flipped by rapidly the impression in your mind is that the characters are actually moving. (They called it a "JoJo book".) Watching this aroused another erection and I had the urge to manipulate my penis again. I tried again hoping to experience the previous thrill but was unable to achieve the same result. I decided to wait a few days and try again. As I walked back home from Jack's I felt exhilarated. All those recent depressing incidents seemed to fade from my mind.

I felt finally there was something to make life worth living and my thoughts were concentrated on when and if I could make myself ...."Come" again.

The next day I was anxious to return to Jack's house to see if he and Dan were again going to engage in this fantastic new activity they had shown me. My hopes were realized when I entered to find them this time with their pants down around their ankles busily stroking away. I joined in and found to my delight I was easily able to "come" in only a few minutes. In the following days and weeks this became a regular routine for the three of us and my ejaculations grew significantly larger. These trips to Jack's house became something to look forward to and my outlook on life was greatly improved. I thought....

"Now I can relieve my loneliness with this new activity and make myself feel good"

To further stimulate this activity we opened a Sears Roebuck catalog to the pages featuring women in braziers, girdles and under garments. After a few days using our imaginations to see the models without any thing on we got the bright idea to place plain white paper over the photos and trace the outline of the female figures. Next we drew in what we thought the breasts and pubic areas should look like. Just the act of drawing in what we thought these areas of the female body would look caused an extreme arousal in our sexual desires. With each passing day we were becoming more and more interested in seeing an actual nude female body. One afternoon we were in the house alone and John's ten year old sister, Martha, was there as well. Martha liked to put on little shows where she would dance and sing. She asked us to watch her perform one of her shows but after the first time she performed for us we became bored with it and refused to watch anymore of her shows. One day she began requesting us to watch her "Newest act". We refused once more. Jack then pulled Martha into another room and discussed something with her in private. Soon Jack came back with a big smile on his face and informed us that Martha was going to put on another show and we were going to watch it. When we began to frown and grumble john said....

"She's going to dance for us NAKED!"

That got our attention. At last we would see a live naked female body. As directed we sat down on the living room rug and waited anxiously for the performance to begin.

Martha entered from the hallway with a sheer silk like scarf draped over her young undeveloped body. She did her best to mimic a ballet dancer with little awkward leaps in the air twirling and dancing in circles. We were mesmerized as she flung the scarf aside completely exposing her nakedness. Her ten year old body had not yet begun it's development toward womanhood. Her chest area was still flat and there wasn't even a sign of "peach fuzz" in her genital area. Still we all found this show extremely exciting and the three of us began "stroking" ourselves. Martha watched as we masturbated. She seemed to be just as fascinated by seeing us as we were by seeing her. Later Jack informed us he had offered her a dime to do the nude show. There were a few more repeat performances with the price going up to twenty-five cents each time. The following weeks we were obsessed with these sexual activities. We somehow located more of the "JoJo Books" to look at. I remembered the "Sunbather" magazines I used to look at when we lived on Fourteenth Street. Although I had not seen any more of these for several years I wondered if there were still some hidden somewhere in the apartment. So while my parents were out to their favorite "bar" I began searching the apartment. I found none of the nudist colony books however in the bottom of a dresser drawer I found a photograph of a naked woman. The photo was from the waist up with her large breasts fully in view. This was not someone I knew or had ever seen before and wondered who it was. I remembered my mother worked off and on at Caton's Camera Shop and she had probably confiscated it from a customer's roll of film. I took it to show to my friends. This was the time in the lives of many of the boys around my age when we were discovering sex and girls. Sex, pictures of naked women, dirty comic books, and anything that pertained in any way to these things were the constant topic of conversations between almost every boy in my seventh grade class. Someone told us of a magical substance called "Spanish Fly" which when consumed by a girl would turn her into a sex maniac. We began feverishly to question the older boys at school to see how we could obtain this wonderful potion or pill so we could slip it to any or all the girls we knew. Unfortunately we never located the illusive "Spanish Fly". We were learning more of the specifics regarding how women became pregnant and how that could be avoided by using a "Rubber". One day a boy brought a package of "Trojans" (a brand name for rubbers) to school. He blew them up to a size representing a large penis and waved them in front of the girls. Most of the girls acted as though they were offended while all the boys laughed. A few girls were giggling as well.

One afternoon at Jack called me into his parent's bedroom and knelt down beside a heat register motioning for me to join him. In those days most homes were heated by coal furnaces located in the basement. The heat was transported from the furnaces via ducts which connected to adjustable registers which could be opened or closed to allow heat into the room as desired. The register in question serviced both the bathroom and Jack's parent's bedroom. There was a flap in the middle of the register that could be moved to change the flow of heat from one room to the other. As I knelt down next to Jack he showed me how he had bent the bottom of the flap slightly to allow him to see into the bathroom from the bedroom. He explained his mother usually took a bath when she came home from work. He planned to wait for a time when his mother was in the bath, and his step dad (Denny) wasn't around, to look through the vent to see her naked. A few days later, while I was at Jack's, his mother came home from work without Denny and followed her usual bathing routine. Jack called me to the bedroom where we positioned ourselves flat on the floor to see through the register. I was able to see his mother naked. She was facing the register.

She was drying herself with a towel completely unaware anyone was watching. Seeing a totally nude woman was extremely exciting but disappointing as well. His mother's naked body looked nothing like the fantasy women we had imagined when we traced them from the Sear's catalog. As his mother began to dress we became nervous and quickly left the bedroom. Jack and I were excited to actually have seen a grown woman without clothes on however the sight did not live up to our expectations. Up to that point, other than his skinny, undeveloped sister, we had only seen glamorized photos of nude women. We were now faced with the reality that all women might not look that good naked.

Chapter 16

LEAVING HIGHLAND PARK

February 1949 arrived and with it came my fourteenth birthday. Grandma came to our apartment in Highland Park and brought a Birthday cake. The biggest surprise of that day was the appearance of my real father. He had never come to see me on my birthday before. I was flabbergasted when he presented a bicycle for my birthday. It was not a new bike but it was in really nice condition. I was quite grateful and thanked him sincerely. This was the first time I had any feeling of warmth toward my real father. I hopped on the bike and went for a ride through the neighborhood to show off my "new" bike. This was a very happy day for me.

A few weeks after my party, my mother informed me we would be moving again. I objected vehemently….

"I am not moving! I finally made some friends here and I joined the Boy Scouts too. I am not going to move. All you do is move to avoid paying all the bills you run up. That's not fair!"

"Well" she said "If you're not moving with us, where will you live? Are your so called friends going to let you stay at their house?"

I knew I had no choice and began to cry. Then she said…

"We are only moving 10 blocks away from here so you can ride your bicycle to school and visit your friends as well."

With that thought in my mind my crying subsided and I gave up my objections. During Easter break from school we made the move to the apartment house on the corner of Linwood and Sturtevant. It was a three story building containing thirty-eight apartments. To enter from the front you passed through a set of double wide leaded glass doors into a vestibule then through a second set of leaded glass doors into a large lobby area with an upholstered divan, three upholstered chairs, a glass topped carved wood coffee table and a fireplace. Although the lobby was quite impressive I cannot recall ever seeing anyone occupying it. There was an elevator at one end of the lobby for tenants who lived in the second and third floor apartments. At the rear of the building there was an alcove with a cement parking area, large enough for a truck, which was designed to facilitate tenants who were moving in or out. The door adjoining this parking area opened to stairways that led to the basement or to the first floor. Our first floor apartment was the one at the top of the stairs. The layout of the apartment was rather unusual. The kitchen, bathroom and living room seemed normal size but the bedroom assigned to me was no bigger than a large closet. It was furnished with a bed about the size of a standard sized cot and still there was barely enough room to stand next to it. The bedroom for my mother and Lester was huge. There was enough room for at least four double beds. I have no idea why these two bedrooms were constructed that way. Our apartment was furnished with basic furniture. The living room contained a slightly worn stuffed davenport and chair. My mother was responsible for collecting rents from the tenants and Lester was to take care of routine maintenance problems, cleaning out the ash residue from the incinerator, removing the "clinkers from the furnace and stoking the "hopper". I was assigned the responsibility of collecting the newspapers etc. from the trash closets. Each floor had a trash closet for tenants to deposit their trash and old newspapers. These "closets" contained a garbage chute for tenants to deposit their garbage. This chute led to an incinerator located in the basement where the garbage was burned. Each day I toured the three floors collecting mostly newspapers and cardboard and brought them downstairs to a large storage room where I was supposed to bundle and tie them. My incentive for doing this was that two or three times a year a man who bought bundles of newspapers would come and pay the going price for the papers I had collected. I was told I could have that money. I also was to receive a weekly allowance of twenty-five cents for trimming hedges, cutting grass, and keeping the sidewalk clear. I spent a few days acquainting myself with the apartment building and the surrounding neighborhood. The nearby homes were larger and much nicer than in other places I had lived. The tenants in my new apartment house included a Michigan state senator (Senator Blondy) and one of the Schostak Brothers.

I soon began to miss my friends and began what would become a daily bicycle ride back to Highland Park to reunite with Jack and Dan to continue our exploration into the delights of sexual self gratification. On one of my bicycle trips I arrived at Jack's house to find his sister again performing her latest dance interpretation while the boys watched. Jack called me aside and asked if I would like to "fuck" his sister. Just the thought of this new experience sent a thrill coursing through my entire body. I excitedly responded "yes". He next informed me I would have to pay him a quarter first. I anxiously handed him the twenty-five cents he requested and he led me to the bedroom where Martha was seated in a narrow straight back chair with an upholstered padded seat. She was bare naked and seemed to balk at allowing me to "do the dirty deed" but Jack reminded her she promised to let both Dan and I do "it". I removed my pants and underwear. I moved closer to the chair she was seated in. My penis was by now firmly erect and I was excited to proceed. However Martha became reluctant and sat upright as I approached. As I grew near the chair I could see I would have to crouch down to match up my penis to the area of her crotch. Finally with much fumbling and awkward maneuvering I attempted to "put it in" but she drew back. By now I was trembling with excitement. With some coaxing from Johnny she scooted forward and opened her legs. I quickly pushed my penis between her legs and immediately "came" Oh! My God! As my sexual frenzy subsided I began to feel embarrassed and guilty. I made some sort of feeble excuse and left shortly thereafter. The next day as my embarrassment subsided I remembered that babies were made this way. Then, I began to worry that I might have made her pregnant. The idea that she could be pregnant dogged me for several weeks. I fretted over how I would explain this to my mother, what would Martha's parents do to me, how could I be a father at my age, etc. Worry, worry, worry! Yet even with the potential difficulties facing me I still spent a lot of time fantasizing about a *"repeat performance"*. A week later at Johnny's house John, Martha and I were in the living room. We talked Martha into getting naked for us and I presented Johnny with another quarter. Martha laid back flat on the living room carpet and I straddled her and attempted to put "it" inside her. As soon as I tried she yelled out in pain. I drew back and waited for her to calm down but as soon as I tried to push she screamed again. She yelled at me to stop. She said "it" was too big and wouldn't go in her. Unable to achieve penetration I gave up in total frustration. This situation completely confounded me. After all I thought....

"Didn't we just "do it" a week earlier? Why didn't she say it was too big then"?

During the following months I spent a lot of time thinking about all that had transpired.

Note: *A few years would pass before my understanding of the physical positioning necessary to accomplish penetration brought me to the realization that during my first so called sexual encounter with Martha, penetration would have not been possible. The only explanation I can offer is that my penis came in simultaneous contact with the warmth of Martha's thighs and the soft upholstery of the chair. Due to my extremely excited physical and mental state this was enough to institute a climax and cause me to believe I had intercourse with Martha. My increasing knowledge also brought me to the realization that all my worry regarding Martha's possible pregnancy was total folly. She was only 10 years old, with no breast development, devoid of the slightest sign of pubic hair and had not yet started her "periods". (I marveled at my own stupidity.)*

My recent introduction to self gratification would remain a significant and necessary urge accompanied however with an ever present feeling of naughtiness. I was becoming less interested in a performance in the presence of others and more inclined to experience this guilty pleasure privately. Group participation in this activity was coming to an end.

When Easter vacation came to an end I resumed riding my bike to Ferris School each morning. After school was out I would usually ride to Jack's house. If I found no one there I occasionally stopped at Dan's house. For the most part, I avoided Dan's place as his folks were usually home and I was afraid of his father. In fact I was afraid of most men. I continued to attend the Boy Scout Meetings and earned a few "Merit Badges" while advancing from "Tenderfoot" to "Second Class Scout". So went my new routine for a couple of weeks until one day at the end of regular class Mrs. Mac Michael (my seventh grade teacher) informed me I was to report to the Principal's office before I left for the day. Apprehensively I proceeded down the hall to the Principal's office wondering what I had done wrong. The Principal made some small talk regarding how I liked school and complimented me on my good grades. Just as I began to relax and started to think I was not in any trouble she asked where I was living now. Unaware that my recent move was any kind of problem I informed her of my new address. My world collapsed as I heard her tell me that my new address was in Detroit and thus I could not continue to attend Ferris School in Highland Park. Dejected and physically shaking, I left her office and rode my bike back to Linwood and Sturtevant. On my ride back I was overwhelmed with grief.

"Once more I was to be separated from my friends."

When I arrived at our apartment I went to my bedroom and lay on the bed sucking my thumb and weeping. My mother asked what the matter was and I began sobbing incoherently as

I related what the Principal told me. I calmed down somewhat as my mother said she would look into the matter to see what could be done. My mother kept her promise and spoke to the Principal. She convinced the Principal to allow me to finish the few weeks left before summer break at Ferris but I would have to transfer to the appropriate Detroit school in the fall. I was greatly relieved by this reprieve and would worry about the new school later.

Chapter 17

Mr. COPP

I was still attending Ferris School when Mrs. Mac Michael informed her seventh grade class we were in for a treat. She led us down the hall to a large meeting room where the students from 5th, 6th and 7th grade had gathered. We were introduced to Mr. Copp who described himself as an expert on photography. After he explained the basic principles on the workings of a camera he took some photographs of the classroom with a camera he had brought with him. He also had all the chemicals and materials required to develop a photograph from the "film negative" which he then used to produce some actual photographs. I watched closely as he went through the entire process and was fascinated as he placed the exposed blank photo paper in the "developer solution". I observed a faint image of the classroom appear and continue to intensify until the picture was crystal clear. He then used tongs to retrieve the photo from the developer solution and quickly drop it into another solution that he called the "fixer". He explained the fixer would stop the picture from overdeveloping. All this was very interesting to me and after his instruction ended he passed out a sheet of instructions explaining in detail how one could develop pictures from "negatives" and a list of the required materials. I thought that if Aunt Doris still worked for her father at Caton Photo she might be able to obtain the things I needed to set up my own "darkroom" for developing pictures. I asked my mother to see if Aunt Doris would get the materials I would need and I would pay for them with the money I had saved from my allowance. A week later Aunt Doris showed up with everything I needed. I immediately began organizing my small bedroom to accommodate my new "darkroom". My mother went through her collection of photographs and gave me several negatives which I anxiously attempted to develop into finished pictures. For the next few days and after a several mistakes resulting in over exposure and under exposure I became familiar with the correct timing of each step in the process which resulted in some good photos. I converted several negatives into finished pictures and was quite proud of the results. I was anxious to show the photographs I had made to Jack and Dan, who had also attended Mr. Copp's seminar. I took them with me on my bike ride to Highland Park. When I got to Jack's house his mother told me Jack and Dan had gone to the drugstore on Hamilton Ave. I rode my bike to the drugstore where I found them along with other kids from the neighborhood. This drugstore was a popular hangout for the neighborhood kids so often we would gather there to consume chocolate phosphates, potato chips and occasionally, when we could afford it, malted milks or milkshakes. As I sat at the counter slowly sipping on a fountain coke I looked out the window and was surprised to see Mr. Copp standing on the corner outside the drugstore. I exited the drugstore, approached him cautiously and pulled out the photographs I had made to show to him. He smiled and said "Hi". He looked at my photos and asked me my name. He then complimented me on the photos and suggested I continue developing more negatives. He mentioned that he would be dropping by this drugstore occasionally and if I had some photos with me he would be glad to look at them and perhaps offer advice to improve my results. I was exhilarated by his approval of my efforts.

During the next few weeks I continued to develop more photos and always took them with me on my daily trips to Highland Park and my frequent trips to the drugstore. Whenever I saw Mr. Copp standing on the corner outside I would go up to him with my photos seeking his approval and advice. Before long he began making small talk about other things as well. Asking what my plans were after school was out for summer vacation, what other hobbies I had, who were my friends and so on. He seemed to be genuinely interested in what I had to say. Jack and Dan soon joined in our conversations and we were all impressed with this kindly older man who treated us as equals.

Conversing with Mr. Copp outside the drugstore soon became a semi regular event. On one of our visits Mr. Copp asked what we were doing for money. We all confessed we were given a weekly allowance to spend. He asked us if we were interested in making some money on our own. We of course were quite interested and wanted to know more.. He explained that each summer he went on a camping trip to Traverse City, Michigan where he picked cherries and was paid a dollar for each bucket of cherries he picked. He told us he could make as much as $50.00 in a week. He said he had his own tent and cooked all his meals over a campfire. He offered that he would like to find some others to join him to share expenses and wondered if we knew anyone who might be interested in going with him. The three of us were quite impressed. My allowance was twenty-five cents and Johnny and Don had similar allowances. The thought of going up north and camping out was extremely appealing to three city boys. We asked him how old did one have to be to go on a trip like this. He replied ….

"Are you boys interested?"

We answered enthusiastically …

"Yes!"

He said he would be willing to take us with him on the trip but we had to have permission from our parents and we would each need to have five dollars for starting expenses. I had been saving part my weekly allowance and felt sure I could come up with five dollars by the time we would have to leave. Jack and Dan were sure they could get the necessary funds as well but getting permission from our parents was another matter. I was not confident my mother would okay the proposed trip but, as she seemed always willing to send me somewhere other than home, I had my hopes up. To bolster my position I decided to have Jack and Dan accompany me when I asked my mother for permission. The three of us sat on the stuffed davenport across from my mother who was sitting on an upholstered chair. It was a hot summer day and she was wearing a brightly colored sun dress. While I was explaining how I first met Mr. Copp at school and that he was willing to take us with him on his cherry picking trip I noticed she was perched toward the front edge of the chair with her sundress hiked above her knees. For a brief moment I thought I could see a dark spot under her dress. I quickly looked away thinking it was my imagination playing tricks on me. When I looked again it was still there. Suddenly all sorts of questions were racing through my mind and I was immediately filled with apprehension.

"My God what am I seeing? Isn't she wearing underwear? Are Jack and Dan seeing this too? Am I crazy? Is she doing this on purpose? What's wrong with her? Why did I bring my friends here?"

I was relieved when she shifted to a different position blocking the view. When she said I could go provided Jack and Dan were allowed to go as well we hurriedly left the apartment. Outside, sure that they had seen the same thing I did, I braced myself for their teasing and ridicule. Surprisingly nothing was said. More questions raced in my head...

"Didn't they see it? Are they too embarrassed to say anything? Are they just being considerate of my feelings?"

After a few days went by and still nothing was said I concluded that either they did not "see" or it was my own dirty mind playing tricks on me.

Jack's folks had already okay-ed the trip but Dan's mother said she wanted to meet Mr. Copp before she decided. The next week Mr. Copp met with Mrs. Mac Cormick and she finally gave Dan approval to go. The three of us were overjoyed. Summer vacation would start in May and I spent the next few weeks gathering and packing all the things I thought I would need for a camping trip. We met Mr. Copp at the drugstore a few more times to discuss details and set a specific date for leaving. Mr. Copp would first pick up Jack and Dan at 8:30 am then pick me up at 9 o'clock on the date specified. About a week before we were to depart for Traverse City Dan informed

Jack and I that his mother had changed her mind and was not going to allow him to go. We were greatly disappointed but Jack and I agreed we still wanted to go. The night before we were to leave I was so excited I hardly slept. I was awake and up at 6 am with all my gear packed and ready to leave the minute Mr. Copp was supposed to arrive. Nine o'clock came and went with no appearance of Mr. Copp and Jack. At approximately 9:30 am there was a knock on our door. I ran to the door excited that they were finally here. Upon opening the door I saw not Mr. Copp but two strange men dressed in suits. One of them asked ....

"Are you Julian King?"

"Yes." ... I replied

"Are your folks home?"

"Yes."

My mother came to the door and asked.... What can I do for you?"

One of the men showed a badge and said.... We would like to speak to you alone."

My mother told me to go to my room and asked the two men to come inside. After a lengthy conversation the two men left. My mother came into my room and I was dismayed to hear her say ....

"Skippy, you're not going on any camping trip."

"Why? What happened? Where is Mr. Copp?"

Then she informed me that the two strange men were police detectives and they were investigating Mr. Copp for child molestation. He had a history of molesting minors and had been arrested and was in jail awaiting the prosecutors' decision on the appropriate charges. Someone had informed the police of our planned trip but the detectives would not reveal who it was. My hopes of going on that fantastic camping trip and earning lots of money were destroyed. My mother began questioning me regarding any inappropriate happenings on the part of Mr. Copp. I told her that nothing like that happened.

"He was always nice to us! I can't believe what they said about him."

My disappointment was crushing. I couldn't (maybe wouldn't) believe Mr. Copp was a bad man. After all, I thought, didn't the school invite him to put on his photography seminar? I wondered who would have called the police. I concluded that it must have been that mean Mrs. Mac Cormick. Several days would pass before I got over the disappointment and gradually came to the realization that Mrs. Mac Cormick….

"May just have saved our lives."

During summer recess I continued my bicycle trips to Highland Park to meet up with Johnny and Don. I also continued to attend weekly troop meetings of the Boy Scouts. As I began to lose interest in my "photography project" my interest in "Scouting" increased and I set a goal of becoming a "First Class Scout". Most of the other boys in the troop wore their Boy Scout uniforms to the meetings. My parents said they couldn't afford to buy one for me and I so I attended the meetings in street clothes. I felt out of place. I decided to spend the money I had saved for the Traverse City trip on a uniform shirt. With at least part of a uniform I attended meetings with a new sense of pride.

Chapter 18

THE SUMMER OF "49"

That summer brought some major changes. A few years earlier Lester had been more or less unemployed and my mother only worked a few hours off and on at "Caton's Photos. We survived with help from my grandma and defrauding the local grocers by running up bills, then moving away without paying them. Rent we owed to various landlords went unpaid. As a child I paid little attention to such things but as an awareness of the world around me increased, my sense of shame was growing as well. I was becoming more aware that the families of friends I knew did not live that kind of lifestyle. Resentment grew within me along with a determination that when I grew up I would never ever live that way. I was realizing that money was power. I vowed I would never be broke and powerless..I determined to save part of the twenty-five cents an hour I earned babysitting for tenants in our apartment building. I devised a scheme to force myself to save. I decided that every time I received a dime coin in change I would put it in a glass quart milk bottle. The money I saved this way was only to be used for very special things.

A radical change in our finances was coming. Due to the daily responsibilities associated with running a thirty-eight unit apartment house my mother had to quit her part time job at Caton's Photo. About the same time Lester became acquainted with a man who was in the furnace repair business. Vic Rashid was his name. Mr. Rashid offered Lester a job cleaning furnaces and Lester began bringing home a weekly paycheck. There was no rent to pay and Lester was receiving a paycheck so the quality of our lives began to improve. The refrigerator now contained food (most of the time). Instead of a steady diet of bean soup we were having steak several times a week and bacon and eggs for breakfast. Along with the improved economic conditions the time spent in the local bars was increasing as well. Lester stopped each night after work and my mother joined him in the evening when her management duties were not as essential. It wasn't long until Lester got the idea to branch out on his own. He had some business cards printed ("General Furnace") with his name and phone number. Now he was in business for himself and surprisingly he began receiving a lot of calls. By default my mother became secretary for this new company. She was kept quite busy answering phone calls for the General Furnace Company. She also had the apartment building's managerial duties to keep up with. I returned early from a visit to Highland park one afternoon to find a colored woman standing at the ironing board busy ironing clothes. My mother introduced her as "Mattie". Mattie came once a week to assist with the household chores. I thought….

"Gee, now we even have a maid. We must be rich"

A week or so later a colored man started showing up at our apartment. His name was Al. Lester was busy with his furnace business and was not available to do some of the heavy chores needed around the apartment building so my mother contacted the Salvation Army and Al was sent. He was supposed to come two times a week to do miscellaneous chores. Al was a friendly fellow and he liked to relate stories of his past career as a lightweight prize fighter. He always seemed to have time to talk to me and I was fascinated by his tales of triumph in the "ring" but as I became more familiar with Al I began to notice the "glaze" in his eyes and the smell of alcohol on his breath when he spoke. Before long he began missing an occasional day when he was supposed to show up for work. When he did show up he was often staggering and sometimes talking to himself. It didn't take long for me to realize Al was an alcoholic and I did my best to avoid him. Finally due to his erratic behavior my mother was forced to fire Al. Shortly after he was let go I ran into him on the street around the corner from our apartment house. He was standing up but slumped against a wall of a nearby business. He was totally drunk but called out my name when he recognized me. I had to stop to say hello as I had been taught never to be rude. Al began his drunken recitation of some boxing match from his past. As he related the tale he also demonstrated the various thrusts, ducks and punches he had thrown at his opponent. Suddenly he swung out and landed a solid blow to my face. I screamed…

"Hey! Al, what are you doing? Stop hitting me! Wake up!"

Al was not only an alcoholic, he was also punch drunk. I quickly moved down the street away from him. As I left him there slumped backwards against a wall he hollered out…

"I'm shorry Skippy."

After our encounter that day I told my mother what had happened. Later that week a new guy showed up to replace Al. I never saw Al again. The new man was called Tee. He was a tall, skinny white man with a southern drawl. Unlike Al he seemed distant and not at all interested in talking with me. Tee seemed much more normal than AL. Tee was not much of a conversationalist but he showed up on his two scheduled days each week and efficiently performed all the duties assigned to him. After he had been working a few weeks at the apartment house some of the tenants became aware of his presence and took notice of what appeared to be his strong work ethic. On the days he wasn't working for the apartment management (my mother) a few of the tenants hired him to do miscellaneous jobs they needed done such as moving furniture in or out. One day one of the tenants (Mrs. Black) stopped by out apartment and told my mother she wanted to have the walls of their apartment painted. She wanted to know if Tee would be interested in doing some painting in their apartment. My mother told her that Tee had done some minor paint jobs in the apartment hallways and that he seemed to know what he was doing. Subsequently Mrs. Black hired Tee to do the painting for her. They arranged a time for Tee to do the job on a weekend when she was going out of town with her husband. They gave Tee the key to their apartment, purchased the desired paint and left it in the apartment. This plan allowed them to be out of Tee's way as he accomplished the task and they would avoid the smell of fresh paint. The neighborhood our apartment was located in was a predominately populated with well to do Jewish families. Many business owners, professional folks and a few politicians resided in the area. I had been in a few individual apartments in our building and had taken notice of the well appointed furnishings and modern appliances contained in most of them. The Blacks apartment was no exception. Their furnishings were exceptional and more than a few original oil paintings hung on the walls. Although the following episode was actually quite tragic at the time, with the passing of years relating this story has provided a great deal of laughter…

The Blacks returned the from their weekend getaway to the shock of their lives. Tee was sitting on the floor of the apartment with his back butted up against the wall a wet paintbrush in one hand and an almost empty whiskey bottle in the other. His eyes were glazed over and he was muttering something indecipherable. There were empty whiskey and beer bottles scattered around the room. Paint had been spilled on the upholstered furniture and in several places on the carpet. The part of the story that was most shocking and yet quite humorous is that in a drunken stupor Tee had painted the walls as instructed however he neglected to first remove any of the oil paintings and apparently painted his way from one end of the wall to the other completely covering any oil painting that was in the way with wall paint. It became obvious that Tee, just like Al, was another alcoholic. To her regret my mother had once again contacted the Salvation Army for someone to assist with the chores around the apartment building. Although as a thirteen year old I was aware that this was a really bad thing to happen to the Blacks I still could not keep from laughing as I related this story to my friends. After that my mother never hired any one through the Salvation Army.

One morning late that summer of 1948 the man that bought the old newspapers I had been gathering from the "trash closets" showed up with a truck to haul away the bundled papers. Unfortunately I had neglected to bundle them. Instead while

I had diligently collected the "papers" each day I had simply carried them down to the storage area and dumped them loosely inside. I was forced to admit to my mother that the papers were not ready to be picked up and begged her to explain the situation to the "paper man" as I was too embarrassed to face him. She convinced him to come back the next day if I would get the papers bundled and ready for pick up. I embarked on the task at hand and spent the entire day stacking and bundling newspapers only stopping for supper. It was approximately 11 o'clock that night when I finished. The following morning the "paper man" returned with his truck and scale for weighing the newspapers. We hauled the "bundles" to the truck where he weighed them. I cannot recall the exact per pound amount I was paid but I remember there were more than 100 bundles weighing around 25 pounds each. I was elated when the "paper man" presented me with $32.00. My weekly allowance was 25 cents and I only earned 25 cents an hour for babysitting. It finally dawned on me that the time I spent collecting and bundling "papers" was definitely worth it. I made a vow to bundle the "papers" at least once each week and not wind up with an almost insurmountable task at the last minute. (I kept that vow for approximately one week). I decided I would keep $7.00 in my pocket and place $25.00 in the "milk bottle" bank with the dimes I had been saving. It was a good feeling to know I always had some money of my own to use for special occasions.

The next day on my Highland Park visit, I proudly informed my friends of my newfound wealth. Jack suggested we ride our bikes out to 8-mile road where Roy's Ranch riding stable was located. We could go horseback riding for $2.00 per hour. Johnny had a job delivering the "Shopping News" once a week and he was paid two cents for each one he delivered. He was due to be paid the next week so he would have enough money for one or two hours of horseback riding. When we asked Dan if he could go, he said he would ask his folks. We got a map and began making plans for the trip to Roy's Ranch. We could hardly contain the excitement that was building with each passing day. The assigned day arrived and the three of us hopped on our bikes and embarked on the first of more than a few long distance bike rides to Roy's Ranch. The "ranch" was a vast wooded area with a creek winding through it. There was a large barn where they kept the horses and a few additional out buildings. Roy was a friendly fellow and, I am sure, well aware that we were naive city kids without any knowledge of what riding a horse entailed. He and an assistant went into the barn and soon reappeared with three horses already saddled. He gave us some rudimentary instructions on handling the horses explaining commands like Gee & Haw etc. He asked that we not attempt to make them run faster by whipping the horses. We of course agreed and kept our promise until we were well out of sight of Roy or any other "ranch" employees. Up to that point, the only horse I had ridden before was on a "Merry Go Round" at Edgewater Amusement Park so I was apprehensive at first. While I cannot remember the names of the horses for purposes of this story, I'll call my horse "Buck". Jack led the way slowly down one of the designated trails through the woods with Dan right behind while I followed on Buck. After we rode along the trail for a while our confidence grew and we began nudging the horses with a slap on their hindquarters. This caused the horses to quicken their pace so we kept it up until Buck broke out in a full gallop. Unaccustomed to this new activity I began bouncing up and down totally out of sync with the rhythm of the horse and nearly fell off. Just when I thought Buck was never going to stop, he finally slowed down to a trot. It was then that I began to sense a painful sensation in the area of my butt cheeks. Jack and Dan had experienced much the same result with their horses and as our hour of riding was close to over we rode gently back to the barn. Although we had sore rear ends and some aches in muscles we were previously unaware of, we would return many times to Roy's Ranch. Successfully venturing some distance from the comfortable surroundings of our own neighborhood instilled an increased sense of confidence in our ability to function independently.

A few weeks later, our newfound confidence was shaken. We all agreed we wanted to go fishing so we got out our map and looked to see where the nearest lake was located. After some discussion, we decided Orchard Lake looked like a good one.

We made plans to ride our bikes there. A few days later we packed a lunch and the three of us embarked on another bicycle trip to Orchard Lake, (fishing poles in hand). We had not yet embraced a complete understanding of time and distance. In actuality, the trip to Orchard Lake was 27 miles. The trip seemed to be much longer than we anticipated and extremely tiring. Before we were halfway to our destination we had finished the lunches we packed, the muscles in our legs were starting to ache and we were tiring rapidly. Sometime around 5 pm, we finally arrived at Orchard Lake. Thrilled at first, that we had successfully completed our mission, we began inquiring of the "locals" where we might rent a boat. Everyone we asked said there were no boat liveries on Orchard Lake. We found an open spot along the shore where we could cast our lines out but the fish apparently were not interested. It didn't take long before we became discouraged and one of us suggested we think about the return home. We considered our situation and the time of day. It dawned on us that it would probably be late at night before we got back home. We would be riding our bikes most of the way on the highway after dark. We had no lights on our bikes and we realized this would be quite dangerous. We decided one of us needed to call home for help. We found a payphone at a local store. Dan was fearful of being punished and would not call. When I dialed, my number there was no answer. Jack's call was successful. He explained to his parents where we were and our problem. He hung up the phone and glumly informed us his folks were on their way but that Denny (his step dad) was very angry. About an hour later Denny and Jack's mother arrived in their four-door Packard automobile. Jack's mother inquired if we were okay while Denny, without saying a word, began piling the three bikes into the car's trunk. We climbed into the back seat and no one uttered a word for the entire trip home. It was dark by the time I rode my bike from Johnny's house back home. As usual, no one was there.

I did get to go fishing several times that summer. Lester's business continued to prosper. Natural gas had recently become available throughout the Detroit area and it was cheaper and much cleaner than heating with coal. Many homeowners were having their coal fired furnaces converted for burning natural gas. Somehow, Lester learned how to convert these coal furnaces to natural gas and made a lot of money doing so. I often overheard Lester on the phone with Vic Rashid so I think he had some involvement in Lester's success. This new prosperity not only meant more to eat but there were other benefits as well. Most Sundays, that summer, Lester would drive my mother and I out to a place called Walt's Landing on Pontiac Lake. Often my grandma accompanied us as well. Walt's had boats to rent, bait for fishing, a nice beach and a picnic area. Les would stop along the way to pick up some beer and we would go fishing out on the lake. Out on the lake it wasn't long until my youthful attention span was exhausted and I lost interest in fishing. I would then request to go back to shore so I could go swimming, visit Walt's playground or play the pinball machine that was located in Walt's bait shop. Les was always accommodating and would row me back to shore whenever I asked. Reflecting back, I wonder if he wasn't just happy to get rid of me. Les liked to fish and drink beer. He would sit in the boat for hours fishing and drinking his beer. Often due to inebriation, he would stay in the sun too long and experience severe sunburns. Many times, I saw my mother treating huge blisters the size of baseballs on Lester's back. How I wondered, could he sit in the sun that long and experience such severe burns without being aware of what was happening to him. Too much beer, I thought.

Summer vacation was drawing to a close and the coming of Labor Day weekend meant I would be attending 8th grade at Durfee Intermediate School. I dreaded another change. I did not want to meet new people or make new friends. I resigned myself to the probability that once more I would be the "new kid" and subject to bullying and ridicule by the "regular" kids. With Labor Day weekend at hand, I spent as much time as possible with my Highland Park friends. Mostly I sought out Jack as I viewed him as a role model. Jack was "cool". He was always in the know regarding the latest teen fashions and he always seemed so very sure of himself. I, on the other hand, was completely lacking in confidence. I was sure that almost everyone I knew or even met was better than me. They all seemed to have normal families. They all had regular meals where moms and dads sat at the kitchen table with their kids. They all had parents that were home at night. None of them went to sleep at night sucking their thumbs at the age of thirteen. Beside all that, I was very small for my age. At the age of thirteen I was still only four foot nine inches tall and weighed ninety-eight pounds. I thought Jack was one lucky kid and I wanted to be just like him. So when Jack let his hair grow longer and combed it into a pompadour with a "ducktail", so did I. When Jack bought a pair of "White Bucks", I bought the same shoes. I tried my best to dress like Jack, talk like Jack, walk like Jack and be like Jack in every way. He was my idol.

Sometimes, when we could convince our respective parents, we would sleep overnight at each other's homes. We would play card games, Monopoly or just horse around in general. On one of those stay-overs Johnny taught me how to play "Black Jack" for money (nickels and dimes). I learned to like gambling. There was one significant occurrence I still remember…. Jack and I were both asleep one night when something woke me up. I thought I heard a noise and got up to see what it was. I went to open the bedroom door and found it was slightly ajar. Instead of opening up the door I decided to peek through the small opening between the door frame and the edge of the door. The opening was only about an inch wide but through it I could see the door to Jack's parent's room was open. I had a partial view of them in bed. Lying on her back was Jack's mother with her legs spread high in the air, naked. On top of her was Jack's naked step dad positioned between her legs and thrusting feverishly back and forth. I became very excited and as I attempted to get a better view I slightly bumped the door. He must have heard something because Jack's step dad reached over from his position atop his wife and was able to push their bedroom shut. The "show" was over. I went back to bed but couldn't sleep. I wondered… *"Did they know I had seen them?* I spent most of the night speculating on what I would say if they brought up the subject the next morning. I also wondered if I might see a repeat performance on another future sleepover.

Jack's step dad (Denny) had a brother living in Indianapolis who came to Highland Park for a visit that Labor Day weekend accompanied by his wife and daughter. The daughter was a pretty girl with dark brown wavy hair and deep brown eyes. She was tall, and slender with noticeable development in the right places. Her name was Marilyn. I was immediately interested in getting to know her but my lack of self confidence and shyness inhibited any thought that she might want to get to know me. Surprisingly Marilyn was not shy and began to strike up a conversation with me. She appeared to like me and we spent a lot of time that weekend talking of typical teenage subjects and discovering what we had in common. Knowing Marilyn would be returning to Indianapolis I didn't want to see the weekend end. As we said goodbye my spirits lifted when she told me she would be back for another visit at Christmas time.

Chapter 19

SCHOOL ELEVEN

Summer vacation was over and it as time to begin school at Durfee Intermediate. Durfee was part of a three school campus located on the corner of Linwood Ave and Collingwood. On the same campus was Roosevelt Elementary (kindergarten through 6th grade), Durfee Intermediate (7th through 9th grade) and Central High School (10th through 12th grade). I walked the seven blocks to school and reported to the office where I was assigned a homeroom. I felt very isolated at first as I knew no one else at this school. Before long I discovered that there would be days at Durfee when I would be the only student in class. The neighborhood around Durfee was inhabited predominately by Jewish people. The Jewish students were excused from school on Jewish Holidays. This left me feeling even more like an outsider. After getting acquainted with the layout of the school and the surrounding neighborhood I decided I would go to school each day and do my best to learn my lessons but would not bother to fit in with other kids at school or in my new neighborhood. Rather I would continue to ride my bike back to Highland Park and maintain the friendships I had established there. I continued the weekly Boy Scout meetings and at one of the meetings Mr. Taggart informed the troop that those of us who attained the age of fourteen would be eligible to be "Explorer Scouts". Explorer Scouts had special privileges one of which was being able to go on camp-outs without having a scoutmaster stay with them. This had tremendous appeal to young teenagers trying to establish independence from the adults in their lives. I began, in earnest, the quest to be promoted to "Explorer". I encouraged Jack to join the "Scouts" too but he didn't seem interested.

With the arrival of fall also came football. Not being able to participate in school sports I never developed a keen interest in sports. Jack however, had a strong interest in University of Michigan football. One Saturday morning he suggested we hitchhike out to Ann Arbor to watch U of M play in one of their conference games. I was always ready to follow Jack's lead and quickly agreed. Off we went, thumbs out high, signaling we wanted a ride. In only a few minutes someone stopped to pick us up. Jack knew the way and after three or four hitches we got picked up by someone who was also going to U of M to watch the game. We arrived a few minutes before game time. I followed Jack as he searched the perimeter of the stadium looking for a spot where we could climb the fence unnoticed. When the right spot was discovered we quickly scampered over the fence and calmly immersed ourselves in the crowd. I knew nothing about football and frankly paid little attention to the game itself however I did enjoy the excitement of being in the midst of thousands of cheering fans. I was glad I came with Jack. When the game was over we hitched back home without any trouble. That fall we would repeat the same trip a few more times with little difficulty. Times were different in that era. There was no mass media to report every single perversion and killing in each and every city or town in any part of the country. Thus the populace was not constantly filled with fear. Drivers readily stopped for hitchhikers and folks were generally unafraid to get into a car with someone they did not know.

That fall for some reason my mother and grandmother became concerned with my small size. It was decided I should see a doctor to be sure my development was normal for a thirteen year old. After a thorough examination by the doctor he left me alone in the examining room to confide his findings to my mother. While alone my curiosity prompted me to look around the room. I opened some cabinet doors and pulled out a few drawers. Upon opening one of the drawers I discovered dozens of small round semi transparent rubbery objects that looked very much like the "rubbers" I had seen blown up and waved in front of the girls at school a few months earlier. I couldn't believe my luck. I excitedly stuffed a handful into my pockets thinking of the fun I would have showing these to my friends. I thought I might even try one on later. As we were leaving I did my best to hide my nervousness over the "significant theft" I had perpetrated. The doctor seemed not to notice. As we were leaving he handed my mother a bottle of pills that I was to take every day. His opinion was that my development was behind normal. The pills, he claimed, were growth hormones and would accelerate my physical development. Some recent limited research on my part indicates there was no real growth hormone pill for the purpose of accelerating growth in humans available in 1948. Still I would grow 10 inches in the three years following.

Later that week when I was at home alone I retrieved one of the pilfered "rubbers", I had secreted under my mattress, with the intention of trying it on. I unwrapped the "rubber" and attempted to put it on. It appeared to be a little small however I was sure it would stretch out to fit. Try as I might I could only get it to go on about a half inch over the tip of my penis. When I tried to pull it on further there was extreme resistance and a lot of pain. I couldn't understand why it would not fit. Next, I thought, it might stretch out enough to fit if I first blew it up like a balloon. That did not work either. I tried several more times to no avail finally in frustration I gave up. One evening, a few days later, I returned from one of my bicycle trips to Highland Park to find Lester and my mother sitting at the kitchen table. Both had big smiles on their faces.

"What's so funny?" I asked.

They both burst into laughter. confused by their reaction I asked … "Why are you laughing?"

Lester motioned at the table where to my dismay several of my "pilfered rubbers" lay in full display. "Where did you get these?" he asked, still smiling.

Feeling heat of embarrassment coursing through my entire body. I thought ….

"Oh my God! How am I going to get out of this?" Playing dumb was my only option.

"I found them at the doctor's office."

"Why did you take them?"

"I thought they were balloons."

"Then why did you hide them under your mattress?"

"I don't know."

While I stood there squirming, they both kept smiling. Lester gave me a knowing look as he asked....

"Do you want to know what they are really used for?"

"Aren't they balloons?"

"No Skippy, they are not balloons. They are doctor's examination gloves."

"What are examination gloves?"

Both Lester and my mother chuckled as he told me...

"Doctors put one on their finger when they stick a finger up your ass!"

Totally mortified. I realized my stupidity. I thought.... *What an idiot I am."*

Desperately trying not to let them find out that I believed them to be "rubbers" I meekly replied.... "I thought they were balloons."

As I walked away Les motioned me closer and smilingly whispered in my ear... *"Did they fit?"*

As Christmas time approached my thoughts turned to Jack's cousin, Marilyn. I remembered she had said they would be returning to spend Christmas Week at Jack's house. I wondered if she would still be interested in spending time with me.

"No!".... I thought.... *"Why would she want anything to do with a scrawny, underdeveloped boy like me?"*

Still my excitement grew as the time for their arrival neared.

"There was always hope."

School let out on Thursday, December 23, so the few students who were not Jewish could celebrate the Christmas holiday. We did not have to return to school till the first week of January 1949. I traveled to Jack's house Thursday afternoon to see when his relatives were due to arrive. Jack wasn't sure but he confirmed they were coming. I spent the next day shopping for a gift for my mother and dreaming of the nice presents I would find under the Christmas tree. With Lester's recent success in the furnace business I believed that this Christmas I would finally see some nice presents. I thought surely this year I would not have to wait until late to swipe a Christmas tree after the "tree" lots were closed. Instead we could buy a "tree" and have it decorated early in the evening. My parents were gone somewhere and I was home alone all day. As the day went on with no sign of my mother or Lester I began to suspect they were at the "bar" again. I made something for my dinner and waited for them to show. Seven o'clock came with no sign of them. Then eight o'clock came and went. At eight thirty I called the "bar" and asked if my mother was there. She came to the phone asking....

"What do you want?"

"When are you coming home?"

"We'll be leaving soon."

"It's Christmas Eve. We don't even have a "tree" yet!"

"Hold on to your horses Skippy! We'll get one on the way home."

Nine o'clock arrived and I called the "bar" again. I was relieved to hear whoever answered say.... "She's not here, they left"

When ten o'clock came with no sign of my parents a seething anger began boiling inside of me.

"What is wrong with them? It's Christmas time! Don't they care? Don't they care about me? Must I spend every Christmas Eve alone while they get drunk with their friends? What kind of life is this?"

I stormed out of the apartment, mad as hell, found the nearest Christmas tree lot, and snatched a tree. By the time I drug it home and put on the decorations it was after midnight and I was the only one home. Disgusted, I crawled into bed, grabbed the satin edge of my blanket and resumed my lifelong habit of sucking my thumb. I awoke Christmas morning to find my parents had made it home at last and still asleep in bed. I went to the "tree" and found a large plain unwrapped box with my name written in pencil on it. I opened it up to find a new Explorer Scout uniform. Although this was the only present from them I was elated. It was something I wanted desperately. I could not believe they paid any mind to my occasional brief comments about the Explorer Scouts. Even though they hadn't bothered to put it in Christmas wrapping I was so happy with this present that my previous feeling of animosity simply faded away.

The day after Christmas I headed for Jack's house. Jack answered when I knocked on the door. I really wanted to ask if Marilyn had come as promised but I simply said ….

"Hi."

"Come on in."

I entered the living room to find Jack's mother, step dad, and Marilyn's parents engaged in conversation, but no sign of Marilyn. I wanted to ask if she was there but could not screw up the courage. I followed Jack as he proceeded through the house to his bedroom. Still no sign of Marilyn. After we were alone in Jack's bedroom, fearful of his answer, I asked …

"Didn't Marilyn come with her folks?"

"Yeah, she's here. She walked down to Simon's Store."

"Did she mention anything about me?"

"Yeah, she told me she likes you and wanted me to call you to come over."

A feeling of cautious confidence crept over me as I waited for Marilyn to return from the store. During Christmas break I spent nearly all my time visiting with Marilyn. We discussed all the things that were important to two young teenagers. Our favorite songs, movies, the coolest new cars, what we were going to be when we grew up etc. Something inside of me wanted to get close to her, to hold her hand but awkwardness and fear of rejection kept me from making such a bold move. When the time came for her family to return to Indianapolis we exchanged addresses and promised to write each other. Then she was gone.

It was January 1949 and school was back in session. Life continued as normal (at least as I knew normal to be). My time was filled gathering old newspapers from the trash closets, some occasional babysitting jobs, daily bike trips to Highland Park, and proudly attending Boy Scout meetings in my new Explorer Scout uniform. At one of the "Scout" meetings I approached Mr. Taggart and inquired if he would approve of the "Explorers" going on a camp out at Roy's Ranch. I told him I had previously asked Mr. Roy if he would allow some Boy Scouts to camp on his property and Mr. Roy said he could not allow that in warm weather months as it would interfere with his horse riding business however he had no objection if we wanted to camp during winter months. Mr. Taggart replied that he would approve provided he supervised setting up the campsite first and once he knew everything was safe and secure he would (as the Explorer Scout charter allowed) leave us on our own. He said we could even use the "Troop's" tent. The only catch was that anyone going on this camp out had to have written permission from their parents. The day for the camp out came in early February and my memory is that there were only five of us that went on the camp out. Mr. Taggart drove us out to Roy's Ranch, helped us unload our gear, set up the tent, and build a campfire. When he was confident all was okay he said goodbye. We got busy gathering up more firewood to last through the night. For some of the boys this was their first trip to Roy's Ranch and they were anxious to spend the day exploring the woods to see if they could spot some wildlife. The temperature began to fall as the sun was descending in the west. Dinnertime was approaching and we were getting hungry. Each boy had been required to pitch in an equal amount of money to buy the groceries etc that we needed. For dinner we had purchased a large box of frozen chicken. We opened the box of chicken, put the chicken in a large pot and placed the pot in the center of the campfire along with some frozen french fries. After what we thought was enough time to cook the chicken we removed it from the fire and waited for it to cool enough to pick it up with our fingers. By then we were all quite hungry and anxiously began to "dig in" to the chicken and "fries". Our hunger was diminishing and we were becoming quite satisfied with our ability to be self sufficient and camp on our own when one of the campers asked….

"What's this pink stuff on the chicken?"

We all took a close look at the piece of chicken he was holding in his hand. There appeared to be some reddish pink juices oozing from the innermost area of the chicken. We all looked closer at our own pieces and saw the same thing. We started pulling chicken away from the bone and discovered it was still cold in the middle and the pinkish hue was actually blood. We realized we had not cooked the chicken thoroughly. It was still frozen in the center. Suddenly we were no longer hungry. The sun went down and darkness surrounded us. It was time to sit around the fire and take turns trying to scare each other with gruesome horror stories we made up as we went along. The temperature continued to drop and we were beginning to really feel the cold. Soon we gave up the "stories" and climbed into our sleeping bags trying to keep warm. We would learn the next day the temperature had dropped to five above. We slept in sleeping bags with our winter jackets and gloves on in an attempt to stay warm. The cold however was unrelenting and it fast became unbearable. Our toes began paining from the cold eventually becoming numb. We had to do something. I remembered that Roy's Ranch bordered on Eight Mile Road and that there was an occasional business located on that highway. We decided to try and find our way through the woods to Eight Mile where perhaps we might find an open business and make a phone call for help. We trudged through the snow and found our way to the corner of Eight Mile and James Couzens highway. Located on that corner was an open restaurant. The sign on the top of the building read "Richards California Twinburger". It was open! We rushed inside grateful to be out of the extreme cold. I spotted a pay phone on the wall and I called home. As I dialed the number, I was thinking …. *They won't answer. They're surely out at the "bar".*

As expected no one answered. I had previously called the "bar" so many times trying to cajole my parents into coming home that I knew the phone number by heart. I decided to call the "bar". I heard the bartender cry out… "Millie, it's your kid on the phone."

Thank God! they were there. I explained the situation we were in to my mother. She said Les would come and pick us up and hung up. The travel time from the bar on Linwood and Clairmont to James Couzins and 8 mile Road should have been approximately thirty minutes. We waited an hour and a half for Lester to arrive. He was drunk. No complaints were uttered as we were so grateful to be on our way back home and out of the cold.

Early the next morning the phone woke me up. I scrambled out of bed to answer it. Mr. Taggart was on the other end. He sounded perturbed when he asked …

"What the heck is going on?"

I apologized and explained the situation as best I could. I said I would go with him to pick up all the "gear" we had left behind. He told me not to worry about it, he already picked it up himself. I thanked him for doing that and told him again how sorry I was. This event ended my venture into "Explorer" scouting. I was the one who brought the idea to Mr. Taggart and I felt responsible for it's failure. Embarrassment kept me from facing him ever again.

Many years later there was much media hoopla as they covered the "Grand Opening" of Northland Mall, the first Shopping Mall in America. It was erected on the property we knew as Roy's Ranch where we had camped one cold February.

Early that spring brought some exciting new developments. The newfound prosperity we were experiencing meant we could now afford things we never had before. I came home one afternoon after school to find a new television. Well, it wasn't actually new, rather my mother had bought it from a tenant who was leaving town and moving out of the Sturtevant apartment building. I believe it was an "Emerson" with a seven inch round screen. I had never seen a television set before. Television broadcasting was in it's infancy. There were only a few channels and a very limited number of programs, all in black & white. At that time you could not simply turn on the TV and instantly find a show to watch. Programming was sporadic. Sometimes, especially late at night, you could find only test patterns to watch. Still I was excited to watch such shows as Ed Sullivan, Arthur Godfrey, Milton Berle and my favorite "Broadway Open House". Broadway Open House was the precursor to NBC'S "Late Night Show". The hosting was alternated by two very funny guys, Jerry Lester and Mory Amsterdam. They interviewed actors, singers, comedians and other notables of that era. They almost always made me laugh but the real reason I was attracted to the show was Dagmar. Dagmar was a big busted attractive, sexy blond. She played the dumb blond part to a tee. I didn't care if she was dumb or smart I just wanted to look at her. Viewing her significantly aroused my male instincts.

Another big development, (perhaps the biggest) was that I would no longer be an "only child". My mother was pregnant and I would have either a brother or sister sometime in July. I wasn't sure how this would impact my life but I remembered how happy I was to spend time with my little cousins Butch and Sue whenever I was at Uncle Red and Aunt Polly's. I was quite fascinated to see how my mother's belly was growing and to be allowed to touch her stomach and feel the baby kick.

Easter was nearing and with money no longer a problem my mother took me to downtown Detroit to buy a new Easter suit. In those days it was more or less a tradition for people to buy new suits or dresses to wear on Easter Sunday. We had been so poor and unable to buy new clothes for so long that I suppose she wanted me to have a new suit for Easter even though I had no desire to wear a suit for Easter or any other time. Grandma joined us and downtown we went to look at suits in various stores. Nothing pleased me. I resisted every suggested style or color. I would not agree with any of their selections, and eventually they grew tired of my obstinance. In the end they made the choice for me. They agreed on a sport jacket and matching slacks that I considered old fashioned. I vowed (to myself) never to wear that stupid outfit. The body of the jacket was gray flannel with huge contrasting beige pockets on each side. There were flaps covering each pocket. There was a strap that went around the middle and closed in the front creating a cinched effect. I was sure no self respecting teenager would be caught dead wearing such an abomination. On Easter Sunday I was sent off to a local church, by myself, wearing the new suit that had been imposed on me. I walked down the street in the direction of the church till I was out of sight of our apartment house. When, I was sure I couldn't be seen I took off the jacket, turned down a side street and slowly wandered around several blocks carrying the jacket across my arm. When enough time had elapsed for church to be let out I returned home. No one was the wiser. I removed my jacket and slacks, hung them in my closet thinking....

"That's the last time I'll be wearing those in public".

I returned home one afternoon In May surprised to find Lester there alone. He informed me that he had taken my mother to the hospital and he needed me to stay and watch over the apartment building while he returned to the hospital to stay with her. He said she might be delivering the baby. I stayed home that night and for the next several days. Someone had to be there to accept the rent checks and try to handle anything that came up until my mother returned from the hospital. When Les brought her home she was quite pale and very weak. There was no baby with her. She told me it was a boy but the baby was born premature and weighed only 4 and a half pounds. She said babies that small had to be put in an incubator and could not come home till he weighed at least five pounds. She named the baby Gerald. Jerry Perkins (my new brother) came home three weeks later. At first glance I noticed his eyes seemed slightly "crossed" but my mother said new babies were sometimes like that and would "uncross" gradually as he grew older I was amazed to see how small and delicate he was. I marveled at his tiny little hands and fingers. There was a small bump in the middle of his little pink face that passed as a nose. I couldn't wait to hold him in my arms. I was fourteen years old and had never experienced a newborn baby up close. From day one Jerry was my brother. No matter we had different fathers he was still my brother and I loved him dearly. It wasn't long before mother and Les returned to their old schedule. I became the babysitter in chief. I learned to give him his "bottle", change his diaper and rock him to sleep. I didn't mind, he was my brother. That summer, my bicycle trips to Highland Park became less frequent due to my new brotherly responsibilities.

Summer vacation was coming to an end and school would soon be back in session. I would be starting ninth grade at Durfee. I decided to make the ride to Highland Park as I hadn't been to see Jack and Dan for a couple of months. I caught up with Jack as he was on his way to see another boy who lived several houses down the block. His name was Karl Audubon. He was a couple years older than we were and as such ran with an older crowd. Jack was attending ninth grade at Highland Park High School and Karl was recruiting him to join Alpha Omega Fraternity. High school fraternities were supposedly banned at that time however Alpha Omega was operating in "open secrecy" anyway. Jack asked me to accompany him so I could meet Karl and he could get to know me. Always anxious to be a part of anything Jack was involved with, I tagged along. Karl was an impressive individual, well groomed, sharp dresser and seemed very sure of himself. I had mixed feelings of admiration and intimidation in his presence. I watched and listened, saying as little as possible while Jack and Karl talked. After we left Karl's house Jack began explaining, what he perceived to be, the benefits of joining a fraternity. For several days he worked on convincing me to pledge Alpha Omega, which I resisted. Lack of self confidence and a fear of meeting new people held me back but in the end, wanting to emulate Jack, I relented.

Jack and I attended the Alpha Omega introductory meeting where, along with other potential pledges, we were introduced to the present members. I heard someone call out the name "Skuppy". At first I thought they were calling me but I soon found out there was a pledge with the name Paul Skupholm and he was nicknamed "Skuppy". I met him later and we exchanged some light conversation regarding our shared nervousness over being accepted into the fraternity. All the pledges were indoctrinated with the so called benefits of membership and given an assignment to accomplish and bring to the next monthly meeting. The first assignment was to memorize, and be able to recite in front of all the members, the Greek alphabet backward and forward. We were also informed that while the introductory meeting was informal the next meeting would require wearing a suit. Remembering the only suit I possessed was my awful, outdated and "corny" Easter suit. I thought ….

"I am doomed".

I spent the next few weeks repeating the Greek alphabet, both out loud and to myself, in an attempt to commit it to memory. When I was sure I had it memorized I began the same process to memorize it in reverse. Jack and I practiced in front of each other almost every day leading up to the meeting. The meeting day arrived and I went with Jack to the meeting place. The meeting was held in the home of one of the members. It was a brick house with large rooms and furnished, in my mind, quite luxuriously. We were led downstairs to a large fully furnished, finished basement where we joined the other "pledges". We were told we would be called one by one to appear before the membership where we would be scrutinized on our appearance, demeanor and ability to recite the Greek alphabet backwards and forward. Although I was totally confident of my ability to meet the Greek alphabet requirement I was filled with dread regarding the appearance and demeanor standards. Every member and pledge at the meeting was wearing a dark, conservative style suit and there I was in this goofy looking two tone suit with large patch pockets. I was first to be called in front of the membership committee. A committee member asked me what my reason was for wanting to join Alpha Omega. At a loss for an answer to this unanticipated question I naively replied ....

"Jack White told me it was the thing to do."

The questioning continued regarding my age, what grade I was in, what school I attended etc. Finally they got to the Greek alphabet which I recited flawlessly. Next they asked to hear it backwards which I also recited flawlessly then, in what I believed was their final attempt to trip me up they asked me to speak it forward and backward all at once. I did what they asked without missing a beat.

"Very good" I heard someone say.... "You are dismissed."

I left the meeting and rejoined the other pledges that were all as nervous as I was. The other pledges asked me what had happened in the meeting. Trying to appear confident I told them they better know the "alphabet deal" but the rest was just routine. When Jack returned from his interview I asked him how it went. He said he had made a mistake on the backward recitation of the "Alphabet" but he was still confident he would be accepted as a member. I was in awe of his self assuredness. Skuppy admitted he too had made a mistake on the Alphabet and was worried he might not be accepted. After all pledges were interviewed the rest of the meeting was dedicated to socializing with the existing members and the other pledges. I felt very ill at ease throughout the entire event and was relieved when the meeting was over. The pledges were informed that those who were accepted as new members would receive an invitation to the next monthly meeting. No invitation meant you were "blackballed".

Jack and I met a few times during the next few weeks to discuss any news regarding our acceptance into the fraternity. I heard nothing for three weeks then a few days before the next fraternity meeting I found Jack at his house looking a little guilty. He reluctantly informed me that he had received an invitation to the next Alpha Omega meeting a week earlier. He also knew that Skuppy had made it in as well. My heart sank as I realized I had not been accepted but then hoping against hope I thought maybe my mail had been delayed. Maybe my invitation was lost. Maybe…maybe… maybe!

The invitation never arrived. I had been "blackballed".

For the next several weeks my thoughts dwelled on what had happened and why. By his own admission Jack had failed the Greek alphabet test yet he was now a member of Alpha Omega while I had performed the same test with no mistakes and I was not.

"What went wrong? Why was I rejected? Was it my stupid suit? Did I say the wrong thing to someone?"

In the end I knew it was me. It was my inability to communicate cleverly like Jack. My lack of "coolness". My embarrassment over this repudiation kept me at home for a while. I filled my time between school and caring for my new brother, in the evenings, while mother and Les were at the "bar". Eventually my need for acceptance from my friends compelled me to make the bike ride to see Jack and Dan. Not finding either of them home I went to the drugstore where they often "hung out". They were not there either. As I stood in front of the drug store contemplating what next to do a car suddenly swerved into the curb in front of me. Jack was behind the wheel with Dan right beside him.

"Hop in." Jack said… "We're going for a ride"

"I didn't know you could drive a car."

"I just learned."

"Where did you get the car?"

"A friend of mine from school let me borrow it."

"Who?"

"You don't know him. Come on get in!"

Afraid of disappointing my friends I reluctantly climbed into the back seat and off we went. When we had gone a few blocks and Jack seemed to drive okay I relaxed a bit. Jack wanted to drive faster than the speed limits in the city allowed so he headed out to Eight Mile road. In 1949 the Detroit city limit ended at Eight Mile and there was little development along that divided highway. Traffic was sparse and there was no posted speed limit at that time and Jack thought he could drive as fast as he wanted. Dan and I became uneasy and began telling Jack to slow down. At first he ignored our pleas and continued his mad dash heading west down Eight Mile. Finally when he noticed the gas gauge was near the "Empty" mark he slowed down saying…. "We better head back" We came to a gravel turnaround and Jack pulled into it intending to drive back to the east but he was going too fast and the car slid sideways on the gravel. He pressed down on the gas pedal attempting to gain purchase and avoid sliding off the gravel turnaround. The car lurched forward and entered the eastbound lane of Eight Mile where we collided with another car going east. Fortunately no one was hurt however the right front fender had been severely crushed into the right front tire and Jack's friend's car was undriveable. As we all stood around dazedly examining the damage the police showed up.

The police investigation of the accident eventually led to the discovery that Jack had not borrowed the car. Rather, he had taken his friend's car without permission. Furthermore the car actually belonged to his friend's father. The cops took us, one at a time, into the back of their police car and began the questioning. I think the cops believed the separate and similar stories Dan and I offered explaining that Jack had told us his friend had loaned him the car and we had no idea it was stolen. The three of us were escorted into the police car. Dan and I were driven to our respective homes where the event was related to our parents. My mother simply said….

"I trust you learned something today."

"I did."

Nothing more was said about this event. The next day I went to Jack's house and found no one home. I went next to Dan's. His mother came to the door when I knocked. She did not look happy. She called Dan to the door and he did not look happy either. He informed me that his parents had forbidden him any further association with me or Jack. Rejected again and dejected over the loss of a friend I went back to Jack's house where I found his parents arriving home from work. His mother told me Jack wasn't home and might not be home for quite a while as he was in jail for stealing a car. She asked me what had happened and I told her what I knew and left.

Now what will I do? These were my only friends. I'm alone again.

For several days I moped around our apartment house collecting the papers from the trash closets, reading books, baby sitting Jerry. I was becoming bored with life in general so when Les asked me if I wanted to earn some money I asked him how? He said he needed a helper on some of the furnace jobs he was working on. I could go with him on Saturdays and I could help carrying in the tools and equipment along with other small tasks. He said he would pay me ten percent of his profit on any job I went on. I had lost my two friends and with little to do I agreed to his proposal. I went with Les several Saturdays that fall. I carried the tools and ran back and forth to the truck fetching whatever items Les needed. After a few jobs Les enlisted me for some other tasks. One of the jobs required re-cementing the firebrick inside the furnace cavity. Due to his large size Les had difficulty reaching in far enough to accomplish this. I was still quite small (apparently the "Growth Hormone" pills had not kicked in yet) and I could actually climb inside the furnace so Les showed me how to remove any loose bricks apply the asbestos based cement and reposition the furnace bricks. I also became involved in jobs that required putting asbestos insulation around the furnace duct-work. Les would fill a large shallow basin with an asbestos solution then I would unroll wide strips of asbestos paper and drag the strips through the asbestos solution, making sure the strips were well saturated. Les would then wrap the strips around the duct-work. It was dirty work but I was earning a lot of money. I continued to save money in my milk bottle "piggy bank".

As winter approached the furnace jobs declined and Les was no longer working on Saturdays. Later that winter Les had fewer and fewer jobs to go on and was spending most of his days in the "bar". My mother was joining him in the evenings and more and more they were coming home drunk which seemed to lead to a lot of quarreling. Les was a big man capable of seriously hurting my mother if he so desired however he was, for the most part, quite gentle. My mother was a small woman, five feet tall, approximately one hundred fifteen pounds, with an aggressive personality. She would start on him about some little thing that he had either done or not done that she was unhappy about while he just smiled or laughed. This reaction on his part only raised her ire all the more and her level of vocal displeasure increased causing him to laugh even louder. I recall seeing her throw various objects at him (missing most of the time). One night she picked up a large marble ashtray and flung it at him. This time she did not miss. It struck him squarely in the left temple and he started oozing blood. My mother started screaming how sorry she was. She tried pressing a towel against the wound but it continued to bleed. She declared they must go to the hospital and they left. I remained at home with Jerry and eventually fell asleep. I awoke when I heard them returning. Lester had a bandage wrapped completely around his head but he appeared to be alright. My mother was still professing how sorry she was and he put his arms around her and said not to worry, he would be okay. Relieved I went back to bed. I awoke in the morning to the sound of Jerry crying. I was very tired and didn't feel like getting up so I pretended to still be sleeping. The crying continued with no response from my mother. I waited some more. Still no response! I was getting more irritated by the minute. All I could think of was that I had been kept up half the night caring for Jerry because of their drunken shenanigans and now they were probably so hung over that they wouldn't get up. It wasn't fair! I was mad! Finally I jumped out of bed, stomped to their bedroom pushed open the door and said….

"Can't you hear Jerry crying."

I saw Lester's face sticking out from the covers at the head of the bed. He was awake. I didn't see my mother. Then I saw my mother's face appear from under the covers but I was puzzled to see her emerge from the foot of the bed instead of at the head of the bed. I thought ….

"What a strange way to sleep."

A few other times I occasionally burst in to find them in this same, what I thought at the time, was a ridiculous way to sleep. It was sometime in my eighteenth year when I realized why they were positioned that way.

The rest of the year was uneventful. Jack was in jail and Dan was forbidden to associate with me. I had not bothered to make new friends at Durfee School nor in the neighborhood where I resided. With no desire to make an attempt at meeting anyone new I filled my time doing the chores I had been assigned, reading books. I even tried my hand at drawing and painting. I started out by drawing copies of illustrations I found in comic books and when gained confidence in my artistic ability I began painting the same scenes using thick water based poster paint. I included some of the better paintings in a few of the letters I mailed to Marilyn. Even now, sixty some years later, I still have a few of these drawings and paintings.

Christmas came that year with all of us playing our usual parts in the same familiar scene. Mother and Les in the bar on Christmas Eve, with me constantly calling the bar asking when they were coming home. Swiping a "tree" late at night, from the local tree lot and decorating it myself with, increasing resentment. The only bright spot was a phone call from Jack. He was at home. He had been home for sometime but he had been grounded for the "car incident". His folks lifted the grounding for Christmas and he wanted to let me know Marilyn was at his house for a visit. The next morning full of anticipation I rode over to John's house to renew my friendship with Marilyn. I believe she was just as happy to see me as I was to see her but the awkwardness of our youth kept us from anything more than smiling at each other. We met several times that week to talk of nothing important at all. She was a young and attractive girl. I was a young and "horny" teenager with not an inkling of how to act upon my feelings. Still I enjoyed being around her and was profoundly sad when it was time for her departure.

Chapter 20

DECLINE

The new year brought little change in the decline of Lester's furnace business. He went out on only a few jobs most weeks and sometimes none at all. He could no longer afford or need me as a helper. The lack of work for Lester meant they both spent more time at the "bar". More "drinking" led to more arguments and more things thrown. Another ashtray collided with Lester's head. Fortunately there was no bleeding this time. Discovering something to eat in the refrigerator was becoming less likely. Sometimes when something to eat was not readily available I would begin to feel one of the weak and clammy sessions that had been a recurring experience for as long as I could remember. One afternoon I experienced one of my frequent spells of low energy. For some reason, for which I have no rational explanation, I thought that a milkshake would make me feel better. I walked across the street to the drugstore where I sat down at the fountain counter, ordered and drank a chocolate milkshake. Even before I finished drinking it I felt the weakness starting to dissipate and my strength returned shortly afterward. I gave little thought to this but from then on I would use this "milkshake medication" to cure many future weak spells.

I saw little of Jack that summer. He was spending a lot of his time with the Alpha Omega crowd and new friends he met at high school. He was chasing after a girl named Carmelita so he was seldom at home when I came by. We began drifting apart. Marilyn did come for a visit that summer and we once more renewed our friendship. One evening we went to see a movie at the local theater. As I sat next to her I wondered what she would do if I put my arm over her shoulder. I started to raise my arm to do just that but then fearful of offending her I withdrew. I repeated this attempt a few times but withdrew each time. I finally summoned enough nerve to place my arm on the top edge of the chair being careful not to actually touch her shoulder. She seemed not to notice so I left it there. After several minutes I allowed my arm to drop down just a little barely touching her shoulder. Again, she did not react to this move. Then, gathering more gumption, I let the full weight of my arm descend onto her shoulder. Still there was no negative reaction from her. In fact she moved a little closer to me. We sat that way for a few minutes then she reached up, took my hand, drew it down and placed it firmly on her breast. This was beyond my belief. I had no idea what to do. I just froze with my hand there, afraid to move it or to say anything. Marilyn said nothing while my hand remained on her breast for the rest of the movie. When the movie was over we left the theater and I walked Marilyn home to Jack's house. We made small talk but neither of us mentioned the fact that she had put my hand on her breast. Still my mind was racing a mile a second pondering the possibilities. What was she after? Why would she do this? How far was she willing to go? When we arrived at our destination we talked awhile and then she informed me her folks were leaving for Indianapolis the next morning. She gave me a hug and we said our goodbyes. Sadly, I made the trip back to the apartment on Sturtevant still puzzled by the developments of the evening and thinking....

"Why did she do that? Was it because she really liked me? Could I have gone further? Did she expect me to? Why would she like me in that way? Why was I such a coward? Would she want to see me again? Will I ever get another chance?"

Doubts and thoughts such as these would tantalize and dog me for months afterward.

With fall came another change of schools. I was starting tenth grade at Central High School which was located on the same campus as Durfee Elementary. At least this change did not involve moving to a new neighborhood. I felt ill at ease at Central High. At Durfee Intermediate School the students were closely monitored and our movements were more regimented while at Central High we were more or less on our own. I had not bothered making friends with any other students at Durfee so consequently I had no friends at Central and was truly on my own. In one my classes I was surprised to see Sandy sitting at a desk (that young girl that innocently asked me to join her in bed several years earlier when we both were very young). When she showed no sign of recognizing me I opted not to say hello. Perhaps she did not remember me or if she did she was most likely embarrassed. At this point in my life I still lacked self confidence and would for years. I soon returned to my routine visits to Highland Park hoping to resume my friendship with Jack. As it happened, when word got out regarding Jack's jail time, he had been ostracized by his so called fraternity brothers. Jack was glad to see me and we quickly renewed our friendship.

It was football season again and Jack and I "hitched" our way to Ann Arbor to see a couple of U. of M. football games. On one of the return trips we "hitched" a ride for only a few miles. For reason unknown the driver did not take the main road but headed instead down an unpaved road then suddenly stopped on the corner of two gravel roads and told us to get out. We were dumbfounded. We asked "why?" He remained silent until we got out of his car. We had no idea exactly where we were but started walking and holding out our thumbs for a ride with each approaching car. There were only a few cars at first, none of which stopped. As we walked further down the road the number of cars diminished. When we had walked a few miles the area seemed to be getting less and less populated with only an occasional house on the road. There were no more cars coming and the cross roads were at least a mile apart. As darkness descended we trudged on. Along the way we came upon a farm house. I stopped and suggested we ask for help but Jack ignored me and kept on walking. My vision was drawn to a light coming from a window that appeared to be from a bedroom. Inside, stood a young full breasted young woman, totally naked. She was standing in front of a basin apparently taking a "sponge bath". I supposed she had not drawn any shades feeling secure in this relatively unpopulated and seldom traveled area. I was drawn to keep watching her and called to Jack to stop but he was several steps in front of me and would not stop walking. Reluctantly I followed thinking …

"We just blew an opportunity to watch a "real young woman" naked."

Finally we came to a paved crossroad with a fair amount of traffic. We caught a ride that took us to Ypsilanti where the driver dropped us at the bus station. Jack called home and convinced his parents to come pick us up. They were not happy! After that I decided not to go to any more football games with Jack and I stopped going to his house again for awhile. This turned out to be a fortunate decision. Days passed slowly and without any friends in my own neighborhood I grew bored. Then one day I hopped on my bike and rode over to Jack's house. Jack's mother answered the door and invited me in....

"Jack isn't here." …. She told me. "He won't be home for some time. Jack has got himself in a lot of trouble and he is in the hospital.

I noticed her eyes begin to moisten as she spoke.

"What happened?"…. I asked

"Jack was in Ann Arbor for a football game and when he couldn't catch a ride back home he stole a car."

She continued…. "He was driving too fast down Michigan Avenue and flipped the vehicle. Somehow he was thrown out of the car and flew into a tree busting his kneecap. He's in the hospital now. They had to remove his kneecap and he will not be able to walk normally again."

When I asked how long he would be in the hospital she said she wasn't sure but when he was released from the hospital he would go to trial for stealing the car so he wouldn't be home for quite some time. Later I learned it wasn't a car he stole rather

I was told it was limousine that belonged to a famous Detroit Tiger pitcher. I seem to recall it belonged to Hal Newhauser. That event would draw to an end my visits to Highland Park. With no nearby friends I became bored and mildly depressed. I withdrew to my small bedroom where I spent a lot of time listening to the radio, reading, drawing or painting pictures once more.

One day in November Lester began talking about going deer hunting up north. He related stories of his hunting exploits in Onaway, Michigan where he was raised. Other than the train trips to visit my great grand parents in Oshawa, Canada when I was very young I had never been very far from home. The idea of traveling to the "wilds" of Northern Michigan enticed me out of the "funk" I had been in since I became aware of Jack's troubles. We began making plans for the hunting trip. Les reminded me I would need some warm clothes and a good pair of boots. I had the warm clothes but needed to buy myself a new set of boots. I had been putting most of the money I earned working with Les, plus my babysitting and paper bundling money, in my "milk bottle bank" for some time and knew I had approximately seventy five dollars saved. This would be more than enough to pay for some new boots. When I retrieved the "bottle" and counted the money there was only thirty dollars in it. At first I was puzzled and distressed, and then I became angry as it dawned on me that "they" probably took it. I approached my mother....

"What have you done with my money?"

"Calm down Skippy. I borrowed it to pay some bills. I'll pay you back at the end of the month."

"That wasn't fair! You should have asked me first."

"I'm sorry. You were not around to ask, when I needed it."

As always I was helpless to do anything about the theft of my money. I spent ten dollars on a new pair of boots and planned on taking another ten dollars with me on the hunting trip. I was highly excited and had everything I thought I would need packed and ready when the day to leave arrived. I had never been in a real forest or seen a wild deer in the woods. Visions of these encounters danced through my mind as we headed north in Les' pick up. This was the first time I had been alone with Les for any significant length of time. I listened intently as he related his experiences growing up in Onaway. There were tales of hunting, fishing and hard work on the farm. I began to "warm up" to him as I thought …. *"Maybe he was not such a bad guy after all."*

There were no expressways in 1950 so it was slow going but we finally arrived in Flint. It was then Les told me he had a sister that lived in Flint. Her name was Ida Mae and we were going to stay overnight at her place before heading farther north. Ida Mae' lived in an upstairs flat with the entrance at the rear of the building, It was in a run down Flint neighborhood. We climbed to the top of the old rickety wooden stairs where Ida Mae stood to greet us. She looked to be an old woman to me however she likely was only in her late "thirties". She had a face that was rounded and pale with hair in pigtails. Ida Mae was friendly and seemed delighted to see her brother. When she bent near to give me a welcome hug I detected the familiar scent of alcohol. After enjoying the dinner Ida Mae fixed for us we retired to the living room. The furniture was old and the upholstery on the davenport was threadbare in spots. The entire flat gave off a musty odor but I was used to all that. I sipped on a glass of iced tea, Ida had offered me, while she and Les discussed "old times" and drank a beer. When they finished their first beer they opened another, then one more, then another. This activity went on late into the night. I was falling asleep sitting up when Ida Mae led me to a bedroom where I plopped into bed quickly falling asleep. At some point I awoke to the sound of their drunken laughter. It was then I became aware of the strong stench of cigarettes emanating from the sheets. Ida Mae had left a light on for me and as I looked at the sheets I could see they had a grayish cast.

I was becoming dismayed with the way things were going but with some difficulty I eventually fell back to sleep. I awoke once more at daybreak anxious to get on the road for deer hunting territory. Les and Ida Mae were still asleep slumped over in the same chairs where I left them the night before. I waited awhile then intentionally coughed loudly to see if they would wake up. Around ten o'clock I tapped on Lester's shoulder. He opened his eyes saying …. "What?"

I told him it was ten o'clock and asked…. "Shouldn't we be going soon?"

He made some kind of a grunting response and started complaining of a headache. He mentioning something about needing a hair off the dog to Ida who had also awoke. Ida went to the kitchen and returned with two bottles of beer. Apparently this was the hair on or off the dog Les had referred to. They drank the beer and soon two more appeared. I was growing impatient and inquired once more ….

"When are we going to leave for deer hunting?"

His answer was …. "Soon."…. but soon never came.

The day and the drinking went on until Les announced it was too late to start out now as by the time we arrived in Onaway it would be dark. We said we would stay with Ida Mae another night and head north early the next morning. Unfortunately the rest of the day and night became a repeat of the previous day and night and the next morning was more of the same. Sad and disappointed I reluctantly came to the conclusion we would never make it to Onaway. I gave up my dream of deer hunting and waited for Les to give up his. Little was said on our trip back to Detroit. When we arrived back home, completely disillusioned, I went straight to my bedroom and locked the door.

Christmas and the New Year came soon after with the same scenario I had become accustomed to. I entreated my mother and Lester, on the phone, several times to come home from the "bar" reminding them had a little boy, Jerry, waiting to spend Christmas with them. Finally in frustration I bundled Jerry up and took him with me to the "bar" to beg them to come home. I thought once I faced them at the bar with Jerry in my arms they would be so embarrassed they would come with me. Instead they just laughed and began bragging to the other "barflies" about their new baby. Lester then ordered a round of drinks for everyone there. My gut wrenched as I watched him play the "big man part". Overwhelmed with anxiety I wondered how could he spend so much money on "drinks" for those barflies when they still had not paid back the money they took from me. I could see it was useless to reason with them and left with Jerry in my arms. I spent another Christmas Eve obtaining a "tree" in the usual way and decorating it alone. The holiday seasons that everyone else looked forward to were fast becoming meaningless to me.

More and more I was home alone caring for Jerry while mother and Les spent their time in the "bar". I didn't resent my time with Jerry but I did resent their drunkenness and incessant arguing almost every night when they returned home. Although I no longer had my Highland Park friends to spend time with having Jerry to take care of kept my mind occupied and eased my sense of loneliness. I had someone to love. Lester's business continued it's steady decline. Being a young teenager my insight into the problems of adults was understandably limited. My thoughts were mostly of myself and how I was being affected by circumstances occurring around me. My desire for independence was gradually developing and with it came typical teenage rebellion.

A check of my milk bottle bank revealed all my money was gone. When I confronted my mother she denied any knowledge of what happened to it. I called her a liar but I was of course helpless to do anything more. Other than a couple dollars I had in my pocket I was now broke and dejected. My spirits rose when I remembered the "paper man" was due to pick up the newspapers I had been collecting. I would have money coming from the sale of the scrap papers. However, once again I had neglected bundling the papers and they were strewn loosely all over in the storage room where I had tossed them. For the next week I spent most of my time stacking the papers and tying them into the appropriate sized bundles. After the stacking and bundling of hundreds of pounds of newspaper was completed I began bundling them once each week so I would be ready when the "paper man" came. I needed the money!

In the meantime things were happening around me that I didn't understand nor pay much attention to. There was some kind of "falling out" between Lester and Vic Rashid. There were frequent phone calls from Mr. Rashid and I overheard my mother saying Les wasn't home even though I knew he was there. Other times I could hear Les shouting at Mr. Rashid on the phone. More than once two men dressed in suits and ties came to our apartment to speak with my mother. They acted very businesslike and had questions regarding some of the residents rent payments. They appeared to be quite serious. I was asked to leave the room each time they came. I was aware of these things at the time but thought little of it. When I returned from school one day I saw the "paper man's" truck pulling out from our apartment building. I was excited to see he had been there to collect my newspapers.

"I was back in the money."

Usually he would pay me about thirty to thirty-five dollars for the scrap papers. I entered our apartment and asked my mother how much I got paid. She said he paid twenty dollars for the papers.

"Why so little? He never paid less than thirty dollars before."

"He said scrap paper prices have declined."

Disappointed I asked….

"Okay where's my twenty dollars?"

"I'm going to have to borrow it for now."

"No! I can't loan it to you. I need it. You took all the money from my milk bottle."

"Sorry, I'll pay you back soon."

"You never pay me back. I hate you!"

I was home one evening "sitting" my brother Jerry when I heard a car motor running outside and someone yelling. I went to the window to see what the commotion was about and saw my mother standing unsteadily beside a car with hands gripping the edge of the open car window. I heard a man's voice yelling

"Get the hell out of my car… bitch."

The driver sped the car off down the alley. I watched for a moment and observed my mother staggering toward the back door of the apartment house. She was weaving severely and then fell to the ground. When she failed to get back up I ran outside to see if she needed help. She was "out cold". I could not rouse her. I gathered her up in my arms and carried her inside. She was a small woman weighing a little more than a hundred pounds. I weighed only around a hundred and twenty pounds myself so I barely made it into the apartment with her in my arms. I headed for her bedroom where I dropped her on the bed. It was then I got the "shock of my life". My mother was wearing a skirt and somehow when I dropped her she fell in such a way that the skirt got shoved up just far enough to reveal she was not wearing any underwear. This confirmed my earlier suspicion that she wasn't wearing underwear that day when my friends were at my apartment.

"My God"! …. I thought ….

"Does she go around like this all the time? Out in public?"

I gingerly grasped the edge of her skirt and pulled it down. Through all this, totally blitzed, she did not wake up. I went and sat down on the davenport my thoughts somewhat muddled and wondering how all this had come about. Then that vague, occasionally recurring memory that I kept pushing away returned once more....

"I am a little baby back in the small bed by the window with a woman lying next to me while Grandma and others are standing just inside a doorway looking concerned."

I mentally struggled to remember more of this event but once again something inside me revealed nothing more and forced further thoughts from my consciousness. I cannot say if it was Lester or someone else who sped down the alley leaving my mother passed out on the cement parking area. What I can say is it would be some time before I would lay eyes on Lester again.

Chapter 21

FORKS IN THE ROAD OF LIFE

I was about to leave for school one morning when my mother announced we were moving once more. I was to come straight home from school to help Uncle Red move the few things that we owned. When I arrived home Uncle Red was there with his car and a small trailer he had rented. I was always happy to see my Uncle Red. He was always ready to help my mother (his sister) and he was the best man I ever knew and the only father figure I had. Together we packed up our possessions and loaded them on the trailer. I assumed we were moving to another apartment or flat but instead we drove to Grandma's apartment. I asked why we were at Grandma's and was told you're going to stay here for awhile. Uncle Red dropped off my mother, Jerry and I at Grandma's and left with the trailer. I wondered what was happening….

"Were we all staying at Grandma's? Where was Uncle Red going with our stuff on the trailer?"

Everyone seemed confused and upset as was I. Grandma's apartment was small. There were two bedrooms but one of them was taken by a boarder named Frank. It was common in those days to rent out a room to gain extra income. I soon learned of our arrangement. My mother and Grandma would share one bedroom that had twin beds and I would sleep on the living room sofa. Jerry would stay in the room with my mother. This arrangement would not last. Problems arose because Jerry was still a baby and would sometimes cry in the middle of the night. This disturbed Frank's sleep. Frank drove bus for the Detroit Transit System and his schedule started early morning. .

This move meant another change of schools and I had to finish 10th grade at Cooley High School. While at Central High

I was totally lost, now I had to adjust to yet another new high school. My longtime friend, Leonard, was a half grade ahead of me at Cooley and knowing we could ride the bus to school together gave me the courage to face this new challenge. On one of the bus rides to school we passed a teenage boy walking. This boy had short blond hair, sharp features and a stern look on his face. The sight of him frightened me.

"Who's that?" … I asked Leonard.

" Bill DeWeese."

"He looks mean."

" Yeah, but he's okay."

Despite Leonard's comment I remained afraid of Bill DeWeese. As a matter of fact I continued to be fearful of all men or boys who, I thought, had a menacing look. Most of them did.

By now the lack of discipline regarding personal hygiene, especially brushing my teeth, had resulted in more discolorization and cavities in my upper front teeth. My shyness and strong feelings of inadequacy prompted me to avoid smiling in order to conceal my dental imperfections. On the occasions when I could not keep myself from smiling I learned to purposefully keep my upper lip down covering my teeth. Extreme shyness, bad teeth, fear of meeting new people and constant changing of schools left me with the decision to keep to myself and not bother trying to fit in or make friends with anyone at Cooley High. This decision was significantly reinforced when one morning at school I saw Skuppy coming down the hall. I would learn he was one of the schools "muckedy-mucks. Due to the embarrassment I felt over the Alpha Omega rejection I spent the rest of my time at Cooley avoiding any encounters with Paul Skupholm. I didn't know it at the time but I would actually remain at Cooley until I graduated. During the three years I spent at Cooley I never attended a single football game or any sporting event of any kind. I never went to a dance, nor attended the Junior or Senior Proms. I simply had no interest in developing any connection to the school or any of the students there. Instead I limited my association to my friend, Leonard, who seemed happy to have me around as well. While it may have just been my own perception I felt isolated from the other neighborhood kids. I was convinced that they were all better than me. I thought ...

"They all have normal lives and live in homes with normal parents and if they ever find out about me I'll be ridiculed beyond belief."

Before long I came to realize that because of his family's odd religious beliefs and his vegetarianism Leonard was somewhat of an outcast as well. We traveled everywhere together. He led. I followed. One weekend night well after dark Leonard and I were hanging out together trying to decide what to do with ourselves (like typical teenagers) when he announced he had an idea for some fun. He said ....

"Come on Skip, follow me."

He led me down Littlefield Ave. to Grand River Ave. then a few blocks down Grand River where a used car lot was located. When we got to the corner across from the "car lot" he told me to wait there. I watched him cross the street to the "lot" then he crouched down and quickly worked his way through the various cars and up to the small office building. He broke a window in the front door and reached in to unlock the door. Once inside I could no longer see what he was doing. He emerged very quickly and began surveying the various cars on the "lot" then suddenly stopped at one of the cars, opened the door, got behind the "wheel" and started the engine. I watched apprehensively as he pulled out of the lot and drove to where I was standing. He pushed open the passenger door.

"Get in." .... He said

"I don't want to be involved in stealing a car. We could go to jail if we're caught."

"They wont catch us. Come on! Are you chicken?"

Young, insecure and mostly afraid of displeasing my only friend, I got in the car.

Leonard turned onto Grand River and headed out of town. His driving was a little unsteady but it was late and only a little traffic was on the road. In nineteen fifty-one the metropolitan Detroit area was nowhere near the size it is today so once we passed Telegraph Road there was almost no traffic at all. At that point Leonard "opened her up". He must have been going 70 miles an hour, maybe more. Afraid this would attract attention I was begging him to slow down before the cops spotted us but he paid no mind to my pleas. A mile or so past Telegraph Road where we passed a roadside diner Leonard hit the brakes and turned the car around. Next he pulled into the diner's gravel parking lot and climbed out of the driver's seat motioning me to follow as he headed for the diner's entrance. Reluctant and frightened I hesitantly followed him into the diner. It was a long narrow diner with booths along the outside wall and windows that looked out on the parking lot. Across from the booths running in the same direction was a long counter with individual seating on stools. A waitress approached the booth where we sat, asking what we wanted to order. Leonard ordered something from the menu she handed us. I was filled with so much anxiety and fear I couldn't even think of eating and said I wasn't hungry. Then the worst scenario I could have imagined came to pass. Through the entrance door walked two uniformed Michigan State Police officers. I knew we were doomed

"They were here to arrest us." (I thought.)

My heart was beating a mile a minute as they neared our booth. When they reached our booth instead of stopping to arrest us they turned and sat down on two counter seats with their backs to us. Still filled with apprehension I said….

"Let's get out of here."

"Calm down Skip. I'm not leaving till I'm finished eating."

"But they're going to spot us and we'll go to jail."

"They don't know anything about us. Quit worrying and stop acting suspicious."

I could not believe how calm Leonard remained through all of this. He appeared to have no fear of the consequences of getting caught. It seemed an eternity until Leonard finished eating. He got up and walked to the exit where the cash register was located and paid his bill. We left the diner and started for home in the stolen car. I was still shaking when he dropped me off in front of Grandma's apartment building. He said he would dispose of the car and advised me to tell no one what we did. I went inside attempting to be quiet so as not to wake anyone. I laid awake the rest of the night worrying about being caught.

I awoke the next day relieved to find everything appeared to be normal. The police had not come to arrest me and Grandma was acting as though nothing was wrong. I went outside to see if Leonard was around but saw no sign of him. I began walking down Schoolcraft Ave in the direction of Monnior school. I walked about two blocks when I spotted a car parked against the curb. I wasn't sure but I thought it looked like the car we had stolen the night before. I did not stop but kept walking. Unsure if anyone was watching I didn't even turn my head to look at the car. I proceeded for another block before turning around to go back home. I did not see anyone else on the street and thought I would get a better look at the car when I passed by it the second time. Still filled with guilt and fear of being caught I made a conscious effort to look straight ahead as I passed the "car". I was alongside the "car" but still looking straight ahead when out of nowhere a police cruiser raced up to the curb, stopping suddenly directly behind the "car". There were four officers inside the cruiser. One of them motioned me to approach the cruiser.

"Where you going?" … One of them asked.

"Just on my way home." …. I responded

"Where you been?"

"Nowhere, just walkin.'"

"Why are you so interested in this car?"

"I'm not. I was just walking by and saw it here."

"Okay kid… Get in!"

I was trembling inside thinking this was it, they had me,

"I'm going to jail."

They sat me in the front seat between two policemen and began asking a series of questions. How old was I? Where did I live? How long had I lived there? Why did I steal the car? Where did I attend school? Who were my friends? Who was with me when we stole the car? What grade was I in? Where was the car when I took it? They obviously were trying to trip me up. I denied all questions regarding the car, acting as though I didn't know what they were talking about. All the other questions I answered truthfully. Expecting that I would surely be taken to jail I was totally surprised when they opened the door of the cruiser and said I could go. I got out and quickly started walking home. I stayed inside the apartment for a while contemplating if I should risk going across the alley to tell Leonard of my encounter with the police. Finally I decided to chance it but when I stepped outside I saw a police car parked in front of Leonard's house. I quickly ducked back inside and stayed there the rest of the day and night. The following morning I knocked on the back door of Leonard's house. His mother came to the door to tell me Leonard won't be coming out today. He's been grounded till further notice. I dared not to ask why as I was sure I knew the reason. Sheepishly I replied okay and left. Two weeks would pass before Leonard would be allowed out. On school days when we got together briefly he explained that when the police questioned him he had denied everything and apparently bluffed his way through it but after the cops left he told me he had been forced to admit his involvement with the stolen car to his parents.

During Leonard's "grounding" I spent much of my time reading books I had checked out from the local library. I stumbled on a book by A. J. Cronin, "The Citadel" and liked it so much that for the next few years I would read all the "Cronin" books available at the library. Reading provided a welcome escape from the reality of my life but I was encountering many new words, the definition of which I was unsure.

Eventually Leonard was released on "probation" with the caution that any more trouble and he might never see daylight again. Leonard introduced me to a few other neighborhood kids. He had only a few friends other than me and it seemed that the friends he had were somewhat odd. They too had only a few friends. Jerry Hopkins was a skinny kid, extremely frenetic and apparently on the verge of mental breakdown. Tommy Thompson another strange kid hardly spoke out loud to anyone. Several years later we would read in the newspaper of some sort of trouble he was in regarding his involvement with spying for the U. S. government. Harvey Hall was a severe diabetic and even though he had to have daily insulin injections I constantly observed him sipping on a large bottle of sugary soft drink. A few years later Harvey and I would become good friends.

I was beginning to feel more independent as I looked forward to my sixteenth birthday. Although I still weighed only 120 pounds I had attained the height of five foot eight inches and was taller than both my mother and grandmother. I had been assigned the responsibility of maintaining the apartment building's furnace. Shoveling coal into the hopper and pulling clinkers became a daily routine. For some reason this new responsibility along with my increasing height gave me a little sense of power.

Summer came and school was out. Leonard's parents were leaving for a long planned, extended vacation and they had made arrangements for Leonard to stay with a neighbor lady that lived on the next block. Leonard was excited to be free from the close scrutiny of his parents for a few months. The neighbor was an older lady who was quite a bit more liberal than Leonard's parents. She allowed him a lot more freedom to come and go as he pleased. Occasionally she would chastise him for staying out too late but she never leveled any punishment and she seemed to like both of us. Awhile back when I had joined the "Boy Scouts" I purchased a "Jungle Hammock" at one of the many Army Surplus Stores that had sprung up around the city after the end of World War II. It was composed of a heavy canvas hammock, mosquito netting sides and roof made of a rain repellent plastic-like material. The hammock was tied between two trees. The roof was tied two feet higher than the hammock itself. Attached to the both the canvas hammock and the roof was mosquito netting with a zipper closure enabling one to get in and out. It was great for camping out during warm weather. Grandma's apartment remained quite warm during the hot summer months as home air conditioners had not yet become affordable for the general public. I convinced her to allow me to string up my "Jungle Hammock" in an empty field just half a block down the alley from her apartment building as it would be a lot cooler than the apartment. Conveniently this empty field was located halfway between Grandma's apartment and the neighbor lady's house where Leonard was staying. We had a great time that summer. We hitched rides on slow moving freight trains sometimes riding several miles unconcerned where they were going. Wherever we finally wound up we knew we could easily hitchhike back home. As much fun as we had during the daytime the hours after dark were even more exciting. Often late at night, I was asleep in my Jungle Hammock, when Leonard would awaken me.

"Let's go do something."

"What do you want to do?"

"I dunno. Just get up! We'll figure out something."

To be able to be out late at night unbeknownst to our parents was exhilarating. It gave us a strange sense of power. For a while we felt completely in control. Free to do as we chose. A huge natural gas storage tank was located a few blocks from Grandma's apartment building. From several blocks away you could see the eight foot tall neon letters across the top that read "GAS IS BEST". I don't know exactly how high it was but once at he top you could see for miles in any direction. We climbed to the top on the steep steel staircase that wound around the side of the storage tank. Leonard led the way up the narrow steps just wide enough to accommodate one person at a time. I have always been somewhat fearful of heights, still I was fascinated when at the top I could see the Fisher Building, General Motors Building, Penobscot Building and the downtown sky scrapers. In the opposite direction I could see where the residential areas ended and farmland began. Leonard, the daredevil, walked over to the very edge of this huge structure and motioned me to follow. Circled around the outer rim was a three foot high metal mesh fence alerting anyone nearing the edge. There was a strong wind that night and I was feeling a little off balance as I approached the edge. Without warning Leonard pulled something out of his pocket, lit it with his cigarette lighter and tossed it over the edge. It fell several stories then there was a sudden flash of light followed by a loud explosion. Leonard was laughing out loud. I asked…

"What was that?"

"That was a Cherry Bomb."

"Are you nuts? We're standing on top of a gas tank and you're lighting off firecrackers!"

As he continued laughing we observed a car pulling into the parking lot below.

Two men got out of the car and began aiming high powered flashlights in every direction. We knew we had to get out of there and scampered our way down the metal staircase. It took several minutes for us to descend to ground level. By the time we reached the bottom the men with flashlights had figured out where we were and began heading towards us. Terrified at being caught we ran as fast as we could. They chased after us but were most likely a lot older than us and soon tired of the pursuit. We escaped.

Another night that summer while asleep I sensed some movement and awoke to find I was swaying back and forth in my hammock. It was Leonard pushing it to wake me up. He had another adventure for us. I followed him to his house where there was an extension ladder stored at the side of his garage. Picking up one end he told me to grab the other end. He led the way down the alley in back of his house. When we had gone about half a city block he stopped and motioned with one finger to his lips for me to be quiet. Then he entered into the back yard of a two story house. He quietly placed the extension ladder against the wall of the house positioning it just below one of the windows on the buildings upper level. Next he climbed up the ladder and looked through the window. He watched for several minutes before he climbed back down and told me to go up to see for myself.

"Why are we doing this?"

"Go up and look. You'll see why."

I was becoming very nervous and just wanted to get out of there before we got caught but, as always, fear of displeasing my long time friend forced me up the ladder. Once at the top through the window I saw a girl standing in front of the bathroom mirror. She was entirely without clothes. Her breasts were fully developed and she appeared to in her middle to late teens. She was in the process of locating and squeezing little blemishes on her face. Torn between the desire to see this naked girl and the fear of being caught after only a few seconds I began climbing down the ladder. As I reached the ground level we heard a muffled cough. We looked in the direction of the cough and saw the outlined figure of a man standing in the dark on his screened in back porch. We grabbed the ladder and started to run out of the yard. Suddenly the flashing red and blue lights of a police car appeared on the street in front of the house. We dropped the ladder and ran as fast as we could. Down the alley I ran, jumped a fence into and through another backyard out to the next street, then down the street. Behind in hot pursuit was a cop. I ducked into and through another yard out to the alley then down the alley. I came to an empty field that was overgrown with weeds. I was running out of breath and ran into the field and flung myself down flat in the weeds. The weeds were sparse and only approximately a foot high. As I lay there one policeman came down the alley while a second policeman walked down the side walk. Both of them aimed their flashlights into the field where I was laying. Some of the beams went directly over me yet miraculously they were unable to spot me. I trembled in fear sure they would enter the field to look more closely but they never did. I watched as they walked away and did not move for what seemed an eternity. Finally I arose from my resting place and crouched down as I made my way back to my "Jungle Hammock" and climbed inside. Just as I began to think I was safe I heard footsteps down the alley. I feigned being asleep acting as though the policeman tapping on my hammock had woke me up. He asked....

"What are you doing here."

"I live in those apartments back there and I'm sleeping here because it's too hot."

"What else have you been up to tonight?"

"Nothin' just sleeping."

"Did you lose your ladder?"

"Huh?"

"Don't play dumb with me."

"I don't know what your talking about."

"Yeah Yeah! Keep it up kid and you're gonna get caught someday and I'll be there."

A shudder of relief coursed through my entire body as I watched him leave. The next day Leonard told me he too had eluded the cops. We went back to see if the ladder was still where we left it but it was gone. When his folks returned later that summer he would deny any knowledge of what happened to the ladder.

Leonard was earning money mowing lawns and doing odd jobs in the neighborhood so he always had some money to spend. Since nearly all my savings had been confiscated by my mother when we were living at the Sturtevant Apartments, I felt a need to find a way to earn some money. Occasions kept arising where I was left out of certain activities because I had no money. I realized that the lack of money was depriving me of options. Having money equaled the ability to decide when and what I wanted to participate in and when I did not. Without money I was not in control of my own life. While walking down Grand River Ave. one afternoon, I noticed a "Now Hiring Ushers" sign in a window of the Tower Theater. I screwed up my courage and decided to apply. I went up to the cashier's window and quietly asked what it was about. She picked up a phone and told someone on the other end that I was asking about the job. Soon a tall thin man appeared and asked me inside. He asked only a few questions and then described the usher's job and informed me the starting wage was 45 cents an hour. He asked me if I was interested and when I said yes he told me he would put me on the schedule starting next week. I was elated. I would have a job some money to spend and best of all I would see all the movies for free. I arrived on my starting day and was given an official looking ushers' uniform and a flashlight. I was proud to escort patrons to their seats and happier still when I saw I was scheduled on weekends for 12 hours which meant would earn almost six dollars that week. After a few weeks I was proud and happy to have saved about ten dollars.

I was growing worried that my mother would ask to borrow the money I saved or simply find where I hid it and take it. I expressed my concerns to my grandmother. Grandma suggested I take most of it to a bank and open a savings account. That way it would not be around where my mother could get at it. She told me the money in the bank would earn interest too. I wasn't sure what interest was but the next day I walked to the corner of Grand River and Meyers Road where I opened a savings account at Detroit Bank & Trust. Then each week I kept three dollars from my pay envelope for myself and deposited the rest in the bank. Each week when I went to the bank to deposit most of my paycheck the teller made an entry in my savings passbook. About one month after I opened this savings account I saw that in addition to my weekly deposits there was an unusual entry of three cents in my passbook. I asked the teller why there was a deposit of three cents. She informed me that it was the monthly interest that was paid on my balance. I was amazed. I could not believe I was being paid money for doing nothing more than saving money. This started the following thinking process....

"I have only about $12.00 saved yet I received three cents for leaving it in the bank. If I save $12.00 every month by the end of a year I will have almost $150.00 saved. With more than ten times as much in the bank I will get ten times the interest every month. Thirty cents interest every month adds up to $3.60 after one year. I'm working for forty-five cents an hour so my yearly interest is equal to eight hours of work. That's almost a week's pay for doing nothing!"

I continued analyzing the possibilities associated with the earning of interest. I began putting pencil to paper and came up with the idea that although it might take several years it was possible to save enough money to enable me to support myself without working at all. I knew it was probably a preposterous notion but this thought settled somewhere in the back of my mind and never left. Thus began my lifelong quest to save money.

Jerry's crying soon became a problem. Frank's sleep was being disturbed almost nightly and Grandma was concerned he might move out. One day a man and woman I did not know arrived at Grandma's for a visit. I was introduced to them but cannot now remember their names. They were neatly dressed, quite friendly and they seemed to be very interested in my little brother. I grew uneasy as I watched these new people utter baby talk to Jerry and hold him in their arms. Remembering that I had planned to meet up with my longtime friend, Leonard, I excused myself and left to meet him. When I returned sometime later the man and woman were gone and there was no sign of Jerry. I asked…

"Where is Jerry?"

Then came my mother's explanation….

"Jerry is with the couple that was just here. They are going to keep him for just a short time until I can find a new place for us to live."

"Why can't he stay with us?"

"Jerry cries at night and wakes Frank up so if we keep Jerry here grandma will lose her boarder."

"This isn't fair! How long is this going to be? When do I get to see my brother again?"

"They will bring him here for a visit once a week on Saturday."

I was not happy with this arrangement but my protestations fell on deaf ears. I felt better when they showed up with Jerry the following Saturday. They came the following Saturday as well and Jerry seemed to be taking all this in stride. But then as I was beginning to relax regarding this arrangement they failed to show the third Saturday. My mother claimed they had called to say they couldn't make it due to illness but they would be there the next Saturday. They came again the following Saturday as promised but I sensed things were changing and I was sure something was wrong when they missed the scheduled visits three weeks in a row. My concern for Jerry was growing steadily. My mother was not even there when they failed to show up with Jerry the third time. This aroused my suspicion that she knew they weren't coming. All sorts of negative thoughts were building in my mind until one day while alone with my Grandmother I lost my temper and began to rant and rave about all the perceived wrongs I harbored toward my mother...

"She's up to something! This isn't right. She's letting Jerry stay with those people too long. She's stolen money from me. She's no good. She's drunk all the time. She was just living with Lester they're not even married."

I was extremely upset and began to cry. I thought, as well as hoped, the revelation that my mother was not married would be a shock and upset my Grandmother, but it seemed to have no effect. I was extremely dismayed to find that instead of being angry she cautioned that I should respect my mother. She and assured me everything would work out for the best. My grandmother and I were there when my mother showed up the next Saturday to meet the couple when they came with Jerry. I was happy to see my brother and he seemed to be doing well. I immediately picked him up and was bouncing him on my knees when I became aware that everyone else bore a somber look and no one was saying anything. The silence was broken by my mother saying....

"Skippy, I have something to tell you. I have bought a small restaurant on Grand River Avenue and I am going to run it alone with the help of Grandma. We will be moving to an apartment upstairs from the restaurant. Because I will be working from early morning till late at night I won't be able to take care of Jerry. This couple has become extremely fond of Jerry. They are "well to do" they can provide many things for Jerry that I cannot. They love him very much and they would like to keep him with them on a permanent basis."

I cannot here adequately describe the anger and disappointment I felt at that point. Repressed resentment raged from the depths of my being as I screamed....

"NO! You can't do that. He's my brother! You can't just give him away. I won't let you. I'll report you somehow to someone. I will find a way to get you in trouble. I hate you"

"But Skip I have no choice. Les has gone to California and I have to run the restaurant and work and Grandma can't keep Jerry here or she will lose her boarder. These people love Jerry and will take good care of him and provide a better life for Jerry than I can."

"I don't care! He's my brother and I love him more than they possibly can. I will watch him when you're at work. I will stay with him at night. I will do whatever is necessary but you cannot give him to these people. I will report them too. There's something wrong here and I will do whatever I have to do to get you all in trouble."

I noticed a look of dismay and disappointment appear on the faces of the couple as I continued my protestations. I am unsure if all I said would have changed my mother's mind however the couple seemed to be moved for reasons of their own. The woman had tears in her eyes as she asked if she could hold Jerry for a minute before they left. I handed Jerry to her and both she and her husband hugged and kissed Jerry goodbye. They left. My mother began to cry. Although I was still angry at the thought that she could let Jerry go I said no more as it seemed I had somehow influenced an outcome where Jerry would remain with us. After everything cooled down somewhat we talked it out and decided that with both my mother and Grandma working at the restaurant they could cover taking care of Jerry during the morning and early afternoon until I got home from school then I would take care of him the rest of the day until the restaurant closed at 8 pm and my mother could be with him. With some occasional difficulty this arrangement worked adequately for a while. It forced significant constraint on my activities as well as limiting my mother's night time visits to the local taverns.

Chapter 22

MOTHER'S RESTAURANT

Uncle Red arrived once more to help us move to an apartment above the restaurant my mother was going to run. It was a small storefront near the corner of Grand River and Ward. Mother and my grandmother cooked all the meals from scratch. My grandmother was an excellent cook and my mother was a good cook as well. The restaurant had counter and stool seating along with a few four place tables and chairs. It was also set up to serve all the popular soda fountain treats such as sundaes, milk shakes, sodas etc. The clientele were mostly other business people located within a block or two of the restaurant. To my dismay I soon realized that one of the regular customers was the owner of the used car lot where Leonard and I had taken one of the cars for a "joyride". I wasn't sure he associated me with that incident but my guilt caused me to avoid him as much as possible. There was a jukebox that for a nickel one could play their favorite song from a selection of the latest 45 rpm records. I was enthralled with a peppy version of "The World Is Waiting For The Sunrise" by Les Paul and Mary Ford. Les Paul had devised a system that allowed him to record, simultaneously, several versions of himself playing the same song on his guitar with his wife Mary Ford doing the vocals. The tempo was upbeat and catchy. This was new music! It was exciting! I loved it and often to the dismay of my mother, grandmother and several customers, would put a quarter in the jukebox to play it six times in a row. I didn't care. I was young and most of the time quite impervious to the sensibilities of others. I also didn't pay much attention to the business. Gradually though I was becoming aware that my mother's mood seemed dour. A pretty good lunch crowd was drawn from the local businesses but there were not a lot of customers for dinner. My mother was opening at seven am. and was closing down at eight pm. When it finally dawned on me that the business was not doing well I tried to help by offering to stay and keep the restaurant open a few extra hours till 10 pm. I would run the soda fountain and sell snacks and cigarettes. She gave me a key and I tried this for a few weeks but only an occasional customer showed up and it proved to be a wasted effort. Sometimes Leonard would show up to keep me company. One night when things were especially slow I decided to treat myself to a milkshake. Leonard was there and I made one for him too. We got carried away and plopped many scoops of ice cream into the "shakes" to make them extra thick. I carelessly wasn't thinking of the costs this was imposing on the business. After several days with nearly nil traffic it was decided to abandon the idea of staying open during the evening hours.

One night after getting off work at the Tower Theater I was experiencing one of the "low spells" that plagued me from time to time. I recalled that milk shakes usually relieved my symptoms of clamminess and weakness. I stopped at the restaurant and used the key I had been given to enter. When I switched on the lights I was surprised to see little creatures scurrying across the counters, tables, walls and floor. I was sickened at the sight of cockroaches everywhere I looked and there were thousands of them. Within a few seconds they were all out of sight. I was amazed to find that our restaurant housed all these roaches and yet this was the first time I encountered them. I began to realize if there were that many of them in the restaurant then most likely they inhabited the apartment above that we lived in, as well.

Upon returning home from my shift at the Tower Theater one weekend evening I was surprised to be greeted at the door by a cute little puppy. My mother told me one of the restaurant customers gave her this dog. She was a six month old Brittany Spaniel and her name was Buffy. I was delighted to once again have a dog in my life. I enjoyed taking her out for walks in the neighborhood and we became friends. After a few weeks I decided it was time to train Buffy to do a few tricks. I taught her to sit and to beg which she learned without much trouble but teaching her to "stay" for some reason, became a problem. I would first get her to "sit" and then place the palm of my hand facing her trying to get her to stay where she was. She seemed to get the idea and complied until I stepped away from her. As soon as I moved away she would get up and follow. After trying this tactic several times without success I became impatient. My impatience slowly evolved into anger. Then for reasons I cannot claim to understand completely, I lost my temper. Perhaps it was the frustration of constantly being subjected to the whims of my so called parents. I was powerless to change the drunkenness, the continual moving, the semi abandonment, stealing my money, and a growing belief that this totally unfair life was beyond my control. All this was boiling up inside me and I can only guess that I was somehow trying to exert some control over the present situation. Without thinking I picked up my little dog and thrust her full force at the floor screaming "STAY". She let out a yelp and lay there whimpering. When I called her to come she struggled to get up and had difficulty walking. Instead of coming to me she limped away toward the bathroom holding up her left front paw. She settled in a small space between toilet and the bathtub. Despite my coaxing she would not come out. A sickening feeling of remorse followed the realization that I had injured this sweet little dog. My mind was racing…

"How bad she was hurt?, How will I explain this? Why did I do this? What's wrong with me?"

When I reached down to pull her out of there she let out a whimper. I sat in a chair and held her on my lap hoping against hope she would be all right but she continued to whimper with even the slightest movement. After a while I carried her to my bed and lay her there. I began to pray that Buffy would be alright but as she lie there whimpering I realized this wasn't going to be the case. My mother returned from work later that evening and in an effort to cover up my foolish action I told her Buffy had fallen down the back stairs and hurt herself.

"What is wrong with her?" My mother asked.

"I'm not sure but something seems to be wrong with one of her legs." I replied

My mother tried to pick up the dog but Buffy cried out in obvious pain.

"Tell me how this happened, Skip."

"I was on the back porch bouncing a ball against the wall and she chased after one of the balls I didn't catch and ran too close to the stairs and stumbled down a few steps.

"Well it's too late to do anything about it tonight so we have to wait till tomorrow. Besides, Skip I have no money to pay for a visit to the vet. We are not going to move her now. You will have to sleep on the davenport tonight. We'll figure this out in the morning"

Guilt and worry kept me awake most of the night. I got up to look at Buffy several times hoping I would see her get off the bed and walk normally. That did not happen. I finally fell asleep. The next morning I overslept and awoke to find Buffy was gone. I ran downstairs to the restaurant to ask my mother where Buffy was. She told me one of her regular customers had somehow made arrangements with a veterinarian to look at Buffy. He had driven the dog to the Vet's office on Eight Mile Road near Woodward Ave. (I am compelled here to tell "reader" that the regular customer who drove my dog to the veterinarian and paid the bill was the owner of the car lot where Leonard and I stole the car!) Extremely anxious to learn what was wrong with my little dog I rode three buses to the Vet's office. Once there The Vet came out of the back room to talk to me. He informed me Buffy had a, badly shattered, broken leg. He asked me how this happened. I told him the same lie I had told my mother. He looked doubtfully at me and shook his head saying….

"I can't see how the leg would incur that much damage from falling down some stairs."

I shrugged and gave no reply. The "vet" informed me he would have to keep Buffy there for a few days to monitor her healing. I left knowing the Vet did not believe my story. During the following three days while she remained at the veterinarian's I was plagued with guilt and remorse. When the day came to retrieve her, I rode the bus to the Vet's. When she was brought out her leg was in some kind of a special cast with a couple of "pins" to secure proper healing. I thanked them for caring for my dog and picked Buffy up to leave. Buffy began to tremble as I held her in my arms. I attempted to sooth her by stroking her back and talking softly to her but she never stopped trembling as we rode the buses back home. Once home I stayed with the dog the rest of the day and night petting her and apologizing for what I had done to her. Even though I doubted she could understand, I vowed never again to hurt her.

The guilt associated with this incident and others to come would remain with me for the rest of my life. A week or so later I returned from work one night and called out for Buffy. There was no response. I looked all through the apartment but Buffy was not to be found. Later when my mother staggered in the door I asked where Buffy was.

"She's gone."

"Gone? Gone where?"

"We can't keep her here anymore. Ish to dangherus for a dog in the city. She's been sent to a farm where she'll have losh of room to run."

"Why didn't you ask me? Or even tell me first?"

"Well Julian, What ever you thought din't madder once Louise in the next apartment tol me she could hear (through the wall) what was goin' on the day Buffy's leg got broke."

I knew my mother only called me by my real name when she was angry with me. So hearing her call me Julian and the neighbor's revelation totally deflated any argument I might have made. My protestations ceased and I accepted another fable about my dog on a farm.

Chapter 23

FRUSTRATION UNLEASHED

After a couple of months of less than hoped for business my mother was unable to make the payments to the people who sold her the restaurant. She received a notice that they intended to take the business back if all the back payments were not caught up by a date certain. There was great disappointment on the part of my mother, grandmother and myself. We all hoped for a sudden improvement in the business but a miracle did not happen and tensions mounted as the deadline approached. While we were all standing in the restaurant doorway one afternoon, I asked if I could go with Leonard to visit another friend of his. My grandmother reminded me that I was supposed to take care of my little brother Jerry. I rudely replied….

"Why can't you watch him one time Grandma?"

"I am here to help your mother!'

"Why? There's no business anyway."

"Don't give me none of your lip Skippy" …. she responded and then added ….

"Don't let him go Mildred.

"Mind your own business."…. I replied

"It **is my business** and you and your friend Leonard have been eating us out of business with your milkshakes at night after were closed."

Embarrassment and anger rushed over me. Without thinking I burst out in a childish tirade ….

"You don't love me! You don't love anyone! You never hug me. I never see you hug my mother or Uncle Red or Uncle Murray. You don't care about anyone. Your just mean."

No sooner had I uttered those hateful words when extreme regret overtook my anger but the deed was done and foolish pride made me leave the scene to avoid further embarrassment. As I began to run upstairs I saw tears in the eyes of the person I loved above all others, my grandmother. In a feeble attempt to redeem myself I did not go with Leonard I stayed home and watched my brother. Although at first angry and resentful, as time passed I pondered on the confrontation with my grandmother. Before long, remorse began slowly building in my psyche.

"I did it again." …. I thought.

"I did not control my temper and hurt my Grandma just like I did with Buffy."

As I thought about all the pain my stupid outbursts had caused, my mind filled with self doubt…. *"Something's wrong with me."*

When my mother closed the restaurant and returned to our upstairs apartment she said ….

"I hope you're proud of yourself."

"I'm not. I'm sorry. I don't know what to do!" ….I replied with tears in my eyes

"Skippy, If you're truly sorry you need to apologize to your grandmother."

I left the apartment and walked directly to Grandma's apartment thinking along the way how to explain my stupidity to my grandmother. I arrived at her front door and knocked. Moments later the door opened and my Grandma stood there her eyes red and moist.

"Grandma I am sorry for what I said earlier. I didn't mean it."

Then from her mouth came the words that seared into my memory to remain there for the rest of my life....

"Skippy, you put a thorn in my heart that will never come out."

I saw the tears forming in her eyes as she shut the door and left me standing there.

Believing I had lost forever the only person that really cared about me I began the journey back to our apartment barely able to hold myself erect. Once there I had great difficulty getting to the top of the stairs. More than once while climbing the stairs debilitating depression overwhelmed me and after a few steps I slumped down to a sitting position. The depression I felt took over my thought process. I simply could not think.

I was sure I was lost. My only refuge had rejected me. I deserved nothing and everything at the same time. Eventually I forced myself up the stairs and entered the apartment. My mother was gone. My baby brother was asleep in his crib. She had left him alone. How could she do that? I picked Jerry up, held him in my arms and began to weep.

It was late October 1951 and the coming of cooler weather meant the furnace at the Littlefield apartments would require stoking the hopper and clinkers would need removing. My mother suggested I go to Grandma's and see if she needed help with those chores. Shame and guilt over the altercation with my grandmother still occupied my thoughts as I walked to Grandma's apartment. I did not knock on her door but went directly to the basement to fill the hopper with coal. I left without speaking to anyone, planning to return another day to remove the clinkers. After a few return trips to repeat these tasks my grandmother appeared in the basement asking if I would like a cup of tea. An enormous feeling of relief coursed through my body. I meekly replied yes. We went upstairs to her apartment and sat at the kitchen table. She thanked me for helping with the furnace chores and we made some small talk but Grandma made no mention of the "incident" then or ever again. I walked home with a lighter foot relieved that maybe I was back in "good graces" with my Grandma but her painful words of hurt will remain permanently etched in my memory as long as I am alive.

The day arrived for my mother to return ownership of the restaurant to the man and wife who sold my mother the restaurant. This event did not go smoothly. As I mentioned earlier this was a time in my life where I paid scant attention to the problems and goings on of the adult world. I was present though when the restaurant keys were being turned back to that couple. I was unaware of all that was transpiring but there was some sort of dispute over the inventory and the man began yelling at my mother. A heated argument ensued and the man's anger escalated. Suddenly with one arm raised and a clenched fist he made a threatening move toward my mother. I jumped in front of him and screamed.

"Don't you dare touch my mother!"

Although he was much bigger than me he backed off but continued yelling obscenities. We left the restaurant and went to our upstairs apartment while he continued his rant. He and his wife attempted to make a go of the restaurant but within a few months it was closed for good.

With winter approaching we needed coal to burn in the furnace that was located in the basement of the apartment building but my mother did not have enough money to pay for a coal delivery. She had obtained work as a waitress at "Gil's Hamburgers". Gil's Hamburgers was a small "counter only style" restaurant serving twenty cent hamburgers, french fries, soft drinks and coffee. The pay was small and tips were few. We kept ourselves dressed as warm as we could as the apartment was almost always cold but on the coldest of nights my mother would give me a quarter to buy a small bundle of scrap firewood that was being sold by a man down the street. I could carry it under one arm so it wasn't much. Only enough to take the chill out of the apartment for maybe an hour and then the cold slowly crept back in. Going to work at the Tower Theater was a welcome relief from our cold apartment. Whenever Mr. Burger asked me to work an extra shift I was happy to accept as it kept me in the warm theater and out of the cold. Once during an extremely cold spell we did receive a coal delivery (paid for by my Uncle Red.) What a delight to have steady heat for a few weeks but when the coal ran out and we were thrust back into the cold once more.

Due to the small pay my mother was earning at "Gils" our cupboards were scant of things to eat. Food was scarce and nothing could be wasted. Breakfast often consisted of a cup of tea and 5 or 6 slices of toast. We did not own a toaster so I made toast by sticking a fork into a slice of bread and balancing it over one the stove's burners till it browned up a little. Sometimes holding it to close to the flame a slice would burn but we couldn't afford to throw it out. I would save the toast by scraping across the top with a knife to remove the charred area then spread it with bacon grease grandma had given us and eat it anyway. Occasionally there would be a box of cereal and some milk available. A close look at the sugar bowl often revealed a few black dots sitting atop the grains of sugar. These tiny spots of black were mouse turds left by the mice that foraged through our kitchen when we were asleep at night. Never mind, we couldn't afford to throw out the sugar. So carefully I dipped the tip of the spoon under the area of the mouse turds, scooped up each turd, threw them out and used the rest of the sugar. Despite the lack of money for food or coal my mother always seemed to have enough money to go to the neighborhood bar. Most of the time when, I wasn't at work, she would ask me to stay with Jerry while she was at the bar.

One Saturday after I got off work Mr. Burger asked me if I would change the letters on the marquis to reflect the new showings starting on Sunday. This was a complicated task involving a high ladder, removing the old steel letters, getting out new letters arranging them to spell out the next day's movies and placing them on both sides of the marquis. This process would take an hour or more however I would be paid $2.50 each time. The movies changed twice a week so I would earn an extra $5.00 each week in my pay envelope. Always anxious to earn money I quickly agreed. That night the temperature was near zero. The metal letters were very cold so I had to take several breaks to warm my hands. It was after midnight when I finished. I walked home and entered the apartment. It was freezing cold and when I called out for my mother there was no response. Jerry was asleep in his crib covered with blankets. I turned on and lit all the gas burners on the kitchen stove to provide some heat for the apartment. Next I ran down the block to the scrap wood guy's place. I climbed over the high fence that enclosed the yard where his wood was stored, grabbed a couple bundles, tossed them over the fence and climbed back out. I ran home and started a fire in the furnace with the stolen wood. The cast iron radiators soon started humming and heat gradually inundated the apartment. Around two-thirty my mother came through the front door.

"Where have you been?" .... I screamed at the top of my lungs.

"I just went for a little drinky poo. Wha's the matter wif you?"

"Your drunk! Again! You left Jerry alone again!"

"I was'n gone long. I only had a couple a beers."

"You're a liar! You don't get drunk on two beers. What is the matter with you? It is zero degrees outside. Don't you care about your little boy? He could freeze to death or get sick from being left in the cold. Your goddamn beer is more important to you than your baby. Go to hell!"

"Don' talk to me like that. I'm your mother. You're s'posed to respect your mother"

"I can't respect someone that's not respectable."

Realizing it was pointless to argue with her when she was intoxicated I gave up and went to bed.

Chapter 24

FLIRTING WITH CRIMINALITY

Like typical teenagers we were sometimes bored and looking for something exciting to do. On some nights Leonard, Jerry Hopkins, some other kids and myself would go carousing for things to do in other neighborhoods Late one night we came upon a fenced in parking lot that housed several small delivery style trucks. There were trucks that delivered soft drinks, bread trucks, and one refrigerated truck. We decided to see if there was anything inside any of these trucks. Some of trucks were unlocked. Some we forced our way into. We found bottles of Birely's Orange and assorted flavors of Nehi soda in one truck. In another truck we came upon a case of a dozen cans of motor oil. The nervousness that accompanies the performance of illegal acts influenced us to quickly abscond with what we could carry We quickly left with the soda pop and the motor oil. We remembered how easy it was to pilfer those trucks and returned again some weeks later. The other boys kept the soda pop and I kept the motor oil which I burned as fuel in the furnace on cold nights when there was no coal or money for scrap wood.

To my surprise Lester was sitting at the kitchen table when I came home from school one afternoon. It had been more than a year since he disappeared and I thought he was gone for good but there he sat looking at me with a slight grin.

"What are you doing here?" …I asked.

"I'm back and I'll be staying here from now on."

"Does my mother know?"

"Yeah she knows and it's okay with her."

"We don't have any money and there's no coal so it's gonna be cold around here."

"Don't worry Skip. Come with me and I'll show you how to fix that problem."

Lester led me to the basement where sat a stack of old automobile tires. He took a knife and began cutting one of the tires into pieces that would fit through the furnace door. He pushed the tire pieces into the furnace, poured some motor oil on the tires and set it them on fire. In only a few minutes the tire pieces were ablaze. We went back upstairs and already the radiators were beginning to burp and hum. In only a short time the entire apartment was toasty warm. I was amazed and grateful that Les knew a way that could keep us warm during that cold winter. I asked him where he got the tires. He said….

"I got them at the tire store right next to the apartment building. They're just scrap tires taken off the cars when people buy new tires."

He was right. There were "small mountains" of old scrap tires stacked up behind that tire store. Our heating problems were solved… I thought... I soon realized there was a problem with using the tires for fuel. The tires burned quick and very hot sending the radiators singing almost immediately. However they also burned very fast and within a couple of hours they were totally consumed and the apartment began to cool again. Still it did provide some relief from the cold for a while. Swiping tires, to burn, from the tire store became a regular routine the rest of the winter. Lester had another trick up his sleeve. There seldom was enough money to spare for purchasing a block of ice to put in the icebox, so without refrigeration, what little perishable food we had in the apartment would often spoil. Lester obtained an orange crate from the local grocery store and mounted it on the outside kitchen window ledge. We could then place any perishables inside the crate and shut down the window down. The cold winter temperature kept the food in the crate from spoiling and we could simply raise the window to retrieve whatever was inside the crate. Gradually my resentment of Lester diminished and we settled into a somewhat normal relationship.

Now that we had the new "window box" to keep things cold I thought perhaps I would find some milk or other perishable items inside that refrigerated truck at the parking lot where we had previously pilfered the soda pop and oil. I returned, with Leonard, one night and climbed over the fence to the parking lot. The refrigerated truck was there along with a smaller milk truck. Both trucks were locked. We decided to break into the milk truck. Inside, along with several bottles of milk, we discovered cartons of eggs, cases of butter and other assorted foodstuff. We grabbed what we could easily carry and fled the scene. Leonard's situation was not conducive to bringing any contraband home so I took it all and placed it in the "window box" at my apartment. Now for a few weeks I had real butter to put on my toast and fresh milk for cereal. I was quite pleased with the situation until a few weeks later. I entered the kitchen one morning to discover a large rat perched on top of the window box with its long tail hanging through the slats of the orange crate. It was a huge rat with a tail almost a foot long. He looked at me but seemed unafraid as he dragged his tail across the open dish of butter and other food inside the crate. A feeling of nausea swept over me as I realized that this rat along with others had most likely visited our window box several times previously and contaminated the same food I had been enjoying for the last two weeks. Aware that food we kept in the window box was attracting these disgusting creatures I decided to remove the crate from the window ledge and reluctantly threw away the food that was inside.

The time my mother spent drinking in the bar increased now that Lester was back. They seemed to be getting along just fine. It made no sense to me and I wondered why on earth Les had left in the first place. They made friends with our next door neighbors, (Louise and Jimmy) who were also quite the drinkers. I arrived home one night to find Jerry alone in his crib. At the same time I heard loud voices coming from the next door apartment. I recognized my mother's voice and went next door intending to scold her for leaving Jerry alone again. As I approached their apartment door I heard my mother scream. I pushed open the door and entered to find Jimmy with one hand on my mother's neck holding her against the wall and his other arm cocked, about to hit her. Although Jimmy was much bigger and heavier than me without hesitation I immediately grabbed his cocked arm and pushed him to the floor. I stood over him with my arm now raised , ready to strike and screamed in his face …

"If you ever touch my mother again I'll kill you. You stupid son of a bitch!"

Louise was begging me not to hit Jimmy while Lester stood there laughing through the entire scene. It was soon apparent all four of them were extremely drunk. Jimmy got up and staggered away while Louise kept asking if he was all right and Lester continued laughing. My mother told me to go home.…

"It'sh okay Skippy It'sh aw'right jus gwan home.

Disgusted with them all I went back to our apartment. The next day Les and my mother apologized to me saying they would not be spending time with Jimmy and Louise anymore.

Late one night Lester told me had a job to do that required two people. He offered to pay me a couple of bucks if I wanted to help him. Always anxious to make some money I said yes. We departed in his old pickup truck around midnight and headed northwest out Grand River Ave. We turned south on Southfield Road which was a divided highway at that time. We came to a small unpaved side street where we turned west. This area was sparsely settled in the early 1950's. We arrived at some kind of construction site. There were all sorts of construction materials stacked everywhere. Lester backed his truck up to where a long iron I-beam laid on the ground. He exited the pick up and walked to the back. Lowering the tailgate he informed me we needed to hoist the I-beam into the back of the pickup. He asked me to go to the back of the "beam". I was to push the "beam" forward as hard as I could once he lifted the front end of the "beam" onto the bed of the pickup. With great effort he lifted the I-beam while I pushed. I was only able to move it forward an inch or so but it was enough to get it barely resting on the edge of the truck bed. Les then came to the back and strained to push it forward. He could only move it about a foot at a time and had to keep stopping to catch his breath before going at it again. Finally he got it all the way on but it was so much longer than the bed of the truck that it teetered a little. After resting a while Les said he thought raising up the tailgate would help secure the "beam" and stop the teetering. When he lifted the back end of the I-beam I was to quickly raise up and lock the tailgate in place. When this was accomplished we hopped in the truck and Lester sped off back down Lyndon with the I-beam bouncing in the back. He seemed to be in a hurry and kept looking behind in the rear view mirror. Everything seemed fine until we came to Southfield Road. As mentioned Lester was in a hurry for some reason and was going too fast when the pickup transitioned from the gravel side street to the pavement of Southfield Road. There was a bounce, then a crashing sound and a loud metallic clang. Les hit the brakes and we looked back to see the iron beam had crushed down the tailgate, slid off the back and was laying in the middle of Southfield. We were about to go back and get it when a car that must have been going at least 60 mph crashed into the beam pushing it forward several yards and lighting up the highway with the sparks created by the friction of the iron beam scraping along the pavement. The car remained upright as it came to a stop. There appeared to be significant damage to the front of the car but the driver seemed unhurt as we watched him get out of the car. Les pushed hard on the gas pedal and sped off fleeing the scene. I said we should stop and see if he was alright but Les confessed he was stealing the I-beam and did not want to wait around for the cops. When we arrived back to the apartment he cautioned me not to tell anyone what happened. I awoke the next morning to the sound of knocking. It was the police at the door. They asked where Lester was. When I told them I had no idea they asked where I was the night before. I lied and said I was home all night. After much more questioning they finally gave up and warned me I could be in a lot of trouble if I was lying. They said they would be back with more questions and I better tell the truth. Les disappeared once more. Several months passed before I saw Lester again.

Chapter 25

THE CAR

I arrived at work one Spring afternoon to find Leonard there dressed in an ushers uniform. I was happy to see he had gained employment at the "Tower". Leonard's boldness always inspired me to try to overcome my inward tendencies. Within a relatively short time we were introduced to another new member of the usher staff. Bill Tucker was a very heavyset teenager with a slight stutter. Due to the largeness of his size we referred to him as Jumbo behind his back. After we became more acquainted with him we found he was quite friendly and soon we were calling him Jumbo all the time. The "Sweet Shop" across the street from the "Tower" was the place in the neighborhood where teenagers met to indulge in various ice cream treats and play their favorite songs on the jukebox. We began hanging out there too. I loved milkshakes but rarely ordered one as I hated parting with the fifty cents that they cost. Priority number one for me was to save money so when ever I was tempted to order a milkshake I reminded myself that I had to work for an entire hour to earn that milkshake. More than once that way of thinking caused me to postpone treating myself. Many times in the future I applied that same logic when considering making large and small purchases.

In late spring after we were out of school for summer recess Mr. Burger approached the three of us at work one day with an opportunity to earn some extra money. The lobby and foyer of the theater needed painting. He proposed to pay us fifty cents an hour to do the painting and it would be cash "under the table" so no taxes would be taken out and the usual limit on hours teenagers could work would not matter. The painting would take several weeks and the painting would be done on weekdays when the theater was not open. Jumbo seemed hesitant but Leonard and I quickly agreed.

"This is a chance to save a lot more money for the car I want."…. I thought.

The paint was provided by the theater owners and Leonard and I began rolling on the paint the next day. Most days I painted from nine am. to five pm. with a short break for lunch. In the beginning Leonard was with me most of the time but after the first week his appearances became sporadic. Still I continued to paint. I wanted money to buy a car. Often Mr. Burger would leave the theater for errands or meetings he had to attend. When he was gone we would sometimes do a little exploring. Alone one afternoon we discovered a way to get soda pop from the pop machine, that was located in the foyer, without putting in any money. We found out there was a lever up behind the dispensing spout that when pushed would cause the soda pop to flow without inserting the required quarter. On another occasion we scoured a few aisles of seats and found a few coins on the floor. We also found a wallet but there wasn't any money in it so we turned it in to the office. The painting project lasted about a month. With the painting money and the five bucks each week for changing the marquis letters I managed to save a little over one hundred dollars. I began looking in the newspaper want ads for cars for sale.

Arriving home one afternoon I was surprised to find my real father sitting at the kitchen table conversing with my mother. I hadn't seen or heard from him since the day he brought me a bike for my birthday. My mother had enlisted him to assist me in my search for a car. I exchanged pleasantries with my father and we made arrangements to meet the following day to look for cars. We spent the next couple of days traveling around to several used car lots to look at cars but the ones I liked were too expensive and the ones I could afford were not to my liking. I decided I would need to obtain more money before buying a car. I began wondering about the money we found on the floor at the Tower Theater.

"Could we find even more if we searched up and down every aisle?"

In the theater there was an area behind the movie screen, hidden by the opening and closing curtains, where a staircase was located that led up to the roof of the theater. A two foot square cap covered the opening to the roof. It was not locked and if you just pushed up on it and maneuvered it to one side you could gain access to the roof. A pipe to drain the water that accumulated on the flat top roof ran down the outside of the building. If someone shinnied up that pipe to the roof they could get inside by lifting the cap and climbing down the metal stairway. Once inside they could open a door from the inside to let someone else in. After explaining this to Leonard we agreed to try it. Late one night we went to the theater after it closed. I was smaller and lighter than Leonard so I climbed up the drainpipe to the rooftop. After lifting the cap I scrambled down the stairs and opened a side door for Leonard. Once inside we began scouring the aisles, with flashlights looking for money. After searching for maybe an hour our score was a few coins and one dollar bill. Not much for the effort we put in but we would try a few more times on other nights. While in there we checked out the store room in back of the candy counter. The actual candy counter was locked and the entire inventory of candy was kept on shelves located below the display area. The theater did not make popcorn on site but purchased it, already popped, in huge bags. Several huge bags of popcorn too large to keep in the counter area were located in the unlocked part of the storeroom. We returned a few more late nights, entered the theater through the roof and searched the aisles. While inside we also filled some shopping bags with popcorn and drained the pop machine soda into a gallon bottle we brought with us. For the next few weeks when food was scarce at our apartment I subsisted on the popcorn and the gone flat by then soda I had pilfered from the Tower Theater. We made the mistake of bragging of our exploits to Jumbo and some others. A few weeks later we planned another late night rooftop entry. As we approached the theater we heard sirens wailing. To our dismay we found our friend, Jumbo, laying on the ground unable to move as men in white uniforms were attending to him. We learned later that Jumbo had tried to shinny up the same drainpipe I had climbed before. I believe his weight, much heavier than mine, caused a screw or bolt securing the drain pipe to the building to break loose while Jumbo was at the very top. He had fallen at least three stories to the concrete parking lot. He would remain in the hospital for more than six weeks due to broken legs and damage to his spine. He would walk with a limp the rest of his life. That ended our late night explorations to the Tower Theater. I realized....

"It could have been me"

My search for a car ended when my mother informed me she knew a man who had a 1939 Ford for sale. He was asking one hundred dollars but would sell it to me for $75.00. With my mother accompanying me I went to look at the car. I decided it would be less risky to buy a car from someone my mother knew so I bought it. My heart was racing with excitement as I got behind the "wheel" and hit the accelerator. My mother reminded me I should drive straight back to our apartment as I did not yet have a driver's license. I obeyed reluctantly. The very next day I rode the bus downtown to the license bureau, took the road test, passed and received a temporary license to drive. When I got back home I immediately jumped in the driver's seat and drove to Leonard's house to show him my "new" car. Leonard hopped in the passenger seat and off we drove to show all our friends. A variety of feelings ran through my consciousness. Pride, independence, power and freedom all went with me as I sped down the road. With a car to go exploring in the summer of 1951 would be an exciting time. I was soon to find out there was a dark side to owning a car as a teenager.... The cops!

Leonard and Harvey accompanied me on my first road trip. We drove to Jack White's house in Highland Park. On the way I was excited at the prospect of seeing him again but disappointed when I found Jack was not there. His mother and step dad began tearing up as they informed me that Jack was in jail again. They said he would probably be released in the next week or so and then surprised me by asking me to come back and reestablish my relationship with Jack, saying that they thought I was a good influence on Jack. I thought …

"These are the same people that shunned me over the false belief I was attempting to break into their house a few years ago."

As we left I assured them I would get in touch with Jack when he got out. Leonard, Harvey and I caught up with Jack a few weeks later when he was released.

The four of us were constant companions that summer. With my "new" car we could travel to places that were previously out of reach. Playing pin ball machines was one of our favorite pastimes but they were illegal within the Detroit city limits. We knew there was a diner located outside the city on the corner of Grand River and Nov Road that had a pinball machine. We made several car trips out to that diner just to play "pinball". One day we drove a little farther looking for more places with pinball machines and discovered a park with a big lake. It was Kent Lake and it was part of Kensington Metro Park. During the next few years Kent Lake would become a favorite and frequent destination. I recall driving with my friends to Kent Lake on the spur of the moment one hot summer night intending to go swimming. It was after midnight and the park closed at 11pm but we entered anyway. We found our way to a beach, jumped out of the car, stripped down naked and ran quickly into the water. No sooner were we in the water when a second car pulled into the parking area. Two young couples got out of the car and proceeded to the water. Apparently they had planned better than we had as they were wearing bathing suits.

"Nuts" … I thought … *"Now what do we do? We can't get out of the water with no clothes on."*

While I was contemplating our dilemma suddenly another set of headlights approached the water. It was the park police! They turned a spotlight on the water and announced ....

"This park is closed. Everyone out of the water immediately!"

The spotlight began sweeping across the water as the two couples departed the water giggling all the way. After a brief exchange with the cops they got in their car and drove off. The cops continued sweeping the water announcing they knew there were others in the water due to the still remaining car. Each time the spotlight came in my direction I ducked under the water until it passed. I assume my friends were doing the same. After approximately fifteen minutes of ducking the sweeping spotlights the park police gave up and drove off. We waited about ten more minutes before we cautiously made our way back to shore. With sighs of relief we dressed and drove away. On the drive home we began to laugh as we thought how we almost had to exit the water naked in front of two girls. Thank God the cops didn't spot us. It was quite late when we reentered the city limits. Previously I had fallen asleep more than once while driving late at night. Several times in the past I was jerked awake when my tires hit gravel shoulders, sometimes on the wrong side of the road. Thank God these occurrences took place late at night with only the occasional car coming from the other direction. We were approaching the corner of Grand River Ave. and Schaeffer when for only a second I dozed off just as another car attempted to pass us on the inside lane. It was late at night with hardly any traffic on the road so I must have wandered out of my lane and side swiped the other car. I immediately stopped and put my head in my hands as a feeling of dread came over me. The other driver stopped got out of his car to see what damage had been done. The passenger side rear fender on my car now had a nice dent in it but the other car had a severe gash on the driver's side front fender along with a broken headlight. I stood on the pavement stunned, wondering how much trouble I was in without any insurance and how on earth I could ever pay for the damage to his car. When, without uttering a word, the other driver got back in his car and sped off. Unbelievable I thought. He didn't ask to exchange information. He just left! At the time we could not figure it out. We were just relieved to flee the scene without having the police involved. Later in life reflecting on this event I concluded that the other driver was either involved in some illegal activity or an illicit affair.

During the next several months the 1939 Ford was driven almost constantly. Unfortunately that much driving meant exposure to the police who seemed to be looking for an excuse to pull over young drivers in old cars. Pull me over they did. I was stopped innumerable times for all sorts of reasons. Often I was accused of driving too fast. Sometimes I was sometimes I was not. The most common infraction was my loud burned out muffler. The real or made up reasons they gave for stopping me didn't matter. The routine was always the same. First they ask for my drivers license and registration. Then with a hostile and presumptive tone and came the questioning.... Where was I going? Where was I coming from? Why was I out so late? How old was I? Where do I have the beer stashed etc. On one summer night I was driving westward on Grand River Ave when I heard the sound of a siren and saw flashing lights in my rear view mirror. I pulled over and watched as a policeman approached. He politely asked for my drivers license and registration. As he was reviewing my credentials I asked if I had done something wrong.

He did not answer but politely asked me to get out of the car. I complied. He then motion to three other officers seated in what I came to recognize as a "Detroit Police Cruiser"

The three cops then began to search my car. They emptied the glove compartment, searched under the seats and under the dashboard. It took two of them to pull the back seat completely out of the car to see under it. When they found nothing there they asked me to open the trunk. Next they proceeded to empty every thing from the trunk. They tossed the spare tire out onto the street followed by the lug wrench and jack. They tore out the mat that covered the trunk deck. They tossed out several other miscellaneous things I had stored in there. The first cop finally announced.... "Okay boys he's clean" Without another word they climbed into the "Cruiser" and left. They left without putting anything back. I gathered up the contents of the glove compartment which were scattered all over the sidewalk. The spare tire, lug wrench and jack were all laying on the street. I spent the better part of an hour cursing those rotten cops while I gathered and put every thing back where it belonged. After finishing the struggle to reinstall the back seat by myself I got behind the wheel and continued westward on Grand River. I had driven no more than ten city blocks when once again I heard the sound of a siren and began to shake as the flashing lights appeared in my rear view mirror. I thought it was the same officers but it was not. It was two different officers in a standard police car. One red haired cop approached with a slightly discernible smile on his face. He began the same routine as the previous cops.

"Drivers license and registration please."

"Why am I being stopped again? I was just pulled over a few blocks back."

"Step out of the car please."

I reluctantly complied only to watch the two officers begin the same search and destroy tactics utilized by the cruiser cops. They too left me with back seat out on the street and the contents of the glove compartment and trunk strewn all over the sidewalk and road. Totally dejected I gathered everything up and put it back. Replacing that back bench seat was the most challenging. I was sure this was not a coincidence. The cruiser cops had radioed ahead to have me stopped again. Their idea of fun I supposed. I was helpless

Most of the time I remained calm and answered the policemen's questions politely but that one cop with red hair seemed to have it in for me. He began stopping me frequently and every time he stopped me he found a reason to give me a ticket. One time I pleaded with him to let me go with out issuing a ticket for my loud muffler. I explained I had to work ten hours to pay for a five dollar ticket as I only made fifty cents an hour. He simply smiled and wrote a second five dollar ticket for a broken tail light. At that point I lost my cool. I could not believe his callousness and I told him so. He smiled at me once more and wrote me a third ticket. The three tickets amounted to a weeks paycheck. I finally realized I could not win and gave up but I never forgot that red haired cop. As far as I was concerned he was one mean heartless son of a bitch! I began to notice that whenever I saw the cops had someone pulled over it was nearly always someone with an old car. Rarely would I see the cops stop someone in a new Cadillac or Lincoln. Over time I came to believe that those with power prefer to prey on the weak.

Despite my problems with the police when I wasn't working I would hop in the car and drive somewhere. It didn't matter where so long as I was on the move. When I was at work Harvey or Leonard would borrow the car and take off for "parts unknown". I found out much later that Harvey would occasionally loan the car to a couple girls he knew. With all the miles being driven it was a wonder that no one, except me, ever had an accident. There were problems with the car from time to time. It was after all quite old and parts often needed to be replaced. I was not mechanically inclined and without a father around to show me the ins and outs of automobile repair I leaned on Leonard who seemed to know everything about fixing many of the problems with my car. With Leonard's help I learned to visit local junkyards to salvage carburetors, fuel pumps, thermostats, fan belts and old tires to use for fixing the problems affecting my 1939 Ford. Two of my biggest problems were replacing the clutch and the transmission. When the transmission failed one day I parked in the empty field behind my grandmother's apartment house and raised it up on cider blocks. We worked for several weeks installing a used transmission that we bought from a junk yard. While I use the word "we" I must confess I did little except to pass to Leonard whatever tools he required to fix the problem. The time came to see if the car would actually run again. I held my breath and prayed while we removed the car from the cinder blocks, started the engine, shifted into first gear and drove forward a few feet.

"By God! Leonard did it."

Surprisingly it actually worked and Leonard had successfully accomplished the installation. I thought, at the time, he was a genius. We were back on the road again and continued our late night forays to such exotic places as Toledo, Ohio where we had heard 18 year olds could buy beer and were even allowed in bars. We were all only 17 years old at the time but were assured by others that we could easily lie about our age and get served. After driving all the way to Toledo and being turned down at several establishments we eventually became tired of being laughed out of every store or bar we entered and drove back to Detroit.... still sober!

During the weeks that my car was out of commission. I stayed at home most of the time. My mother was still working behind the counter at Gil's Hamburgers and she had found a nursery school to place Jerry in while she was at work. She rode the bus with Jerry in tow, to the "school" each morning. Because the school closed down before her shift ended the plan was for me to pick him up each afternoon. Thinking I could use my car to pick him up I originally agreed to this plan however with the car out of service I had to use the bus system to pick him up and bring him home. Before long I realized my mother was often late getting home and I spent many hours at the apartment alone caring for Jerry. To fill the time I returned to reading books. I re-read some of the books I had previously received as gifts for birthdays and such. I also had a few comic books I could read again. Many comic books had advertisements for a "Charles Atlas" body building course. Charles Atlas was well known body builder. I did not have money to spend on the course but concluded that it had something to do with muscle tension.

I recall the headline claim was that his program could turn a weakling into a big strong man. Several times a day, for a few weeks I stood in front of a mirror and flexed each of my muscles firmly for as long as I could. Perhaps it helped. Perhaps it didn't. But it was a source of humor for my friend Harvey who caught me in the act one day and immediately loudly exclaimed....

"I was once a 95 bound weakling! Now I am a 200 pound weakling! Charles At Last"

While enduring an occasional ribbing from Harvey I continued the flexing sessions for a few months. I also visited the local library and for whatever reasons I had in mind at the time I checked out a book about Sigmund Freud. It was a time in my young life that I doubted most everything about myself.

"Why had I never heard from my Daddy? Why did my real father leave? Why was my mother always pawning me off to others? Why was I rejected by Alpha Omega? What was wrong with me?"

I had, somewhere, heard about Freud and psychoanalysis. Perhaps I thought I could learn some things about myself. Why I was so shy. Why I lacked self confidence. Why was I who I was. I would spend the next few weeks retrieving and avidly reading more and more books by Freud and other specialists in the field of psychiatry. While I grasped some of the ideas in these books I was often at a loss due to lack of understanding some of the words. While searching the rack of paperback books at the local drug store one day I spotted a book "Building Your Vocabulary". I purchased this book, took it home and began reading it in my spare time. I learned the definition of words such as misogynist, altruism, paranoia and many other words I came across while reading the psychiatry books. I studied this book for weeks improving my ability to comprehend the meaning of many other words I had heard before but was never exactly sure what they meant. Obtaining knowledge of several words I previously did not understand or had not even heard of brought with it, ever so slightly, an improvement in my self confidence.

Late one summer night Leonard, Jack, Harvey and myself decided to go out cruising in my car. For a few weeks I had been having trouble getting the car to start. It probably needed a new battery but I was reluctant to spend the money for one until I was sure that was the problem. Most cars at that time had standard transmissions. A car could be started by putting it in gear, pushing in the clutch, pushing the car forward a few yards then quickly letting out the clutch. The four of us pushed the car down the alley where it was parked, popped the clutch and drove off. Like most teenagers we had no definite plan. We simply wanted to enjoy the feeling of freedom and independence the car provided. We eventually found ourselves driving down Eight mile road. It was a divided highway and the north border of the city of Detroit at that time. There was no posted speed limit. The speed limit was "Whatever was safe and proper for the current road conditions." We thought this would be a good place to see how fast the car could go. Off we sped with the accelerator pushed to the floor. After driving a several miles suddenly the car engine sputtered and died. We coasted to a stop in the far left lane. The car had overheated and we had to let the engine cool before we could start it again. With only an occasional vehicle on the road that night we thought we could just stay with the car in the left lane till it cooled down. After about fifteen minutes we tried to start the car but the battery was dead again so we began pushing the car in an attempt to start it by popping the clutch. Harvey was a diabetic and lacked the strength to push so we had him get in the driver's seat ready to "pop the clutch" while Jack and I began pushing the car. Jack and I were at the back of the car pushing. I was on the passenger side. I looked back and saw another car coming toward us at a high rate of speed. The oncoming car was in the same lane we were in. With no battery power we were without lights and I was fearful that he might not see us. I ran to the right side of the car and began waving my arms and yelling. He apparently did not see me or the car as he rapidly approached, still in our lane. Surely I thought the driver would see us and switch lanes, but he didn't. A split second before crashing into our car he swerved trying to avoid the collision. Everything happened so fast it is hard to describe what actually occurred but as he was swerving I leaped backwards onto the running board. I heard the crash as his car ripped off the rear fender on the side of the car where I stood. I felt the whoosh of air as the other car passed by me within inches. Then I heard the scraping sound as the other car sideswiped my front fender. It is almost beyond belief that the collision resulted in ripping off the rear fender and sideswiping the front fender while I stood on the running board between the two fenders sustaining not so much as a scratch. This event along with other happenings caused me to believe I won't be taken until it is my time.

Chapter 26

GAMBLING

While sitting around one fall afternoon wondering what to do with ourselves Jack proposed we go to the horse races. No one wanted to pay the cost to park or the entrance fee at the track but Jack suggested if we ride the bus to the Detroit Race Course we could probably find a way to sneak in. Off we went on the bus to the "track" We scoured the perimeter chain link fencing and discovered an obscure point, behind a large stable, where we climbed over unnoticed. Once inside we slowly worked our way from behind the building and into the main area. We blended into the crowd that had gathered to view several horses coming out of the stable. We watched excitedly as the horses passed by. Most of the horses seemed quite docile as they trotted by but one of the horses appeared greatly agitated. It was stomping its hoofs and whinnying loudly. The handler was having trouble keeping the horse from jumping out of line. The four of us all came up with the same idea…. *"This horse was ready to run!"* We decided immediately that we should bet on this horse. No one had the two dollars required for a minimum bet so we began counting our money. I had fifty cents Jack had a quarter Leonard had fifty cents and Harley contributed the remaining seventy-five cents. We pooled our money and gave it to Jack, who looked the oldest and possessed the confidence, to place the bet. We did not even know the horses name but we noticed his number. The horses were out on the track and the start of the race was imminent as Jack got in the bet line. The line was long and we were worried the bet window would close before Jack could get our bet in. While Jack was in line we went out to the edge of the track and saw the odds board. We were dismayed to find the horse we were betting on was a ninety-nine to one shot. Suddenly we didn't feel so smart. We began thinking we were fools to pick a horse just because he was acting rambunctious. No sooner did Jack get the bet successfully placed than the race started. After all these years I cannot describe the play by play of the race. I can only tell you when the race was over, the P. A. system blurted out the result. It was a photo finish and our horse was involved. We waited for what seemed an eternity while the judges reviewed the finish. This was our first time at a race track. We knew nothing about the procedures and technicalities involved. Finally the announcement came. It was a "dead heat" between our ninety-nine to one shot horse and another two to one shot. The odds on our horse had dropped considerably by the time the race began, still we were elated to actually win some money. Jack cashed in the ticket and we received thirty-eight dollars back for our two dollar bet. We split the winnings proportionately to the amount we put in and left the track vowing to return. This seemingly fortunate result would be the hook that drew me into many more future trips to the track.

Chapter 27

REJECTION

In late summer that year one of the girls that worked behind the candy counter at the "Tower" called me aside to tell me that a friend of hers wanted me to ask her for a date. This surprised me as I felt my bad teeth would turn off any girl who might possibly be interested in me. Still I thought perhaps my conscious effort to avoid smiling and keeping my upper lip down may have prevented her from seeing the large cavities and greenish condition of my teeth. Her friend's name was Mary Muller. I knew who Mary Muller was. She attended most Saturday matinees at the "Tower". I had noticed her and was quite attracted to her but I never considered she might feel that way about me. She was a petite girl with long dark hair, soft brown eyes, a nice figure and a very pretty face. While taking tickets at the "Tower" one Saturday Mary approached and handed me her ticket. Somehow I screwed up enough courage to carefully smile at her and say "Hi". She smiled back at me and proceeded onward down an aisle to select a seat. After completing the task of taking tickets it was my job to take a position at the opening of one of the aisles that lead into the seating area. I took note of the aisle Mary walked down and I selected that aisle to monitor. During the intermission Mary passed by me on the way to the candy counter. She smiled once again but said nothing. I wanted to say something but could not muster the courage. Soon thereafter as she was returning to her seat she stopped and asked me my name. Thus began a short conversation after which I built up enough confidence to speak to her again on her next visit to the "Tower". The fall semester at school was just around the corner and some of the "Tower" employees were planning an outing to Boblo island as a farewell to summer celebration. When Mary was at the Tower one Saturday I casually mentioned this planned event to her. I was overjoyed when she inquired if she could go with us. I replied positively and informed her of the date and time we planned to leave. Boblo was an island located near the mouth of the Detroit River. Getting to Boblo required a boat ride from downtown Detroit. The Boblo Boat was moored at the foot of Woodward Ave. I rode the bus downtown with Mary and while walking to the boat dock we had to pass by the Vernor's Ginger Ale bottling plant right next door. We stopped and treated ourselves to a Vernor's Cream Ale (a delightful concoction of Ginger Ale and dairy cream). We continued on to buy our tickets and boarded the boat. It was a leisurely eighteen mile trip down the river to Boblo Island. We spent some time observing the homes and businesses that dotted the Canadian shoreline. On the lower deck there was an observation point where we could look down into the engine room and watch the huge engines running as it propelled the craft through the water. There was a snack bar for refreshments and a dance band played on one of the decks. I wasn't much of a dancer but gave it my best effort when Mary asked me to dance. We were filled with anticipation as we heard the hum of the engines lower and the forward movement of the boat slow to a crawl. Next the boat made a wide turn and began maneuvering to the dock. We waited anxiously then hurried down the gangplank and along the dock to touch ground on Boblo Island. We started out as a group to stroll and explore the "Island. There was an amusement park with several rides. We rode the roller coaster, dodgem cars, and one called "The Whip". There were pony rides, a roller rink, a dance pavilion and picnic grounds. Mary and I elected to take a ride on the little trackless train that made a tour of the island. This was not my first Boblo experience. My grandmother had taken me to Boblo a few times before. It was always a grand time. Mary and I became better acquainted as we wandered about the "Island that day. I got the distinct impression, even though I found it hard to believe, that she liked me. We spent a wonderful day together. My confidence was really high. So high that on the return boat ride I offered to pick her up each day after she got out of school and drive her home in my car. My spirits rose even higher when she told me she would like that. I got out of Cooley High at 2:30 pm while Mary left Mckenzie High at 3:30. For the next several weeks I met her after school and drove her home every day. I now had a girlfriend. Life was good (for a while).

I continued working at the "Tower" evenings and weekends and attending eleventh grade at Cooley High. In early Fall, one Saturday night around midnight, Leonard and I got off work and went to the small parking area in back of the Mobil gas station located next to the "Tower". The manager of the gas station had granted us permission to park our cars while we were at work. We climbed into Leonard's 1940 Buick coup and pulled around to the front of the gas station which was now closed. Like typical teenagers we were not anxious to go right home. We remained parked by the gas pumps for approximately ten minutes discussing what to do next when a police car pulled in beside us. One officer rolled down his window and asked ...

"What are you boys up to tonight?"

We explained that we worked at the "Tower" and were just talking.

"Why are you sitting in front of this gas station?"

We continued to explain that we had been given permission to park in back of the gas station while we were at work and we were simply listening to the radio and discussing what to do next.

"Well you can't stay parked here."

We replied that we would be leaving right away. We watched as the police car pulled out of the "station" and proceeded down Grand River Ave. As they were leaving Leonard said....

"Why don't we follow them and see where they're going."

"I don't think that's a good idea."

Despite my discouragement Leonard pulled out behind the police car and started following. Leonard stayed about two blocks behind following the patrol car which was traveling at a normal rate of speed. When they made a sharp right turn onto Plymouth Ave. we did the same. We paced them as they continued west at the same normal speed for several blocks then suddenly they accelerated and made a quick right turn at the corner of Schaeffer Highway. Seeing this Leonard hit the gas pedal hard and sped up to the corner. Grabbing the suicide knob, he had mounted on the steering wheel, he whipped around the corner with tires screeching to find the road totally devoid of vehicles. Nothing! No police car in sight. Leonard slowed to crawl. We looked in every direction but saw no sign of the police car. At this point we were driving north on Schaeffer. Empty fields, that were yet to be developed, separated the neighborhood to the west from Schaeffer. An alley bordered the edge between the housing area and the open fields. Leonard had equipped his Buick coup with a spotlight which he turned on and aimed at the empty fields. Then we saw it. The police car was parked in the alley with it's lights off. Leonard put the spotlight directly on the cop car and laughed. He continued to drive very slowly rotating the spotlight to keep it focused on the cop car as he continued down the street. Suddenly their headlights came on. Gravel flew as the police car screamed out of the alley. Leonard burned rubber as he flew up to the corner of a side street and dashed west into the neighborhood. The cops followed. Both cars were traveling at a high rate of speed. The chase went on for some time as Leonard, driving extremely fast, sped recklessly down several neighborhood streets randomly deciding to turn right or left at each corner we came to. We could see the flashing red and blue lights of the cop car in close pursuit two or three blocks behind. He continued to zigzag, up, down, back and forth on neighborhood streets with cars parked on both sides. After several of Leonard's evasive maneuvers I looked back to see, unbelievably, there was no cop car in sight. I breathed a sigh of relief and thought …

"Thank God we got away"

We were only a few blocks from Plymouth Road when Leonard suddenly stopped the car in the middle of the street..

"What are you doing" … I asked….. "We've eluded them! Let's get out of here!"

Then came the words that I will never forget…,

"Let's give them a chance to catch up."

"You're absolutely nuts! Come on Leonard! Plymouth Road is two blocks ahead. Let's take it and get the hell out of here."

Leonard kept the car stationary for what seemed an eternity until we saw the cop car come wheeling around a corner three of four blocks behind. The chase resumed. This time Leonard screamed off onto Plymouth, turned left, raced east up to Schaeffer and ducked into a gas station that was located on the corner. He parked next to the gas pumps attempting to feign a customer buying gas. The cop car passed by heading east and I thought we had eluded them until the patrol car reappeared slowly heading back our way. To my dismay they pulled into the gas station, exited their car and approached.

"You guys think you're pretty smart. Dontcha?"

With no response from us he continued….

"We are gonna show you just how smart you really are."

They rustled us out of the Buick and into the police car. We were taken to Schaeffer Station, finger printed and booked. We were falsely charged with "Suspicion of breaking and entering" They knew we were innocent of that charge but apparently decided we needed a lesson. We were put in separate jail cells. I kept thinking, naively, they couldn't keep us long because after all …

"We were innocent of the charges"

I was sure they would let us out in the morning but morning came without our release. I became extremely distraught and disoriented as it became uncertain when or even if we would ever be let out. I remembered my commitment to pick up Mary after school. How would I explain this to her. On Monday morning we were finally released. Driving home I told Leonard off…

"What the hell was wrong with you? It's your fault we went to jail." Leonard just laughed. Sometimes I wondered if he was all there. I was greatly relieved to pick up Mary Monday afternoon and told her nothing of the weekend events."

With my own car to drive around in schoolwork became a distraction that fall. I was always anxious to get out of school, pick up my friends and take off somewhere (anywhere) in the car. I stayed out late almost every night then could not wake up in the morning and was often late for school. Sometimes I would be so late that I just decided to skip that day. I had always been keenly interested in achieving good grades but now school seemed boring. Most of the teachers were old and boring as well. I neglected homework assignments. In fact during the three years I eventually spent at Cooley High I never turned in a single homework assignment. Whenever I was in the classroom I listened intently to everything the teacher said. I had been blessed with an excellent memory and the uncanny ability to discern what was important to remember and what was not. With this ability I could almost predict what questions would be asked on all the tests. This resulted in great test scores which tended to compensate for my lack of turning in homework assignments. There were fifty or more students in most of the classes I attended. As long as I got by with good test scores I pretty much went unnoticed in the day to day classroom interactions. One teacher proved to be an exception to my general opinion of teachers. Mr. Nesbit taught English literature. He made a point of querying all the students in his class on a regular basis. He had assigned the class to read Shakespeare's Macbeth which I failed to do thinking I could simply listen to what he had to say about it in class and then excel on any test he might come up with. In the class of fifty plus students I felt the odds were good, on any given day, he would not call on me. The day came when my theory turned out to be wrong. That day I was the first to be called on…

"Julian! Explain for us what Shakespeare was attempting to show us in his tale of Mac Beth?

I stumbled and mumbled a totally inadequate response. Then I felt his wrath.

"Julian! Your response makes it clear to me that you have not the slightest hint of a correct answer. You have not even opened the book. Have you?"

"No."

"Mr. King I'm going to ask you this same question in class tomorrow and you need to have a satisfactory answer if you want to continue in this class."

He calmly informed me in front of the rest of the class that there was no room in his classroom for students who thought they could bluff their way through. Either we paid attention and came to class prepared or we might as well leave right now and accept a failing grade. I was mortified in front of the entire class. His response caught me off guard. In other classes, when caught without an adequate answer, the teacher simply ignored me and moved on to question another classmate. I was intensely ashamed and sat down without another word. I pondered this unexpected development the rest of the day. I wanted to graduate and I did not want to risk failing this class. Embarrassment was followed by anger. I resented being made a fool. I made a decision to not let this stand. I spent that afternoon and evening reading and rereading "Mac Beth" until I felt ready to answer Mr. Nesbit's question or any other he might pose. In class the next day as promised Mr. Nesbit called on me first with the same question. I was ready with my answer….

"Shakespeare was giving us an example of how ambition carried too far can lead to destruction."

He paused a few seconds the smiled and said….

"Very good Mr. King"

I felt vindicated however I could not risk finding myself without an answer to Mr. Nesbit's future questioning. I would rise to this challenge! While I ignored assignments in other classes I made a point of studying and preparing for Mr. Nesbit's class. Subsequently I became his star pupil and he used me as an example for the other students to emulate. Had I encountered more challenging teachers, like Nesbitt, I might have been a better student.

While driving Mary home from school one afternoon she told me her biology class was going on a field trip to Rouge Park the next day. She asked me to go with her. I asked how could I go when not only was I not in her class but I didn't even attend the same school. She said she had permission to bring me along so it would not be a problem. We agreed to meet later and discuss it. That evening I went to meet Mary at her next door neighbor's house where she was babysitting. Mary appeared at the front door when I knocked. She came outside and we went to sit in my car that was parked at the curb in front of the house. Inside the car she snuggled up close to me while we discussed the arrangements for us to meet at McKenzie the next morning for the field trip. After we sat in the car awhile I put my arm around her and we kissed. Everything seemed fine. I almost could not believe my luck. Here I was with this pretty young girl who actually seemed to like me. At that moment I was tremendously happy. We met the next morning, boarded the bus and proceeded to Rouge Park. Once there we spent the day walking along several trails observing the flora and fauna. Mary brought a camera and was taking lots of photos of various plants and things that interested her. Looking back at that day I cannot explain what was going through my mind at the time but for whatever reason I began making fun of different photographs she was taking. I mistakenly supposed she knew my few sarcastic remarks were an attempt to be funny. When she didn't laugh I tried even harder without much success. The call to return to the bus sounded. We arrived back at school, got in my car and I drove Mary home. I kissed Mary goodbye not knowing it would be a while before I would see her again.

The next afternoon, following my normal schedule, I drove to McKenzie to pick up Mary. She was not waiting in the usual place so I waited for her. The throng of students, who were always there, gradually disbanded but still no Mary. Perhaps, I thought, she was kept after school for some reason so I continued waiting. After waiting for an hour I drove to her home. I knocked on her door. Her father came to the door gruffly asking….

"What do you want?"

"Is Mary home?"

"She's home but she's not coming to the door!"

"Could you tell her it's Skip?"

"She knows who it is. Don't come back here! I don't want you bothering her."

I did not think arguing with Mr. Muller would be to my advantage so I turned back to my car and drove away in disbelief. That night and all the next day I was worried about this development. I was anxious for school to get out so I could pick up Mary and find out what the problem was. Mary, again, was not in the area where I normally picked her up.

I questioned some of the other students as to Mary's whereabouts. No one had an answer for me. I waited until there was no one left to ask. I saw no point in going to Mary's home again. I had no idea how to proceed. I left discouraged and dejected. I repeated this scenario the rest of the week to no avail. I had hopes she would come to the Tower that weekend but she did not appear. I continued visiting her school off and on for the next couple of weeks but never caught sight of her. Totally devastated, bewildered and depressed once again

I withdrew to contemplate what had happened. I wondered what had I done ...

"Had my sarcasm the day of the "field trip" angered her? Had she finally noticed I was covering up my cavities with chewing gum? Had someone told her of my weekend in jail? Had her father learned of this and forbade her seeing me? Or could it simply be she realized who I really was? A nobody going nowhere without any prospects for the future. My real father deserted me, my Daddy didn't care about me. My mother constantly tried to dump me off. Why should Mary be any different?"

Other than my time at work or school I remained in the apartment for the next several weeks running these possibilities through my mind. I returned to reading my vocabulary builder and more books on psychoanalysis from the library. Friends stopped by attempting to lure me out of my funk but I felt no ambition to leave the apartment. Harvey and I had become good friends and I felt comfortable telling him of my plight. I asked him, if he happened to see Mary, to try to find out what the problem was. A few days later Harvey informed me that he had spoken with Mary and she told him she was mad at me for ridiculing her on the field trip. Several weeks passed and I was slowly getting over Mary's rejection when Harvey arrived at my door. He handed me an envelope. It was addressed to Skip King with a return address for Mary Muller. My heart began pounding as I read the letter inside.

"Dear Skip, I am so sorry for what I have done. It was a mistake to stop seeing you. I don't know what got into me but I miss you and want to meet you to discuss getting back together. Please meet me after school tomorrow at our usual place." .... *Mary*

My spirits soared as I realized I had not lost Mary. I had not done anything wrong. She still cared for me. I wasn't a loser... *"Thank you Lord."* The rest of the day and all night I could think of nothing else. I would meet Mary. We would work it out. Everything would be normal again. The next day I didn't go to school. I was too excited. I spent the day preparing what I would say. I took care to wear my best clothes. I carefully combed and re-combed my pompadour until I felt it looked just right. The anticipation of reconnecting with Mary was dominating every second as I made the drive to McKenzie. I purposely got there early and anxiously waited for school to let out. Soon students began exiting the school a few at a time followed by larger groups. I watched intently hoping to catch first sight of Mary. The throngs of students gradually dissipated until there was only an occasional few. Still no sign of Mary. Puzzled and disappointed I finally left.

"Perhaps", I thought, *"She's sick and didn't attend school today."*

I drove back to my apartment planning to return to McKenzie the next day. Later that afternoon Harvey stopped by. When I recounted the day's events I thought I noticed the slightest glint in Harvey's eyes. With high hopes I returned to McKenzie the following day hoping to see Mary at our old meeting place. Once again I waited but she did not appear. After a few more days of extreme disappointment I came to the conclusion that Mary had deliberately done this to hurt me. I knew it was my own fault for hurting her feelings on that field trip. Now she was just trying to get even. I was filled with remorse thinking….

"I was going out with the prettiest girl in the neighborhood and all my friends were envious of me. Everything was great. Why did I screw it all up with my sarcasm?"

It appeared she was deliberately avoiding me so it would not do any good to keep returning to McKenzie. I decided to wait a couple of weeks before making another attempt to see her. That did not work either. I was having a hard time accepting that she could be so callous as to tease me with a letter indicating she wanted to renew our relationship. I routinely confided my despondency to Harvey which for some reason he did not seem to take seriously. Finally, one day, he burst out laughing at me and confessed that he had written the letter himself and signed Mary's name at the bottom. He thought it was a good joke. When I refused to believe him he asked me if I remembered seeing a postal stamp on the envelope. I could not recall whether or not there was a stamp. For a while I had trouble believing his story but eventually it made sense. I wondered what was wrong with me. How could a girl I thought was fond of me suddenly discard me without explanation and someone I thought was my friend play such a cruel joke without regard for my feelings. Harvey's idea of a joke was cruel and I remained disenchanted with him for several weeks. For a while I lost interest in most everything. School was boring, work was humdrum the excitement of driving new places in my car lost it's luster. I retreated to spending my time at home reading the books by Freud and his contemporaries.

Chapter 28

NEW DISCOVERIES

At work one evening Mr. Burger called me upstairs to his office. I didn't know what I might have done wrong but I was sure he was going to fire me. He did not fire me. He told me the head usher was leaving and asked me if I would be interested in the position with a ten cent raise to fifty-five cents an hour. Surprised and overjoyed, I quickly accepted. As head usher there would be a few new responsibilities. I would be responsible for accepting the admission tickets from the patrons. I would monitor the Men's and Lady's room to be sure they were always in proper condition. I would be in charge of the other ushers. Most importantly, after the box office closed Mr. Burger, the cashier and the candy counter girl went upstairs to his office to balance the night's receipts. I was responsible to collect the admission charge from any late comers and give them their ticket stubs. I had observed George, the previous head usher, pocket some of the late admissions for himself. This was fairly easy to do with the manager up in his office. Adult admission was seventy-five cents and while I turned in most of the late sales to Mr. Burger I often was able to put an extra dollar fifty in my pocket. This positive development improved my disposition and drew me out of the funk I was in. Going to work gave me something to look forward to.

At the Tower one evening an older lady and her husband entered the theater and approached me holding a thin, flat cardboard box. When I held out my hand to accept their admission tickets they looked puzzled and hesitated. Mr. Burger then appeared behind me informing me to allow them in without a ticket. I wondered what was going on but did as he told me. I watched as they walked through the foyer. Just before they entered the seating area the lady handed the box to Mr. Burger.

He took the box and went to his upstairs office. This was curious to me but who was I to question Mr. Burger. After the second feature had begun I was at my post at one of the aisles talking with Leonard when Mr. Burger came down from his office with that box the lady had given him. He opened it and asked us if we would like to sample a slice of pizza. It was the early "50s" and pizza was not yet a household name. We had never heard of something called pizza. We asked...

"What's pizza?"

He told us it was an Italian dish. Cautiously we took a small bite of the cheesy concoction. We smiled as our taste buds encountered the delightful combination of tomatoes, cheese and bread. We quickly devoured the remaining slices. It was absolutely delicious.

"What is this? Who made this?".... we asked.

"It's pizza!"

Mr. Burger told us he made a deal to offer the lady and her husband free admission whenever she brought him one of her home made pizzas. We wanted more and immediately began the quest to find a restaurant that offered pizza. They were few and far between but eventually we discovered "The White Spot" a restaurant that made pizza. It was on the outskirts of town so we would drive out there and each order our very own large pizza. A pseudo contest took place to see who could eat their entire pizza alone. It almost always ended in a tie.

Saturday matinees at the Tower were always challenging. The patrons were almost exclusively children and young teenagers. There was always a lot of "horsing around" and the occasional fight. The ushers were assigned to keep things under control. One of the regular attendees was a thin gawky looking young girl named Judy who looked to be about twelve or thirteen years old. We soon realized that there was always a commotion in close proximity to wherever she was seated. She was frequently changing seats and the laughter and commotion followed wherever she went. One Saturday while attempting to quiet things down I walked down the aisle to where Judy was seated to discover the boy she was sitting next to had his fly open and she was manipulating his penis.

"Hey" …. I shouted …."Stop that"

Judy just laughed and giggled as she continued stroking. I grabbed her by the arm and escorted her out of the theater. Apparently she was doing the same thing to other boys causing disruptions wherever she sat. I would learn shortly after she was slightly mentally retarded and the young teenage boys called her "Jack off Judy". At this point in my life I was still a virgin and although I could not allow this activity to continue I was envious of the boys who sat next to her.

There was another young girl who showed up every Saturday and always caused trouble. She was not anything like "Jack off Judy" but she liked to get into arguments with other kids and she would become quite loud at times. Several times I cautioned her to remain quiet or I would have to eject her from the theater. She was a feisty twelve year old girl with a sharp tongue, named Shirley. One Saturday afternoon when she refused to stay in her seat and be quiet I told her she had to leave. As I walked her to the exit she started to taunt me saying I was a jerk, adding she had a beautiful sister about my age but her sister wouldn't be caught dead with a dope like me. She went on saying her sister wouldn't go out with me even if I was the last man on earth. From then on, at every Saturday matinee she made it a point to remind me that her beautiful sister would never even look at me. Considering the condition of my teeth I had no doubt that she was right. About that time, still wondering if my bad teeth had something to do with losing Mary, I had made an appointment with the neighborhood dentist, Dr. Sklar, to have the large cavities filled and my front teeth cleaned of the greenish tartar.

Winter was drawing near and the nights were steadily growing colder. My mother was still working behind the counter at Gil's Hamburgers. Her paycheck was minimal. A counter girl at a fast food joint received very little in tips so money was scarce. She couldn't afford the price for a delivery of coal. The little heat we had came from the twenty-five cent bundles of scrap wood when she could afford them and the old tires I swiped from the gas station. The furnace would run out of fuel during the night so we piled on all the blankets we had. My mother continued her usual pattern of stopping at the bar every night after work. Just like the winter before I would often come home late and find the apartment close to freezing and Jerry alone in his crib. Jerry was not always alone. One weekend night I arrived home quite late to find a man standing in our apartment doorway. As I climbed the stairs I could see he was leaning forward through the doorway with his head bent down kissing my mother and saying goodbye. My mother was wearing only her panties and brassier. I was filled with shock and disgust. Immediately I screamed....

"You're nothing but a whore! You make me sick! I hate you!"

My mother remained silent as the man who apparently already got what he came for scurried down the stairs. I went to my room slammed the door thinking....

"Was there no limit to the depths she would sink."

The next day nothing more was said by either of us. I did not know if having been caught somehow was a relief to her but it wasn't long before I began awaking to find other strange men in the apartment. My mother would explain this by telling me that these men had no home to go to and needed a place to sleep for a night. By then I had become inured to her antics and gave up my protests.

Other than buying gas for my car and the cost of an occasional sundae or milkshake from George's Sweet Shop I continued depositing much of my weekly pay in the bank. I had enough money saved by now to afford paying for a delivery of coal but swiping old tires from the gas station was more preferable as I was determined to keep saving. Having money in the bank eased my feeling of insecurity. Still I was growing more concerned for Jerry being alone on cold nights and needed to find a solution to this problem. The old tires burned extremely hot and quickly sent the radiators singing but they also burned very fast and only provided heat for a few hours. I came up with the idea that if we had some coal to burn we could burn the tires during the time someone was awake and then pile in some coal just before we went to bed. The coal took a lot longer to burn and would last through the night. I made a deal with my mother to pay half the cost of a coal delivery if she paid the other half. She agreed and this solution worked fairly well for a time. I compensated for this crimp in my saving plans by driving my car less often and saving money on gasoline. I would hitchhike to and from school instead of driving and I would curtail driving my friends everywhere they wanted to go. My friends weren't thrilled with my new resolution and still wanted to go "cruising" hither and yon. Jack suggested we siphon gas from other people's cars so we could go out driving whenever we wanted. Leonard and Harvey agreed. They all seemed to know what siphoning meant and late one night I leaned how this was done. I knew it was wrong to steal gasoline and I was fearful of getting caught yet I went along with this idea. I was sure being the only one with a car was the main reason I had so many friends. Without the availability of my car I wasn't sure they would spend as much time with me. Siphoning gas became a regular routine. We were careful not to target the same cars each time. With this solution to my money problem we were back to our nightly excursions.

Getting up in the morning for school had always been a challenge for me even when my mother was around to wake me up. Running around with my friends till all hours of the night did not make waking up for school any easier. I frequently overslept and was late for school. My first class was American History. Due to my unusually good memory I had done well in earlier history classes as I could easily recall important dates and events. I did not care for the teaching style of Mrs. Brown, the teacher of this class. She seemed quite old and she seemed not to be excited about the subject she was teaching. She would slowly stroll around at the head of the classroom while giving a lecture on some important historical event. Her speech pattern was slow and deliberate with long pauses in the middle of a sentence. She would often wander to the windows staring out into space while relating a story. Then would come a long pause in her story. At times she seemed to be in a trance of some sort. I found this unbearable. I may have come late but I did come to class with the hope I might learn something. These pauses sometimes lasted for several minutes. The class sat waiting to hear the conclusion of the talk which sometimes simply did not come. Late night carousing the night before coupled with Mrs. Brown's frequent trances made me prone to falling asleep in class. More than once Mrs. Brown awoke from her trance and saw me nodding off. She was already irritated by my late arrivals to her class and apparently sleeping in the middle of one of her so called lectures failed to improve her opinion of me. Finally she warned me that one more late arrival would result in a failing grade. Not wanting to endanger my ability to graduate the following year, I vowed to get up on time for school every morning. This vow was soon broken and I had to develop a new plan. Rather than arriving late when I overslept, I would simply skip the entire day. After all Mrs. Brown's ultimatum was about being late, not about missing school entirely. My mother, understanding my problem, cooperated with this strategy and wrote the necessary notes explaining I was too sick to go to school. This led to a new problem. One afternoon I was called to the vice-principles office and told I was going to be suspended from school and thus have to repeat eleventh grade. Normally I would not have the gumption to defend myself and simply accept my fate but this threat meant I would not graduate on time. I was shocked out of my normal shyness and almost without thinking I responded to the Vice Principal's statement....

"Why?"

"You are missing too much school. You have already missed 20 days of school this semester."

"So what?"

"You cannot be getting passing grades with that many absences on your record."

"Have you even bothered to look at my grades?"

He then requested an assistant to retrieve my records. After reviewing my grades he turned to me and said....

"How you are maintaining a B average with all these absences is beyond me! Instead of suspending you right now I will give you another chance with this caveat. Mrs. Brown does not want you in her class so you will have to accept a failing grade from her and you must continue to maintain passing grades in all your other classes.. Should you miss one more day of school I will reinstate your suspension."

I thanked the vice principle and promised not to miss another day of school. I managed to get to school on time for the rest of the semester and was passed into the twelfth grade despite the failing grade from Mrs. Brown.

Spring arrived and one afternoon Mr. Burger assigned me the task of raking up the winter's debris that had accumulated on the grassy area adjacent to the west side of the Tower Theater. It was a rather large area so at one point I took a break from raking. As I stood leaning on the rake I noticed a young girl standing a short block away across Fullerton Ave. I remember she was wearing a lavender colored dress. From this short distance I could see she was quite attractive and had long very dark brown hair. I felt an immediate attraction to her and continued to watch. Disappointed as I watched her walk away I thought ....

"Now there's a girl with "class".

I wondered who she was and how I might possibly meet her but then I thought, what good would it do for me to meet her. She would not be interested in someone like me. It was obvious, in my mind, that a girl that beautiful would have her choice of handsome well to do boys so my chances were nil. Still awestruck by her beauty I continued to gaze at her until she walked out of sight wondering to myself …

"Would I ever see her again."

While still "down in the dumps" over the rejection from Mary Muller I started thinking about Jack's cousin Marilyn again. I began contemplating making the drive to Indianapolis to see her. Looking back now it was a silly idea but perhaps I was seeking some kind of acceptance. I mentioned this idea to Leonard who immediately agreed to accompany me. With this encouragement I began to formulate a specific plan. The main stumbling block was the cost of the gasoline necessary for the trip there and back. I had earned a week's paid vacation from the Tower Theater and thought that would be the ideal time for the trip. With my vacation pay and other funds I had available I had seventy dollars. The plan was set. The night before we were due to leave Leonard suggested we fill some 5 gallon cans with gasoline and put them in the trunk as insurance that we had enough gas for the trip. He knew of a large parking lot where O. H. Frisbee moving vans were parked. These trucks had huge gas tanks so we could easily siphon enough gas to fill a few 5 gallon cans. We retrieved a gas can that Leonard's father kept in his garage. We informed some other friends of our plan and with their help we came up with four 5 gallon cans. Late that night Leonard, Jumbo and I drove my 1939 Ford to the O. H. Frisbee lot and began siphoning to fill the cans with gasoline. While we were siphoning the gas a man approached. We thought we were caught however the man strolled by us without a word, apparently unconcerned with what we were doing. After we loaded the four gasoline filled cans into the trunk we could see there was room for one more can. Jumbo then announced he knew of another can sitting outside his neighbor's garage. We decided to go get it. We retrieved this last can and returned to the O.H. Frisbee parking lot. We parked, exited the car, can in hand, and started walking to the "lot". A lone figure appeared out of the darkness walking down the sidewalk towards us. As

264 Julian W. King

the figure drew near we could see it was a policeman. We stopped in our tracks afraid to move. The uniform began speaking.....

"Hi boys. What are we up to tonight?

"Er, Uh, nothing much."

"Where you going with that gas can?"

"Er, Uh, we ran out of gas and just walking to the gas station."

"There's no gas stations around here."

"Oh."

At that point two other officers appeared from behind us. One of them said....

"Okay boys we know what's goin' on here. Let's cut the bull! Open the trunk."

We opened the trunk revealing the four gas filled cans. One cop asked what we intended to do with all the gasoline. I told him of our plan to drive to Indianapolis. He laughed and said ....

"Are you nuts? Don't you realize you would be driving in a death trap? All it would take is for someone to crash into the back of your car and all that gasoline would explode."

"I didn't think of that." ....I meekly answered.

With that the three of us were taken to Schaeffer Station, finger printed and booked. We were told to empty our pockets whereupon the officer saw I had seventy dollars in cash. He laughed out loud saying ....

"What kind of screwball are you? Instead of using the seventy bucks in your pocket to buy gas you were going to risk your life driving around with a trunk full of full gas cans."

We spent the next three days and nights in separate cells only allowed out to be interrogated by detectives regarding numerous other crimes recently committed in the area. After accusing us of various specific larcenies, which we emphatically denied, we were threatened with jury trials and long jail time. The time I spent in jail seemed an eternity to me. I was convinced life as I knew it was over. Monday morning one of the detectives opened my cell door and told me to follow him. I went with him back to the interrogation room where Leonard and Jumbo were already seated at a table. I was told to take a seat next to them. On the other side of the table sat two more detectives. The stern looks on the faces of two detectives sent shivers of dread through my entire body. I was prepared for the worst. One detective asked if we were prepared to plead guilty to stealing gas from the "Frisbee" moving vans. Resigned to our fate we all nodded or spoke in agreement. A faint grin momentarily crossed the lead detective's face as he spoke …

"Mr. Frisbee has a deal for you boys."

We remained apprehensively silent as he continued….

"Mr. Frisbee will drop the charges against you on one condition."

We were three naive teenagers with no idea of what was coming but anxiously agreed to any conditions, no matter how drastic, just to get out of jail. A detective knocked on the door apparently as a signal. The door opened and a middle aged man in a business suit entered the room. The detective spoke….

"Boys! I want you to meet Mr. Frisbee."

We hung our heads. Mr. Frisbee smiled and said….

"Hello boys. Listen I will agree to drop all charges on one condition.

Full of dread and apprehension we fearfully waited for him to reveal whatever terrible condition he was about to impose on us. He continued....

"The three of you come to my house and have dinner with my wife and I next Thursday."

We were dumbfounded. It seemed almost impossible that we could get out of the mess we had gotten ourselves into by acceding to this simple request. We quickly agreed to his terms. Mr. Frisbee handed us a slip of paper with directions to his house and the time we were to arrive. He shook our hands and left. We were released from custody and left Schaeffer Station in semi-shock and disbelief of our good fortune.

I dreaded having to face my mother with what had happened but she already knew. Several of the cops from "Schaeffer" regularly stopped at Gil's Hamburgers, where my mother worked, for coffee so they knew my mother. They had told her of my problem. I was thoroughly ashamed to face either my mother or grandmother but all my mother said was....

"Did you learn anything?"

Apparently she had elected to do nothing to help get me out in hopes I would learn a valuable lesson. I did! I vowed never to do anything that would risk putting me back in jail. A vow I would pretty much keep for a long time. The three of us were elated to be free again and agreed to meet at my apartment on Thursday for the drive to Mr. Frisbee's house. Leonard arrived on Thursday afternoon and the two of us waited for Jumbo to arrive. He did not! We finally left for "Frisbee's" without him. Mr. Frisbee's house was located in an upscale neighborhood in northwest Detroit. It was a huge two story brick house encompassed by manicured hedges and carefully attended landscaping. We knocked on the door almost wishing no one would answer. Mr. Frisbee opened the door and smilingly invited us in. We entered cautiously still suspicious of his motive for wanting us there. I was so nervous and worried about what was going to happen next that I did not take particular note and cannot accurately describe in detail the inside of his house. Suffice it to say I had never been in a house so large and so opulently furnished. He introduced us to his wife who was the epitome of graciousness. We retreated to some sort of sitting room and were invited to sit down. After several minutes of small talk a maid appeared announcing that dinner was ready. The meal was served by the uniformed maid. So concerned with the next shoe to fall I ate but cannot even tell you what it was. More small talk ensued....

"Where do you boys live? Do you have jobs? How are you doing in school?"

We replied politely to all their questions without any embellishment hoping to get out of there unscathed. After dinner Mrs. Frisbee announced they had a movie to show us. We were escorted into a den where a large white screen had been set up. We took our seats as the movie began playing. It was a homemade movie of a voyage the Frisbees had made around South America. Back then only the very rich could make such a journey around South America. Household movie cameras were not yet able to record both motion and sound so Mr. Frisbee narrated as the scenes changed. We sat attentively still wondering what punishment was in store for us. Finally the movie came to an end and it appeared to be time to leave. Mrs. Frisbee bade us goodbye, wished us the best and left the room. Mr. Frisbee walked us to the door bidding us goodbye. He shook our hands gave us his business card and said....

"Thank you for coming boys. If there is anything I can ever do to help you boys with anything at all please do not hesitate to call me.

We thanked him for dinner and left. Outside we let out a huge sigh of relief. We could not believe our good fortune. That was it! He wanted us to have dinner with them and nothing more. We were stunned. Considering we had tried to steal all that gasoline from him how could he be so nice, so forgiving, so without malice.

"What a nice man!"…. I said to Leonard who totally agreed.

Up to that time we had not taken into account the effect our actions had on the people we were stealing from. The graciousness of Mr. and Mrs. Frisbee caused us to reflect on our recent activities.

Our days of siphoning gas were over.

Chapter 29

DARKNESS AND LIGHT

The season opened at the Detroit Race Track and Leonard, Harvey, Jack and I were anxious to try our luck once more. School was out for summer recess and our daytime hours were free. Not wanting to spend the money for parking fees we rode the bus to the DRC and climbed the fence to avoid paying the entrance fee. We were confident that pooling our money to bet on the horse that appeared the most animated and energetic would once again be successful. After all, we thought, it had worked once before. However after this strategy failed for several races we soon realized that winning our very first bet on our first trip to the track was simply dumb luck. We left the "track" broke that day. Some of my confederates became discouraged and swore off any more trips to the race track. I, however, was enthralled with the excitement generated by the running of the race itself. My heart thumped in my chest as I watched those large powerful, beautiful animals thunder around the dirt track leaving clouds of dust in their wake. I knew I would return. In preparation for future visits to the "track" I began researching the sport pages in the three major newspapers, The Detroit News, The Free Press and The Times. All of them had a handicapper's column with that day's selection of winners and comments on certain horses that would run that day. I kept track of how often each handicapper predicted a winner. I decided to look for a race where all three handicappers predicted the same winner and to bet only on that horse. This strategy got me back at the track again, often accompanied by Jack White. Before long I discovered the impact of betting odds. When all the handicappers picked the same winner the majority of wagers would be for that horse to win thus driving down the "odds". Many of the winners Jack and I bet on went off at 3 to 2 odds meaning if we bet $2.00 and our horse won we only got $3.00 back. Although we often bet on winners our small profit was offset by the occasional losers. The result of my strategy was sometimes we came out a little ahead, sometimes a little behind but we were not getting rich by any means. Still, the excitement of being at the track enticed me to return almost every day with or without Jack. Due to my frequent presence at the race track I was beginning to become familiar with many of the horses and which jockey had ridden on them in previous races. I also began studying "The Racing Form" to see more of the recent performances of certain horses I was interested in. I was learning how certain horses performed under different track conditions. Some ran better than others on muddy tracks. Some were fast starters and on six furlong races could jump to an early lead and hold it. These same horses would peter out and fade to the back of the pack on one mile or longer races. Often the jockey mounted on a horse impacted it's performance. After several weeks I became confident that I knew enough about certain horses to make some of my own predictions. I limited my betting to the races where I had some familiarity with a horses recent performances and was reasonably confident of it's chances to come in the money. I did not win every time but I enjoyed some success with this plan and by the end of most weeks I was coming out ahead. My overall weekly profits were exceeding the pay I was earning at the "Tower". I began contemplating the possibility of quitting my head usher job. I arrived early on a Saturday before the theater was open. While waiting outside my heart quickened when I looked across the street and saw that same pretty girl with the long dark brown hair walking by I watched in awe as again she walked out of sight. I thought

"No way will I ever meet her"

Mr. Burger arrived and I turned in my notice. I went without a job but that summer my winnings provided me with enough spending money to purchase gas for my car and the other things a teenage boy might need. I was even able to keep adding funds to my savings account which was of prime importance to my peace of mind.

The fall of 1952 arrived and with it came new problems. The "track" would soon be closing and I was without a job. I was dismayed with the thought of returning to school for my senior year. I looked forward to the prospect of graduating the following spring but school has become so boring for me that I could barely stand it. I wanted to quit but was too embarrassed to face my mother and grandmother. I continued my routine of attending classes, neglecting homework assignments, and getting by with good test scores. Leonard, in the meantime, had also quit his job at the "Tower" and had begun "setting pins" at the Ambassador Bowling Alley located on Schaeffer and Fenkell Rd. He informed me that they needed another pin setter. I went there with Leonard one afternoon and met Herb (the owner). Herb was an old paunchy guy with a balding head and a bulbous, pock marked nose. He interviewed me briefly and asked to look at my hands. (My hands were quite small for a man.)

"You think you can set "pins" with those little hands?"…. He asked.

"I guess so."

"The pay is fifteen cents a line. If you're interested show up tonight at 6:30 pm and we'll see how you do."

Although he reeked of alcohol and appeared to be an alcoholic, I would soon see he was totally in control of his senses. I arrived early that evening and Herb assigned me to an alley next to Leonard. Leonard demonstrated the process of picking up the fallen "pins", quickly shoving them into the openings on the "rack" then pushing down on the bar which set the pins upright on their designated spots. I watched Leonard as he picked up four pins" at a time (two in each hand) and thrust them into the "rack". When I tried to do the same I realized Herb was right! I found it extremely difficult to handle four at a time. I was however determined to keep this job somehow. The first Bowling league started at 6 pm but some bowlers came early to throw a few practice balls. During practice I was awkward at handling the "pins" and struggled to keep pace with the bowlers. As bad as I was during practice I was even worse when the actual league began. I was too slow and the bowlers were becoming aggravated waiting for me to reset the "pins. Several times Leonard jumped into my "pit" to help me and somehow I got through the ten frames that comprised a game. I struggled through the second league which began at 9 pm. My fingers were bruised and sore when it was over. I went up to the front counter with Leonard to collect my pay. A line was defined setting "pins" for one bowler bowling a complete game. We were paid fifteen cents per line so setting pins on one alley for the two leagues netted me a buck seventy. Herb paid us cash (under the table) so there were no deductions. Leonard was able to handle ten bowlers on two alleys so on a normal night he earned "three forty". I determined I was also going to be able to handle two alleys at a time. I was up to speed in just a few weeks. Often on a "League" night one of the pin setters would fail to show up leaving two lanes without a pinsetter. Herb assigned Leonard and I on either side of the two unmanned bowling lanes and had us set pins on our own assigned lanes then jump over and set the pins on the adjacent unmanned lane. Covering three lanes naturally slowed the process down and sometimes the bowlers had to wait a few extra seconds for the "rack" to come down and set up the pins. It was a difficult task and the bowlers complained but we liked the extra money we earned. I was earning double what I made at the "Tower" and feeling quite flush. I was able to keep adding to the savings account at Detroit Bank & Trust and still have a substantial amount of cash in my pocket.

With this improvement in my financial situation I loosened up a bit on my spending. George's Sweet Shop, directly across the street from the "Tower", was a favorite hangout for "teens" in the "Fiftys". Hamburgers, milkshakes, sundaes and soft drinks were their specialty. Previously I had not been anxious to spend money and was reluctant to join others at the Sweet Shop. With more money in my pocket I began frequenting the "Sweet Shop" with Leonard, Jack and Harley. Increased trips to the "Sweet

Shop" brought me in contact with wider circle of acquaintances and I was becoming more comfortable meeting strangers. This was a time when most teenagers were acutely aware of their appearance. Girls were girls and boys were boys and we dressed in a manner that emphasized our respective genders. Neither boys nor girls came to school wearing blue jeans. Girls came to school wearing cardigan sweaters with long skirts or dresses that ended below their knees. The boys mostly wore dress khakis and sweaters. We wanted to look good. A boy wouldn't think showing up for a date without wearing a suit and tie. We took pride in how we looked and dressed. Now that I was interacting with a larger circle of kids I became more conscious of how others, were dressed. I believed most other kids my age came from better homes with normal lives and I wanted to appear, at least, to look as though I was as good as they were. I was making good money at the bowling alley and felt that I could afford to splurge a little on some new clothes. Apparently Leonard was of a similar frame of mind. We began trolling through the downtown haberdasheries looking for the latest styles. We cruised through all the men's stores. Harry Suffrin's, Hughs & Hatcher, Hudson's to mention a few. I recall that almost every time we entered a store there was a salesman ready to pounce….

"What can I help you with today?"

"Nothin' we're just looking."

"Let me show you some of our newest inventory of suits."

"No thank you. We are only looking today."

"We have some nice"…. blah, blah, blah etc."

On and on it went at every store we entered. We wanted to be able to browse freely without pressure. We were relatively new at this and wanted to see what was available and not be pushed to buy something we weren't sure of by some obnoxious salesman. After touring almost every downtown men's store that day, we entered Hughes and Hatcher. For whatever reason we had thought Hughes and Hatcher was too upscale for our budget so we had avoided going in. Surprisingly no salesman immediately jumped out at us and we were able to walk around looking at things unbothered. Eventually an older gentleman approached and asked …

"How are you fellows today?"

"We're fine." …. We cautiously replied.

"Well I don't know what you're looking for but…."

At that pointed out where the various departments were and said….

"If you find something you like my name is Howard and I'll be over in the fitting department."

With that he left us on our own. We spent a good deal of time perusing the suits, ties and dress shirts never once pestered by Howard. We found some suits we liked but the price tag was more than we wanted to spend. Charcoal gray suits were the latest fad and we had found them in a few other stores with a slightly lower price. It was nearing closing time and we decided to wait till the next day to make up our minds. As we left Howard waved goodbye and thanked us for stopping. We were very impressed and appreciative of the treatment we received from him at that store. The following day we both came to the same conclusion. We were going back to Hughes and Hatcher and buy our suits from Howard. When we arrived the next day we found to our dismay Howard was not there. When another salesman offered to help us we told him we had already decided on our purchase but we wanted Howard to wait on us. He informed us that it was Howard's day off and he would not be back until the next day.

"We'll come back."

The next day we returned, found Howard there and each bought a new suit along with some dress shirts and ties. Howard thanked us graciously and we left feeling really good about ourselves and our new suits.

Shortly after my new found willingness to spend money more freely there was an unfortunate occurrence at the bowling alley that would reinstate my frugality. It was one of those nights when two of the pinsetters failed to show for work. Leonard and I each assumed the responsibility to cover an extra alley. The "league" started at 9:30 pm and many of the bowlers liked to have a few "drinks" while they bowled. Some were inebriated before they arrived. We were jumping back and forth between the three "pits" doing our best to keep up with the bowlers however it was a difficult task and sometimes a bowler had to wait a little longer than he thought necessary. As the night wore on we became a little tired and we slowed up a little. A few of the bowlers became impatient and were looking down the lanes, scowling and waving their arms in our direction. We were doing the best we could and ignored them for a while. As the bowlers grew more frustrated they began expressing their frustration by throwing the bowling balls extremely hard to get our attention. The slow pace angered one of them enough that he decided to throw his ball while I was still standing in the "pit". As I was pushing the pin setting rack down I looked up and saw a bowling ball halfway down the alley coming fast. I knew I would not have time to jump out of the way before the ball hit the pins so I held the rack down and let the ball hit the "rack". The ball hit the rack with a loud bang which brought Herb out from behind the counter. Herb talked to the bowlers and then walked down the alley to ask me what happened. I explained the situation. Herb's attempts to calm everything down worked for a short time but then another bowler pulled the same trick. When I saw another ball coming at me I jumped out of the way letting go of the rack too soon and the unset pins spilled out all over the alley. Pent up anger overtook common sense. I grabbed the bowling ball and threw it, with all the strength I could muster, back down the alley toward the bowlers who were busy laughing and not paying attention to the ball coming at them. It grazed the leg of one of the bowlers and the rest of them jumped out of the way. I watched as one of them charged down the "alley" with clenched fists. I pushed the rack down and held it there preventing him from getting to me. He was cussing loudly and screaming various threats at me when Herb ran down the "alley" and eventually calmed him down. Herb chastised me and cautioned against any more shenanigans. When I went to the front desk to collect my night's earnings Herb told me not to come back. I was through working at the Ambassador Lanes.

If I was to have money to spend I needed to find a job or I could withdraw some money from my savings account at the bank. That idea held little appeal for me. Aware of my joblessness my mother informed me there was an opening at "Gil's Hamburgers". I was reluctant at first not knowing anything about cooking "burgers" or "fries" but my mother said….

"It's not difficult to learn and they'll show you how to do everything."

I went for an interview with "Gil" himself. Gil was a middle aged man with a pleasant demeanor and the interview was brief and easy. I was to report for work the following day. Thus began my career as a "short order cook". As promised I was shown all the ins and outs of frying "burgers". Close attention was required as the grill was huge with as many as thirty hamburgers frying at one time. They taught me how to operate the "deep fryer" for "French fries", draw sodas from the fountain dispenser, use the commercial Bunn coffee maker and take customer's orders. It was a simple operation and I was at ease within a few days. Last of all I was shown how make out customer's bills, collect the money, ring it up on the "till" and make change. After working at "Gils" for a couple of weeks I began thinking about all the money I was putting in the cash register. I recalled hearing Lester joking about how bar tenders, at some of the many taverns he frequented, were "knocking down." When I asked what "knocking down" meant Lester explained that sometimes, when no one was looking, a bartender might not "ring up" the money paid by a customer but instead pocket it for themselves. This was accomplished when a customer would place the exact amount of money for their bill on the bar and leave. While at Gil's I took note that at very busy times, when customers left the exact change, other employees were not always ringing it immediately in the till. Instead they just placed the money and customer's bill on the back counter next to the cash register without ringing it up. Sometimes there would be several bills and cash sitting next to the register waiting to be rung in when things slowed down. I wondered if it was all being "rung in. I watched closely for a few days and had my suspicions but was unable to discern, for certain, that anyone was "knocking down". I considered this strategy for awhile before deciding to try it myself. I wasn't greedy. My first attempt involved pocketing only a small amount. One day during a lunch rush there were three or four tickets waiting to be rung in. I waited for the rush to end and when I thought no one was watching I rang up all but one ticket and put a quarter in my pocket. I waited apprehensively for someone to say something but it seemed no one had noticed. After a few days went by without any repercussions I gained enough confidence to attempt another "knock down". This time I pocketed fifty cents. Again I heard nothing and felt sure I had got away with it once more. I set both a goal and a limit of pocketing at least, but no more, than a dollar a week. Two girls came in for lunch one day. They seemed to be in high spirits laughing and giggling as they entered. They looked to be about my age and smiled at me as they placed their orders. I served their orders and presented them with their separate bills. They each placed the correct change on the counter and continued eating and giggling. It was busy and I placed their tickets along with the exact change on the back counter next to the till. When I thought no one was looking I rang up only one of the tickets slipping the money for the other ticket into my pocket. The two "gigglers" finished eating and left. Having performed this maneuver enough times before, I was no longer worried about being caught. The following morning my mother came home from her night shift at Gil's looking very concerned about something. As I prepared to go to work for my day shift she informed me I did not have to go to work that day. I had been "let go". She said Gil had called her into his office and told her I had been extremely rude to one of the customers. I could not believe what I was hearing. I was sure I had not been rude to anyone. There had not been an incident of any kind that could even remotely construed as rude. When pressed, my mother revealed that the problem involved Gil's daughter who had been in the restaurant with a girlfriend for lunch the day before. The knowing look on my mother's face let me know she knew something but wouldn't say. As I reflected on the events of the past few days I surmised that Gil's daughter had observed my thievery and reported to her dad. A little more reflection brought me to the conclusion that Gil had suspected me and sent his daughter to verify his suspicions. An enormous feeling of guilt swept into my consciousness as I realized not only was I out of a job but I had also put my mother's employment at risk by my foolish actions. My spirits sagged. I lost two jobs in a row with no one to blame but myself. I began to regret quitting my job at the "Tower".

The gray November skies brought colder weather and the need to keep our apartment heated. My mother was still strapped financially and a bin of coal remained unaffordable. I was unemployed and unwilling to spend money on coal or bundles of wood when I could swipe old tires from the tire store right next door. We made it through most of the winter burning the tires I cut up but then an unforeseen catastrophe occurred …. The cut up tires burned hot and fast causing the water contained in the "boiler" to turn to steam which then traveled up the pipes to the radiators. In no time at all we had heat but the problem was that the tires were consumed very quickly and when they were burned out the heat source was gone and the apartment would again grow cold requiring another trip to the basement to put more tires in the furnace. I came up with the idea that if I put a lot more cut up tires in the furnace they would last longer and I would not have to make as many trips to the basement. One night I filled the furnace to the brim forcing in as many chunks of tire as would fit inside. Soon I heard the water rapidly boiling. Upstairs I found the radiators singing loudly. I went to bed. During the night I awakened to a very loud bang. It sounded like it came from somewhere below. I listened for more bangs but when I heard no more I went back to sleep. The next morning I awoke to a cold apartment and much commotion outside. The furnace boiler had blown up and the basement was filled with water. Instead of all those many tire chunks taking longer to burn up they burned just as fast but with greatly intensified heat that the furnace system was not designed to withstand. The landlord was there along with personnel from the fire department and various city inspectors. They soon ascertained the old tires I had been burning emitted a heat too intense for the old furnace to accommodate, eventually giving way. We were told we had move out willingly or face eviction.

I don't know how my mother found a new place for us to move to but the following day my steadily reliable Uncle Red showed up with a U Haul trailer and helped us move the few things we owned to our new abode. It was very small building behind a large two story house. It looked like a garage because in actuality it had been a garage at one time. During the hard times of the "Great Depression" many home owners converted their garages to living quarters either to accommodate less fortunate family members or simply to raise money by renting it out. We were now living in a single car garage. It was in rather "run down" condition. A nine by twelve carpet had been laid down over the concrete floor. There were threadbare spots in the carpet allowing the concrete to show through. The nap on the arms of the sofa was worn bare. There was one tiny bedroom, a very small living room, a kitchen area with a narrow apartment size range and sink. There was no room for a table in what was called the kitchen as it was only four foot wide. There was barely enough room to squeeze by the kitchen sink to get the "bathroom" which had no bath tub or shower only a lonely toilet that barely fit in the tiny space provided for it. The only way I could clean myself was to stand by the kitchen sink and wash my body with a washcloth. Eventually I found this method inconvenient and inefficient. I began to find more and more reasons not to do it. I slept in the bed at night while my mother was at work and she slept in the bed during the day while I was at school. Not taking a regular bath produced an increase in body odor which apparently my mother became aware of. She suggested I might want to drive to Grandma's apartment and bathe once a week. I followed that regimen for a few weeks but then something went wrong with my car. It wouldn't start so if I wanted a bath I would have to walk to Grandma's. It was winter and trudging through the snow to Grandma's was a bleak prospect which I often avoided. Instead, I washed up at the kitchen sink sometimes going for weeks without a bath or shower. Recent events had me in a funk. My car wouldn't start, I had no income and I got myself fired from two jobs. It was my fault we were kicked out of our upstairs apartment. It seemed everything I did turned out wrong. For an extended period of time I did not much care about anything. I paid little attention to my appearance. My previous interest in dressing to look good around friends and acquaintances no longer mattered. My grades were suffering at "Cooley". I spent most of my spare time in our little garage house reading. When friends came by coaxing me out I found excuses not to go. I was of no use to anyone.

In my last semester of twelfth grade at Cooley one of the elective classes I chose was "Public Speaking" I thought it might help me with my shyness. I attended class regularly and listened intently to the teacher. One of the tasks was to write a speech and then deliver it aloud to the class. I cannot remember now, the details of the speech I wrote but I sat in dread of being called upon to deliver it. Each day one of my classmates was called to give their speech after which the teacher commented on it's merits. I prayed every day at class not to be called on but my time finally arrived. Speech in hand I stood in front of the class trying to begin but I could not stop shaking and nothing would come out of my mouth. After several minutes of not speaking the teacher told me to go back to my seat. After class the teacher called me aside and informed me she would give me another chance to deliver my speech but could not give me a passing grade if I did not recite it in front of the class. Although I knew I would get a failing grade discouraged and disappointed in myself I gave up attending the class.

That spring at school an announcement over the P.A. system informed students that the following day would be "College and Career Day". Seniors would be excused from regular classes and were to report to their home room for counseling on college applications or other future goals. No one in my family had attended college nor did I even know anyone who had gone to college. No one had suggested or discussed college with me so I had only a vague idea of what college was all about or what was involved. The library books I had been reading, by Freud and others, inspired a keen interest in psychiatry. I entertained the idea of attending college with the notion that I could one day become a psychiatrist. Thinking about this possibility lifted me from my "down in the dumps" mental state. I had something to look forward to. The next day I went to school and waited for my session with my school counselor who I was led to understand would offer advice on how to go about applying to whatever colleges were best suited to advance whatever goals one might want to pursue. My counselor, Mrs. Sullivan, was (in my young eyes) an older woman. She had solidly gray hair in pigtails wound tightly around her head. One student at a time was called to a table where they spent several minutes in consultation with Mrs. Sullivan. After waiting somewhat impatiently for more than two hours I heard my name called. My visit with Mrs. Sullivan was brief and to the point. Apparently she had already reviewed my school records. I sat down. She looked me straight in the eye cited my attendance record and announced I was wasting my time trying to get into any college. I meekly countered with the fact that I was maintaining a "B" average in spite of my poor attendance. She then reminded me of the History class I had failed. I attempted to explain that I had deliberately dropped out of that class but she interrupted me citing my failing grade in Public Speaking indicated I might not even graduate. This took me by surprise. I knew I had not been doing well but I thought I was at least getting passing grades in all other classes. Mrs. Sullivan seemed uninterested in anything I had to say and dismissed me. I left school that day totally dejected. My little bubble of hope had been burst. Through most of high school I had been totally bored. I found many of the teachers uninspiring and had done only the bare minimum hoping to get by and graduate. Now, according to Mrs. Sullivan that was in jeopardy. Now that I believed college was out of reach graduating lost it's importance.

Final exams were nearing and my chemistry class teacher called me aside to warn me I was about to fail her class. I had turned in no homework assignments. She asserted I was inattentive and often fell asleep in class. I needed the credit from her class in order to graduate and I couldn't bear the thought of having to repeat twelfth grade. I was sick of school and desperately wanted out. She said my only chance to pass her class was to get a passing score on the final exam. If I could pass the final she would pass me with a grade of "D". I showed up for the final exam along with several other students. I was the only one taking the exam for the purpose of avoiding a failing grade. All the other students were hoping to score high enough to have their grade raised to an "A" or "A+". Some of the answers were obvious but many of them required using common sense and reasoning. When finished I turned in my test and left without any idea of whether I passed or failed. The following day in chemistry class the teacher passed out the test results to all the other students but not to me. She asked me to wait until she had conferred with all the other students. I supposed she did not want to embarrass me in front of the others. This, I was sure was bad news. When everyone else had left it was my turn. She called me up to her desk looked at me quizzically and said….

"Julian! Why on earth didn't you show what you knew in class?"

"Huh?"

"Julian! You scored an "A" on the final exam. You scored much higher than all the other students even though many of them were already getting an "A" and were just here to raise their grade to an "A+". I can't even accuse you of copying from some other student when your test score is so much higher than all the other students taking this final. I cannot believe you had all this knowledge and did not demonstrate it in class. Based on this final exam I have decided to raise your grade two levels. You will see a "C" on your report card."

Greatly relieved I thanked her, knowing I had made several educated guesses at some questions and could not believe my luck. Was I just lucky or had I been absorbing the necessary facts without even knowing it. That was a good day for me. I could be sure to graduate and finally be free of this uninspiring tedium called school.

Graduation was just around the corner and most students were circulating autograph books to collect notes and comments from other students for the purpose of remembering them in the future. I had so little interest in being a part of Cooley High School that I had not bothered to obtain one of these "books". I was embarrassed when a few students offered to sign my book. I made the excuse of forgetting it at home. The next day I brought an Autograph Book to school but I was reluctant to ask anyone to sign it. Actually after three years at Cooley I had not made friends with any other students and felt awkward asking anyone to sign my book. Only after someone asked me to sign their book did I muster the courage to ask them to sign mine. I can hardly remember anything written in that book with one exception. A girl that sat next to me in biology class asked to sign my book. She wrote....

"To Julian, The best looking boy in Cooley High"

My face flushed as I read her comment. I thought why would she write such a thing? Did she think that was funny?

Was she being sarcastic? I did not let anyone see what she had written.

A trip to Washington DC was planned for the graduating class which of course required more money than my mother could afford. Although I was quite interested in seeing Washington DC. I was not willing to take the money from my bank account to pay for the trip. On graduation day I strode across the auditorium stage to receive my diploma while my mother, grandmother and to my surprise my real father looked on. Graduates were excitedly exchanging invitations to graduation parties their families were hosting. A few invitations came my way but without a party of my own I was unable to reciprocate and declined. After the ceremony was over I was anxious to celebrate my freedom. Like most thoughtless young people I spent as few minutes as possible receiving congratulations from my family before speeding home to change into everyday clothes and meet my "all important" friends. While I was there Harvey stopped by asking me to go golfing. I had only been golfing a few times at Palmer Park Golf Course and wasn't very good at it. I was not really anxious to go golfing but my persistent desire to be accepted by others took sway and I agreed. Neither of us were any good at the game. We either sliced or hooked our shots into the rough, the woods or just duffed the ball a few yards down the fairway. At Rouge Park Golf Course there was one unusual hole where the tee off was located at the bottom of a hill. The fairway began at the top of the hill several feet above the tee off. The ball had to be hit very high in the air in order to reach the fairway. I teed off first. I was delighted when I hit the ball high enough to barely make it to the top of the hill where it rolled out of view. Harvey was not so lucky. He miss hit the ball and it sailed to the right into the rough at the bottom of the hill. We both searched for his ball in the high rough for several minutes. I decided to climb up the hill to locate my own ball while Harvey kept searching. I found my ball which had landed approximately three yards beyond the crest of the hill. When I turned to yell back to

Harvey I saw him standing at the bottom of the hill about to swing a club at his golf ball. Then I heard him shout …

"Watch this King, right between the eyes"

With that he swung at the ball. I watched as the club hit the ball. I could see the ball coming fast and straight at my head. It was hit so hard and fast that I could not get out of the way. The ball hit me just below my left eye. It struck me with so much force that it drove me backwards off of my feet. I did not fall from loss of consciousness but rather from the force of the ball. Harvey came running up to see if I was okay claiming he was only joking and couldn't believe he had actually hit me. We left the golf course without finishing the round. We met up with Jack White later that evening. By then my left eye had turned various shades of purple, yellow and blue. Jack laughed when we told him about the earlier event at golf. Jack told us he knew of a graduation party that we could go to in the downtown area. That evening the three of us proceeded downtown. I began to have second thoughts when we found the address of the party was in an apartment building located in a deteriorating neighborhood. Jack bound up the stairs and knocked on a door while I followed apprehensively. A smiling young man opened the door. I was surprised to see he was "colored". Today we would refer to the young man standing there as African American or Black. He invited us in. The apartment was filled with dozens of young "colored" boys and girls all in a celebratory mood. Jack seemed to know some of the partiers and he and Harvey quickly blended in with the crowd. Unsure of myself, as usual, I held back responding only when someone else initiated a conversation. Most of the people that talked to me wanted to know how I got the "Black Eye". Soon I was surrounded by several colored girls, all giggling and flirtatious, asking me questions about my "black eye". I thought …

"What's going on? Why are these colored girls so interested in me?"

They were asking me questions about the other guy and how bad had I hurt him. Not understanding, nervous and embarrassed

I avoided answering. I quickly excused myself and sought out Jack and Harvey strongly suggesting that we get out of there. They laughed at first but after repeated insistence they reluctantly agreed and we left. Once outside they began pointing at me, laughing and explaining that they had spread the word that I was a prize fighter. They had those girls believing my black eye was a result of a boxing match I was in earlier that day. I did not see the humor of it at all.

It was the summer of 1953. I was eighteen years of age and just released from the confines of school. I had no job but decided I would not look for work that summer. Instead I would enjoy the summer using the money I had been diligently saving for the last few years. I began frequenting the Detroit Race Track when it opened for the season. I resumed daily reading of the newspaper's handicappers and the Daily Racing Form to refresh my knowledge of the jockeys, the racehorses and their trainers. The knowledge I gained from the frequent visits to the "track" the previous year served me well. I spent a lot of time at the track that summer betting on the horses. I was not always a winner but I came out ahead often enough that I seldom needed to withdraw funds from the bank.

My success at the track was the only bright spot in what I perceived to be my dreary life. Without a job to go to or school to attend I had virtually no regimen to follow. Left with a lot of time to think I began to ponder the situation I was in and the totality of my existence up to that point in time. It was not good. I had a real father who I only saw sporadically. He might come to visit me or take me fishing one day but then I might not see him again for a year or more. According to my mother he almost never paid the measly six dollars a month child support. Was I to believe he really cared about me? I held out hope for years that my Daddy would come back and find me but I never heard from him again. So much for loving your Daddy. My mother spent all her free time hanging out and drinking in bars with other men she picked up, sometimes bringing them home. I was living in a garage and sleeping on a couch. There was no way to shower or bathe. The mile long trip to Grandma's for a bath didn't seem worth the time anymore. There was no such thing as a regular dinnertime gathering. Comparing my situation to observations I made while visiting the homes of my friends depressed me. They lived in nice neighborhoods in regular houses or apartments with bathtubs and real bathrooms. They had fathers that held regular jobs and mothers that stayed home, kept house, and cooked regular meals. They had set meal times where they sat and ate together discussing the events of the day. I both envied and resented the normalcy that they seemed to enjoy. My resentment was deepening and I was becoming withdrawn. I tried avoiding my friends but they still kept coming by. *"Why?"*, I thought, did they bother.? I was just a nobody living in a garage with nothing to offer. Still they came.

One afternoon Jack and Harvey stopped by coaxing me out. Jack had just bought his first car and wanted me to take a ride in his 1945 Chrysler so I went. We cruised around the neighborhoods showing off his "new" car. While driving down Fullerton Ave. we passed two girls walking down the street. Harvey exclaimed …

"Hey! Stop I think I know one of those girls."

Jack backed up to where the girls were walking then paced the car's speed to match the girls progress as they continued walking down the street. Harvey leaned out the window and announced …

"Hi, Judy!"

I was sitting in the back seat feeling embarrassed. I avoided eye contact with the girls. Judy recognized Harvey and Jack (they had met each other the previous night at George's Sweet Shop). A short conversation began with Harvey asking where they were going and then offering to drive them there. Judy quickly agreed but the other girl was reluctant. Judy assured the other girl that she knew us and we were okay. After some additional prodding from Judy the second girl agreed and they both got into the back seat with me. Judy next the window and the second girl right next to me. A quick introduction revealed they're names were Judy Troshinski and Gail Starr. My shyness made me hesitant to look directly at them. I kept my head down for a while. When I finally turned to look at the girl sitting next to me my heart leaped. I could not believe what I was seeing. I was sitting next to that attractive girl I had seen in the lavender dress, while raking leaves at the "Tower". She had long dark brown hair and deep soft brown eyes. She was even more beautiful up close. Judy immediately began chattering on about something but sitting so close to this attractive girl I was too enthralled and nervous to take note. While driving to their friend's house Jack, always the outspoken, charming fellow never at a loss for words, began setting the stage for another meet up with these girls. Although Judy was extremely outgoing and very friendly she was a little overweight and her loquaciousness was a turn off. I knew Jack would not be interested in her so it seemed obvious to me he would set his sights on Gail. Jack's spiel was always so impressive I thought there was no point trying to compete. Surely I had no chance with her. I remained quiet. We dropped the girls off at their friends house with the understanding we would see them the next day at the "Sweet Shop". The following evening Jack, Harvey and I drove to the 'Sweet Shop". I was sure the girls would not be there but Jack believed they would show. As we passed through the entrance door I spotted the girls sitting in a booth. I felt another skip of the heart. We joined them in their booth and gave the waitress our orders. We sat talking while the jukebox played songs by the Four Aces, The Gaylords, Johnny Ray, the Four Freshmen and others. Jack spearheaded the conversation with an eye to future get-togethers while I sat silent. Several times during the next few weeks we would meet or run into Gail and Judy along with another girl, Judy Giles. Somewhere along the line the conversations evolved into a plan for a picnic out at Kent Lake. While I was anxious to be involved with any event that brought me in contact with Gail, I was deeply concerned about being seen in a bathing suit. Since moving into the "garage" I had been neglecting my personal care. I knew my physical appearance had been deteriorating but had not much cared. Upon close examination I became aware the lack of regular bathing had caused the pores on my knees and elbows to accumulate myriads of tiny blackheads. Blackish soil marks had built up below my ankles in the concave of my feet, and in the crevices of my ears, Thick black material had accumulated between my toes. I decided I either had to "fix" myself or just give up and decline to go on the picnic. There was something about this girl that drew me to her. Even though I thought I had little chance with her I felt the slightest sliver of hope the few times I had been near her. I did not want to pass up a chance to be close to this girl. I thought I must at least try to make myself presentable. I began making the trips to bathe at Grandma's several times to scrub my feet, knees and elbows. It took several attempts but I finally was able to clean the stains from my feet. My knees and elbows were much more difficult. The minute blackheads were embedded in my pores and had to be individually squeezed out. I would work on my knees until they became sore from the pinching. Then I started on my elbows until the pain was too much. After a few hours respite I would start again. I repeated this process several times every day but a few black dots remained on my knees. The hair in my armpits presented an even bigger problem. Not washing my underarms for so long had allowed a thick coating of film to accumulate on the individual hairs and no matter how much I scrubbed them it would not come off. Squeezing each individual hair one at a time between my thumbnail and the nail of one other finger and scraping the coating off was the only way I could rid myself of the disgusting result of neglecting my personal hygiene. Sometimes I became so disheartened with the difficulty of correcting the condition I had fallen into I almost gave up. Still I was driven by a need to see how things would play out between Jack White and Gail. Perhaps, if I was still around when she eventually saw through his usual "line", I might have a chance.

The day for the planned picnic arrived. Leonard joined us and we picked up the girls. Seven of us piled in my 1939 Ford (three in the front seat four in the back). Off we drove west on Grand River to Kensington Park where Kent Lake was located. I observed that the beach was quite full and was still conscious of a few of the deeply embedded black heads I hadn't been able to scrub off my knees. I suggested we avoid the crowds and have our picnic in the woods. The others agreed and we climbed up a grassy slope into the wooded area where we found an opening to lay out our beach blankets. After we unpacked and ate our picnic lunch we relaxed a little, exchanged stories and jokes. I watched carefully but saw no indication that Jack and Gail were hitting it off. In fact I was surprised that she seemed somewhat interested in talking to me, though I was sure she was only being friendly. All in all it was a great day. Everyone seemed to enjoy the event and on the drive home we all agreed we should do this again. On our next trip to Kent Lake, Leonard and his girlfriend, Helena, came separately in his 1940 coup. After a few trips to the "Lake" Leonard suggested going to Burroughs Farms. Leonard was working for Burroughs Corporation and one of the benefits of his job was free admission to "Burroughs Farms" a vast private park exclusively provided for Burroughs employees. It was located a little further west of Kent lake near the small village of Brighton Michigan. Alternating trips to Kent Lake and Burroughs Farms became a regular event for us that summer.

One summer night Harvey and I were out cruising around in my 1939 Ford. I was driving the car while Harvey was asleep on the passenger side. We were headed northwest on Grand River. The last thing I remember was passing the Riviera Theater on the corner of Joy Road and Grand River when I was suddenly jerked awake by a heavy thump. Instant reflexes told me to grab hold of the wheel and immediately swerve to the left. Within a split second there was a second hard thump. As I regained consciousness I saw that we were in the middle of the intersection at Livernois and Grand River. I pulled through the intersection and drove to the curb. Still dazed we got out of the car to examine the cause of the thumps. The right front wheel had a dent in the rim and the right rear wheel had an almost identical dent. I looked back and realized we had apparently struck the pedestrian "island". (Note: Some wide avenues in the city took so long to cross that people were unable to cross all the way before the traffic light changed. In those cases a concrete "island" was constructed in the middle of the crosswalk to provide a safe place for people to wait for the light to change again. Harvey and I walked back to look at the Livernois "island". The "island" was approximately five feet wide and ten feet long. A steel street light pole was located 6 inches from the edge of the "island's" curb. I began to tremble as the realization hit me. While asleep at the wheel I had stuck the "island" with both the front and back wheels without hitting the light pole located six inches away. Other than the two dented rims the car was not damaged. I shook my head in disbelief. Apparently while asleep I had traveled approximately ten city blocks without hitting anything until I was snapped awake by the wheels striking that island at Livernois. We proceeded home in silence, awestruck by the event and thankful to be alive.

As planned the next morning the "group" met up and made the trek to Kent Lake. We spent, what had become, a normal day in the woods with a lot of banter, jokes, and flirting. The big surprise came when we were leaving and found my car with two flat tires. The front and back tires on the passenger side were completely flat. I realized the dented rims from the previous night's accident had resulted in a slow leak. We inflated the two tires with a tire pump Leonard happened to have in his trunk and drove slowly back to Detroit stopping a few times to pump more air into the slowly leaking tires. After spending the next day visiting some local junkyards I found the right sized rims and replaced the damaged ones.

It was beginning to dawn on me that whenever we were on one of our summer picnics to Kent Lake or Burrough's Farms Gail was always in close proximity and friendly. I wanted desperately to believe she liked me but I still remained unsure of myself. Fearful of rejection I dared not to get my hopes up. On the we return from one of these picnics the grand surprise came without warning. We were about to drop Gail at her house. Harvey, Gail and I were seated in the back seat. Gail was about to leave the car when she suddenly turned my way and leaned over to kiss me for the first time. A feeling of lightness overcame me. I felt as though I was floating in air as I kissed her back. The kiss she gave me seemed passionate. I had only kissed a few girls before but never a kiss such as this. My confidence soared as I thought no girl had ever kissed me like this so she must truly have feelings for me. I watched as she walked down the gravel driveway to her house. I could barely contain the happiness coursing throughout by being. I could hardly wait to see her again.

Gail was a part time employee at "People's Outfitting" in downtown Detroit. I knew she rode the bus to and from work and the bus stop she used was just down the block from "Georges Sweet Shop". I began making it a point to be at the "Sweet Shop" around the time I thought Gail would be passing by on her way home. Perhaps, I thought, she might stop in and I would get to see her. She did stop in some days but not always. I positioned myself in a booth facing the large front windows so that I could observe the passers bye. Filled with excitement at the prospect of seeing her once more my heart pounded as I waited. On the days she came in the thrill took me to the highest heights. On days she did not appear the disappointment drove me to the deepest depths. Our relationship was progressing slowly. It was a time when most boys my age had a steady girlfriend. The custom was to offer a "Friendship Ring" to the girl they wanted as a "steady". She would accept and wear it if she wanted to go steady. My friend Harvey and others were telling me that Gail wanted me to ask her to go steady but I remembered Harvey's fake Mary Muller letter joke. In spite of my doubts I bought a "Friendship Ring" in case I ever summoned up the nerve to ask her. I had the ring with me at all times planning to ask Gail to wear it but something always held me back. I was afraid she might say no and her rejection was something I could not bear.

"What would I do if she said no?"

Every time I knew I was going to see her I practiced, in my mind, how I would ask her to go steady but each time lost my nerve. Over and over my friends asked ...

"Did you give her the ring?"

They all laughed at me when I told them.... No."

I carried the "ring" in my pocket for nearly three months before gathering the nerve to ask. I was trembling inside as I waited for her answer then elated when I heard her respond yes. Our connection grew stronger from that point on.

Gail invited me to dinner at her house so I could meet her parents, her brother and her sister. I was in for a couple big surprises that night. The first surprise was her little sister Shirley. It **was the very same** Shirley that harassed me at the "Tower" telling me about her beautiful sister that ...

"Would never have anything to do with me."

The second surprise was Italian spaghetti for dinner. Gail's mother was of French and Italian heritage. My mother was of Scotch and Irish descent. Italian cooking she knew nothing of. The only spaghetti I had eaten was out of a can or the awful stuff the served at school lunches. I hated it. I recalled throwing up the last time I had eaten spaghetti for lunch at Brady school. I began to sweat thinking ...

"What am I going to do? I can't offend her parents but I cannot stand the thought of eating spaghetti! How do to get out of this?"

As we sat down for dinner I began making comments about not being very hungry and suggested I would only take a small portion of spaghetti. Instead of passing the dish around the table for us to serve ourselves Mrs. Starr simply dished out the noodles and sauce herself. I looked down at my plate to find a mountain of noodles and a sea of spaghetti sauce. I thought ...

"My God! I will never survive this. This girl is so important to me that I cannot risk insulting her mother. I am going to have to get through this somehow."

294 Julian W. King

I slowly wrapped some sauce covered noodles around my fork and tentatively placed them in my mouth.

"Not so bad." ... I thought then as I took another fork full.

"Gee! this is good."

I discovered that real Italian spaghetti was in fact delicious. I finished the original "mountain" of spaghetti in short order then asked for a second helping. To this day "real" spaghetti remains one of my favorite meals.

Fall was upon us and my summer of indolence was over. It was time for me to find a job of some sort. When I began perusing the want ads in the local newspapers. I became acutely aware of the importance of a college education. My innate lack of self confidence coupled with limited education and no particular skills made the act of applying in person for a job a fearful task so I spent several days reading the "Help Wanted" advertisements without ever actually going or calling for an interview. Jack was looking for work as well and one day he told me there was a factory close by on Meyers Road that was hiring. He was going to apply there and asked if I wanted to go with him. We applied together and after a quick interview by the plant supervisor (Al Vercillino) we were both hired the same day. The factory was an aluminum extrusion plant. Large aluminum billets were heated to a high degree then forced through various dies to form 25 foot long strips of shaped aluminum. Next, while still hot and malleable, each end of the formed strips was clamped into the jaws of a stretching machine that pulled in opposite directions forcing the aluminum strip to straighten. After cooling long enough to retain their intended shape the strips were stacked in separated layers eight feet high onto a wheeled platform which was rolled into a huge oven where they underwent the heat treating process which gave the strips rigidity. Lastly the rigid aluminum strips were cut into specified various lengths that would eventually be used to form aluminum ladders, storm doors, windows and many other aluminum products. I was introduced to the cutting station where a quick instruction had me cutting the strips into a predetermined length. I would spend several days in one place pushing the button that cut the strips to size then stacking them up on a dolly that once filled would be rolled away and replaced by another empty one. It was boring work but I wasn't qualified for much else and the pay was a dollar and a quarter an hour enabling me to begin rebuilding my savings account which had declined over my summer of leisure.

Jack and I were assigned to the same shift so we would ride to work together every day. His car was not running at the time so I would pick him up for work each day. Before long this became a problem as Jack had often overslept and was not ready to leave when I got there. This resulted in our being late for work several times. Within the first month we were called to the office and warned about our tardiness. We promised Mr. Vercillino we would be on time from then on however a few days later Jack overslept again. I threatened to go without him but Jack begged me to wait for him. I did not want to lose my job but I didn't want to lose my friend either so I waited while he hurriedly dressed. We jumped in my car and sped off to work only to be a couple minutes late. When nothing was said to us we thought we got away with it. Jack was ready for the next few days but then once again I arrived to find him still asleep. Again I waited. Again we were a few minutes late. We went to our posts and began working hoping our late arrival had gone unnoticed. All went as normal until lunch time when the shop foreman, Bill, stopped by and gruffly said….

"Hey assholes, Vercillino wants you in his office."

Apprehensively we proceeded to Mr. Vercillino's office where he invited us to sit down. He smiled politely and said he had noticed that we were both very good workers, followed instructions well and got along well with supervision. We began to relax while he continued…

"I am going to do you boys a favor. I am going to give you the opportunity to find a job that you will like. This will be your last day at Winterseal so that you can go out and find some work that you enjoy. You see boys when you have some kind of work or a job you really like you can't wait to get to work each day. You are nice young men but this job is not for you. Find something you really want to do while you're still young. I wish you a great future."

We were dumbstruck. We had just been fired but somehow felt like Mr. Vercillino had done us a favor. Later in my life his words would have even greater meaning for me.

Once more I am out of work and still faced with little to offer to any prospective employer. The weather was turning colder and I stopped at my grandma's apartment a few weeks later to see if she needed the stoker filled or clinkers carried out. Apparently she had mentioned to Aunt Rea that I was looking for a job. Aunt Rea's son, Raymond, was part owner of "H.J. Mc Carty Wholesale Tool Distributors". I had met him a few times and called him Uncle Ray but knew little about him. Grandma informed me I should go to his place of business to apply as he might have a job for me. Having met Uncle Ray before I was less fearful of applying and anxious to find work. I went to "H. J. Mc Cartys " the following day. I was interviewed and hired not by Uncle Ray but his manager. I would be paid forty-five dollars for working forty five hours a week (eight hours Monday through Friday and five hours on Saturday). The business involved filling orders that came from hundreds of hardware stores. I would pull the specified tools from the shelves load them on a hand truck and bring them to the packaging station to be packed and then shipped out via UPS or some other trucking company. A few days after I started working there Raymond Heimstedt wandered into the stockroom waved to me then walked back to his office. I would have little interaction with him during my time working at H.J. MCs Cartys. After I had worked at "Mc Cartys for several months I was given a new responsibility. As I mentioned previously most of the large orders were shipped out by a trucking company but there were a few (maybe even a dozen or more) small hardware stores located in the sparsely settled lake areas outside of Pontiac that were delivered using

"Mc Carty's" own company truck. Another employee, Warren, made these deliveries once a month. When Warren left their employment I was told I could take over his deliveries if I could get a chauffeurs license. I applied, received the required license and was promoted to delivery driver. I looked forward to the days for these deliveries as the route took me out of the city and out by Orchard Lake, Union Lake, Pontiac Lake and many others. I was a city boy but driving by the lakes and vast open areas along the way brought back memories of my days on the farm.

Gail continued working at "Peoples" part time while also attending Immaculata High School and I continued working at Mc Cartys. We were very much in love and our conversations occasionally drifted to the topic of marriage. I was eighteen years old and Gail was at the tender age of sixteen. Life's experiences had advanced my maturity beyond that of an 18 year old. Unlike myself Gail seemed to have a stable, loving family life although her folks were of very modest means. Gail had started working when she was fifteen so she could pay for the tuition, books and uniforms required to attend Immaculata High School. I did not completely understand all the ramifications of married life. I only knew I wanted to get away from the life I was presently stuck in. I had to believe no matter what the future problems might be, a life with this girl I was in love with, had to be better. I cannot speak for Gail but I was deeply in love and wanted desperately to be with Gail and even more desperately to start a new life. By then Harvey, Jack and Leonard all had "steadys". According to them their relationship with their girlfriends had advanced considerably further than mine. They started boasted about their sexual exploits thinking, I believe, that I would join in and reveal similar intimate details. When that proved fruitless they began querying me specifically about what Gail and I were doing. They had trouble accepting the truth that I had no sexual contact with Gail. Each time I was with my friends they taunted and laughed at me saying I was a fool for not "putting the make" on Gail. Although I secretly had the most intense desire to "be" with her I strongly retorted that she wasn't that kind of girl and I had too much respect for her to attempt anything like that. I proudly announced we were waiting for marriage. That spring and summer they continued to make fun of my old fashioned ideas. The bond between us was growing stronger as time passed. The more I got to know her the deeper in love I fell. I was spending a lot of time at her house getting to know her mother and father. I liked them a lot they were very nice and accepting of me. On Sundays they often went on fishing trips to nearby lakes. Before long they began inviting me to go with them. Gail's Dad and I shared a common interest in fishing and we became friendly.

Gail's mother grew up in Saginaw, Michigan. She was one of ten children born to Raymond and Anna Bricault. Ray Bricault was well known locally as an artist. He was quite adept at painting beautiful scenes and portraits on canvas. The local newspaper ran an article about him featuring some of his oil paintings. In addition to his paintings he earned a few dollars painting signs for local businesses and playing drums in a local band. Several of the Bricault children still lived in Saginaw and every summer, usually on Labor Day weekend, they held a Bricault reunion at one of the area parks. It was quite a large event with all the Bricault families and friends gathered together. Each summer Gail and her parents drove to Saginaw to join the festivities. It was late summer 1953 and the date for the "reunion" was approaching. To my surprise, I think at Gail's urging, I was invited to go with them. I anxiously accepted and we made the hour and a half trip to Saginaw in her parent's car. The day before the planned reunion we arrived at her grandparent's house where I soon met the Bricault clan. Many of Gail's Aunts, Uncles and cousins were already there. I watched in awe as each one of relatives embraced Gail and her parents with great hugs and kisses. Reticent to meet new people I tried to stay in the background to avoid being noticed. However when they approached and lavished big hugs on me I quickly realized I was not to be an exception. The Bricault's open demonstration of affection for each other surprised and amazed me. My family was not given to such outward displays of feelings. Taken aback at first I soon began to feel welcome. The annual Bricault reunions became something I looked forward to.

We stayed the night at Gail's grandparent's home. The house had many small bedrooms. I was assigned to one with a twin bed while Gail slept in another room. Late that night I lay in bed thinking how lucky Gail was to have such a wonderful and normal family. It was well after midnight when I sensed someone in the room. It was Gail. She leaned over to give me a kiss. Delightfully surprised I said....

"What are you doing?"

"I wanted to kiss you goodnight."

"You can't be in here!"

"It's okay. they're all asleep."

"What if someone catches you in here? You've got to get out of here." It's to risky."

She kissed me a second time and left. Unable to get to sleep I spent most of that night thinking about what had just happened. Believing that someone could love me had always been difficult for me but considering the chance she had taken I had to believe her professions of love were, in fact, real. The reunion the following day was a blast. I met and was greeted with hugs by many more of the Bricault clan. Lots of Italian food, baseball, horseshoes, other games and family camaraderie made for a happy day. Running through my head, on the trip home, was the continuing thought…

"How fortunate Gail was to have such a large gregarious extended family."

The Labor Day holiday was over. Gail returned to classes at Immaculata High School while I returned to work at McCarty's. Our relationship grew steadily albeit slowly over the coming weeks and months. We spent many hours just talking, becoming familiar with each other's concerns, personal problems, and our future goals. Our discussions of marriage were becoming more serious. I wasn't sure if we were talking reality or fantasy but as our conversations progressed I became more and more sure this was the girl for me. She was not only attractive in outward appearance but her thoughts and goals were closely aligned with mine. We spent as much time with each other as circumstances allowed. Kissing and hugging was becoming more intense as the months passed. The passion I felt to "be" with her was nearly unbearable still I dared not touch her in an inappropriate way. I loved her so much I thought my life would be over if I did anything offensive that might cause her to lose respect for me. We were modestly "necking" in my car one night when Gail brought up the subject of religion. Gail was Catholic and although I had spent very little time in any particular church, I had been baptized Episcopalian. Gail's religion was important to her. Mine was not. The "Church" frowned on marriages of Catholics to non Catholics and she wanted to be married in the Catholic Church. I had attended Mass with Gail a few times. The Mass was in Latin and I was quite in the dark as to what most of it was about but nothing was going to get in the way of the life I hoped for with Gail. I agreed to go with her to see a priest at Epiphany Church. Father Scherzer was a very serious man. He listened intently as we related our concern about a future marriage in the church. When we were done he explained the "Churches concern regarding the stability of the marriage, any children that might come along and other reasons why the "Church" preferred both parties to be Catholic. He gave me some pamphlets and books to read before I made any decisions. I had already decided to convert before I began studying the materials the priest gave me. After a couple of weeks spent reading these religious books, short stories and poems I found that a lot of what I read made sense. When I returned the materials to Father Sherzer and informed him of my commitment to convert to Catholicism he told me I would have to take "instructions" in the faith, make a "Confession", and be "Confirmed" by the Bishop. I agreed and began the process. Once a week I would spend an hour with Father Scherzer discussing and being queried on that weeks study lesson. I was on my way to being a Catholic.

As I was growing older the infrequent contacts with my real father became even more infrequent. That was not a big concern for me as I had very little motivation to see him anyway. One afternoon I was sitting in a booth at "The Sweet Shop" when I was surprised to see him walk in and sit down next to me. After an awkward greeting he began the usual small talk. How was I, what have I been doing etc. I told him about my job at Mc Carty's and my new girlfriend Gail. He apologized for not coming around for a while explaining he had been busy with some problems at home. Eventually the conversation led to the one thing in which we shared an interest. He asked if I had I been fishing lately. When I told him I hadn't, he suggested we plan to go fishing together. At that time of my life, like most teenagers, I was enjoying my freedom and very much into spending time with my friends. Family, pretty much, was secondary, however I reluctantly agreed to the idea. We set a specific time to meet for the fishing trip the following Saturday. I thought no more about the fishing trip. The next Saturday forgetting the plans with my father I attended the prearranged session for "instructions" with Father Scherzer. Afterward I went to the "Sweet Shop to see if Gail or any of my friends were there. I saw Harvey in a booth and sat down across from him. He smiled and said....

"Your father was here looking for you."

"Oh my God! I forgot all about meeting him."

"He asked if I knew where you were and I told him you were at "instructions" to become a Catholic. He did not look happy."

Although I felt bad about standing my father up I shrugged it off thinking we could always go fishing another time. I justified my faux pas by reminding myself he had gone for years without contacting me. Later, at home, my mother informed me my father had been there looking for me. She knew I had stood him up and she told me that he said he was very disappointed to hear I was converting to Catholicism. I asked why he even cared what church I went to. She told me that my father hated the Catholic religion because his second wife (Anna) was a Catholic and, according to my mother, after being married to my father for several years Anna had fallen in love with someone else and recently divorced my father. My father and Anna were not married in a Catholic Church so the "Church" never recognized their marriage thus the Church permitted her to divorce my father and still be married again, in the "Church". Which she did. My father did not want the divorce. He believed Catholics were not allowed to divorce and felt the "Church" was being duplicitous by allowing Anna to marry again. I absorbed all this information but thought it didn't matter much to me. As far as I was concerned the relationship with my father was one of obligation rather than any deeply held feelings on my part. What I did not know was that I would never again see my father alive.

I continued with the series of "Instructions". At one of the lessons Father Scherzer announced that next week I would make my "Confession". I strongly hoped that I could just go to church unannounced one day and make an anonymous "Confession" to one of the other priests at Epiphany but it seemed that Father Scherzer wanted to hear my "Confession" himself. I could not summon the courage to refuse so I reluctantly went to Epiphany on the assigned day and took my seat in the "Confessional. I wanted to make a sincere confession but I was overwhelmed with embarrassment at the prospect of revealing all my misdeeds. I was physically shaking as I slowly began. I tried to avoid any specifics and generalized my infractions. I had told lies, taken the Lord's name in vain, disrespected my elders, and so forth. As I went on eventually the guilt I felt overcame my fear and it all came pouring out. I told of breaking my dog's leg in a fit of temper, stealing the car with Leonard, stealing gas, stealing the "late ticket sales at the Tower Theater and slowly, reluctantly I got to the "dirty things". I was still quivering as I revealed the encounters with Martha, spying on Jack's mother, repeated masturbation and the lustful thoughts I was having regarding the girl I was in love with. How, I thought, could I be forgiven for all these transgressions? Yet Father Sherzer (the priest) said I was! I left the confessional that day with a lighter heart vowing to avoid the re-occurrence of these sinful deeds.

For a short while I kept that vow.

I began attending Mass with Gail every Sunday. In the month of May 1954 I was "Confirmed" in the Catholic faith. In my mind wanting to be a good Catholic was often challenged by an intense desire to be liked and accepted by my friends. The temptations of youth were ever present. Late one summer night I was riding around town with Leonard in his car. We were "shooting the breeze" about nothing in particular. Busy talking and not paying particular attention I began to notice some familiar buildings. We were in downtown Detroit. We drove several blocks past J. L. Hudson's and then Leonard turned onto a dark unlit side street. Surprised at the surroundings I asked ….

"What are we doing here?"

"Let's see if we can find us some whores."

"Are you crazy? I don't want to find any whores."

"Maybe you don't but I do."

Despite my objections he continued driving slowly up and down various side streets without finding what he was after. Suddenly out of nowhere a "colored man" appeared rapping on the windshield and asking. ….

"What are you boys up to tonight?"

"Oh you know." ….. Leonard replied.

"You boys looking for some fun tonight?"

"Yeah.".... Said Leonard.

"I know what you boys want. Follow me."

With that he jumped in a car that was parked close by and took off. Leonard followed. The "colored man" led us up and down several blocks finally arriving in a parking lot adjoining what looked like a high rise apartment building. He got out of his car, walked over to us and said we should come with him into the "building". For some reason I was becoming suspicious. When the man began walking toward the "building" I quickly warned Leonard not to follow. He ignored my warning and got out of the car asking me to go with him. I pulled out my wallet, quickly jammed it into the coils under my seat and followed Leonard into the apartment building. The man was waiting for us next to the elevator. He had taken off his shirt and stood there in his undershirt with his suspenders hanging loosely at this side.

"Why did he take off his shirt?..... I thought ... "That makes no sense. Something's wrong"

He motioned us into the elevator. We got off on the seventh floor where he began his spiel....

"Boys, Some of these girls have been known to take advantage of their clients. Sometimes they've stolen a clients money and run off without providing the agreed service. My job is to protect youse boys so give me your wallets and money. I'll hold it for you. That way it'll be safe till your done with the girls."

I was sure something was wrong but afraid to confront this man directly I nudged Leonard hoping to get his attention. Ignoring my nudge, he took out his wallet and handed it to the man. Next the man held out his hand for my wallet. Extremely frightened by then I told him I did not carry a wallet. He then asked for my money. I told him I did not have any money. He laughed and said....

"How you gonna get any girls with no money? "

"I don't intend to "get" any of these girls. I'm just keeping my friend company. "

"Look boy I is just tryin" to protect you boys. You mus" have some money on you."

I repeated my denial.

"Come on boy. Why don't you empty your pockets and show me."

I turned my pockets inside out revealing they were empty. Seeming to accept I had no money he turned to Leonard and told him to go down the hall to a specified room where a "girl" was waiting for him. The man said he would meet us at the main floor elevator when Leonard was finished. He then got on the elevator and left. As Leonard started down the hall to the specified room I told him…

"No one will be there. You've been had."

The room Leonard was to go to was quite a distance down the hallway and around a corner. After a few minutes Leonard reappeared declaring disappointedly that he knocked several times but no one answered. We descended to the ground floor and found no one there. We returned to our car to find it had been broken into, The contents of the glove compartment were scattered all over the car floor. The back seat had been dislodged. The trunk was pried open and it's contents in disarray. Apparently while the "colored" man had our attention up on the seventh floor his partners had plenty of time to break into our car and search for any money we had hidden. Apprehensively I looked under the passenger side seat and was shocked to see my wallet still stuck in the coil springs where I had jammed it, with the money still inside. I thanked my lucky stars that they did not find it. We drove home in silence. We had both learned a little more about life that night only Leonard had paid a much bigger price for that lesson. There would come a time later in life when we could laugh at the events of that night.

During the fall and winter months of 1953 the time Gail and I could be together was limited. We were both working and Gail had to study for school, still we were growing closer. My feelings for her deepened with every day that passed. I wanted always to be near her, to see her, to touch her or just hear her voice over the phone. Together one night we agreed we would marry as soon as she graduated from high school. We both started saving in earnest for our marriage. Preoccupied with work and spending any free time I had with Gail I paid little attention to whatever was going on with my mother. Then one day she was taken from work to Mercy Hospital with some kind of stomach problem. She was there for three or four days. The "1939" Ford had finally gone to the junk yard so a bus ride was the only way I could get to the hospital. I was a resentful, selfish young man only concerned with my own life and (I am now ashamed to admit) I never took the trouble to visit her in the hospital. After she recovered and returned home I sheepishly apologized and asked what had happened. She told me she had peritonitis in her abdomen. A doctor I would get to know later treated her even though she could not pay him. If it wasn't for Doctor Montante she might have died.

A few months after the hospital incident we moved again. We were back on Grand River in, what had become normal for us, an old run down apartment building with worn out furnishings. There were two bedrooms so at least I had a bed to sleep in. Since I no longer had a car, being located on Grand River was convenient for catching a bus to work each day and I could easily walk to the "Sweet Shop" or to Gail's house. Returning late one night from a visit to Gail's house I encountered a strange phenomenon. I was about to climb the back stairs to our second floor apartment when I had a strange feeling that something was different. Looking up the stair case I observed what I can only describe as a cloudy or misty humanistic form hovering in mid air at the top of the stairs. I stopped to watch, attempting to discern what I was seeing. The form remained there several seconds wavering slightly. Then as I slowly ascended the stairs the ghostly form began fading and suddenly whisked off into the darkness as if by a strong wind. I stopped at the top of the stairs completely puzzled over what I had just seen. I had trouble sleeping that night. Curiously enough the following week my Aunt Rea passed away. At the time I did not see a connection with the two events.

There was a big surprise awaiting me when I returned from work one afternoon.

I was not accustomed to finding my mother at home in the afternoon. Normally she would be at work, or if not, she could be found at Burns Bar relaxing with a few beers. On this particular day I came in the apartment thinking no one was there. As I passed my mother's bedroom door I thought I heard a sound. I stopped to listen and heard....

"Oooh! Fuck me. Fuck me. Oooh! Fu-fu-fuuck me! Don't stop, come on fuuuck me more!

Prurient interest held me there for a few seconds before the realization that it was my mother's voice coming through the door stunned me back to reality. Never had I heard any woman express herself in such a vulgar manner. In those days even my male friends rarely used "Fuck" in their conversations. Totally disgusted I felt a pit in my stomach. I assumed she had picked up another bar bum and brought him home. I went to my room and slammed the door.

"What a slut"…. I thought.

A while later I heard noise in the kitchen and came out of my room to find a man standing at the stove. It was Lester. He was back again. Realizing it was him in the bedroom with my mother lessened my disgust somewhat, but not completely. I wondered how Les could just keep disappearing for months, sometimes a year or more, then show up one day and immediately resume life with us like he had never left, but that was my mother's problem. Lester's proclivity for booze had not subsided. He was drinking more than ever. I arrived home one evening to find Les there with Jerry in his arms. Les was drunk and staggering. He was laughing while tossing Jerry in the air and catching him. He continued laughing when I asked him to stop several times. I became nervous when he nearly missed catching Jerry and I called the police. I answered the door when the police arrived explaining why I called. They then spoke to Lester asking....

"Who's apartment is this?

"It's mine." .... Lester answered

"No it's not. It's my mother's" .... I retorted.

When Lester told the officer he was married to my mother and Jerry was his little boy I objected....

"He's drunk and he's endangering my baby brother."

"Listen sonny, this isn't your apartment and it's not your kid so shut up right now or you'll be the one going to jail"..... The officer said.

I gave up reluctantly but at least Les had stopped tossing Jerry in the air.

Chapter 30

Hard Lessons

It was early summer and the Detroit Race Track was open for the 1954 season. I had done well betting on the horses the previous year and was anxious to try it again. I reminded myself that we were saving money in earnest for our marriage and couldn't risk losing money on the horses. I had to be cautious. Leonard showed up at my apartment one morning with a book about gambling. The book described how you could earn a modest living betting on the "Horses". The theory the book proposed went like this….

"First select a "Handicapper" from one of the major newspapers and only bet on the horses that Handicapper" projects to win. Next decide how much you want to win each day. Assume you want to win $10.00 each day. If the odds on the horse you're betting on are 5 to 1, you bet $2.00. If that horse wins you're ahead $10.00 and you leave the 'track" right then. However if the horse loses you are behind $2.00 and on the next race you bet enough to win $12.00 (Your original goal of winning $10.00 plus the $2.00 you lost on the first race). Suppose the next horse you bet on is two to one. You would then have to bet $6.00 in order to win the necessary $12.00. If your horse loses the second race you have to consider the "odds" and bet enough to win $18.00. Under this system you keep adding all your previous losses to the goal of $10.00 and continue betting the necessary sum until you have a winner. If you followed the system correctly once the horse you bet on wins you win back all your previous losses plus the $10.00 and go home happy." The book also cautioned not to place a bet if the odds are even money and don't attempt to run this system more than once a day. Lastly one should have at least two thousand dollars before trying this system. Of course I did not have the suggested funds but the idea intrigued me. I decided I would check the three city newspapers each day to compare the success rate of all the handicappers. After two weeks I discovered that all three handicappers had at least one winner every day. Going through my mind was the thought that ten dollars a day was more than I earned working at McCarty's.

Dedicated to saving money for our marriage, I couldn't just quit my job until I knew this betting system worked. I could however put it to the test on weekends. I got off work at noon one Saturday and hopped on the bus headed for the "track" ready to give the system a try. I lost the first and second race but won the third race and was $10.00 ahead. I left the track excited at my good fortune. The following Saturday I returned to the track and was once again successful. My confidence was building. This was easy! On my third visit to the track I lost the first 4 races. The odds on the handicappers' pick for the fifth race were 3 to 1. A ten dollar win plus the $32.00 I had already bet and lost required me to bet $14.00 on the fifth race. I was becoming anxious. I had come to the track with $50.00 (a week's paycheck). If I didn't win the next race I was out of money. I went to the betting window and with great trepidation made the required bet. I thanked god when I won that race and left for home. That experience made me realize I could not do this with only fifty dollars. I began thinking about the three hundred dollars I had in the bank and the money Gail had saved too. I nervously explained, to Gail, what I had been doing and broached the idea of combining her savings with mine to pursue what I believed was a sure fire system. I cannot tell you with certainty whether she was as excited as I was but she did agree and $350 was added to the bankroll. After successfully working this system a few more weeks I was "riding high". A few times when Gail wasn't working she went to the "track" with me. I was so sure of this system that on one occasion we took a taxi cab to the "track". I simply added the cost of the cab fare to the amount I had to win that day. Being able to do this only once a week was frustrating but I was not ready to quit my job yet. Then a new idea occurred to me…

"Why not use this same system at the "Trotters"

Instead of a jockey mounted on a horse, a "trotter race" had the jockey sitting on a two wheeled carriage, called a Sulky, pulled by a horse. The "trotters" ran at Northville Downs (at night). I could work during the day and go to the trotters at night. Winning ten dollars six days a week would profit me sixty bucks every week. I had to try it. For a month or so it worked. I felt like I was on easy street. There were times when I had to wait several races for my win. Sometimes the odds were such that I had to place rather large bets but I always won by the end of the night. I gradually became accustomed to bigger and bigger bets sometimes finding myself at the one hundred dollar window. I remember a time or two when I was accosted by other, obviously desperate, men begging me to tell them the winner I had just bet on. They were sure I was in the "know" because they observed me placing big bets. Apparently a lot of people were watching me. On more than one occasion I found myself sitting next to and discussing the race with some of the owners of a horse. I was feeling like quite the "Big shot" when one day I went without a winner. Down over a hundred bucks I was scared. The next night the system called for a bet of over two hundred on the first race. I was shaking as I placed the bet and continued shaking as I watched the horses run. My horse won, thank God. Instead of being frightened by this close call I grew more confident in the system. After all I thought…

"Didn't the book say the handicappers rarely went three days without picking a winner."

I continued my nightly trips to the "trotters" experiencing more long winless stretches but eventually winning the ten dollars I was after. On another night once again I went without a winner. I was unfazed by this. It happened before and I got through it. The following day with each race I bet on and lost I was sinking deeper into the hole. I could hardly believe it when I went second day without a winner! I had lost over three hundred dollars. That night I stayed up late, pondering my situation....

"I still have almost three hundred dollars left. Should I quit now? How can I explain this to Gail? How did I ever get into this?"

Reluctantly I came to the conclusion to follow the system. But I didn't follow it exactly. The book said not to bet on any race where the odds were even money but every handicapper in all three newspapers picked the same horse for the third race the next day. The racing form revealed that this same horse had easily won every race he had been in that season. I decided this horse was my only chance. Saving my money for the third race I did not bet on the first two races. Observing that the handicapper I had been using did not have a winner the first two races helped to bolster my resolve to bet on the third race. The odds dropped to even money on the horse I was to bet on. Despite the system's warning about even money bets, sure this horse was a winner, I went to the '"window" anyway and bet all our remaining money. I won't bother the reader with a blow by blow description of the race. Suffice it to say he came in second. I was dead broke. Barely able to stand or even think I trudged in shock to the bus stop and made the ride home thinking all the way....

"How could God do this to me? God doesn't love me. He hates me!"

The thought of telling Gail what happened filled me with dread. I was sure that would be it for us that she would be done with me. Not only had I lost all my hard earned savings but hers as well. I felt worthless.

"How could I have been such a fool?".... I thought

There was no way out of it. I had to tell her and face the consequences. I first told my mother what I had done. I was surprised when, expecting to hear her chastise me, she simply posed the question I heard so many times before ...

" *Well Skippy* did you learn anything?"

Next I went to Gail's house. Afraid to face her parents I asked her outside to explain and apologize for losing all her money. I was prepared to hear her tell me to "get lost", we were through. Thank God that did not happen. I could see the disappointment in her eyes but still she wrapped her arms around me and consoled me. I wept in shame. I knew I couldn't possibly deserve such a wonderful girl. Gail's acceptance of the circumstances, I had put us in, was accompanied by my own self condemnation. I remained depressed and unable to think clearly for several days. As before, I eventually snapped out of it and started thinking ....

"How can I repair the damage I had done? No matter how long it takes I must somehow replace the money I lost."

Aware there was no way to recover the money all at once I dedicated myself to rebuilding our savings and found every possible way to conserve on spending. I hitchhiked to and from work to save bus fare. I packed my lunch instead of eating out. I began scouring newspapers and advertisements for coupons. Gail and I rarely went anywhere other than her place or mine. No more movies. No more milkshakes at the "Sweet Shop". On rare occasions when I found myself in a restaurant with friends I would either claim I wasn't hungry and not order or search the menu and choose the least expensive offering. It was slow going but at least I was saving.

I earned a few dollars working occasionally with Lester on Saturday afternoons. When Lester's furnace business did not "take off" right away he would go out in his pickup truck to drum up some business. He would cruise through high end neighborhoods looking for houses with chimneys in disrepair. He would then "pitch" the home owner on the so called danger these chimneys posed explaining he could fix it right now for a reasonable price. The vast majority of the time it was only an appearance problem with no real danger to the chimney but his sales pitch often convinced women. It seldom worked when husbands were home. When he got an okay to do the repair he used his ladder to get to the roof. My job was to get whatever tools or materials he might need and hand them up to him. Lester paid me 10% of his profit. He must have been a good salesman as he usually obtained a few jobs each day. The problem was that once he had a few paid jobs he wanted to stop at the nearest "bar" for a "drink" or two (or more). I soon learned to have him pay me immediately after each job as he often drank up all his earnings that same day.

At work one day my determination to rebuild my finances took a wrong turn. It was time for me to drive McCarty's delivery truck on the run out to the Pontiac area. I watched as a large order for Damman's Hardware was being packed. Most items were packed in big boxes but I noticed an electric saw was packed alone in a small package. I began thinking about the value of that saw and thought about swiping it.

"Maybe the hardware store would not check the order, maybe they would think it fell off the truck or maybe they would think McCarty's made a mistake filling the order. There was no way they could pin it on me. I could keep it a while and sell it later."

After the order was loaded onto the truck I drove a couple blocks, stopped, got out of the truck then took the package containing the saw and hid it in an alley. I made all the deliveries as usual and returned to McCarty's. Later that day after Mc Carty's closed I retrieved the package. When I got to work the next day there was a lot of activity in the office. Everyone was busy making phone calls, searching through files etc. There was some kind of "hubbub" occurring. Uncle Ray was in the storeroom talking heatedly with the man in the packaging section. Attempting to act normal I asked…

"What's going on?"

Ray appeared to be very upset as he related that Dammon's had reported a saw missing from their order. He asked if I knew anything about it. I played dumb, denying any knowledge of a missing saw. Ray stared at me for a moment then walked away. I wondered did he suspect me or was it just my guilty conscience. After the passing of a few days the subject of the missing saw subsided but my guilt did not ....

"I repaid the man who gave me a job when I needed it, by stealing from him."

Gail and my grandmother were the two most important people in my life. I was very proud to have such a beautiful girlfriend and I wanted my Grandma to meet her. We went to Grandma's apartment one evening for a visit. Grandma seemed to approve but looked tired that evening so we didn't stay long. A few weeks later my mother told me Grandma was in the hospital. Gail and I went to the hospital to see her. Uncle Red, Aunt Polly, Uncle Murray and my mother were all there. Grandma looked very pale and barely spoke. I stayed a while then left feeling deeply concerned. Two or three days later, at work, Uncle Ray called me to his office and told me I should leave now and go to my grandmother's apartment. When I arrived to Grandma's apartment my mother and her brothers were all crying. Grandma was lying in her bed quite still. She had just passed away. I stood in a corner of the room grief stricken, stunned, and sobbing. Uncle Murray came over put his arms around me and whispered words I will never forget. He said....

"Your grandmother spoke of you just before she died."

"What did she say. I asked sobbing.

Your grandmother said... "Skippy is going to be a great man someday."

I was glad to know she had thought of me in her final moments but too overwhelmed with grief to grasp the impact of those words. Later in life I would often recall her utterance and contemplate it's meaning. During the next few days time seemed to pass very slowly. I can't remember any specific happenings or people at the visitation or the funeral service. I was too dazed by my loss. I only remember the trip to Grand Lawn Cemetery.

Preferring to remember her alive I never returned to her grave site but a week has not passed since then that I have not remembered her with love, appreciation and her dying comment on my future.

A few days later my mother, her two brothers and their wives gathered at Grandma's apartment to decide what should be done with her possessions. I was invited as well but arrived at the apartment later, after I got off work. As I walked up the stairs to the apartment I thought I heard loud voices but they became quiet as I entered. Some sort of tension was in the air but I asked no questions. Uncle Murray approached me asking if there was anything of Grandmas that I wanted. I remembered the set of Encyclopedias and the set of Charles Dickens novels that I had often looked through as a young boy and asked for those. After I was there for maybe an hour everyone was preparing to leave. I was headed down the back stairs carrying the books when all hell broke loose. My mother was screaming at my Uncle Murray. Uncle Red was yelling too. I was unable to decipher the actual words being spoken but it was clear that my mother and Uncle Red were extremely angry with Uncle Murray. Later I asked what the commotion was about. My mother answered with a vague reference to money that was supposedly for me to attend college but she would not be specific. Whatever the problem was from that day forward my mother and Red were united against Uncle Murray. My mother never spoke to her brother, Murray, again. I found this situation distressing. How, I wondered, could this close knit family who gathered joyfully together on holidays and birthdays simply fall apart at a time when they needed each other more than ever? I loved my Uncle Murray. He was the uncle who gave me money for candy when I was little but I was powerless to affect my mother's position. I would see my Uncle Murray only once more, years later.

The year 1954 gave credence to the saying (things happen in threes). After my grandmother's death Gail became more important to me than ever. Without her I had no one I could turn to. Once more she sustained me in my grief. After she forgave my foolish losses at the track I had to believe she truly loved me. Our physical relationship continued to grow. We had been seeing each other for more than a year and although our kissing and hugging was becoming quite passionate I still had refrained from any attempt at overtly touching her sexually. The day, or should I say the night, finally came when my desire overcame my best intentions. We were sitting looking out the window of my apartment that evening watching the cars traveling up and down Grand River Avenue when for a reason I cannot explain I reached over and touched her on the area of her breast. I had not planned it. It just happened suddenly without any aforethought. When she did not immediately push my hand away I looked in her eyes for her reaction and saw tears forming in the corner of her eyes. Feeling guilty I withdrew my hand and waited for her to caution me but she said nothing. Soon thereafter she said she had to go. Little was said as I walked her home thinking maybe this was it! I was relieved when at her front door she did kiss me good night. I slept little that night alternately despairing over the thought of losing this wonderful girl but excited that at least she had not yet chastised me. Wondering if she would still want to see me I called her the next day half expecting the worst. When I asked if I could come by and pick her up in my car she responded yes.

"So far so good." …. I thought.

Things went on in as usual for the next few days and when nothing more was said about the "groping" incident my confidence increased. One night we drove out to Rouge Park and parked on a secluded street. We began with the usual "necking" but my passion soon moved into overdrive. My extreme desire to touch her again was countered by the fear of offending her. Then It came blurting awkwardly out of my mouth….

"Would it be okay to touch your breasts again?"

I regretted asking as soon as I said it but when she softly responded yes my regret turned to joy. Together we unbuttoned her blouse and unclasped her brassiere to expose her delicate breasts. I stared in awe at the most fascinating sight I had ever seen. She allowed me to touch them and eventually to kiss them. I could not recall anything in my entire life, up to then, that brought such joy, such sheer delight. How I loved this amazingly beautiful girl. How, I also thought, could I be so fortunate to have so wonderful a girl actually care for so undeserving a person as me. The physical aspect of our romance progressed rapidly after that night. We were just a hairbreadth away from actual intercourse. Hormones were raging through my body and my passion was excruciating. I began feeling sharp pain in my groin area. Leonard said I had the "nut ache" and sex was the only cure. Gail observed me wincing in pain one evening and asked what was wrong. With some hesitation and embarrassment I related Leonard's explanation. Gail did not respond. A few days later Gail told me the date for the Bricault reunion was coming soon. I half expected her to ask me to go with her but instead she said she was not going to go with her folks. I thought this strange but didn't ask why.

The day before her parents were leaving for Saginaw Gail proposed I come and stay overnight at her house. Surprised and delighted by this invitation I quickly accepted. We had been going together exclusively for well over a year without having sex. Secretly I hoped that this could be the "day" but dared not bring the matter up. That night at Gail's house my excitement was such that the exact details of how we fumbled our way into bed together are still a blur. What I do remember, and will treasure forever, is the absolute thrill of knowing the girl I loved more than life was laying in her bed waiting for me. We made love for the first time that night. I am unable to summon the words to describe the myriad explosions of passion and the ultimate joy of acceptance I felt that night. For most of my life I felt unsure that anyone could really care for me. She had given herself to me and finally I found a love I believed I could trust in.

With the final barrier crossed it became easier to cross it again.

With very little money a motel was out of the question so our trysts had to take place in the back seat of my car. We both knew how babies were made but I guess we did not think it was that easy. We were very young and careless. For my part I suppose I still had that youthful feeling of invincibility. I cannot tell you I thought about it at the time but Gail was raised Catholic and I was a recent convert to Catholicism. The "Church" forbade contraception and maybe that influenced our lack of taking any "precautions".

"I simply have to disengage prior to climax" ... I thought.

A valuable lesson awaited in the future.

It was early December when Gail came to me with a seriously concerned look on her face. When I asked what was wrong she told me she had missed her "time of the month" and had made an appointment to see Dr. Montante. There were many reasons to hope Gail was not pregnant. She was still in high school and would not be able to graduate in June. There was the extreme embarrassment associated with out of wedlock pregnancy in those days. How was I going to face her parents? With all this so new to me I wondered if I would have the courage to live up to these new, unknown responsibilities. I prayed for her not to be pregnant so that none of this would matter. I attempted to bargain with fate, making promises that I would never again engage in sex with Gail until we were married. I pleaded with God not to do this to us. My pleas went unheeded. Gail returned from her Doctors appointment with a worried look on her face that told all.

Somehow I had prepared myself for bad news. I had already been through many unwelcome changes and disappointments in my short life. Many of these changes gave me pause for a while. In various ways I would attempt a retreat from the world but eventually some kind of internal stubbornness would resurface and I would reluctantly rejoin the living. This however, was a different matter. This involved someone I loved. There was no time for me to wallow in my own disappointment. I had a wonderful young woman to be concerned with. She would have to face her parents, her friends at school. She was looking forward to graduation and now she would have to drop out of school. There was no place in society then, for a girl to continue her schooling while pregnant. Especially not in an all girl Catholic school like Immaculata. Knowing it was important for me to conceal my trepidations and present a good front I consoled the best and sweetest friend I ever had....

"Don't worry we will get through this. We were planning to marry next June anyway. We love each other."

We got through the initial shock and made a plan to confront our situation. First I would tell my mother Gail was pregnant, Gail would tell her folks and then we would go to father Sherzer for guidance. The time arrived when I was to accompany Gail to explain our situation to her parents. Anticipating the wrath of her father I went to her house trembling with fear and embarrassment. I was surprised at the absence of malice and relative calmness of her folks. Her mother looked disappointed but said little while her father simply asked my intentions. I explained we were definitely going to marry. He shook his head and simply said ....

"Well you two made your bed and now you're going to have to lie in it. This is your problem! Don't expect to bring her back home if it doesn't work out."

The realization that her folks were not going to stand in the way of our marriage was a great relief. I was still shaking when I left their house that day grateful but with apprehension of what the future held.

Embarrassment and fear of recrimination almost kept me from going to see Father Sherzer however I knew we had to be married in the "Church" so there was no alternative. Surprisingly there was no lecture forthcoming from the Priest. He just listened calmly while I explained our plight then when I finished he asked me what our plans were. After I told him we wanted to marry he suggested I return with Gail so he could speak to both of us. When we returned a few days later Father Sherzer questioned us regarding the seriousness of our commitment. He seemed most concerned that we were totally committed to raising our children in the Catholic faith. We assured him that was our intention and received his blessing for our marriage. He further advised us to refrain from committing the sin of fornication so we would be free of sin when we entered the sacrament of marriage.

Arrangements were made for the wedding to take place in the middle of January. For a few weeks we remained chaste but with so much planning to do we often found ourselves together and eventually the passion we felt for each other became unbearable.

We were married at Epiphany Church by Father Flanagan on Saturday January 15th, 1955. It was a small wedding. Nothing fancy. There was no money for a wedding gown or a tuxedo. Gail wore a lady's suit she already owned and I wore one of the suits I had bought that day with Leonard at Hughes and Hatcher. Neither Gail's house nor my apartment was big enough to host all the families and friends for any kind of reception so it was decided to host Gail's side of the family that afternoon at her parent's house and my side of the family would come to my apartment that evening. Around midnight we made our goodbyes and departed. We drove out Grand River Ave. to Telegraph Road and found the City Motel. We rented a room for four dollars where we spent our one night honeymoon. We had very little money and could not afford to miss work the following Monday. My Uncle Red 's house was nearby so on Sunday and we drove there and spent a few hours visiting with him and Aunt Polly after which we returned to my mother's apartment to begin our life together.

We had a myriad of problems ahead of us. Due to losing all our money on my racetrack folly we were starting out with a total of thirty-eight dollars. We had a baby coming and no insurance to cover the hospital and doctor bills. We needed a place to live. Thankfully the mother I had spent most of my teenage years resenting now offered to let us with stay in her apartment. We agreed to pay ten dollars a week to help with groceries and bills. Gail would continue to work at "Peoples" as long as she was able and I was still employed at "McCarty's". With both of us working we could barely get by but when the time came that Gail couldn't work any longer we would be in financial difficulty. I decided to request a raise in pay at "Mc Cartys. I explained that now with a wife and a baby on the way I needed to make more money. I foolishly added that if I could not get a raise I would have to begin looking for another job. My request was turned down without explanation. Surprised and disappointed at first, I gave some thought to the reasons my request was denied…

"Was my threat of seeking employment elsewhere offensive or was it more likely I was a suspect in the case of the saw that went missing."

Either way I was probably responsible for the situation I found myself in. Later that week I spoke with Leonard. When I told him I was going to start looking for another job he informed me that "Winterseal" was hiring. I said….

"You know I was fired from there. They won't take me back."

"I have a hunch they will rehire you if I put in a good word for you."

True to his word Leonard recommended me. I went for an interview a few days later. I explained how I had learned a lesson from my past failure. I was thrilled when they hired me. I gave notice I was leaving "Mc Cartys" and started at "Winterseal the following week. "Winterseal" paid $ I.75 an hour which meant I would earn $70.00 a week. Twenty-five dollars a week more than I earned at "Mc Cartys". Also in addition to the hourly pay a bonus plan had been enacted since I last worked there. All of the finished "extrusions" produced each week were weighed. There was a certain weight quota the factory was expected to attain. When the amount of production exceeded the set quota a bonus was paid to the employees. The amount of the bonus was based on how much the quota was exceeded. I immediately noticed an enthusiastic attitude on the part of most of the employees. They seemed to enjoy their jobs and wasted little time accomplishing the tasks at hand. I received a pleasant surprise in my first paycheck. The bonus that week was $55.00 on top of my regular pay of $70.00. I was overjoyed. I earned nearly three times as much as Mc Cartys paid me. It was clear then why the employees went so enthusiastically about their jobs. There was however one drawback to working at "Winterseal". Bill, the shop foreman was extremely aggressive, rude and without respect for the employees. If he wanted something done he loudly barked commands usually accompanied with vulgar epitaphs. He would refer to us as…. "Stupid assholes, lazy bastards, worthless fuckers" or worse. We called him "Wild Bill". I did not like being treated this way but decided to restrain my objections as I desperately needed this job. I vowed instead to be a model employee. I applied myself diligently to whatever task I was assigned.

I was not going to waste the advantage this big increase in earnings provided by spending it all. I decided instead to, at the very least, save all the bonus portion of each paycheck and more when possible. Gail and I would continue residing at my mother's apartment awhile longer allowing us to conserve expenses. I rode to work with Leonard for several weeks.

In early summer Gail quit her job at "Peoples" due to her advanced pregnancy. Now that she was spending more time at home Lester asked her to act as secretary for his fledgling furnace business. He had a partner he called "Lucky" working with him. He was running an ad in the newspaper and he needed someone to answer phone calls. He paid her a small amount for each "lead" she provided. This was a good arrangement for both of them but Lester was drinking more heavily and his

324 *Julian W. King*

work ethic was suffering causing Gail to take angry calls from Lester's customers. One morning Gail noticed Lester frantically searching through the cupboards. Then she saw him drinking from a bottle of imitation vanilla. Lester and "Lucky" often stopped for a "drink" at nearby bars and never got to work that day. Lester's drinking was causing friction between him and my mother. I returned from work one afternoon to find Lester on the couch with his pants below his knees and a strange woman underneath him. The woman jumped up shrieking, hurriedly dressed and ran out the door. Lester just looked at me and laughed. He staggered drunkenly after her laughing all the way. I had always thought Les just liked to drink a lot but I was realizing Lester really was a true alcoholic. A few days later the police arrived at the door and arrested Lester. Apparently Lester and Lucky were taking deposits from customers, then, instead of showing up to do the job they went to the "bar' and drank up the money. Unfortunately for them one of the customers they defrauded was the wife of a police detective and he made it his business to catch them. Lester and not so "Lucky" went to jail.

After working at Winterseal a couple of months I noticed the assistant plant foreman (Lynn) often stopped by to observe me working. I began wondering if I was not performing up to expectations. Concerned that I might be fired, I concentrated on doing everything correctly. This job provided a tremendous improvement in our finances. I knew, without insurance, we had some big expenses confronting us when the baby was born and I could not afford to lose my job. A few days later I found out why I was being watched. The plant production was exceeding the capacity of the heat treat oven. The "ovens ran constantly during the day and afternoon shifts but it wasn't enough. The "ovens" would have to run 24 hours a day in order to handle the amount of extrusions but they could not be run without any employees to monitor them. They needed two employees to insert and remove the loads of aluminum from the heat treat ovens every four hours. I was asked to work on a new midnight shift along with one other employee. His name was Ed. The two of us would be on our own without any supervision. Apparently I had been watched to evaluate my work habits. When we were not moving loads of aluminum in or out of the "oven" we were expected to keep busy sawing long strips of aluminum into specified lengths. Each night we were given a quota to meet. We soon discovered that just one of us could easily meet the quota set for both of us so we would take turns running the saw while the other took a nap in the back. It was a great arrangement.

Changing to the midnight shift posed a problem. Leonard continued to work days so I no longer had a ride to work. Aware of my plight, that night my mother mentioned my problem to some of her "bar" friends. One of them had a 1936 Ford for sale. He agreed to sell it to me for $60.00. Although the automobile was 19 years old it was in good condition. I completed the purchase and my transportation to and from work was secured. I continued working the midnight shift at Winterseal. We lived with my mother a few more months in order to save the money we would need to pay for the new baby. My mother advised that I should purchase some life insurance so Gail and the baby would be protected should something happen to me. I bought a $20,000.00 whole life policy from Metropolitan Life and began paying an $8.00 a month premium.

I liked the money I was earning at Winterseal but I didn't feel comfortable with the way "Wild Bill" treated the employees. I also had the feeling that I was smarter than most of the workers there and began thinking that I did not want to spend my life working in a factory. I saw an ad in the newspaper spouting the benefits of a career as a radio and television repairman. I answered the ad and a representative from Radio Electronics Television School appeared at my door. He convinced me this would be a great career for me. After completing the two year course I would be a qualified technician in this rapidly developing industry. I paid the $375.00 fee and signed up. My classes at "RETS' were held from 6pm - 10 pm so they did not interfere with my midnight shift at "Winterseal". Coincidentally the John C. Lodge expressway opened about the same time. This enabled me to drive nonstop to downtown Detroit where RETS was located. Amazingly the drive downtown that previously took nearly an hour could now be made in less than 15 minutes. I began the training with enthusiasm. I always liked learning new things and had no difficulty comprehending the textbook explanations and theory of electronic principles. My enthusiasm dampened when it came to actually working on the physical insides of radios or television sets. I discovered I did not enjoy soldering together tiny little wires, resistors, capacitors etc. I would continue attending the school for more than a year but eventually I decided this field was not for me and dropped out. While returning home from RETS one night I was driving too fast as I turned a corner. The car skidded and rammed into the curb. Afterward I discovered the car would not turn left correctly. The repair shop diagnosed it as a bent tie rod. When I attempted to turn left the turning radius was so wide that I could not make it around a corner and still remain on the pavement. The cost of repair was more than I had paid for the car. I began thinking I should buy another car but before I could accomplish that Gail's "time" came.

Mt Carmel Hospital was located at Outer Drive and Schaeffer. We got into the car and began the drive. Normally I would drive north on Schaeffer and simply turn left into the hospital parking area. Then I remembered my car could not turn left. Not able to follow the usual route I continued a mile west of Schaeffer to Greenfield then turned right, continued past Outer Drive to Mc Nichols, turned right again to Schaeffer where I made another right turn. At this point I was going south on Schaeffer allowing me to make a right turn into the hospital parking lot. This roundabout circle of right turns got us there in time without having to turn left. Our son was born on August 8th, 1955 at Mt. Carmel Mercy Hospital. Gary was a healthy baby and everything seemed to be going our way. We had saved enough to pay Dr. Montante, the seven hundred dollar hospital bill and still have a few dollars left in the bank.

Chapter 31

MOVING UP UP AND....

We decided it was time to move into our own apartment. We rented an upstairs flat on Stoeple close to Lawton Avenue for sixty dollars a month. The owners, the Isopi's, resided downstairs. They seemed like nice people and even allowed us to use the wringer washer they had in their basement. This was a great help as there were many cloth diapers to wash several times a week. Other than driving a car that could not turn left, life was running smoothly. Due to the fantastic bonus plan at work we had saved a lot of money and decided we needed a better car. Up to that point in life I had been driving very old cars. There was always something going wrong with them and I spent so much of the last few years with cars that did not run properly, wouldn't start in cold weather or just broke down when you least expected it. I was tired of it all. I wanted a car that I could depend on. In late September I bought a brand new 1955 Chevrolet Model 210 for $1750.00. Driving it off the lot I felt like I was in heaven. No longer would I have to push my car to get it started. No longer would I have to frequent the junkyards for used tires, batteries and auto parts. No longer would I have to get my hands dirty or bruise my knuckles working under the hood of a rundown "junker". I had a new car. I had money in the bank. I was somebody!

With our improving finances we began thinking about buying a house but we didn't think we had enough for a down payment. Gail posed the idea that we could accumulate our savings faster if she got a job. I was working midnight shift and got out of work at seven a.m. If she could find a job, working days, I could be home with the baby during the day. With two paychecks we could quickly save enough for a down payment. Within a few weeks Gail obtained employment as a secretary at Vinco's Corporation and we were fast approaching our goal of owning our own home. Everything was flowing our way for several months until March 1956 when we discovered Gail was pregnant again. This came as a shock and I could not believe Gail could be pregnant again so soon. I was dismayed at first but quickly self rationalized that I always wanted a nice family with two or three kids so what if it came quicker than expected. Gail continued to work at Vinco's and I resigned myself to remaining at Winterseal although the verbal abuse from Wild Bill was weighing heavily on my mind. Several other Winterseal employees were grumbling about the bad treatment and someone arranged for meeting with a union representative. I attended the meeting and listened to the union's presentation. They began with promising that the union would put a stop "Wild Bill's" verbal abuse. If we were not treated with respect we could go to the union for redress. They continued with more promises that all sounded good but when they began deriding the entire management structure I recalled that Al Vercillino had treated me well and had given me a second chance. They even spoke his name claiming he sits in his office smoking big cigars and laughing at us peons. I was unimpressed with the obvious demagoguery and distrusted any organization employing such tactics. I quickly departed and did not attend any more union meetings.

Terri our second child, a girl, was born on November 8, 1956. Vinco's allowed Gail to take a maternity leave for two months. She returned to work at Vinco's a month after Terri was born. Terri was a beautiful child but she cried a lot more than Gary had. We got along with the Isopis for several months but then something went wrong. Their attitude towards us changed conspicuously. I was never sure what irritated them. Perhaps they were unhappy with our increasing family or the baby's crying. I only know they had withdrawn from, what had been, up to then, friendly conversations whenever we encountered each other. Then one evening I went to the basement to find Gail bent over a wash tub. I could not believe what I saw. She was scrubbing dirty cloth diapers on an old fashioned scrub board. With two babies, now, there were several diapers to wash every day. (Disposable diapers were not available in stores until the 1960's.)

"Gail! Why are you doing that? Why aren't you using the washing machine?"

"Mrs. Isopi said she doesn't want me to use it anymore."

Watching the girl I loved scrubbing diapers by hand confirmed my determination to own our own house and move out of this flat as soon as possible. With two incomes and the bonuses from Winterseal we would soon be rid of the inconsiderate Isopis.

While leaving work one Friday Wild Bill called me aside to say....

"Listen King, Were shutting down the midnight shift so you are working days starting Monday. 7a.m. sharp!"

"Hey Bill I can't work days. My wife works days and I have to be home with my kids while she's at work."

"Tough shit asshole! That's your problem not mine. You be here 7a.m. sharp Monday."

Gail and I discussed and thought about our problem over that weekend. I decided to quit my job at Winterseal. As I would discover over the years I spent with Gail she supported me (and has always supported me), right or wrong, in big decisions. It was a difficult decision but in the end I had enough of Wild Bill's foul mouth and disrespect for the workers. I did not show for the Monday day shift. I spent the next week searching the newspapers for job openings. When I went to pick up my final paycheck on Friday Wild Bill was waiting for me.

"What happened to you King?"

"I quit."

"You could have given me a notice!"

"I gave you just as much notice as you gave me about changing shifts."

"Good luck shithead."

"Same to you asshole."

Always unsure of myself I rarely took an aggressive stance in my defense but occasionally when pushed to the limit I would explode.

Thus ended my factory career. I looked ahead to finding a job where I could use my brain rather than my brawn. This turned out to be much more difficult than I imagined. There were several help wanted ads in the "papers" but I did not want to return to factory life and most of the non-factory positions available required some experience. During the next few months I spent a lot of time at home searching the Want Ads for a job I thought I was suited for. I went to a few interviews without success. I suppose my insecurity and lack of self confidence was not impressive and did not serve me well.

Searching the want ads one day I noticed a large display ad extolling the virtues of a revolutionary machine that would soon be in demand in every household. Interviews for salesmen were being held at the luxurious Lee Plaza Hotel. With nothing to lose I showed up at the designated time and place. There were dozens of others there anxious to find out more about this opportunity. A distinguished gentleman introduced himself. He first explained he was part of a very successful family that had been written up by none other than Life Magazine regarding many business successes. He had large reproductions of that article posted on the walls of the meeting room. I was initially impressed. He touted this new machine saying it could be used as an air conditioner, hair dryer, de-mother, upholstery cleaner and much more. He then introduced someone claiming to have sold several of these machines earning thousands of dollars a month. According to him, they were in high demand and easy to sell. Shortly thereafter an assistant rolled out the revolutionary machine. It was in the form of a small canister resting on casters. Extending from the canister was a corrugated hose ending with a pointed attachment that was aimed toward the audience. The presenter pressed on a switch whereupon a flow of air wafted in the direction of the onlookers. It was a hot day and the airflow had a cooling effect. The presenter immediately began extolling this as one of the many features of this "revolutionary" machine. I was puzzled as to why several people were grumbling to themselves while heading for the doors. About the same time I overheard someone leaving comment....

"It's just another vacuum cleaner"

I remained enthused and curious. I stayed to hear more and was eventually convinced that selling these would be easy. I really needed a job so I decided to give it a try and signed up for training. I attended one day of training and was issued a "Filter Queen" to use as a demonstrator, with the understanding that I could purchase one at a discount price of $250.00. I would be selling them for $350.00. I was assigned a territory and a day later I was out knocking on doors with my spiel ready to present to anyone who would let me in their home for a demonstration. I spent the day without success. Doors were slammed in my face over and over. I was cursed at and otherwise insulted in several different ways. I returned home dejected but I could not allow myself to give up. I needed to earn money somehow to support my little family. For the next few weeks I screwed up the courage to continue trying with pretty much the same results. No sales! Finally a man invited me in and I presented the demonstration as I had been taught. It took an hour and a half . I thought it went well and fully expected to make a sale. I anxiously waited for a positive response. Then the man said....

"Sorry! Fella I don't have the money.

This was too much. I did not have constitution to withstand this much rejection. I decided to give up on door to door sales and vowed to never try this kind of selling again. I needed to return the Filter Queen demo but my embarrassment over my failure was such that I could not face anyone at the office. I mailed in a check for $250.00. At least I now owned a Filter Queen vacuum cleaner which we could use for the next twenty-five years.

At one point I went to an interview at an insurance company. I was ushered into an office occupied by two men in business suits. The manager invited me to sit down. It was a short interview. His first question asked was ....

"What do you think you have to offer this company?"

I thought a few seconds and unable to offer anything solid (I thought and at that time truly believed that being in my early twenties if I received the proper training I could serve this company for more than forty years.) I answered.... "My youth."

At that point both the manager and the man at the other desk began laughing.

"Thanks for coming in. We'll let you know.".... He said still chuckling to himself.

Totally embarrassed, I left without responding. This event crushed what little hope I had left for finding a job. I began to spend my days at home kidding myself that I was still looking for a job when in fact I did not possess the courage to go for another interview.

While at home alone one afternoon Jack White and Jumbo showed up at my door. As they sat down on our sofa I detected a slight smile on both their faces. I asked what they were grinning about. Jack said Jumbo wants to show you something. At that point Jumbo laid a magazine on our coffee table. There was a photo of a scantily clad young woman on the front cover. It was a recent issue of "Playboy". I had heard of this new publication started by Hugh Hefner but never seen one before. I was somewhat surprised at the cover but it was a *pleasant* surprise. After we spent several minutes flipping through the pages anxiously viewing photos of young ladies in various stages of undress we reviewed and laughed the cartoons scattered throughout the magazine. When we were done Jack got around to the real reason for his visit. He wanted me to go with him to the race track. I quickly told him I could not go. I was sure he knew about my losing of all our savings at the "track" a few years ago. Knowing Gail would never forgive me if I lost money betting on the horses I again refused the invitation. Jack was persistent. He explained that I did not have to bet but just help him with advice on the races. As always, reluctant to displease my friends, I gave in. Once at the "track" in order to fight back the temptation to begin betting I kept myself busy making a chart listing the "win", "place" and "show" results of each race. After the first few races had run I began perusing the thousands of discarded betting tickets scattered all over the floor with the improbable notion I might find a winning ticket. After scouring the floor for about an hour without success I was about to give up when I spotted a ticket that at first glance seemed to match with a second place winner on my list. I picked it up, looked at it closely, confirmed the numbers for the race and the horse then checked the date. It appeared to be valid but I wondered....

"How can this be? Something just doesn't make sense. Can I really be this lucky?"

So with great trepidation I approached the "pay" window, cautiously placed the ticket on the counter and waited for the clerk's reaction. I fully expected some sort of negative response from the pay clerk but was totally surprised when he counted out $12.50 and pushed the cash toward me. I grabbed the money and hurried away to disappear into the crowd fearing he would ask for the money back. Before I caught up with Jack a thought occurred to me ....

"What if whoever through away that winning ticket had bought more than one ticket? Maybe there was another ticket lying on the ground."

I had to go check it out. Back I went to the area where I found the ticket. I searched the floor area over and over without success then about to give up unbelievably I found a second valid ticket on the exact same race and horse. So excited by this second find I got down on my knees and began turning over the tickets that laid face down while several onlookers stood by making disparaging comments. Embarrassed but not deterred I actually found a third valid ticket. By then the last race of the day was just finishing. I cashed in the two additional tickets and caught up with Jack. I decided not to tell him of my good fortune with the thought I might return and try this again and I didn't want him competing with me. Barely able to contain myself on the way home I kept repeating to myself…

"Don't say anything."

I sat in silence on the drive home contemplating the unlikely events of the day. How, I wondered did it happen that someone would toss away those winning tickets. It made no sense. Still it happened, so there had to be an explanation. Eventually I reasoned out a plausible scenario. (Here, I remind younger readers that casinos were non existent in those times) The the only legitimate outlet those wanting to gamble were the horse races so the "track" was a very busy place. If someone wanted to place a bet on a horse to win they had to go to one of the betting windows that sold only "Win" tickets. Likewise if they wanted to make a "Place" bet they must go to the window selling only "Place" tickets. The same applied to "Show" bets. There often were ten or more betting windows with three or four designated to sell only "Win" tickets. Three or four windows selling only "Place" tickets followed by the windows selling only "Show" tickets. There were huge crowds attending the horse races. During the last few minutes before the start of a race it was common to see very long lines of betters at each of these windows. Due to the hustle and bustle of the crowds the lines were never simply straight and organized, rather the lines were long, winding and serpentine. It was in the realm of possibility that a better could get in a line that appeared to lead to one of the "Win" windows but due to the wandering formation of the line of betters it actually led to the "place" window. A hurried better might not notice he arrived at an unintended window and walk away thinking they had a ticket to win. Then disappointed when his horse comes in second he tosses his ticket away believing he lost. This would explain why I found the valid tickets. I burst into our apartment excited to relate the happy events of the day but before I could say anything Gail snapped at me....

"Where have you been all day?"

I explained in detail how I had been at the race track and found the three tickets worth almost forty dollars. Instead of sharing my glee over this result she seemed aloof. I got the impression she did not believe my story. She reminded me of my vow not to bet on the horses again. I swore to her I had not made a bet on any horse. She said she believed me but remained distant.

Later that evening Jack and Jumbo returned asking about the "Playboy" magazine. He wanted it back. I began looking around the house casually at first. When we did not find it we began an in depth search but still it was nowhere to be found. Gail had gone grocery shopping. As they departed I promised to ask Gail if she put it somewhere. When Gail came home I asked her if she had put the "Playboy" somewhere. Her response was immediate and terse ....

"I threw it out!"

"Why did you do that?"

"I won't have that trash in my house!"

"It wasn't mine. It belonged to Jumbo."

"I don't care. I threw it out."

At that point I realized Gail's distant attitude was more about the "Girlie' magazine than about my race track adventure. I said no more about it and apologized to my friends. The next day without telling Gail I returned to the "Track" determined to see if the good fortune of the previous day could be repeated.

The last race of the day was just starting and I had closely scoured the floor for hours without success when a suspicious ticket hit my eye. I stooped over, picked it up and compared it to the "list" I made. It was a ten dollar place ticket and appeared to be valid. Instead of immediately running to the pay window I decided to continue looking in the same spot. There only a few inches away laid two more identical tickets. When I was sure there were no more there I went to the pay window. The thrill I felt by this second stroke of good fortune was accompanied by a vague feeling of guilt. The look of suspicion from the cashier as he counted out $84.00 was probably just in my mind. I left for home to relate my continued success only to be greeted by another questionable look from Gail. I returned to the "track" a third time on my quest for discarded cash-able tickets. Once more I struck gold. By the end of that third day I found two "Place" tickets and four "Show" ticket worth a total of $66.00. My glee over finding payable tickets three days in succession was somewhat tempered by the knowledge that it was the last day of the racing season. I would have to wait till the following spring to try again. My luck at the racetrack during the past three days resulted in recovering two hundred dollars but it still didn't relieve my persistent feeling of guilt over losing all the money Gail and I had saved for our marriage on a foolish racetrack betting scheme. Much of the next sixty or so years would be spent in a attempt to redeem myself.

The End Part One

Part Two

Chapter 1

PROVING WORTHY

Across from our upstairs flat on Stoepel Street lived a young couple like ourselves. One day Frank Pees walked across the street, introduced himself and invited us to a backyard picnic where we met his wife, Linda. Within a few weeks we became quite friendly. Frank had just started a new job with the Jewel Tea Company. His job was driving a medium sized dark brown panel truck on an established route, delivering coffee, tea and other non perishable goods to housewives. It was the "Fifties" and most married women could still be found at home. In the course of getting to know each other I mentioned I was having difficulty finding a job. Frank suggested I apply at the Jewel Tea office as they were looking for route salesmen. After a few days of Frank's continued encouragement I summoned up the courage to venture into the "Jewel" office. There I was shown a short film summarizing the company's history explaining the company was started in 1899. The founder drove a horse and wagon delivering coffee, tea and spices to housewives. Over the years more and more items were added to the grocery line and it now included almost every non perishable item you could find in a super market. Later a catalog with more than five thousand items of clothing, bedding, small appliances and more was added. Jewel also offered to sell these catalog items on credit. It was further explained that should I be found qualified for this position a minimum of two weeks on the job training would be provided.

Next I was led to a small office room and given a written test to complete. A few of the questions pertained to how one would handle difficult situations involving customer relations, however most of the questions were mathematically oriented. Shortly after completing the test I was ushered into a large private office where behind his desk sat Frank Phelps, the Detroit Division manager. After introducing himself he began surmising my just finished test. He sat quietly for a while with one elbow propped on the desk while he continually rubbed his forehead. Finally he spoke ....

"What do you think about the film explaining our company history?

"I thought it very interesting."

"Would you be desirous of entering our training program?"

"Yes, I believe I would."

"You did quite well on our little test Mr. King."

"I did?"

"Yes, you got all the math questions correct and missed only one of the others."

He continued .... "Julian, here is a brochure that contains some information regarding our benefits plan, starting wage and possible promotion paths. I would like you to take it home, read it thoroughly and talk it over with your wife. If you are still interested in a career with "Jewel" call me and I will set up a time for you to spend a day riding with one of our route salesman. That way you can see exactly what this job entails prior to accepting a position with our company. You will not be paid for that day but it will help you decide if this is what you want."

I thanked Mr. Phelps and left. While waiting for Gail to return from work I carefully reviewed the brochure Mr. Phelps had given me. In it I discovered that "Jewel" provided medical insurance, life insurance, paid vacations and best of all was 'J.R.E." (Jewel Retirement Estates). J.R.E. was a profit sharing plan that employees could contribute to. Based on an employee's contribution and the company's profitability "Jewel" would also contribute to J.R.E. Recent history indicated that the company contribution often exceeded the employee's contribution. A chart showed the amount one could expect to retire with at age sixty-five. According to the chart if an employee started working for "Jewel at age twenty-one and contributed the maximum (3%) of his paycheck every week until age sixty-five they would have one hundred twenty-five thousand dollars to retire with. This seemed to me, at the time, to be a staggering amount of money. I was enthralled with such a huge retirement sum. Working for "Jewel" had to be my best opportunity. With a wife and two children that depended on me, I had to have health insurance. This company offered me more security than I had ever known in my entire life. My starting salary was to be seventy-five dollars a week. That was quite a comedown from my previous earnings at Winterseal. Many of my friends were earning close to one hundred dollars a week at the major auto plants but I just could not go back to the dull non challenging drudgery of factory work. When Gail agreed I called Frank Phelps to tell him I wanted to take that trial ride. It was arranged for me to meet Leonard Lukas the next morning.

Mr. Lukas was a supervisor for "Jewel". He appeared to be a very pleasant man with an outgoing personality. He had a demeanor quite suited to dealing with the housewives one would encounter on the sales route. He showed me a sales card that illustrated that weeks grocery specials and an oblong aluminum carry basket that contained displays of the different catalog items that were on sale that week. Upon entering the "Jewel delivery truck I was immediately struck by the distinct aroma emanating from inside the vehicle. It was a most pleasant smell of various food products blended together with freshly ground coffee. Even today that aroma is still fresh in my memory. At the first five or six customer's homes Mr. Lukas ran the show.

When the customer answered the door and invited us in he began by pulling displays out of the aluminum carry basket. First he unfolded a cardboard display with swatches of material showing the different colors of blankets on sale that week. Next he opened a tri-folded cardboard display that unfolded to show an actual little girls dress along with huge glossy photos of additional dress styles and colors. The "Jewel" merchandising department was very clever at creating easy to use displays for the route salesmen to present to the customer. After showing the customer the displays and taking orders for the next delivery he used a pencil to add up the total the customer owed for that day's order plus any budget payment due. A few customers paid with a check but most customers paid in cash requiring Lukas to make change from a large leather pouch most Jewel salesman carried. It became apparent that mathematical prowess was a vitally important skill for a Jewel salesman. Note: small hand held calculators would not be available for many years to come. After watching Mr. Lukas at several stops he informed me that it would be my turn to make the presentation to the next customer while he observed. As I walked up the sidewalk at the next stop with the fifty pound basket in hand my body began trembling inside. Somewhat fearful, as well as shy, about how to get through the expected presentation I kept my head lowered as Mr. Lukas knocked on the door. A slightly plump young lady about my age answered the door and asked us in. With my head still lowered I set her order on the table and began taking out one of the sales displays to show this customer. When I finally looked up to observe her reaction to the display I was immediately taken aback. I could not be absolutely certain but this customer was a spitting image of Mary Muller. A few years older and several pounds heavier but the eyes and face were the same. I thought I noticed a look of recognition on her face. Visibly shaking and with my voice breaking, I attempted to emulate the spiel I had watched "Lukas" present. Half way through my feeble presentation Mr. Lukas stepped in and finished for me. When we left I was mortified and apologized to Mr. Lukas who told me not to worry about it. He claimed the same thing happened to many other potential salesmen. He said I should just watch him for the rest of the customer calls. The thought that it was Mary haunted me the rest of that day. If it was her she was married now and the child I heard crying was most likely hers as well.

At the end of that day, although filled with doubts, I hesitantly informed Lukas I wanted to enter the official training program. That evening a call came from Lukas. I was to meet him and the company auditor the next morning to be audited on to the #27 route and begin my future with "Jewel". The next two weeks were spent training with Leonard Lukas. The sales collections of the #27 route were the lowest in the entire Detroit Division averaging only $475.00 per week. There was nowhere to go but up. Leonard Lukas immediately told me I was to carry the display basket at every stop. He soon had me making complete sales demonstration at every home accompanied by a helpful critique afterwards. I fumbled a lot especially when customers asked a question that I couldn't answer. My innate shyness did not lend itself to have quick on my feet responses. At the end of each nine to ten hour day I spent another hour being shown how to complete the daily paperwork and balance the money collected with the orders paid for. Instruction on weekly paperwork followed for a couple hours on Saturday morning. At the end of the training period I felt ready. The keys to the truck were given to me and I began running the route alone the following Monday. I started out with great enthusiasm expecting to immediately improve the route's sales and collection average. The truth is that I seemed to have a great deal of difficulty getting customers to pay attention to my sales pitch. Instead they wanted to talk about various other things of interest to themselves. Initially I made the mistake of wanting all the customers to think well of me so I spent too much time listening to what they had to say resulting in very little in sales and great loss of time. Records of all the customers were kept in sales books. There were approximately fifty customer accounts listed in each of ten books sorted by geographical areas. The plan was to call on all the accounts in one book in one day. Working five days a week it took two weeks to cover the entire sales route.

Eventually I arrived at the house of the customer that resembled Mary Muller. I was hesitant to make the call and sat in the truck a long while summoning the courage necessary then walked slowly up to the front door and knocked. No answer! Sometimes a customer might be in the backyard or down in the basement doing the laundry. Not wanting to have to make a callback later I found that walking around to the side door and knocking again often got results. When there was no answer at the front door I walked slowly around to the side door but as I was about to knock I could see through the door's window that the customer was lying on the kitchen floor, flat on her stomach and scuttling backwards. I watched in disbelief as she pushed herself backwards toward the basement stairway then down the three steps to the landing that was even with the side door entrance. She paused a moment then, still on her belly, manipulated into position to slide down the longer stairway to the basement. About halfway through her downward slide she looked up and saw me standing outside the door. Feeling embarrassment for both her and myself I quickly turned away and retreated to the Jewel truck. I sat deep in thought for a several moments then drove away. I knew then it really was Mary Muller. I assumed she was too embarrassed to face me.

"Why else would she go to such an extreme to avoid me?" .... I pondered.

After I finished calling on my customers that day I thought for a while then decided to mark her account closed. I would never stop at her house again. Now and then I wonder what happened between us. Was it my fault? Did my sarcastic nature drive her away? I'll never know but it doesn't really matter because subsequently I met a truly wonderful girl who I believed loved me and that I loved more than life.

On the Jewel route I seemed to be treading water in the quest for a sales improvement. More than a few months passed and instead of a sales increase, my route sales collections declined to $450.00 per week. The fact was that I was simply uncomfortable as a salesman. I did not have the confidence needed to be able to take control of the conversation with the customers. Instead of trying to make sales I found myself losing valuable time listening to customers ramble on about whatever subject they wanted to talk about. Discouragement with my lack of success made it harder and harder for me to start work. I kept finding excuses to put off starting my daily calls. I was sitting in a restaurant one Spring morning, drinking a cup of coffee and trying to build myself up to starting the route when Frank Pees walked in and sat down on the stool next to me.

"What's up?" .... He asked

"Nothing much. Just getting ready to start my route."

"I hear the Silver Bass are running over in Amherstburg. What say we forget work and go fishing?"

(Note: For a few years I had been going fishing for Perch or Silver Bass during the Spring spawning run when they were in the mouth of the Detroit River. Fishing results were poor due to serious pollution on the Detroit side of the river but still relatively good on the Canadian side. I would drive over the Ambassador Bridge to Amhurstburg, Canada and rent a 20 foot fishing boat at Duffy's Landing. It was important to get there early as often all the boats were rented.)

Dreading work anyway, I agreed. I mentioned to Frank the boats might all be rented out before we could get there. We decided to call Duffy's. They were out of boats. Not wanting to miss out on this short lived run of Silver Bass we came up with an alternate plan. While not ideal we could rent a boat on our side of the river and motor across to the Canadian side. We began our quest to find a boat to rent. We soon discovered that apparently several other fisherman had the same idea. Everywhere we went all the boats were taken. We tried on Grosse Isle then continued south on Jefferson Ave. stopping at every boat livery along the way, without success. We were about to give up when we found a boat livery about five miles south of the mouth of the Detroit river at the Point Mouilee wetland that connected to Lake Erie. We thought we could motor through the swamp to Lake Erie then cross the big lake to the mouth of the Detroit River eventually getting to the desired fishing area. We entered the boat livery and inquired about renting a boat. The owner replied he had rented out all his large boats but he also had a ten foot dinghy for rent. He informed us it was too dangerous to take such a small boat out on the big lake and he would only let us rent it if we promised we would stay within the canals that ran through Point Mouilee wetlands. Thinking we had already wasted much of the day searching for a boat to rent we decided we may as well spend the rest of the day fishing the swampy canals of Point Mouilee. We reluctantly agreed. After clamping my 3 ½ horsepower air cooled Clinton outboard motor to the back of the dingy we got out our fishing gear, boarded the ten foot craft and proceeded through the marshy canals to a spot where we had the "big lake"in view. We dropped our lines and fished a short while without even a bite. We were getting restless and eventually looked at each other simultaneously thinking the same thought…..

> "Let's go for it."

I started the outboard and we motored out to Lake Erie. (Later that day we would realize the stupidity of taking a ten foot flat bottom dingy with a meager 3½ horsepower outboard motor out on one of the Great lakes.) We headed north for five or six miles through the big lake toward the Detroit River. The moderate motion of the waves made it slow going and It took much longer than we anticipated. We finally arrived in the mouth of the river and cruised upriver to a spot near Bob Lo Island where I had fished a few times before. We baited hooks and dropped our lines. As I relaxed and looked around I thought it was curious that although we had found it nearly impossible to locate a boat to rent, the number of fishing boats on the water was rather sparse. Normally during the Silver Bass "run" this area of the river would be jammed with boats. I wondered ....

"Where are all those fishing boats that were rented out earlier that day?"

I soon saw the answer. As I continued to scour the river I noticed several boats speeding in the direction of Duffy's. When my gaze turned eastward toward Lake Erie I could see a dark bank of clouds moving swiftly in our direction.

"Frank!" .... I said.... "We better get out of here. Those dark clouds are heading our way. We don't want to get caught in a storm in this little boat."

Without hesitation we pulled in our lines. I grew concerned when my outboard motor failed to start after cranking it several times. Finally it started and we began heading southward toward Pointe Mouilee. As we left the mouth of the river to enter Lake Erie the storm was upon us. We were faced with a five mile journey through very rough seas. It was so rough that I had to face the small craft east headlong into the crest of each wave to avoid being swamped sideways. Then as the crest passed and we entered the trough of each wave I immediately steered the boat southward toward our destination. There was no choice but to continue this long and extremely harrowing process and hope against hope we could make it. I decided to stay close to the shore in case we were swamped. The waves became stronger as we traveled south. The crest of the waves seemed at least five feet and pushed our little craft even closer to the shore. As we neared shore we were faced with two harrowing problems. First the wave action was such that we were nearly swamped at the top of the wave but then our craft was hitting the sandy bottom once the crest passed. Either way I knew we were in great danger. I realized I had to steer our little craft far enough away from shore that we no longer hit bottom yet hope we were close enough to at least have a chance to swim to shore if the worst happened. Back and forth we went, crashing east through the crest a few seconds then south in the trough a few seconds. We battled this storm for more than two hours, praying all the while. Finally near exhaustion we were in view of the Point Mouilee wetlands. A tremendous sigh of relief emanated from both of us as we entered the relatively calm waters of the swamp. When we finally reached the shore of the boat livery we exited the boat and both collapsed on the ground thankful to still be alive. We laid on the ground a while gathering strength to load up our car and head home. I thought....

"Once again I miraculously eluded what could have been my finality".

The next day I resumed my sales calls on the Jewel route but was now a day behind schedule. I had to work on Saturday that week to catch up on my calls. During the next few years I often found myself having to run my route on Saturdays as a result of taking days off during the week to go fishing or to partake in other diversions. My sales collections were well below the division sales average of $700.00 per week. I was becoming depressed and thinking maybe it would be wise to quit before they fire me but at the same time I was acutely aware that I had a family depending on me. One morning I was stunned to see Frank Phelps appear at the door of my truck as I was about to start my route. He stepped into my van, smiled and while rubbing his forehead he asked....

"What seems to be the problem Mr. King?

"What do you mean?"

"Well Julian, you have been out on this route for a while now and instead of bringing the sales up they are declining so it would seem something isn't working."

Caught off guard by his surprise appearance, various excuses coursed through my mind as I struggled to find an answer to his question. After a sustained pause I confessed what I thought was the truth....

"Mr. Phelps, although I have been inspired at all the sale meetings, whenever I try to apply any of those suggestions or techniques I cannot seem to get the attention of my customers. When I first started on this route I was so anxious to be liked and accepted by the customers that I let them dominate the conversations. Instead of spending time explaining why they should purchase whatever I am selling I wind up listening to them tell me about their own personal interests. I simply don't know how to regain control."

"Mr. King let me ask you a question. If you could start over on a different route do you believe you could avoid the trap you fell into and obtain better sales results?"

"Yes, I think I could."

"Well there is an opening on the "#21" route adjacent to this one. The sales on the #21 route are almost as poor as the route you're on now. I want you to spend the rest of this week considering whether you can seriously do a better job on a different route. If you decide to give it your best I will approve your transfer to that route."

I realized I had few options if any. I had a wife and two children depending on me. With only a high school education and no training or skills to offer to any employer, there was no choice to make. I decided I must accept the transfer. I also knew I could not fail this time.

The following Monday I was audited off the #27 route and on to the #21. I psyched myself up mentally and began my route calls determined to be in charge and not let the customers dominate the time. That worked! Not allowing the customers to control the conversation resulted in a lot of time saved. Instead of completing all my sales calls around 6pm, I was able to finish calling on each customer by around 3pm. This provided me at least three more hours to go back to the homes of customers that were not at home the first time I called. Thus I was able to contact more customers each day and that led to higher sales and collections which helped to increase my confidence level. Within a few months I had increased my weekly sales collections to the company average of $700.00. At meetings I received praise from Lukas and Phelps and felt much better about my future.

Chapter 2

TWO FAMILIES ONE HOUSE

One evening Gail and I discussed our financial situation. It was part of our youthful dreams to own a house of our own but we were not sure if we could afford it yet. We saved a few dollars while we were both working but her maternity leave from Vinco's would end soon and she most likely would not be able to return to work. With only my income from Jewel we could not save enough to afford purchasing a house. If Gail could somehow continue working we could probably save enough for a down payment in one year but we had a problem. If we both worked days who would watch our babies? At that time Gail's Mom & Dad were struggling financially as well. Her Dad had no employee benefits of any kind. He had worked as a freelance tailor most of his life. When he was still tailoring at Harry Suffrin's in downtown Detroit at the age of 66, he was struck by a car while crossing Woodward Ave. He did not incur any broken bones but he had a very bad scrape on one foot and was unable to wear a shoe. He thought he would be back to work in a few weeks however after several months the sore on his foot had not healed. Gail's parents were not wealthy. Gail's father had no paid sick days or a pension to collect on. Without health insurance their meager savings were eroded by several visits to the foot doctor. We became aware of how seriously bad off they were when we stopped to visit and found Gail's father sitting in his chair wiping tears from his eyes. He would not say what was wrong but Gail's mother confessed they had to claim "welfare" benefits earlier that day. Mr. Starr was a proud man and at that time in our society there was a stigma attached to being on welfare. Mr. Starr was ashamed.

At some point Gail had a conversation with her folks. It was discussed that if we moved in with them Gail's Mother could watch our two babies enabling Gail to continue working. We would pay them rent, share household expenses and both parties would save money. Gail's paycheck would go in the bank to save for a down payment on a house. It seemed a good idea at the time. A few weeks later we left the Stoeple flat and moved to the house Gail grew up in on Sorrento Ave. This arrangement was highly beneficial to both families and worked fine at first however after several months signs of tension arose. There were no significant disagreements, rather trivial little things began to irritate Mr. Starr. As I reflect back I know that I should have been more tolerant. I should have realized that suffering with the pain of a seriously injured foot would likely cause anyone to be somewhat impatient. When I first began dating his daughter Mr. Starr had always been nice to me. Most Sundays he took his family out to local lakes or rivers to go fishing. Although he did not know me well at the time, he often invited me to join them. Eternally anxious to be anywhere Gail was , I always accepted. Before we were married I spent many Sunday afternoons fishing with the Starr family. I decided to make an effort to ease the natural occurring tension that develops when two families try living in the same house. I invited Mr. Starr to go fishing with me to Amherstburg where the Perch run was underway. I knew he loved to go fishing and was surprised when he declined so I pushed him more than once for his reason. He remained quiet. Later, Mrs. Starr told Gail the reason....

"Our Social Security check doesn't come till next week and your father doesn't have the money to buy the six dollar Canadian fishing license."

That revelation, along with previously finding Mr. Starr's total dismay over collecting welfare, reinforced my belief that working for "Jewel" was a smart choice. The "Jewel" retirement program would ensure that I would never find myself on welfare or at the mercy of a government check.

While living with Gail's folks I became acquainted with some of the neighbors. A fellow about my age lived across the alley from us. His name was Kenny Ludke. He was short, muscularly built with dark, close set eyes and sharp facial features. I had seen him before in the vicinity of the "Sweet Shop" but he had "that "look" that had I always interpreted as being threatening so I had avoided him. After I got to know him I discovered that Kenny was quite friendly and we became good friends. As the tension with Gail's folks grew I began spending more time visiting with Kenny. We often played cards at his house or went to a local tavern to drink beer and shoot pool. Always conscious of the money I was spending I drank very slowly. Kenny often downed two or three glasses of beer while I drank just one. We continued to save money while the strained relations at Gail's parent's home were becoming increasingly uncomfortable. In the early spring of 1957 we decided it was best to start looking for a house of our own. We began searching the "Want Ads" hoping to find a house we could afford that was located reasonably close to Gail's folks house so that her mother could watch our kids while we both continued working. We found a house for sale on Appoline only two blocks away. The price was six thousand dollars with a six hundred dollar down payment on a six percent land contract. It was a beveled clapboard house that sat on the back of the lot. It had two small bedrooms and one bathroom. There was no basement. The natural gas floor furnace was situated in the crawl space and located centrally in a small hallway that adjoined both bedrooms, the kitchen, living room and bathroom. Lacking experience in buying a house I called on my Uncle Red for advice. He had sold his house on Hubble and bought a new house on Tireman Street close to Rouge Park so I knew he had some experience in buying a house. I valued his opinion. I met him at his house one weekend afternoon and we drove out to a newly built subdivision on the outskirts of Detroit. He showed me a brand new house as yet unsold. It was about the same size as the house on Appoline with two bedrooms and one bath. Like the house on Appoline the price was six thousand with ten percent down but unlike the Appoline house there was a gas furnace in the full basement with ducts to send heat to each individual room. This new house was very tempting. After touring the new house we went back to Uncle Red's house where I sat and visited with him and Aunt Polly for a while.

As the evening progressed I noticed my uncle seemed to be somewhat fidgety. After a little time passed my uncle announced he he had to go to the store and asked me to accompany him. We drove off in his car and parked in front of a local "bar". He smiled mischievously and said....

"Let's go in and have a couple beers."

I followed him inside where he took a seat on a bar stool. I took the stool next to him. He ordered three bottles of beer. The bartender placed one bottle in front of me, one in front of Red and a third bottle in front of a man sitting to my right. When I paid no attention, thinking the third man must be a friend of his, Red spoke....

"Do you know that guy sitting next to you?"

I turned to look. I was happily surprised to see my Uncle Murray. We shook hands and talked a while. He asked how I was doing. I asked him the same. I felt a little awkward but was so very very glad to see him. I always liked my Uncle Murray and still had no inkling of what caused the family rift. I was happy to know, at least the two brothers had made up. We finished our beer and Red said we had to get back home. I shook Murray's hand again and we left. Uncle Red drove straight home and did not stop at a store! At the time I did not quite understand all that happened that evening. With the passing of time I came to realize that Uncle Red had reconciled with his brother and made a conscious effort to reunite me with my Uncle Murray but for some reason did not want Aunt Polly to know about it. Unfortunately I would never see my Uncle Murray again.

That new house was a much better value than the one on Appoline but it was several miles away. If we bought the new house it would be difficult to have Gail's mom baby-sit Gary and Terri. After some thought we came to the conclusion that having close proximity to Gail's mom who could watch our children while we both worked took precedent over the advantages of the newer house. In late spring of 1957 we moved into the Appoline house and settled in. We soon discovered a few problems. Both bedrooms were just seven by nine feet. So small that a double bed would not fit. The only way we could even fit a three quarter bed along with a small dresser was to position the bed sideways against the wall. To make the bed we had to pull it away from the wall and make one side then push it back against the wall to make the other side. Upon opening the oven of the stove that came with the house we found it littered with mouse droppings. The house was inundated with mice. One of my first tasks was to find and seal the several obscure places where mice had gnawed though the baseboards to gain entry to the house. We had very little furniture to start with but Uncle Red gave us an old sofa and chair he no longer had use for, along with an old kitchen table and chairs. It was a meager start but we were happy to be in a house of our own. Despite the fact that the Appoline house would present many more serious problems in the coming years I always reminded myself it was a large step up from my own previous life.

Chapter 3

INCREASING RESPONSIBILITY

A few months after moving to Appoline we had another surprise. Gail was pregnant with our third child. I thought.....

"This is unbelievable. How can she keep getting pregnant so fast? I know how babies are made but this is ridiculous."

I began to doubt Father Sherzer's claim that God will not give you more than you can bear and I began to question everything....

"How am I going to get through this? Gail will have to quit work. How can I support three kids on just my paycheck? We only have two bedrooms where will they all sleep? What is the point of trying? I can't win!"

After days of being somewhat depressed I recalled my personal commitment to being a responsible person and snapped out of it. I realized Gail was facing the very same challenges and my love for her had not diminished. I had no choice. I could not run. I had to find a way to make this work. Gail might be able to work for another four months but then we would be down to one paycheck. If we were to survive it would be necessary to make every dollar count. I had to come up with some sort of budget. I listed all the bills we would have to pay and wrote each one on a separate envelope. Based on a four week month I ascertained how much money from each week's paycheck I needed to put in each envelope in order to meet all the bills and expenses that would be due. I wrote the calculated amounts on each envelope. I thought a small surplus might build up as during the course of a year there would be a few months with five paychecks. My weekly take home pay was $55.00 and my envelope budget went like this Land Contract - $15, Electric - $8, Heat - $8, Water - $2, Insurance - $4, Clothes - $2, Car - $4, Food -$8 and Entertainment - $2.

After the budget was finalized I set a goal to try and cut back on the actual amount spent in each category. Keeping the thermostat low in winter might keep the heat bill below the projected cost. Holding grocery shopping below the $8.00 budget by only buying what was on sale would save money. I could save money on gasoline by watching how much I drove my car and so on. Putting money in the bank each week was always important to me but I could not fit that in our budget. I had however previously devised a strategy to force myself to have some money saved at the end of each year. On my weekly deductions for the Internal Revenue Service I only claimed one of my children so I could expect a refund on my income tax each year that I could put into savings.

Then at a most opportune time a way to supplement my income knocked on my door. It was Ray Lowery. Ray worked for Jewel as a Direct Salesman. I had met him briefly at one of the monthly sales meetings. A Direct Salesman was someone who went knocking door to door trying to convince people to become a regular customer on a Jewel route. At times new customers are needed to replace the regular customers who move away or quit for various reasons. The Direct salesmen were paid a flat amount for each customer they signed up. They had no guaranteed salary. I invited Ray in. He sat down made some small talk for a short while before asking me to follow him out to his car. While opening his trunk exposing some brightly colored six foot runner rugs he asked ….

"Would you like to make some extra money?"

Before I could answer he continued ….

"I have a hundred of these rugs. They're called Rainbow Runners. I can sell them to you for a buck apiece then you could sell them on your route for three or four dollars."

"What if I get caught? Jewel would fire me."

"They won't catch you. There are rugs in the Jewel catalog similar to these. If management stops by your truck they will think it's a rug from the catalog."

"What if I can't sell them all?"

"Hey! Skip if you sell twenty-five rugs at four bucks apiece you've got your money back. After that it's pure gravy."

After weighing the risk compared to our need for extra cash I agreed to buy Lowery's rugs. I loaded the rugs into my Jewel truck and the next day began showing them to my customers. Surprisingly I sold twenty-five rugs the first week eventually selling them all in only one month. The extra cash came in handy. After a while I learned another "trick" that provided a financial benefit. Whenever shampoo or some other product was on a buy one get one free sale. I would order several more than I actually sold and keep them in stock. Sometime later when a customer ordered one of those products at regular price I filled their order from the extra supply. Managing my inventory that way caused an "overage" at the twice a year "Jewel" company audits of my route. Being intuitively very good at math I was always able to have an approximate knowledge of the amount of these overages. This presented me with the opportunity to occasionally take home (without paying) a box of cookies, detergent or something from the general merchandise catalog. I knew that was not completely honest but faced with serious financial challenges, I felt it necessary to do whatever I could to survive.

The winter of 1957 exposed a few more problems with our house. Sometime in the past one of the previous owners added on a large addition to the original house. This addition was constructed with four large wide windows, two on each side. It adjoined the original small kitchen. It was large enough to accommodate our automatic washer and still leave room for a kitchen table and six chairs. The original floor furnace was not designed to produce the heat necessary for the expanded space so on very cold winter days the inside walls with the four windows actually had ice build up on them. During the winter we avoided using that room except to have our meals. The water pipes in the crawl space were another problem. They froze up during the deepest part of the winter more than once requiring me to crawl under the house with a blow torch to heat up and defrost the pipes. We soon learned the grate covering the floor furnace got very hot and we could not step on it without wearing shoes. On many occasions I would seriously regret not going with the nice new house my uncle had shown me.

Our third child, Cheryl arrived in March 1958. She too was a beautiful baby. Now there were three kids to fit in a small bedroom. We purchased a bunk bed for Gary and Terri to sleep in. Cheryl would have the crib. While not overjoyed with three kids to support I was glad to have a healthy baby and I loved her as I did the first two. With three children still in cloth diapers the washing and drying was enormous. We had purchased an automatic washer on credit when we bought the house but Gail was drying the clothes on wash lines strung out in the front yard. In the winter we ran lines back and forth through the combination kitchen/utility room to dry clothes on. This was already unmanageable even before Cheryl was born. Gail was coming to her wits end and I knew something had to be done. I began the search for an automatic dryer. Gail and I were totally adverse to buying things on credit. We promised each other not to buy on credit without the approval of the other. As Christmas neared that year without asking her, I made the decision that Gail's Christmas gift would be an automatic dryer.

Two days before Christmas, while I was at work, two men in a truck pulled up in front of our Appoline house. One of the men knocked on our front door. When Gail answered the door one of the men said ….

"We have a delivery to make here."

"There must be some mistake. We didn't order anything"

"The order is for this address!"

"What is it?"

"It's a brand new Norge automatic dryer."

Gail was overjoyed and watched in amazement as the men installed the dryer. To this very day Gail claims that dryer was the greatest Christmas gift she ever received.

With three children to care for Gail was not going to return to Vinco's. We had been pretty good at sticking to our budget. Instead of shopping for the specific groceries we desired we diligently planned our meals around whatever was on sale that week. The weekly treat for us was one 6-pack of six ounce "cokes" and a large bag of potato chips. This frugality freed up a few extra dollars for entertainment.

My friends Leonard, Harvey and Jack were all married by then. I was best man for both Leonard and Harvey. Jack had moved to California a few years earlier. Leonard and Harley occasionally stopped by to keep in touch. One day Leonard called me to tell me his mother had passed away. He was my oldest friend and to support him I attended the funeral. He was extremely distraught. I saw him collapse in tears in front of his mother's casket sobbing out how sorry he was, how he wished he had been a better son and begged her to forgive him. Watching him go on like this for a considerable time moved me to think about my own relationship with my mother. I did love my mother but had deep resentment inside me for the lousy upbringing and depressing life I was forced to endure with her. Still, as I watched Leonard's breakdown I thought to myself....

"I don't want to someday find myself with all the regrets and recriminations Leonard apparently has. When the time comes I am not going to find myself feeling guilty the way Leonard feels now"

Some months later while Leonard and I were having a few drinks in one of the local bars the subject of my mother came up in our conversation. I made, what I thought was a mild derogatory remark about what a mess she made of her life and mine. Without warning Leonard jumped from his chair pushed me against the wall with one of his hands on my neck while he slapped me across the face saying ....

"Don't talk about your mother that way! She's just a lonely woman who likes her sex!"

I was dumbfounded. I couldn't understand what the basis for him to make such a statement about her loneliness and sex was or why he reacted so strongly. Then as quickly as he exploded he calmed down and apologized. I thought ....

"Something's seriously wrong with Leonard. Still... he is my oldest friend."

There was another unusual incident involving Leonard that concerned me. I was visiting him and his wife at their house when Leonard began bragging about buying a motorcycle and joining a motorcycle club. He wanted me to buy a motorcycle and become a member too. When I informed him I wasn't interested he began to extol all the benefits the club offered.... parties, racing competitions, get-togethers with sexy women. I thought it strange he said that in front of his wife but she just laughed. Then he opened a photo album and retrieved a photo of a woman sitting on the edge of a bed totally naked. Items in the photo's background revealed it was their bedroom. He said benefits such as this would be available to members. Next came an even bigger surprise. Leonard whispered something to his wife. She smirked and nodded. He asked if she was sure. A slight giggle accompanied her second nod. Then he pulled out a photo of his wife nude from the waist up with her breasts on full display. I did want to continue looking but was overcome with embarrassment. He again suggested that I along with Gail should join their club. I made up some excuse about being afraid of riding motorcycles and said I had to be somewhere else. I left in total shock of what just transpired. Although we had been friends for as long as I could remember I decided it best to avoid him for a while. Several months would elapse before I would hear anything of Leonard then one morning going through my mail I opened a letter. It was from Leonard. He explained that he was in some kind of mental rehabilitation hospital and did not expect to be released for sometime. He wrote ....

> *"As my oldest friend would you please look after Helen and see if she needs any help."*

His plea to help his wife greatly concerned me. What would I do if she needed financial help. With a wife and three kids I was struggling to keep my own head above water. Still, feeling I couldn't ignore the situation I drove to their house. Helen greeted me at the door and asked me in. She introduced me to her parents who were there. I informed Helen of Leonard's letter and asked what was going on. Helen related in a matter of fact manner that Leonard was "losing it". According to her at some point he had purchased a gun. She continued to explain that he would sit in his chair watching "Westerns" on television with his gun at his side. Then one night while watching a gunfight on television he pulled up his gun and started shooting live bullets at the television. She did not say who called them but the cops came and took Leonard away. Then she grinned and matter of factly blurted out....

"He's in the Loony Bin now."

Her sudden declaration made me feel uneasy and I was thinking it was time to leave but remembering Leonard's request I asked Helen if she needed any financial help. She replied....

"Absolutely not! My parents are here and they'll help me with anything I need."

I left somewhat relieved but puzzled over Helen's blasé attitude. Several months later I received another letter from Leonard informing me he was released from the hospital and had moved to Chicago. He did not say why but I assumed he may have relocated in an effort to avoid the embarrassment that would necessarily accompany any explanation of what happened.

Harvey came knocking on my door one Saturday afternoon with a surprise. Jack was back in town. In fact he told me Jack had returned from California several months ago. My excitement at the thought of seeing my old friend again was tempered by the disappointment to learn he had been back for quite some time yet failed to contact me.

"I thought I was his best friend?"

I went with Harvey to an upstairs flat where Jack was living. Jack introduced me to Liv a girl he met and married while in California. They had two children. We renewed our friendship and reminisced over some of our past experiences. Jack explained he had not contacted any of his old friends since moving back to Detroit. He had obtained a position as office manager with Pepsi and had been extremely busy. This revelation amazed me. I knew he hadn't graduated high school. He hadn't even finished ninth grade. I asked ….

"How on earth did you qualify for that kind of a job?

"It's not difficult. You just apply for it."

"But you have no experience in that field!"

"They don't know that."

He laughed as he explained that when he filled out the application he claimed to have a business degree from a college in California. He bragged he had done this with several firms and he said in some cases the company would not bother checking his references and even when they did it might take weeks or months before they get a reply to their inquiry, if at all.

(Note: It was the mid "fifties". Computers, cell phones and all the means of instant communication of today were not available then.)

According to Jack he had obtained (and lost) several good jobs using this technique. He unabashedly admitted that eventually his inability to perform in the position he had lied his way into became obvious or the check on his reference came through. Either way he was exposed and dismissed but that did not bother him. He would just go on to deceive another employer. (Still the old smooth talking Jack.) While we visited with Jack a furniture van pulled up in front of the building. Jack had bought some furniture from one of those "No money down, no payment for six months" furniture companies and it was being delivered. We decided to get out of the way of the delivery guys. As we were leaving Jack suggested, and we agreed, to get together the following weekend. A week later Harvey and I returned to Jack's flat and knocked on the door. No answer. We knocked a few more times without a response when a man from the downstairs flat appeared saying ….

"Those folks moved out a few days ago. They sold all their furniture and I think they went back to California."

Harvey and I looked at each other both realizing nothing had changed it was the same old Jack. He had bought a houseful of "no money down furniture", immediately ran a want ad, sold it, pocketed the money and left town. I began to rethink those past years of my idolization of Jack.

Other than the occasional visits with Leonard, Harvey and Kenny Ludke we were kind of a keep to ourselves young couple but we did get to know Dick Moore, one of our next door neighbors. Dick had been dating Gail's old friend Judy Troshinski for quite some time. When they married Judy "Tro" became our neighbor. Through Judy and Dick we met and became friends with many of their friends. The Maibergers, The Rollets, The Goodwillies and others. We all became good friends. We played card games, went on picnics and were invited to join them at house parties and, picnics. We were asked to join the dinner club they had formed. Everyone took turns hosting and making dinner for all the club members. When our turn to host came, Gail planned to make a special dish of Chinese Pepper Steak. The morning of the day that the guests were to arrive the old sofa Uncle Red gave us collapsed. A support slat on one side that held up one of the cushions broke in half. I tried several ways, unsuccessfully, to fix it. In the end I resorted to placing a box full of books under the broken slat to support the cushion. I was devastated. All of these friends were financially better off than we were. They lived in bigger houses, drove newer cars, and had better paying jobs than I did. Now they were to come to our older, smaller back of the lot house and I was sure they couldn't help but notice our broken down furniture. I felt embarrassed but there was no way out of this predicament. As our guests arrived a few at a time I was on pins and needles anticipating some sort of derogatory remarks. After dinner was finished Gail received several positive comments on her Pepper Steak. The evening progressed with jokes and laughter and surprisingly not a single reference to the sad state of our davenport. What a relief and how happy I was to find such nice friends. Other than Leonard and Jack, during my childhood years I was moved around so often that it was difficult to develop permanent friendships thus as a teenager and young adult I cherished any friends I made. Leonard was living in Chicago and Jack was back in California so these new friendships gradually assumed more importance to me.

Our fourth child, Cynthia arrived in August of 1959. Unknown to us an unwelcome companion came home with her. Cynthia seemed unusually cranky and "out of sorts". The very first day at home whenever I tried to hold her she would cry out. By the second day we noticed a small reddish spot on the upper part of her left leg. When we touched that area of her leg she screamed. By the end of her second day at home there was some swelling and a pimple had formed there. The morning of the third day the pimple and swelling had increased. By that afternoon her leg had swollen to almost twice it's normal size. We immediately took her to the hospital emergency room where the problem was diagnosed as staphylococcus. (We would later learn "Staph", as it is often referred to, is a bacterium frequently contracted In hospitals.) The doctors informed us that this was very serious and potentially life threatening for so young an infant. Explaining that her leg might have to be amputated and even then there was no guarantee she would survive they asked permission to operate on her leg. We had no choice and assented. Cynthia would stay at Mt. Carmel hospital for a week while the doctors attempted to battle the infection. The doctors had to lance the large "boil" to clear out the infected pus that had formed. We were on edge for the entire time praying to God to spare the life of our beloved baby girl. Cynthia survived but would bear a five inch jagged scar on her left leg as a result. Unaware of this disease at the time, both Gail and I had touched Cynthia's leg putting us in contact with the infection. Shortly thereafter we both developed Staph-like boils on our faces and elsewhere. They were extremely painful and it would take two years and hundreds of dollars for prescriptions before we eradicated it from our bodies. Fortunately my improving route sales provided an increase in my take home pay and the health insurance "Jewel" provided covered the hospital and doctors bills.

The arrival of Cynthia meant Cheryl would have to move out of the crib so we needed another bed. Anticipating Cynthia would also eventually grow too big for a crib we bought a second bunk bed. Four children in one small bedroom was a tight fit but they were all still little. I knew this arrangement would not work for long but it was what we had to do at the time.

Chapter 4

STEPPING UP AND DOWN

In the early years of my life, likely because of constantly being shifted from one place to another, I had not formed good habits of hygiene (especially brushing my teeth). I can't remember my mother reminding me to brush every day. On the farm, without the availability of running water, baths were once a week and brushing your teeth was not a priority. Whenever I was with my grandmother, she would remind me but then I would be back with my mother and the ritual was forgotten. Neglecting to brush my teeth resulted in lots of cavities and an accumulation of greenish tartar. More than once during my younger years my grandparents paid to have my teeth cleaned and my cavities filled. As I grew into my teenage years I became more conscious of how I looked. I explained earlier in this story how, without money for dentist visits, I tried to hide this problem with gum or by consciously keeping my upper lip down but I was not always successful. With my growing family and so little money I went for years without a visit to the dentist resulting in the slow deterioration of my teeth. Fillings eventually loosened and fell out. Once more I was back to keeping my lip down and plugging my cavities with chewing gum. The ramifications of this strategy are revealed in the following …..

Opportunity presented itself in 1959. While about to call on one of my best customers I observed a car pull up behind my Jewel truck. Before I could retrieve this customer's large order the doors of that car swung open and Len Lukas emerged along with another man I did not know. Lukas introduced me to Howard Rodenbough. Lukas explained to me that Frank Phelps had retired and Mr. Rodenbough was our new Division Manager. Mr. Rodenbough was out contacting all the route salesmen on their routes and wanted to accompany me on this sales call. Now, it happened that this particular customer and her husband had nine children thus their need for groceries, clothes and various household items was huge. Consequently I almost always had a big order to deliver to her. I knocked, the door opened and she invited us in. Once inside I set down her order and began showing the sales displays and impulse items. She bought several of my impulse items, ordered four dresses from the fold out display of children's dresses and several other items from the Jewel catalog. I took her grocery order for the next delivery and added up her bill including her ten dollar budget payment for a total in excess of thirty dollars. She paid her bill and we departed. Outside her house Mr. Rodenbough seemed greatly impressed. Probably due to the fact that the average "Jewel" customers bill was less than six dollars. Relieved to hear them say they were leaving I watched as they drove off. I continued on my route glad that I had not made any significant errors in front of the Division manager and thought little more about their visit.

At a sales meeting a few weeks later Mr. Rodenbough called me aside and asked if I had any interest in advancing my career with "Jewel". I was surprised by this inquiry. Of course I replied yes! Rodenbough further explained that a supervisor's salary was $100.00 per week. He said there was an opening for a supervisor and again asked if I was interested. When I replied affirmatively arrangements were made to audit me off my route and audit on a newly hired salesman. At the next sales meeting I was introduced as a new supervisor and assigned to lead a group of eight route salesmen. I received no training in the "art" of supervision but was simply told to contact each of my salesmen on their routes and pass along some of the sales techniques that worked for me. Without any actual skills in the supervisory field I fumbled my way through as best I could hoping to somehow improve the sales results of the men assigned to me. At that time I was only twenty-four years old and significantly younger than all the route salesman in my group. I had the uncomfortable feeling that due to my young age some of them did not hold me in the highest esteem. Still I was determined to try and gain their confidence. Several weeks later an opportunity arose. One of my salesmen was scheduled for a vacation. His name was Bud Whirlow and this particular salesman was number one in sales and collections for the Detroit district. His average collections were $1000.00 per week. As supervisor It was my responsibility to run his route while he was gone. Anxious to make a positive impression I was determined to contact every one of his customers and maximize the sales and collections on his route. When I did not find customers at home I would make back calls again and again until I found them home. My efforts on Bud's route that week resulted in collections of $973.00. When Bud returned from vacation he seemed very pleased and thanked me profusely.

Some big changes were announced at the next sales meeting. Although he had only been Detroit Division manager for a few months Frank Rodenbough announced he was being transferred to some other district and Earl Smythe was our new Detroit Manager. We were introduced to Russ Maclinchy who would fill a new position of "roving supervisor". By the end of the meeting all the new changes had me feeling a little disconcerted when to my surprise Bud Whirlow stood up and paid me a great compliment. He told everyone there what I had accomplished while he was on vacation and announced that never in more than 20 years had any supervisor running his route ever come close to the results I achieved for him. His praise significantly buoyed my spirits and I left thinking this would put me in good stead with the new manager. A few days later Earl Smythe phoned me and asked me to meet him for dinner. I was excited by his invitation thinking he had been impressed by Bud's positive reference regarding me. At dinner it was just the two of us. We enjoyed some small talk as we consumed our dinner. When we finished eating Mr. Smythe began inquiring as to my future plans with Jewel. Then, just as I was beginning to feel good about our dinner meeting, Earl Smythe suddenly dropped the hammer ....

"Julian, there is going to be a reorganization of the Detroit District's management. Detroit will be divided into three supervisory groups instead of the present four. So we will be eliminating one supervisor. I am requesting that you to go back to running your old route. Russ Maclinchy has years of supervisory experience and will take over your group. You will like Russ. Did you notice what a nice smile he has?"

The devastation was complete. I sat In total shock unable to respond. After several seconds of silence, Mr. Smythe said….

"Julian take the rest of the week off and think about it. I would like to see you back on your old route where I know you'll do a good job."

My mind went blank. I couldn't or didn't reply. As I got up to leave it seemed my body had taken on such extreme weight that I could hardly lift my feet to take each step toward the door. Driving home all I could think of was …

"Failure! I was a failure! What will Gail think of me now?"

My walk up the dirt driveway to our house on Appoline seemed to be in slow motion. Finally I entered the house and flopped down on the couch in total silence. Several times Gail asked what was wrong before I could even speak. A few tears left my eyes as I relayed the events of the dinner with Earl Smythe. As always Gail gave me her total support telling me not to worry everything will work out. I spent the rest of the week depressed over what appeared to be my failure. I played the conversation over and over in my head trying to divine any meaning to Smythe's comments. I recalled his comment on Maclinchy.

"Did you notice what a nice smile he has?"

I wondered why would he comment on Maclinchy's smile. Eventually it dawned on me.

"That was it!!"

I realized that without being too direct he was making a point about *my* smile. He was right. There was a problem with my smile. I was not facing the fact that the cavities in my front teeth had once again became prominent. My teeth had deteriorated over the years and the fillings had fallen out. I was once again under the delusion that others would not notice my teeth if I kept my upper lip down or covered my mouth with my hands whenever I laughed. My stupidity and neglect probably contributed more than anything else to my failure. I continued to be depressed over the demotion but at least I had discerned the probable cause. The following Monday I reluctantly returned to running my old route. I thought ….

"What else can I do ? I have a wife and four children depending on me. This is all I know."

After resigning myself to the reality of my situation I resolved to visit a dentist, have my teeth fixed and return to operating my old route that had fallen back into the dumper again. Aware that my demotion was primarily my own fault a long lingering depression haunted me. Still, back on the route the customers were happy to see me back and despite my unhappy state of mind I quickly brought the sales and collections back to the level I had enjoyed before. Many more changes took place in the following six months. Though I understood Smythe had good reason for dropping me from supervision I still took solace when he was removed as Detroit District Manager. Perhaps, I thought, I could build a better relationship with Lloyd Woodruff, the new manager.

Chapter 5

FRUSTRATION & TEMPTATION

Somewhere along the way to my Catholic conversion I had accepted as faith that God would not give someone a burden more than they could bear. This concept was put to the test that year. In early summer of 1960 came another blow. Gail was pregnant with our fifth child. Reeling with disbelief my psyche was screaming ....

"No! No! No! This cannot be possible! I am only twenty-five years old and I will have five kids. It just cannot be possible. God would not do this to me!"

But he did!.

Gail and I had tried to be good Catholics. We had not used any sort of birth control. Perhaps, my unusually strong libido was natural or maybe it was an outlet for the frustration of years of deprivation, first as a child then followed by the challenges of raising a family at so young an age. I can only say that "being" with Gail provided relief from the very difficult conditions I found myself in. Gail was my savior. At night when she held me all my troubles were forgotten for that short while. Still something had to be done. We simply could not have another child. Up to then I had been a loyal Catholic. I had taken my family to Church each Sunday, refrained from meat on Fridays and observed Lenten restrictions. My faith was wavering. I felt like giving up. There was no point to life. It was just setback after setback after setback and no matter the effort I was pushed down again and again. I slacked off on my church attendance. More of my time was spent going to the "bars" with friends and drinking more than I should.

At times I went with Kenny and Harvey to a "bar" on Fort Street that featured music by a live band. This "bar" had a large dance floor and drew a lot of young women many of which apparently liked to dance or possibly just wanted to connect with other young men. Before long Harvey and Ken became very friendly with a couple of the regulars. A few weeks later they boasted about having intimate relations with some of those girls. Encouraged to approach various girls, I refrained. I cannot say there was never any temptation on my part but being shy and awkward around the opposite sex kept me from immediately acting on impulse. With a few minutes to think I came to my senses. I knew not a single girl there or anywhere, for that matter, was worth risking my marriage. Still I returned with my friends to that dance "bar" several more times. Perhaps I enjoyed savoring the possibilities but eventually I tired of the atmosphere and the class of people there. I stopped going there.

Once Harvey's car was out of commission and he asked me to drive him to Fort Street. I reluctantly agreed. I thought I was taking him to that "bar" but instead he directed me to an apartment house. He told me to come with him to one of the apartments. Always easily led I followed. One of the girls from the Fort Street "bar" resided there. I had seen Harvey with her before. She offered us a beer. We sat and shot the breeze for a few minutes and then Harvey said ....

"Wait here Skip, I'll be back in a few."

I watched as the two of them went through a door, shutting it behind them, into what must have been her bedroom. I drank my beer and waited patiently. Thirty minutes or so passed until Harvey reappeared saying it was time to go. In the car he sat quietly as we made the drive back. It seemed obvious what had taken place in the bedroom but curious to hear Harvey's explanation I asked....

"What was that all about?"

Harvey just smiled with no response.

On another occasion Kenny and I were at a local "bar", shooting pool and drinking. We had consumed more beer than we could handle when. Suddenly Kenny announced he was going to go look for his dad. Kenny's alcoholic dad deserted his family years ago. Kenny resented his father but still tried to catch up with him off and on to see how he was doing. Kenny knew most of his father's usual haunts. We found him sitting at the "bar" at the first place we stopped. He walked up and placed his hand on his father's shoulder. His Dad looked surprised when he turned and saw Kenny. They did not embrace each other rather just exchanged smiles. The bartender strolled over saying ….

"Hey Lucky, you ready for another?"

Then it hit me, the bartender called him Lucky! I took a second look at the drunk sitting at the "bar" and realized it was Lester's old partner in crime … Lucky.

"Oh my God." ….I thought. *"Why didn't I realize this before now?"*

Kenny's last name was Ludke. Lucky was a natural nickname for his father yet it never occurred to me that they were related. Kenny's dad turned to look at me and said ….

"Hi Skip, How ya doin?"

"I'm okay. How you doin"? Heard anything of Les lately?"

"I don't see much of him anymore but I heard he's down on skid row now."

While I never had any strong affection for Lester he still had been a part of my life for some time and somewhere deep inside I cared what might have become of him. Kenny bought us all a drink and after some small talk we bade goodbye to his father, again without any embrace. Kenny remained quiet driving back. We returned to the bar we left earlier, shot some more pool and continued downing beer. A young woman looking a little distraught was perched on a stool at the end of the "bar". Kenny soon entered into a conversation with her. I saw him buy her a couple drinks but didn't think much of it. We were about to leave at closing time when the bartender called Kenny aside and whispered in his ear. Kenny walked over and spoke to the distraught young woman. She slid slowly off her bar stool and followed us out. The three of us, totally inebriated, climbed into Kenny's car and took off. Half dazed by drink I paid no attention to where we were going until we arrived at a seedy motel on Telegraph Road. Kenny registered for a room, got the key and escorted the young woman into a room. My head spinning from the all night consumption of beer, I nodded off while I waited in the car. I awoke as Kenny reentered the car declaring ….

"Go on in Skip! She's ready. She said you can do it too but she doesn't want you to try to kiss her."

"What is all this? You just screwed that girl? Why on earth would she let you do that and why would she let me screw her too? I don't get it!"

"She's an alcoholic, has no money and no place to live. She needs a place to sleep tonight so I offered to get her a motel room if she "put out" for us.

I had never had sex with anyone but Gail and temptation did present itself. After hesitating a few seconds, in spite of my strong and ever present sex drive I said….

"Let's get outta here."

Later I would learn Kenny was having difficulty at home. He suspected his wife was having an affair with a neighbor. (Later it became apparent that she was.)

Kenny was drinking too hard and often coaxed me to join him. Kenny, Jumbo, and I were drinking (more than we should again) in a "bar" on Livernois one night when Kenny suddenly

jumped up and rushed out of the "bar" to his car without saying
a word. Surprised by this sudden departure we quickly followed.
Kenny sped off at a high rate of speed before we could settle in
the car seats. He accelerated in excess of seventy miles an hour
down city streets posted at 35 mph, running several red lights
and causing other drivers to swerve out of the way or screech
to a stop to avoid a fatal collision. He arrived at his apparent
destination and screeched to a stop in a downtown area known
as "skid row". He immediately jumped out of the car and ran
into the closest "bar". He never uttered a word during this entire
episode. He hadn't bothered to park but left us siting in the
car in the middle of the street. Jumbo and I were completely
at a loss. We had no idea what the reason was for his irrational
actions. I walked apprehensively into the "bar" Kenny had just
entered to ask him what was happening. Kenny waved me off,
without a word . Kenny ran out of that "bar" and into another
"bar" right next door. I gave up. We decided to leave Kenny
there on "skid row" and drove his car back home. We both felt
lucky we survived Kenny's reckless drive. At seven o'clock the
next morning the the phone rang. It was Kenny pleading with
me to bail him out of jail, which I did. He never explained his
actions and I did not ask. He repaid the money I put up for his
bail and we remained friends but I was leery of Kenny for a long
time after.

My recent demotion at Jewel and impending arrival of our
fifth child was weighing on my mind and to add to my concerns
the brakes gave out on our Chevy. The cost to fix the brakes
was prohibitive. Always reluctant to withdraw money from our
savings I started thinking....

"Jewel" allows me to keep my Jewel truck at home. "I can
use the truck to go to run any errands that need doing, so the
brakes can wait for now."

During the next several months the Jewel truck was our
only means of transportation. We packed all the kids in the
truck to go visit friends, Grandma and Grandpa, and even to go

to church on Sunday. I was often embarrassed to be seen using the truck by people I knew. I was also aware I would be in big trouble if "Jewel" discovered I was using the company truck for personal use but I was young and willing to take this and other risks that I know now were foolish.

My friend Kenny, who I hadn't seen for a while stopped by our house wondering if I was avoiding him. Reluctant to admit the truth I explained that because my car was broke down I was stuck at home. Kenny told me he could fix the brakes if I paid for the parts. I bought the required parts and the following weekend We jacked up the car, which had sat idle, at the curb in front of the house, for several months. I stood beside the car and handed Kenny whatever tools he asked for as he worked on the brakes. He did get my brakes working again. It was something to do with brake shoes of which I knew nothing. Our friendship resumed and we began our trips to the bar to shoot pool. I was also drinking way more than I could reasonably handle. Drinking too much led to lots of arguments with Gail. Sometimes the arguing escalated to pushing and shoving. So drunk was I one night that I have an unclear recollection of the exact circumstance that caused my unforgivable reaction. Gail and I were in bed arguing. I cannot even remember what it was about but it advanced to the point that I lost my temper and smacked her across the face. The next morning the result of my drunken stupidity stared me in the face. Gail had a "Black Eye". Although I apologized, communication between us was sparse. Unsure if she forgave me I spent a few days feeling very low and reflecting on what I had done. Filled with regret every time I looked at her and the condition of her eye I began to doubt my sanity. Gail never brought it up again but the atmosphere at home was cool for a while. When, alone, I reflected on my actions....

"Why in the world would I strike this girl I loved so much? This girl, the only girl who cared for me, the only hope I had for a normal life, my reason for going on. How can I expect her to forgive me? How could I be so stupid? We worked so hard together to make

a life together. Gail bore the brunt of raising the kids. To save money she cut all the kids hair, mine too. She sat long hours at our sewing machine making the kids clothes. She washed all the diapers and clothes, cooked all the meals and basically cared for our family of seven while, when I wasn't at work, I was running around to "bars" with Kenny."

For several days every time Gail left the house to go shopping or visit her folks I wondered if she would return. Perhaps, I thought....

"She had enough of my stupidity. What would I do if she didn't come back?

The thought of being alone again was debilitating. How could I face another day without her? She understandably remained wary of me for some time and I was beginning to doubt she would ever forgive me. I cannot now explain the thought process that resulted in the what follows but while Gail was out of the house with the kids I began writing down what I was feeling. I still have the little 3 x 5 inch memo book I wrote in. Her are exactly the thoughts I had scrawled down....

"My love for you is so deep I can hardly bear to continue this way yet to ignore the problem only compounds it and later it will be worse than it is now. So I continue straight down the road to nothing for I know not which turn will lead me home. Admittedly I am lost. My conclusion it seems is that there is no real love at all, but only a love of convenience. As long as we don't rock the boat everything is fine but nowhere in my limited observation do I see any love that is constant & unwavering. Between man & wife or lover, between parents & children, between God & man it is all the same. Love is what they all want given to them & will reciprocate as long as they receive it. But when they do not get this love they soon stop loving also. Regrettably I cannot omit myself from the above condemnations."

I could not forgive myself back then and even as I write this story (60 years later) I still can't forgive myself.

It took a while but eventually the tension diminished and we continued our life and struggles together. In my earlier years I imagined and hoped for an idyllic life with a wife and children far removed from the problems of my childhood but I was learning that problems were a continual part of simply being alive. Apart from the problems brought about by an individual's own actions, other problems would arise over which a person had no control.

Chapter 6

CONFLICTION

Sitting in my living room chair on a Saturday afternoon I looked out the window to see a large figure of a man standing on the sidewalk in front of our house. He gazed in my direction a few moments then began meandering slowly up our long gravel driveway. As he drew closer I realized I knew him. It was Lester. As soon as he stepped on our porch I opened the door and asked him in. He sheepishly said hello and entered. I invited him to sit down and asked how he was. He replied softly that he was okay. He was neatly dressed and appeared to have recently shaved and combed his hair but I did not think he was "okay". He looked to have aged much more than the six years that passed since I had last seen him. He had lost some weight and most notably there was a large indent in the top right side of his forehead. It was round and deep about the size of a golf ball. I asked what happened but he shrugged it off saying he fell and hit his head. I assumed it was the result of some sort of altercation down on skid row. Lester sat quietly and seemed not to want to engage in a lot of conversation but after awhile he inquired about his son....

"How is Jerry? How is Millie?

"They're both fine."

"Where are they living now?"

Then I remembered, my mother had made me promise not to ever tell Lester where they were living. She said it would cause too many problems. Young and unthinking, at the time, I agreed and made that promise. Deeply torn between my empathy for Les and the promise to my mother left me in a terrible bind. With much doubt about what to do I said....

"Les, I am so very sorry. If it was up to me I would tell you but my mother made me promise not to tell you where she is and I have to live with her in my life so I just cannot. I am truly truly sorry."

I saw his head lower slightly and his shoulders shrug inward. After a moment of silence he spoke without a hint of animosity.

"That's okay, Skip, I understand."

A minute or so passed before Les slowly arose from his chair, politely said goodbye and left. I was deeply saddened as I watched the hunched up form of what was once a strong virile man walk slowly down the driveway, away from my house and probably out of my life forever. Like so many other things, I have done or not done, much later in life I would regret not telling Les where his boy was.

About the same time Gail's father was facing serious problems with the foot he injured in the Woodward Ave. car accident some years back. Despite several doctor's treatments it would not heal. Mr Starr was in his late sixties and his health was complicated with a recent diagnosis of diabetes. His foot continually grew worse and eventually it turned black and gangrene set in. It became necessary to have his leg amputated just above the knee. The recovery and mental adjustment to his circumstances became a large burden on Gail's mother and a great concern for Gail regarding both her parents.

In late December Gail gave birth to our fifth child Robert. There was nothing unusual about the birth and the baby appeared to be a normal. Soon after we brought him home from the hospital we noticed he was having problems keeping his formula down. He kept spitting up after every feeding. We tried a few different formulas but he continued to regurgitate them all. He was not gaining weight. At three weeks of age he was still at his original birth weight. Dr. Montante had him admitted to Mt. Carmel Hospital for observation. A few days later he was diagnosed with "Pyloric Stenosis" a blockage in the digestive system that prevented milk or his formula from leaving the stomach and into the small intestine. He continued to lose weight and immediate surgery was necessary. After the surgery was performed Bobby remained in the hospital 10 more days. We went to visit every day. Seeing this tiny baby with tubes in his feet and head was heart wrenching. Totally helpless all we could do was pray for him to survive. He was left with a large jagged four inch scar on his little abdomen but thankfully he did survive. When he was released from the hospital and we were able to bring him home he was so thin and gangling he made us think of a baby bird squawking in his nest. We were so glad to still have him. Bobby moved into the crib and Cindy moved to the bottom bunk bed. Five children in one small bedroom seems nearly impossible in today's world. We endured those crowded conditions a few more years while in the back of my mind I was aware this arrangement couldn't last much longer.

A family of seven presented several challenges the least of which was the strain on finances. There was also not enough room in our little house. There was not time enough to provide the individual attention each child might want or need. There was not enough time in the day to judiciously settle every child's perceived transgression by one of their siblings. By necessity we had to develop a disciplined approach to managing our family. It was the only way we could continue to effectively function. We knew our children would think some of our decisions harsh or unfair but we had no choice. I was acutely aware that my own upbringing involved strict discipline from my grandmother who I was quite sure loved me and a total lack of discipline from my mother who seemed not to care much what I did or what might become of me. I trusted our children would come to understand at some time later in life but not then.

The only time Gail and I could be alone was in bed together at night. Holding her close enabled me to forget the myriad of problems and responsibilities that swirled in my head throughout the day. That, of course, led to the problem of our ever growing family. A solution had to be found! My adherence to the dictates of the "Church" were weakening but Gail still felt strongly that artificial birth control was wrong. With another child absolutely out of the question Gail began paying extremely close attention to the "Rhythm System". We had been trying that system of birth control for a few years but it obviously had not worked or maybe in our passion we had made too many exceptions. There would be no more. I cannot speak for my wife but the years of frustration of laying night after night next to her unable to act upon the extreme desire I felt became nearly unbearable. At least though, abstinence gave us relief from an ever increasing family, for a while.

Chapter 7

A SIGN OF STRENGTH

Once again there was another change of "Jewel" managers and Ronald Degenz was sent to Detroit to replace Lloyd Woodruff. At the monthly sales meeting he introduced himself and explained *his* agenda and *his* goals for the Detroit Division. His speech left no doubt in anyone's mind that things would be done his way, or else! Ron was a large strongly built man with narrow set piercing blue eyes. He carried himself with an attitude of superiority that I had come to recognize, and resent, in most everyone that occupied a position of authority. When he introduced himself his tone of extreme confidence lacked even a hint of friendliness. I thought ....

"This isn't my kind of guy but so what, the only time I'll see him is at sales meetings."

For a couple of years I continued to run my route, ignoring the negative impression I had of Mr. Degenz. Going to work each day was growing more tedious. I was running a successful route and generally respected by management and other route salesmen but there was no challenge in it. Playing poker and going fishing provided diversions and relief from the daily humdrum. At one of the monthly sales meetings Mr. Degenz brought up an incident that occurred between another route salesman, John MacNaughton and the company auditor. I knew MacNaughton from other meetings and he was a nice easy going guy. I liked John. The reason for the incident was of little importance but when John softly stated his side of the dispute. Mr. Degenz rudely interrupted him and declared loudly ....

"If you're going to dispute our auditor's decision we don't need you on our sales team!"

For whatever reason Degenz's statement aroused a strong resentment in me. I had enough of his arrogant and bullying style. Without considering the possible ramifications I immediately stood up and loudly retorted....

"If you don't need John then you don't need me either."

I barely got the words out of my mouth when Degenz responded to my outburst.... "Hold on! Hold on! Let's all calm down. Okay, we need both of you. Maybe I was hasty. Let's all relax and go on with the meeting"

I cannot explain why I blew up at that meeting. As a young man I was usually timid and allowed others to push me around but on rare occasions, when I had enough, I sometimes exploded with defiance. Perhaps that was what I was feeling. From that point on I avoided Degenz as much as possible. Degenz's management style had one beneficial affect on the route salesmen. We were united in our dislike and resentment of Jewel's management. After sales meetings we would gather at the closest "bar" drink a little too much and grumble about our jobs in general. Degenz continued as the Detroit Division manager and I continued to run my route though it was becoming increasingly more difficult with time.

Chapter 8

THE CAPE COD HOUSE

The year 1963 brought some significant changes. Our youngest son, Bobby, would be three years old in December. He was growing too big to sleep in a crib. Five little children in that small bedroom was not going to work much longer. Something had to be done. We had to find and move to a bigger house. One we could afford. We began the search in early spring. With the help of a real estate agent we found a Cape Cod style house located on Ferguson Street, a few houses south of Puritan Ave. This was, at that time, a very nice neighborhood in northwest Detroit. It was a two story brick house with three bedrooms and a finished basement. It seemed a perfect solution for our expanding family and we had enough savings to cover the down payment however the one hundred dollar a month payment posed a major psychological problem for me. Always cautious where finances were concerned I was reluctant to make the decision to buy. Once again I turned to my Uncle Red for advice. After he looked at the house on Ferguson and I explained our financial situation he said....

"Skip, you simply have no choice! You cannot remain in that small house on Appoline. You are making progress with your job at "Jewel". Stop worrying and just make the move. It will work out."

I wanted someone to bolster my lack of self confidence and his encouragement was what I needed.

We decided to sell the Appoline house but before we found a buyer my mother informed me she knew a couple that might want to rent it. I was hesitant to enter into any sort of deal with friends of my mother as they were usually "bar flies". Lester was long gone but she continued her drinking ways. For quite a while her regular haunt was Betty's Bar on Grand River Ave. where she met another regular patron. He was a rather nice old Polish fellow named Tony. He too was a steady drinker but unlike Lester he held a steady job. My resentment toward my mother was reinforced by the her frequent requests for my brother Jerry to spend time at our house. I loved Jerry and was happy to have him visit but was reminded of all the times I too was pawned off to relatives. Her modus operandi obviously had not changed. On one occasion she asked us to watch Jerry for a week while she and Tony went on vacation. We were glad to do it but when the week was over they did not come to retrieve Jerry. Ten days passed with no sign of them. After two weeks we became concerned and drove to the "trailer" (mobile home) they lived in. I knocked loudly three times. The door finally opened and there they were the two of them both so drunk they could barely stand. They muttered something incomprehensible. Livid with anger and disgust, I yelled....

"You better get sober and pick up Jerry by tomorrow or else!"

It was an idle threat but it worked. They showed up the next day meekly apologizing. I said little in response. They took Jerry and left. I continued to harbor a deep feeling of resentment toward my mother but also believed my children should have contact with their grandmother even if the prescribed way to visit her on her birthday or Mother's Day was to take them to Betty's Bar. The children loved these trips to Betty's Bar where Tony (and other patrons) bought them pop and potato chips. Blissfully unaware of adult problems my children loved their grandmother and Tony. Eventually they married and Tony became Grandpa Tony.

After considerable thought and with much trepidation we agreed to rent the Appoline house to my mother's friends for sixty dollars a month. The rent they paid covered our Appoline land contract payment each month. Seemingly a great arrangement at the time. We made the move to the house on Ferguson. We were overjoyed with all the room this new home provided. It felt like heaven compared to anywhere else I had ever lived. We bought new furniture and located some of the older things down in the finished basement. Not only did we now have room to invite friends for visits or parties but we no longer felt embarrassed by the humble surroundings we had on Appoline. We enjoyed having Gail's parents, my mother and Tony, my aunt, and uncle, cousins and many others for holiday gatherings. Because of my childhood experiences Christmas get togethers were especially important to me. Unfortunately my mother's drinking was very important to her and led to extreme frustration on my part. All too often when invited for one of our children's birthday parties or Christmas dinner my mother and Tony either failed to show up or arrived very late and inebriated. Eventually both Gail and myself became exasperated with her lack of concern for her grandchildren's feelings. My frustration came to the boiling point on a Christmas day when they failed to appear on time for dinner. We had grown used to their untimeliness and went ahead with dinner without them. The children were anxious to see their grandparents as well as anticipating the presents they would bring. I grew more and more tense as the day and evening wore on without their appearance or even a phone call to explain their absence. Sometime around nine o'clock in the evening two of my children were fighting over one of their toys when the doorbell rang. Gail opened the front door and my drunken parents entered just as I was sending the two arguers to their room. My mother interjected saying....

"Oh Skip, thash' not right. Don't do that to your kids. Ish' Chris'mas."

I blew up and screamed....

"Who do you think you are? Mind your own business! You have no right interfering with my handling of my own children.

I'm sick of you're not showing up on time. Don't come to my house drunk anymore."

Without a word in reply they turned and left. Later, when I cooled down I felt bad about shouting at my mother but also thought she left me no choice. A few weeks passed before the hurt subsided and our relationship returned to a sort of normal.

Chapter 9

AQUIRING BUSINESS ACUMEN

Soon after we moved to Ferguson I was called to a special "Jewel" meeting where it was announced the name of the company had been changed to "The Jewel Home Shopping Service". A new compensation plan was also unveiled. It was called the "Jewel Franchise Plan". Under this plan route salesman would be called "Franchise Operators" and Franchise Operators could earn substantial bonuses for controlling inventory, customer loss and bad credit debt. Each route would be audited twice a year. The audit would determine customers lost, customer credit accounts fallen into "bad debt" and the amount of investment the "company" had in inventory and credit balances. Based on the results of each audit a route salesman had the potential to earn monetary rewards in addition to their weekly earnings. I looked forward to this new compensation plan. I had already deduced how to determine any overage or shortage that existed prior to an official audit. I believed that I could do a rudimentary analysis of my route a few weeks prior to a company audit and correct any deficiencies before the official audit. I began in earnest a quest to maximize my income through control of the factors that led to a profitable route for the newly named "Company" that I continued to think of as "Jewel Tea". I was careful in extending credit to customers. I made extra efforts to treat customers respectfully. When an audit was scheduled I first analyzed my route to determine how many customers I had gained or lost. I marked a red dot on any accounts that had fallen into bad debt to alert me to make a special effort to get those payments up to date. Thus began an extended period of highly profitable audits of my route. "Jewel" also established the "Distinguished Franchise Operator Award" plan. Over the following years I managed my route to be profitable for more than ten consecutive audits. I was awarded special engraved watches, clocks and trophys. Most important of all was the big improvement in earnings. One of the salesmen, who had the third highest sales and collections in the entire country, approached me and asked ....

"How do you do it Skip? My sales and collections are nearly double yours yet with all the bonuses that you earn, your income is higher than mine."

I was glad to be making progress financially but the daily routine of running the route eventually began to take it's toll. I kept finding it more and more difficult to put on my salesman's face and begin making my route calls each morning. I was seeking reasons to put off starting my route each day. If I learned the Perch were "running" in Amherstburg or fish were biting any where else I would take a day off to go fishing. Playing poker for money was another way to divert my mind from the fact that I was unable to derive real satisfaction from my chosen profession. Often I would play cards til early morning and then be too tired to run the route. Still I knew I had customers out there that expected me to arrive with their orders for coffee and other groceries. When I got a day behind on my deliveries I would make up the day by working Saturday. Gradually over time I got behind more than just one day and eventually, though it might seem hard to believe, I was as much as ten days behind on my route calls. I was able to conceal this fact from the home office by creative book keeping and submitting fictionalized reports of sales and collections all the while maintaining a decent sales and collection average derived from the route calls I actually did make. It did not occur to me then, that my ability to manipulate all the paperwork and weekly reports in such a way that the Jewel Home Office was not aware how far off schedule I was on my route was in fact a detriment to my potential success. While I was able to fool "Jewel" there was still the problem of the actual customers who were not getting their orders on time. I was fielding angry calls from customers who needed the orders for things they ran out of. I was constantly running around to bring orders to certain important customers that I did not want to lose. All this added to my inner frustration with the job that I both desperately needed yet could barely bring myself to do. (Looking back now I realize had I actually ran my route properly on time each day I might easily have been one of the top route salesmen in the nation with significantly higher earnings.)

Chapter 10

LOSS

A significant event occurred late in 1963. After knocking on a customer's door I heard her ask me to come in. I entered and stood in the doorway. Mrs. Florina (the customer) was sitting in front of the television. She looked up at me with tears in her eyes and muttered....

"They've killed President Kennedy."

I stood there in shock and disbelief for a minute as I heard the television broadcast the voice of Walter Cronkite, cracking up as he provided sketchy details of the assassination. It was more than I could handle at the moment. Filled with confusion and dismay I excused myself and left. I sat in my Jewel truck trying to process the sudden unexpected news before driving back home. I was so depressed I could make no more calls that day. I did not have a strong opinion on politics but my grandparents were democrats and it followed that my mother leaned toward the Democrat Party so I considered myself a democrat as well. The first time I voted was in 1960 for John F. Kennedy. He was young and full of promise. I was thrilled when he won the election. I believed he would enact things to help people like me with their lives. I resented republicans such as Senator Gerald Ford who stood in opposition to legislation that I thought might make my life better. Kennedy's death was a bitter loss. My mood along with the mood of almost everyone I encountered was dour for quite some time.

My disposition did not improve with the news that the couple who rented our Appoline house had moved out. Upon inspecting the now vacant Appoline house we discovered it in shambles. There was a large hole in the bathroom floor where a toilet leak had been left unrepaired for so long the flooring had rotted out. There were burns in the carpet, broken door hinges and areas where it seemed someone punched their fists into the wall. I had not followed my instincts regarding not to rent to barflies. The drunks had destroyed the house. I had neither the time nor skill to perform the needed repairs. The cost of hiring someone to fix the problems was exorbitant so we put it up for sale "as is". We sold it for three thousand dollars (half what we paid). The wisdom of my decision to buy the old house on Appoline instead of the new house on the outskirts was highly in doubt.

Chapter 11

ANOTHER LOSS

Mr. Starr's condition continued to deteriorate. Following a short period of depression, after his leg was amputated, his spirit returned and he learned to function using crutches. For a few years he joined us for all the usual birthday and holiday celebrations and he enjoyed spending time with our children whenever we asked Gail's mother to babysit. Unfortunately the very same conditions that led to the amputation of his right leg began to appear again on his left foot. Sores that would not heal eventually became gangrenous and eventually there was no choice but to amputate once more. He seemed to take it like a "trooper". Gail visited him every day in the hospital. I accompanied her most of the time. He survived the surgery but he was very weak and somewhat disoriented. It was heartbreaking to see him laying there with both legs gone. On the last day I saw him alive I went to the hospital with Gail to see him. We visited a while then after Gail gave him a kiss and we started to leave he suddenly screamed out....

"WATCH OUT! YOU ALMOST FELL INTO THAT HOLE."

"What hole?"

"IT'S RIGHT THERE! CANT YOU SEE THE FIRE?"

His continued screaming brought a nurse who calmed him down. When we thought he was okay we left. At the time we thought he was simply delirious, probably from the medication. Now I wonder. Mr. Starr never recovered from his ordeal. In February nineteen sixty-five he passed away in the hospital. He was a good father in law.

Chapter 12

OPPORTUNITIES?

In the course of running a route eventually some customers move away, or quit. To maintain the number of customers needed, Jewel had a separate team of "Direct Salesmen". The "Direct Salesmen" were sent to designated routes where they "cold knocked" on neighborhood doors and presented a "spiel" to the housewives in an attempt to convince them to become a regular "Jewel" customer. One day while calling on one of these new customers, sales basket in hand, I knocked on the door. I heard someone ask me to come in". I entered the house to find a young woman, wearing a very short skirt, sitting on a couch and smiling coyly at me. I introduced myself and began my sales presentation. When I knelt down to retrieve one of the displays from my sales basket I looked up to see that same coy smile on her face as she sat with one leg perched loosely over the other. A significant portion of her bare leg was in view. I perceived this to be intentional and became very nervous. I diverted my gaze, hurried through the rest of my sales pitch, excused myself and left. Puzzled by this development and thoughts regarding what it meant or what might I have done plagued me for the next few days. I came to the conclusion that no matter if this woman really wanted something from me, it would be asinine to act on it and put my job at risk. More importantly I would not jeopardize my marriage. Two weeks later I arrived back at the same customer's house. I was still pondering the possibilities but after several knocks there was no answer. As I was leaving a neighbor lady accosted me saying....

"There's no one living there now. She filed for divorce and moved to New Hampshire a week ago."

That revelation convinced me she was seriously trying to start something. I was relieved she was gone and temptation along with her.

The new year brought some good news. Ron Degenz was transferred out and we had a new Detroit Division Manager. Cliff Anthon seemed to have much more knowledge, experience and understanding of the route salesman. He was a welcome change. A month or so after he took over management of the Detroit Division he called me aside at a meeting and asked if I was current on my route. I perceived a twinkle in his eye as he informed me he had received a few calls from customers complaining they had not been getting their orders on time. This revelation struck a nerve. I knew Mr. Anthon was "on to me". I could not continue neglecting my route. I had to get current with my calls. I began the process of catching up by not making call backs on customers that were not home. Running through all customer calls only once enabled me to finish that days calls early and then I started on the next days calls. I also worked every Saturday. Following this regimen, within a month I was able to get current on my route. The following explains why getting current on my route turned out to be more beneficial than I had ever imagined.

Starting some time in my early teens I began having trouble with my left knee. I had no idea why but it often ached severely and gave out occasionally, without warning, causing me to fall down. I learned to live with what I referred to as "a trick knee." I never knew when my knee would malfunction and more than once fell while trying to cross busy major thoroughfares with cars whizzing by. Shortly after my marriage to Gail, I stumbled and fell. My knee locked up in a bent position. No matter how hard I tried I could not unbend my knee. The pain was excruciating. I laid in bed hoping that with time it would unlock, to no avail. Gail called her mother for advice and her mother contacted a chiropractor. At the time it seemed altogether improbable but that chiropractor made a house call to see me. After some preliminary questions he began massaging my leg, telling me to relax. A few moments later, just as I relaxed. He grabbed my foot and quickly lifted it upwards then snapped it back down. I heard a loud crack accompanied by a sharp pain and my knee was unlocked. My knee still ached but I was able to stand and walk normally. The chiropractor wrapped my knee with an ace bandage and prepared to leave. When we asked how much we owed he said....

"Two dollars."

That was unbelievable. He drove to our home, fixed my knee, including an Ace bandage and only charged two dollars. With no health insurance, at the time, that was a godsend. Unfortunately a few months later my knee locked again. We enlisted the service of that same Doctor who once more used the same technique to free up my locked knee. I continued to experience "trick knee" problems for several more years but for a long while, at least, no locking up.

By 1966 I had become better acquainted with Cliff Anthon. He seemed to understand the problems and frustrations of a route salesman. I grew to like him. That year my knee problem intensified. I was walking through the living room when suddenly I fell down. I attempted to get up but found I was unable to straighten my bent leg. It was locked in an acutely bent position again. The pain was unbearable. Gail somehow helped me to our car and drove me to the emergency room at Mt. Carmel Hospital. X rays were taken and I was admitted to the hospital. The following day Dr. Silber interviewed me. I gave him the history of the my knee problems. After reviewing the X rays of my knee he informed me I had "joint mice". I was at a total loss.

Joint mice?

Dr. Silber explained that at some point in time I had sustained an injury to my knee and chipped off a tiny piece of bone from one of the bones in my knee joint. He continued to explain the each time that chiropractor had snapped my leg, to unlock it, he most likely chipped off another tiny piece of bone. The bone chips calcified over time becoming small round marble like balls residing in the middle of my knee joint causing the bones in my knee joint to slide out of their normal position. That caused my knee to fail and me to fall. An operation was required to remove the "mice". I would have to be off work for at least eight weeks. I notified Cliff that I needed some one to run my route. Thank God I had caught up on my calls.

The operation was a partial success. Dr. Silber informed me he was able to remove five of the calcified balls but there were still five or six located on the back side of my knee he could not reach. He advised me to watch for a while to see how my knee held up. If I had more trouble I would need a second operation going in from the back to remove the rest of the "mice". Fortunately, for the rest of my life I never experienced the sudden falling down or locking of my "trick knee" again. I would however continue, from time to time, to feel extreme aching in that same knee.

Several routine blood tests were performed during my hospital stay revealing that I suffered from hypoglycemia (low blood sugar). When some of the symptoms of hypoglycemia (extreme weakness, clamminess, sweating) were explained to me I realized these were the very reasons I was taken to so many doctors and hospitals as a young child. The diagnoses that were made of polio and rheumatic fever were incorrect. With that knowledge I understood why I continued to experience these same conditions. It explained the "milkshake medications" I had discovered on my own. I remained in the hospital for ten days and was told not to return to work for at least eight weeks.

Relieved of the daily responsibilities of work I now had more time to spend with my kids and Gail. Being separated from Gail during my hospitalization had greatly increased the passion I always felt for her. Almost immediately upon my return home we abandoned our previous caution regarding intimacy. Not surprisingly several weeks later Gail informed me she was pregnant. I was disappointed with that news but, unlike previous times, not despondent. Our financial situation had improved somewhat and I was no longer plagued with worries regarding my ability to support my large family. Gail gave birth to our sixth child, in December 1966.

No sooner was Geoffrey home from the hospital when he began to exhibit some familiar symptoms. Like his brother Bobby he was regurgitating his "formula" and not gaining weight. He too was diagnosed with pyloric stenosis and admitted to the hospital for surgery. Unlike his brother, due to medical progress, he was only in the hospital for three days. Instead of the long jagged scar on his abdomen the scar was a barely noticeable neat, thin line only two inches long. Geoffrey was a happy addition to our family. His brothers and sisters were six to twelve years older and all seemed fascinated to have this new little person in our family. Within a few years Gail and I would experience the *"joy" of five teenagers in one household!*

Gail and I maintained contact with our old friends and the newer ones we made. I occasionally talked on the phone with Leonard who was still living in Chicago, played cards with Harley, and went hunting with Kenny. The Goodwillies, Moores, and Rollets introduced us to Saturday night "Treasure Hunts". A Treasure Hunt is more accurately described as a contest of solving various puzzles, each of which take you to a destination where you get another puzzle to solve. A series of ten or twelve puzzles leads you to a final destination where the winners are announced and prizes are awarded. We teamed up on these "hunts" with Ted and Wanda Rollet and became very good friends. The Rollets lived in Southgate, Michigan and were active in a community actors group. They put on amateur plays and musicals. We attended some of there plays. It happened that on one of the plays we did not go to they met someone who they thought might be related to me. On one of our frequent visits Ted Rollet, who had a wry sense of humor, asked me....

"Skip, do you have a brother named Frank?

"Yeah, a half brother I haven't seen since we were kids."

"Well I met a guy named Frank King at the play that we put on last week. I thought you might know him. His father was there with him and his name is Julian King"

I tried not to show it as my heart slowly sank. With apprehension I asked....

"Did you tell him you knew me?"

"Yes, I told him I had a friend called Skip and his real name was Julian King too."

"Did they ask anything else? Where I lived or phone number or anything?"

"No."

For years I tried not to think about my father. Now he was back in my thoughts....

"Face it he doesn't give a shit about you! He could have asked Ted where I lived. He could have asked for my phone number! My number has been in the phone book constantly ever since 1955 along with my address. He obviously knows my name. He could have looked me up anytime he wanted to but he didn't. He doesn't care! Why? What is wrong with me? Why doesn't my father care? My Daddy could have found me just as easily but he didn't either. It must be me. I guess I'm worth nothing to them."

I could easily have allowed myself to become depressed but then I thought about Gail....

"She must love me. She stuck by me no matter what. I am not going wallow in self pity. I know how to dismiss from my life those who don't care. I will stay strong for those who do."

It took a few days but I got over the hurt, for a while.

Before long, restlessness drove me to venture out of the house to play poker or go fishing. On my way back home from an evening of poker I noticed a large sign that read.... "Piano Bar". I always liked music and loved to sing to myself alone or when driving in my car. I would sometimes join in singing along when a group of people were singing but I lacked the courage to ever sing alone in front of anyone. The sign was on the front of the "Sip and Chat Bar" located on Greenfield Ave. just south of Plymouth Road. I decided to stop and go in to see what it was all about. Music was emanating from the finger tips of a woman who sat behind a piano bar that was surrounded by a few patrons sitting on bar stools. I sat down at the piano bar and listened for a while. A few of the sitting customers were singing along with the song being played. Occasionally Dorothy Conrad (the piano player) would call a singer up to sing solo at the microphone that stood next to her piano. Sitting there a while I slowly relaxed and started humming with the songs, then began singing along, quietly I thought, with others. With two or three beers in my system I was enjoying myself and feeling somewhat anonymous. I was shocked into reality when Dorothy pointed directly at me and said....

"You have a nice voice, young man, it's your turn. What song do you want to sing?"

I stammered a reply....

"Uh, er, no! I can't sing."

"Nonsense! I know you can sing. I could hear you just now! Get up here!"

Embarrassed and shaking all the while, I forced myself to go to the "mic". I was so nervous I cannot even remember what song I sang. I was happily surprised to hear a loud applause when I finished but relieved when I could sit back down. I listened to a few more singers while I consumed a few more beers and, oddly enough, when Dorothy called me to sing again, I willingly returned to the "mic" and sang without nervousness. That night was the first of many trips to the "Sit and Chat". I got to know Dorothy Conrad and became one of her many regular singers. I grew up hearing my mother sing around the house and knew she had a nice "voice". My Uncle Red also was a good singer. More than once I heard the story told that Uncle Red had actually sung on the stage of the Fox Theater in downtown Detroit. It was said that because he had a family to support he had turned down offers to join a professional band. I decided to invite them both to come with me and spend a night singing together with Dorothy Conrad. I was delighted when they agreed to come. We had a great time singing that night. It took some coaxing at first but eventually they both got up to sing and the crowd loved them both.

After several weeks of singing at the "Sip and Chat" I became friendly with a lot of the folks who were regular "followers" of Dorothy Conrad. Most of Dorothy's fans were older but I always got along well with folks older than myself. Among her "regulars" were two women, Marilyn and Sandra. Neither of them were singers but they were there most every night. They both seemed to enjoy hearing me sing, especially Marilyn. I often heard them asking Dorothy to have me sing a song. When I was singing Marilyn watched intently and continuously smiled at me. I loved to sing and naively presumed she simply appreciated my voice. One night, after I had stopped several times to sing with Dorothy, Marilyn was there again. She invited both my wife and I to a party she was having for some of her "Sip and Chat" friends. We decided to attend. The party was in Marilyn's finished basement. It was a small gathering. Sandra was there along with two other couples. They were all older than us. Marilyn, I found out, was not married. We engaged in normal conversation and some jokes were exchanged. Every one seemed to be having a good time. After imbibing a few drinks I needed to relieve myself and was directed to the upstairs bathroom. Upon returning to the party I encountered Marilyn on the stairs to the basement. The stairway was narrow and Marilyn blocked my way. She smiled at me curiously and did not move out of my way. I stood somewhat puzzled wondering what was going on. I thought she acted that way because she had too much to drink. Then she spoke....

"I like you, Skip."

I was sure, then, she was drunk and responded....

"I like you too."

"You know you can have your way with me. You can do anything you like to me."

This caught me by surprise. I fumbled for some kind of response and said....

"Marilyn, you know I'm married. My wife is right downstairs, for God's sake!"

"I know your wife is here. It doesn't have to be now. You can have me anytime."

I repeated that I was married, not interested and pushed my way by her. Shortly thereafter I made an excuse saying I felt unwell and we left. Most likely, she was offended. I continued my appearances at the piano bar but I never saw Marilyn again.

As my recuperation from surgery drew to a close I dreaded the return to my route. I began thinking about ways to avoid continuing my career with Jewel. With only a high school education and no training or experience other than sales my options were limited. I had determined long ago that having money empowered a person to make decisions, that they otherwise could not. To that end we had been saving what ever amount of money in any way we could for a long time and we had around eight thousand dollars in the bank. I started wondering if owning a business might be a way out. While searching the newspaper I came across a Kampgrounds of America advertisement for franchisees. As a family we had used camping as a way to vacation without spending a lot of money and the children had seemed to enjoy it. I contacted K.O.A. for more information. Their representative showed up at our door a few weeks later. He extolled the virtues of owning a K.O,A. Franchise. We were excited by the prospect of owning a business that would get us away from the city and closer to the outdoor life. Our enthusiasm grew after we traveled to a K.O.A. Campground several miles north of Detroit to see an actual operating franchise. Our contemplation of buying a K.O.A. franchise involved giving up the security that Jewel offered. We would no longer have health insurance, a regular paycheck or a retirement plan. Those were the very reasons I had become a Jewel salesman in the first place. Could I give up that security? There was one other problem. The franchise fee was a few thousand dollars more than we had saved. The only way to come up with the required amount would be to cash in my J.R.E. funds. The problem was my J.R.E. Account was not fully vested yet and I would lose a substantial portion of the accumulated funds. I struggled with those questions for the next several weeks. While still mulling over this opportunity the time came to return to running my route. The sales collections on my route had declined significantly. Within a month of my return I had my results back in the top ten. Then without any inkling came a surprising development that put a dent in my plans for my career as a campground entrepreneur.

Maybe it was because Mr. Anthon observed the quick decline of my route's results while I was recuperating and the swift recovery of the results when I took back over. Perhaps it was because of my history of several extremely profitable audits. I cannot know for sure but for whatever reason he contacted me on my route one afternoon and asked if I was interested in a promotion to supervisor. I told him no, explaining I had failed at supervision once before and I did not want to be humiliated again. Mr. Anthon assured me he would personally guide and train me through the process of becoming a successful supervisor. I was at once both overjoyed at the prospect of a second chance and fearful of another failure. He suggested I think it over and discuss it with my wife before making a final decision. We had to decide whether to pursue the K.O.A. dream or see if I could redeem myself in the roll of supervisor. Gail, as she always did, encouraged me to do what I thought best. She knew I was totally bored with running a route. In the end I simply could not give up the security Jewel offered. I called the office a few days later and told Cliff Anthon I accepted his offer. After being audited off the route I arrived at the office ready to put on the face of a supervisor.

Cliff Anthon was true to his word. He spent many hours working side by side with me. Interviewing new applicants was my biggest challenge. It didn't matter whether I was interviewing an inexperienced twenty-one year old or an experienced man in his fifties I still felt intimidated by them. Cliff worked on my self confidence by reminding me I was a successful route salesman with several profitable audits under my belt. He had me sit in on every interview he held with prospective salesmen. It took a while and I still harbored deep feelings of inferiority but I learned to act the part of a successful interviewer.

I was assigned a group of eight route salesmen to supervise. I thought of them as equals and found working with them satisfying and relatively easy. I imparted a few sales techniques that worked for me on my route and got along well with the salesmen in my group. As I eased into this new supervisory roll I thought that helping my salesmen to operate their routes for better audit results would earn them more bonuses and make me look better in the eyes of upper management. I dedicated myself to making an advance analysis of each of my routes a month prior to a scheduled audit. I used Hi-Liters to mark any account that either inactive or were "bad debt". When one of my salesmen was running his route he would notice the hi-lighted accounts and know action was needed. It wasn't always possible to cure the deficiency but being aware of the problem meant more of them were corrected. Some of my salesmen, for the very first time, earned a bonus at audit time. After a few years of using this technique to successfully lower the level of bad debt four more routes were added to my group. Even with the additional routes I still had the lowest average of bad debt in the Detroit Division. Soon Cliff Anthon was asking me how I was able to keep bad debt so low. When I tried to show him my method he seemed not to have the patience to go through it all but encouraged me to keep doing whatever was getting results.

One of the benefits of being a supervisor was a company car. A company car was a Godsend. We never had two cars before. When needed I had used the Jewel truck as a second vehicle.

Chapter 13

EXODUS

It's true what they say, time goes by fast when you're busy, and I was staying busy. Busy with work, busy playing cards, busy going fishing, and busy with the routine of raising a family. Almost overnight it seemed that five of my little children were either in or about to enter their teen age years. There was a lot of the typical teenage rebellion. Too much to go into here. Suffice it to say that as parents, in an attempt to preserve our sanity, we tried to maintain the discipline required to manage a large family such as ours. Unlike most families of today's modern world, with only one or two children to contend with, there was not enough time in the day to devote to every real or often imagined crisis that continually cropped up in the lives of each individual child. It was clear to see our kids did not appreciate our rigid approach but we hoped someday they would benefit from a disciplined upbringing.

There was a lot of tension. Our teenagers must have been as frustrated with us, as we were with them. Added to my personal frustration was the fact that I was becoming bored with my supervisor's job. For relief from the boredom I resorted to the usual distractions, fishing and poker. Too many times I played cards till all hours of the night and early in the morning, Sometimes too tired for a normal work day I began faking my way through by claiming I spent the day riding on routes with some of my salesmen when in actuality I spent only an hour or so with them. I would look for an out of the way place where I would park and sleep in my car to recover. It was time for a break!

It had been a few years since I had taken a vacation. A "Jewel" employee could opt not to take vacation time and still receive the vacation paycheck. In accordance with my philosophy of saving money I had let my vacation time accumulate with the idea of taking the pay at some time in the future. It was at the point that I needed some time away from my job so we decided we would take a week long trip to Washington State where Gail's mother was living. Some time after Gail's father died her mother met and married Robbie Robinson and moved to Bremerton, Washington. We packed our luggage and six kids (Jeff was just six months old) in our old Chevy station wagon and began the drive to Bremerton. Adding the two weekends to my one week off work we had just ten days to complete the trip. We were all excited to embark on this adventure. Other than trips to Canada none of us had ever traveled outside of Michigan.

Full of anticipation we began our cross country trek. We made it as far as Wisconsin the first day where we pitched our tent near the Wisconsin Dells. The next morning we continued along I-90. For the next two days we covered more than a thousands of miles. Constantly in awe of an ever changing topography we had never before encountered. Viewing the Badlands of South Dakota and the driving through the mountains of Idaho and Montana were unforgettable experiences. Another experience I will never forget was my Chevy station wagon losing power just outside of Billings, Montana. We limped into town to the nearest "garage" where I was informed that we had "blown a head gasket". I did not even know what a head gasket was let alone understand what was required to fix it. We camped overnight there while the mechanic installed a new head gasket and claimed he cured the problem. I paid the mechanic for his work, an expense I had not counted on, and we continued our journey the next morning. After three days traveling we arrived in Bremerton.

The next four days were spent visiting with Gail's mother, her new husband and Gail's sister Shirley who had made the trip from San Diego to join us. We were shown the local sites and enjoyed an impressive trip into the forests of the Olympic Mountains. Our time in Bremerton was all too short. Today, it seems quite foolish to spend six days driving for only a four day visit but the sites we saw and the memories we now cherish made it all worthwhile. We bade our goodbyes with kisses and hugs and began our return trek.

We got almost as far as Seattle before our car started exhibiting the same loss of power it had in Montana. In the middle of Seattle the car conked out for the second time. With no place nearby to camp we were forced to rent a motel room for the night. More unplanned for expenses! Money was getting tight! The next day I learned the reason for the two breakdowns. A warped engine head. Apparently the mechanic in Billings had simply installed a new gasket on the warped engine head. That did not solve the problem because the warped head would cause the new gasket to blow again and it did. The Seattle mechanic first fixed the head and then installed a new gasket. We were on the road again but we were way behind schedule. I had to stay behind the wheel for very long arduous hours stopping only for gas, fast food and short rest breaks.

We were forced to an unexpected stop in the middle of Minnesota. Late in the evening as the road took us along the shore of a small lake I noticed the sky was completely overcast and the air was so heavy you could feel it. The sky had a strange orangeish pink hue that seemed to coat everything we looked at. In the distance we could see several vehicles stopped along side of the road. Out of caution I slowed down, then noticed our car losing traction and slip sliding left and right. I pulled over on the shoulder, exited the car to investigate and immediately slipped on the gravel. Gaining composure I looked down and saw what caused me to slip. It appeared to be some kind of squashed lizard-like animal. I believe they were salamanders. Looking around further I saw hundreds, maybe thousands, of crushed salamanders with their guts strewn all over the highway smashed to slimy smithereens by the car wheels they had encountered. They were everywhere, as far as one could see. One could not take a single step without stepping on their crushed bodies. The other cars had slid on the slimy mass of dead bodies causing the drivers to pull over. That was one of the strangest scenes I ever experienced. To this day I have not discovered the reason why or what would cause thousands of these creatures to expose them selves all at once in the same location. We paused awhile amazed and puzzled, then slowly picked our way past the devastation and continued homeward.

Despite all the problems with the station wagon we made it to Bremerton but the old "wagon" seemed to be running sluggishly as we made our way back through Illinois. I decided I would sell it when or if we made it home. We were relieved and happy to see the "Now Entering Michigan" road sign as we left Illinois behind. Our happiness soon faded when we heard an alarming report as the radio played the evening news. There was rioting in the "colored" neighborhoods of Detroit. The radio broadcast announced that the disturbance broke out when Detroit police raided a "bar" on 12th street and Clairmont. Unbelievably this was one of the "bars" I had visited as a child, begging my mother to come home. Gail and I were distressed to hear this but we were confident it would subside and our mostly white neighborhood would surely be safe. During the several hours of driving it took to complete our return home we listened intently to the radio for more news of the rioting in our beloved city of Detroit. Once home we immediately turned on the TV and watched the devastation in horror. The riots continued for 4 or 5 days with massive looting and deliberately set fires destroying much of the"colored" neighborhoods, causing several million dollars of property damage. Michigan National Guard troops were brought in to quell the disruption and a curfew was imposed.

Still young and impervious to the real danger I ignored the curfew one evening when Harvey informed of a poker game and we drove to the game's location several blocks south of Livernois and Grand River. The game started about 6 pm and broke up around midnight. On our return home as we turned west from Livernois onto Grand River a military vehicle was crossing the very same intersection. There were six, maybe a few more, uniformed soldiers standing at alert in the back of the vehicle armed and ready. We were terrified thinking they might arrest us for violating the curfew. We drove slowly past them expecting to be stopped but they just stared intently in our direction without taking any action. Relieved to have gotten away with this infraction I decided not to challenge the curfew again. In a few days everything calmed down but the City of Detroit would never again be the same. For the next few years there existed a large undercurrent of frustration and dissatisfaction within the minority community. At the same time the possibility of another violent outbreak remained prominent in the minds of the largely white middle class. These factors eventually combined to determine the future of the city. At the time I pretty much dismissed Detroit's problems. They were not my main concern. Supporting my young family was uppermost in my mind.

In 1970 my oldest son, Gary, was fifteen years old and he began attending Cooley High School. Cooley was the same high school I graduated from in 1953. I had my own personal problems at Cooley but I still considered it a good school and a relatively safe environment for my children. Before long outside forces changed my opinion. The was a general feeling within some of the minority community that their children were not receiving as good an education as the children attending mostly "white" schools. This perception was fueled on by certain politicians anxious to curry the minority's votes. Growing pressure led to an attempt to better integrate some Detroit schools by "busing". The student body at Cooley was changed dramatically by "busing" in students from minority districts. The young students were not prepared for such a sudden and dramatic change. Racial tensions mounted, fights broke out and bullying was common. Twice my son was held up at knife point for his lunch money. Similar problems occurred at the elementary schools. My daughter Terri was chased by a gang of boys and had to climb out a ground floor window to escape. These occasional Incidents were a growing concern for us. Fortunately a new opportunity laid in the not too distant future.

One evening Cliff invited me, and my wife, to dinner where I was introduced to "Jewel's" Vice President of the Midwest Region, John Ellen It was a rare treat for us to dine at Topinka's Steak House as Gail and I rarely went out to dinner and when we did we couldn't afford to order steak. I might have enjoyed the meal if I had not been so very nervous at meeting a company vice president. I was on pins and needles waiting for something momentous to occur. I feared the napping in my car had been discovered but nothing of import was discussed that evening, only small talk. All through dinner I wondered what was behind the invitation and was greatly relieved when the evening ended without incident.

A few months later Cliff told me the company wanted to create a profile of all supervisors. This involved some voluntary tests and interviews. I saw no reason to object and agreed. On the day of the "interview" I met alone with two men that I did not know. They introduced themselves and slowly eased me into a conversational style interview, at first asking seemingly unimportant questions....

"Who is my favorite person? Who do you most admire? What do you like to do in your spare time? What do you hope to accomplish in your career with Jewel? What is most important in your life?"

The interview lasted more than two hours with many more benign and unobtrusive questions. Gradually the questions became more pointed....

"What do you think of Mr. Anthon's management style? Why do you think you failed in your first attempt at supervision? What are your career goals with Jewel?"

I answered as truthfully as possible while being aware the "wrong" answers could be detrimental to my possible advancement. After the interview was over I went to another room where I was handed a written test with all sorts of questions. Some related to math, some concerning language and definitions and some were problems requiring the use of logic. I was also shown a series of several complicated designs, that looked like some sort of modern art, then asked to select the two most similar to one another. There were several other facets to this test and in many cases I admit to having to make an educated guess at the answer or solution. When finished I was quite unsure of my performance on this difficult and comprehensive test. I asked Cliff when I might find out the results. Cliff said the test and the interview would be sent out for evaluation and we would get the result in a week or so. In the office, about a week later, Cliff informed me the written test was an intelligence test and it revealed I was in the 98.5% quartile. Puzzled by this information I asked what being in the 98.5 % quartile meant. Cliff said....

"It means only 1.5% of the people who have ever taken that test, scored higher than you!"

I had difficulty accepting that information. I always felt that I was smart but, aware I lacked a college education, never considered I could rank higher than most in the area of intelligence. When I asked Cliff about the results of my interview with the two men. He said their report was in my file at the home office in Barrington then tried to change the subject. When I pushed him a little on the matter he said....

"One of the their conclusions is that you are "highly punitive".

"Highly punitive? What does highly punitive mean?"

"I don't know, Skip, I'm not familiar with the term either!"

I was puzzled. I wanted to know what "highly punitive" meant. Most people that I asked had no answer but when some one said it meant I was sarcastic I tentatively accepted that explanation. I returned to my regular supervisory duties but the term "highly punitive" remained in the back of my mind.

A few weeks later I was invited to another dinner meeting. This meeting was with Cliff, John Ellen and Robert Woodsome. Mr. Woodsome was the president of Jewel Home Shopping Service. In complete awe of Mr. Woodsome I sat quietly, speaking only when a question was asked of me. Having dinner with the president of "Jewel" put me in such a state of unbelief I remember almost nothing that was said. I do recall Mr. Woodsome mentioning something about playing Bridge. (I had told those two interviewers I played Bridge in my spare time). I was relieved when dinner came to an end. I prayed I had not made any major faux pas. I remained curious regarding the reason for the interview, the test or the meetings with Jewel "higher ups" but heard no more for several weeks.

John Ellen was back in Detroit for the once a month meetings with Cliff and I was asked to sit in with them. Cliff took me by surprise with a question....

"How would you like to join the Vice President's staff?"

Caught totally off guard I fumbled to reply....

"Staff? What's that? I don't know what that means!" At that point Ellen entered the conversation explaining that as a member of his staff I would be given special assignments such as training new supervisors, holding management classes or just about anything else he needed done. It could involve some occasional travel to the home office in Barrington, Illinois. I paused a moment trying to regain my wits and responded....

"I am very interested in being on your staff but I would like to discuss it with my wife first."

Ellen was fine with my response but said he needed a definite answer the next day. I told Gail of this surprising offer and as always she agreed. I accepted and within a week I was given an assignment in the Barrington teaching a class for new supervisors. During the next few months I was given various special duties many requiring very long hours and overnight stays away from home. The promotion to "staff" was fortuitous providing a definite relief from my earlier boredom that, if continued, might have led to my downfall.

John Ellen announced a get together weekend for all his staff to be held in Traverse City, Michigan in September. We stayed overnight in waterfront cabins. Charter boats were rented and we all went fishing for Lake Trout on Lake Michigan. I had not met any other "Staff" members previously but became acquainted as the day wore on. There was an outdoor barbecue dinner that evening and plenty of beer available. Ellen was downing quite a few of them. It was obvious to me he was intoxicated. I drank very little as I did not want to make any mistakes or create a bad impression. I was having a quiet conversation with another "Staff" member when from several feet away John Ellen barked out loudly....

"Hey! King fetch me a beer.... **NOW!**"

A wave of embarrassment passed over me as I had never heard him speak in that tone to anyone else. I dutifully retrieved a beer from the refrigerator. He took the beer I handed him without a smile or a thank you. Later as I considered the incident I wondered if I was being tested. It took awhile before I dismissed the event as unimportant.

Later that fall, while on assignment in Barrington, John Ellen escorted me to the office of Robert Woodsome. We shook hands and the usual small talk took place. While complimenting me on the work I had done he continued to explain that the Vice President's staff was only an interim position. Mr. Woodsome began inquiring about my goals within the Jewel organization. He asked if I aspired to be a Division manager someday. When I replied that I would he asked if I was willing to move to a different city or state to pursue that goal. I told him....

"Yes but of course my wife has to be comfortable with making such a big move."

After agreeing that the wife's acquiescence was essential he laid out his proposal....

"Julian, there is an opening for a supervisor in Oklahoma City. It involves supervising a group of 18 route salesmen. The routes are spread out over half the state of Oklahoma ranging from the northern Texas border to the southern border of Kansas. Due to this vast geography you would have a much bigger and different challenge than you faced in Detroit. Proving you can manage a group this large would be a significant step in your quest for higher responsibility."

There was no doubt in my mind that this was a turning point in my Jewel career. It was now or never. It was clear that if I wanted to advance I had to either accept this new challenge or go back to being a supervisor. Trembling with both excitement and apprehension I struggled for a response. I told Mr. Woodsome I was very interested but reiterated that I needed to first discuss it with my wife. Woodsome then added....

"Mr. King, here is another bit of information that might affect your decision. The Oklahoma City Division Manager is .... Ron Degenz."

The world, I thought I was living in suddenly crashed around me. I could not believe what I heard. I considered Ron Degenz as the epitome of everything I disliked and resented in a manager. I asked myself....

"How could I possibly work under that man again?"

Trying not to reveal my state of semi-shock and hoping to find a way out of what I considered an impossible situation I decided to tell Mr. Woodsome of my previous confrontation with Ron Degenz. Woodsome informed me that he and Degenz had already discussed that occurrence and Ron very much wanted me to join him in Oklahoma. Woodsome said he needed an answer in the next few days. Still in a daze, I thanked him and left.

On the return flight to Detroit I gave a lot of thought to Woodsome's proposal. I knew this was an opportunity to prove myself and, if successful, maybe move up further to a Division Manager position. Also I considered the deteriorating conditions in Detroit and moving to Oklahoma could be a solution for the problems my kids were facing in the Detroit schools. Leaving all my friends and my mother, despite my ambiguous feelings toward her, was a difficult decision. One I could not make without Gail's input and agreement. We mulled it over for a weekend and, over the strenuous protestations of my children, decided to accept the offer.

Woodsome said it would be a month or more before the transition would occur. In the meantime I continued the various duties on Ellef's staff. One of those staff duties was to train a new route salesman in northwest Detroit. While stopped outside a customer's house and explaining some paperwork to the trainee I noticed two men walking along, one on each side of the street. Each man had a large bag, slung over their shoulder, filled with what looked like newspapers. They walked up to each house and slipped one of the "papers" in each door way. I realized they were delivering "The Shopping News". The men that were recruited to deliver these "papers" were usually poor souls that were picked up down on "skid row" and driven out to assigned neighborhoods. They earned "drinking" money distributing these bags full of "papers". My heart sank as the bedraggled man on my side of the street drew near. I could see it was Lester. What a dilemma? I really wanted to speak to Lester but with this new salesman right beside me I was embarrassed. I turned away hoping Les did not see me. He walked by seemingly not to have noticed me. That was the last time I saw Lester. It is another sad, long, lingering addition to my list of regrets. Over my eighty-plus years I have observed others waste whatever potential they might have had, over addiction to various substances, but none ever saddened me more than watching Lester's slow steady decline into total alcoholism. While not my father, He was in my life more than any other man. I learned a few things from him. Mostly what not to do.

The time arrived for me to make the transition to Oklahoma City. We "listed" the house on Ferguson for twenty-five thousand. A few "going away parties" were held by my friends and one by my "Jewel" salesmen. The plan was for me to work in Oklahoma for two weeks then fly back to Detroit every other weekend. Jewel would pay all my motel bills, meals, and airfare until the house was sold. Selling our house turned out to be much more difficult and complicated than we expected. The demographics in Detroit were changing rapidly. Likely due to "bussing", and other problems, many middle class occupants that could afford it, were selling their homes and relocating to the suburbs. Thus there was a glut of houses listed for sale making it difficult to find a buyer. Six long and difficult months went by before we were able to sell our house. Gail was alone to deal with all the usual problems that are inherent in a family of six. For my part, I knew I would find it difficult being alone and separated from my family, especially Gail.

I drove to Detroit Metro airport with Gail and the kids in the car. We kissed and hugged goodbye. I boarded the plane and was off to Oklahoma City. During the plane ride, although it was too late, I started second guessing myself....

"Was I doing the right thing? Would I be capable of suppressing my disdain for Ron Degenz? Why on earth would he want me on his management team? Is this a ploy to get even with me for challenging him at that meeting years earlier?"

After indulging awhile in self doubts I garnered up the resolve to succeed convincing myself, I could do whatever it took to excel in this new assignment.

Chapter 14

OKLAHOMA

Ron Degenz was there to meet me when I arrived at the Oklahoma City airport. He was very friendly and seemed quite enthused to have me on his team. He drove me to his house where he introduced me to his wife and children. Mrs. Degenz had a supper prepared for us. After we enjoyed some small talk Ron provided me with an overview of what the challenges were and gave me copies of the files on the men I would be supervising. I was one of four District Managers working under Ron Degenz. Ron informed me that he had just taken the realms of the Oklahoma City Division. He said he was assigned there to address the problems of the low sales average and very high level of bad debt pervasive on most of the routes. After dinner Ron drove me to the office where he handed me the key to a 1970 Ford Falcon, my company car, and the key to the office. I located a motel that I would use as a home base to reside in until Gail could sell our house and join me.

A sales meeting was held a few days after my arrival where I was introduced to the salesmen in my group. I was somewhat surprised to see their wives at the meeting as well. The meeting went just fine. The salesmen and their wives all seemed welcoming and friendly. When the meeting was over one of the men called me aside and explained that due to the widespread territory of the routes they seldom saw each other so they had a tradition bring their wives and going to dinner together after every meeting. I was invited to join them and I did. Going to these dinners afforded me the opportunity to get to know more about what the men and their wives were interested in. I still remember most of their names but the Mc Cook brothers stand out in my memory for reasons I will relate later.

Two of my eighteen routes were without a salesmen. My first assignment was in the small city of Duncan where I was tasked to run the route myself until I could interview, hire and train a new route salesman. I drove approximately ninety miles south of Oklahoma City to Duncan, found a motel to stay in and placed an advertisement in the local newspaper. I ran the route during the day, answered phone calls from applicants and held interviews in the evening. Several weeks passed before I hired a salesman for the Duncan route. Another two weeks were spent teaching the paperwork and training him to run the route.

As soon as I felt this new salesman was capable to go on his own I began traveling around the state making contact with some of the other established route salesmen in my district. My plan was to follow my proven program of analyzing each route prior to every scheduled audit. Doing that always worked well for me. I thought that showing the Oklahoma salesmen how to earn bonuses at audit time would improve their morale, cut down on turnover and best of all lower the bad debt on their routes. It took some time for this to take effect but each time one of my routes was audited the bad debt level was lower and many of the salesman began earning bonuses. In most cases it was the first bonus they ever earned.

The Duncan route proved to be a continual problem. I spent a lot of my time in Duncan hiring and training new salesmen, some of whom quit a few weeks after I left them on their own. Over and over I made the trip to Duncan attempting to recruit a solid route salesman. Stuck in Duncan for weeks at a time but still determined to continue analyzing all my routes I traveled all over the state making contacts and analyzing their books on Saturdays and Sundays. Often I worked more than seventy hours a week but staying constantly busy kept me from thinking about not having my family there with me.

For six months, other than flying back to Detroit every other weekend, I spent my nights in various motels around the state and ate my meals in restaurants. It was a lonely life. At night with no one to talk to I had time to think. *Maybe too much time!* It had been so many years since that vague childhood memory tried to enter my consciousness that I had forgotten about it. Once more, as I lay in bed half asleep one night, it made another attempt but for reasons I still do not understand something inside me refused to let it fully emerge. Instantly it was again forced back out of my thoughts (for a while).

The flight home every other weekend to be with Gail and my kids for two days was a welcome respite from the Oklahoma grind and helped to keep me sane. During this time Gail was a real trooper. While she was putting up with the typical teenage minor rebellions she was also dealing with city inspectors who demanded all sorts of corrections to conform with regulations on the sale of a house. We finally accepted an offer and sold the house for seventeen thousand dollars. Five thousand less than it was appraised at six months earlier.

As previously agreed Jewel paid for Gail and the kids to fly to Oklahoma City and join me. We located a nice three bedroom house to rent for two hundred dollars a month. I continued my quest for success traveling all over the state, hiring, training, analyzing route books and holding sales meetings while Gail bore the brunt of responsibility for managing the family. I believed that I was meeting all the goals that "Jewel" had sent me to Oklahoma to accomplish. My program of analyzing the route books and educating my salesmen on the importance of controlling certain important factors, had reduced their bad debt significantly. More bonuses were being earned and morale rose accordingly.

Several times a year sales contests were sponsored by "Jewel" to motivate the sale of various merchandise. Lawn chairs in the spring, blankets in the fall and so on. I am compelled here to relate an incident that, though devastating at the time, in retrospect seems quite humorous. It was a contest for the sale of "Corelle" dinnerware. Jewel was introducing Corelle, a new product at that time, to it's customers. "Corelle's" claim to fame was that it looked and felt just like real china dinnerware but, unlike real china, it was practically unbreakable. In preparation for introducing this unbreakable dinnerware at our monthly sales meeting I took a plate home and dropped it, several times, on our tiled kitchen floor. Sure enough it did not break. I was sure I was ready to dramatically demonstrate this remarkable new product. So there I was at the office, holding the monthly sales meeting in front of 18 route salesmen, their wives and Ron Degenz. While explaining the fantastic unbreakability of this new "china-like" dinnerware I held it up, paused a moment, for dramatic effect, then dropped it in front of everyone. *Catastrophe!* It shattered into what seemed like a million pieces. I stood there shocked, dumbfounded and speechless. Everyone, except me, was either chuckling or outright laughing. Ron Degenz rushed to my rescue, immediately took another plate held it up over his head and dropped it. A sigh of relief emanated from me when thankfully that one did not break. Although I considered my presentation a failure and was sure my group of salesmen would certainly not win that contest, I was wrong. My salesmen outsold every other "group" in the Midwest Region and won the event. In fact, during the two years I spent in Oklahoma my "group" won every contest of every kind held by "Jewel". My "group" had the highest sales average, the largest increase in sales, the lowest bad debt, and the highest profitability in the Midwest Region. I felt confident that I was achieving the objectives that "Jewel" expected of me thus putting me in good stead for the next step up in management.

"Jewel" held a management conference twice a year. These regional events were hosted by the Regional Vice President and attended by the Division Managers and District Mangers like myself. They were held at various locations around the midwest and I looked forward to these events as a break from the daily routine. One of these conferences took place in Lake of the Ozarks, Missouri. Ron Degenz drove his car there and I rode along with him. During the long drive and we discussed several subjects and my plans for the future. I began to feel more relaxed with Ron so I decided to ask.....

"Ron, did you see the report on my interview in Detroit where it said that I was extra punitive?".

"Yes I read it."

"What does extra punitive mean?"

"I'm not sure but it might mean you tend to strike back when criticized."

Sensing he was uncomfortable talking about it I decided to drop the subject. Still, I was bothered by being labeled with a phrase of which I did not know the implication. The conference was fun and educational. Days were filled with informative seminars but evenings we were on our own. One night we attended a show called the "Ozark Opry". This was a hilarious take off on Nashville's "Grand Old Opry". Another evening several of us piled into cars and made the drive to St. Louis where a few us us made the climb to the top of the Gateway Arch. It was a fun to get away and an opportunity to spend time with others that shared similar challenges and responsibilities. Each morning, while I was there, I noticed John Ellen with another man, tennis raquets in hand, strolling toward the tennis courts. I didn't think much of it at the time but later that year at another conference I saw the same guy, with Ellen again, playing tennis. I asked Degenz who that man with Ellen was. According to Degenz he was a District Manager from Dallas and like me, on track to potentially rise to Division manager. I would see them together on many more occasions during the two years I spent in Oklahoma. Two of the longest years of my life.

My disenchantment with Oklahoma began very slowly. The weather was not to my liking. Too hot and windy for too long. Too many tornado threats and the lack of Michigan's vast greenness were all little things gradually weighing on me. I was also becoming concerned with our finances. Our monthly rent in Oklahoma was two hundred dollars compared to our payment of one hundred dollars a month back in Detroit. Utilities and other expenses seemed to be higher as well. Dawning on me was the fact that since I moved to Oklahoma I had not been able to continue with my goal of always saving at least some small part of my income. I decided to ask for a raise. Degenz told me all raises had to be approved by Ellen I spent a few weeks struggling to gain the courage to phone Mr. Ellen Finally, I called him to request a raise and explain my situation. I was pleased, at first, to hear him agree to a ten dollar raise but disappointed to hear him tell me that the ten dollar raise above my $200.00 weekly salary would be deducted from the bonus I was due at year end. In effect I was not getting a raise at all. I reminded myself that if I achieved the position of Division Manager the starting salary was four hundred dollars a week. I swallowed hard, determined to do everything I could to achieve that goal.

The Duncan route continued to be a problem. I was back down there again hiring and training a new salesman when Ron Degenz showed up one evening with Dick Britain. Ron introduced us and we went to dinner together. While we ate Ron revealed there was a proposed plan to merge the Oklahoma City Division with Dick Britain's Kansas City Division. It hadn't yet been determined who would be in charge of the merged division but Britain was being introduced to all of Ron's district managers and vice versa. After dinner as we stood in front of my motel room Ron asked how progress was going on securing a steady salesman for the Duncan route. While I was relating some of the difficulties, I saw Britain hold out his hand out and start rotating his thumb over the top of his loosely closed fist. He chuckled and then asked....

"Hey King! Do you know what this is?"

"No. What is it?"

" It's the smallest record player in the world playing.... My Heart Cries For You." I always had a good sense of humor so I laughed, then without missing a beat I held my hand straight up with my palm open and began flapping my fingers up and down. I smilingly asked....

"Hey Dick! Do you know what this is?"

"No."

"It's me waving bye bye to you."

We were actually in the process of saying our goodbyes anyway so I thought it was a suitable joke at the time. Later events would cause me to doubt the wisdom of my actions.

A few months later in Galveston, the company held a deep sea fishing trip for contest winning district managers. It was a fantastic trip. I caught eighty-four Red Snappers. Some, two at a time, which I later cooked and served to my group of route salesmen at a backyard picnic. After the fishing was over we were treated to dinner at a local restaurant where again I saw Ellen with that same Dallas district manager. I thought I should find out how I stood in comparison to this guy from Dallas. I knew my group was leading in sales, lowest bad debt and leading in all important management factors but still wondered how these achievements compared to Ellef's apparent "buddy". When I inquired Degenz told me not to worry. According to Ron, year over year sales in Dallas were flat, bad debt was high and Ellef's protege wasn't doing too well. Those comments lessened my concern.

The following week Degenz called me to meet him at the office in the evening where he introduced me to Mr. and Mrs. Schulman. Ted Schulman had answered an advertisement that Ron had placed in the Oklahoma City newspaper. Schulman had recently moved from California and was interested in taking over the Duncan route. He once taught school in Lawton, Oklahoma (a town not far from Duncan) so he was familiar with the area. Ron wanted me to meet him and see what I thought. Schulman came to the meeting wearing a suit, he was well spoken and I thought that if Schulman had been a teacher he must be somewhat intelligent. He appeared to be a good prospect. Ron said he had already checked Schulman's references but said it was my decision. Two weeks later the Schulmans made their move to Duncan. Once again I checked into the Duncan Holiday Inn and spent two solid weeks there training Schulman to run the route and do the paperwork. After two weeks training he seemed to be doing fine so I left him on his own.

All the routes in my group now were running with regular salesmen so I was happy to be able to base myself back home in Oklahoma City where I could at least spend some evenings with my family. With me spending so much time traveling, things had not been easy for Gail. We had not purchased a car of our own so the company car was our only means of transportation. I was often gone on company business so Gail had to walk to get groceries and other things she needed.

Our oldest son Gary was seventeen and he and his three sisters were separated in age by only a few years so Gail was contending with all these teenagers primarily by herself. Gary had been saving fifty percent of the pay he earned working at a local super market. This was a regimen we had set for him starting with his very first job delivering newspapers in Detroit when he was twelve years old. With our goal for him to attend college we had purchased a college endowment policy from Metropolitan Life when he was born. The rapid increases in the size of our family and my meager paychecks did not allow for the same endowment policies on all our children but in those days men were considered the bread winners and women mostly cared for the home and children. I hoped that Gary would want to go to college and the money he saved along with his endowment policy would help pay the tuition. Gary had different ideas for the money he had saved. He wanted to buy a motorcycle. When I tried to dissuade him by pointing out how his savings would help pay for college he informed me he did not want to go to college. He seemed to be serious. This hit me hard. It was a huge disappointment. Circumstances had prevented the fruition of my youthful illusions of becoming a psychiatrist. I thought it important that if I couldn't send them all, at least my oldest son should go to college. It became apparent that was not to be.

I was working late one day in the Oklahoma office, doing analysis on one my routes. Ron and rest of the office employees had left for the day and I was alone. I knew there was a personnel file in Ron's private office. I was curious about what might be in my file. I tried his office door and found it unlocked. I entered. Nervously searching through his file cabinets I found the one marked Julian King. The only thing of significance was a copy of the report from that interview in Detroit with what I had since derived were most likely two psychologists. Now I thought....

"I'll find out what "extra punitive" means."

Concerned with what was in their report I began reading it slowly. Their conclusions were that family was of utmost importance to me. That my approach for helping the route salesmen in my group was treating them as team members and would go to great lengths to help them succeed but did not want to waste time on those who seemed unwilling to make an effort. The report also stated that I was extra punitive. Unfortunately I found no answer to my puzzlement.

The following day while back working in the office Ron called me aside. He told me that as part of my development the company wanted me to take a Dale Carnegie course. When I asked how much it would cost he said that the company would pay the tuition. I agreed and began attending twice a week classes. There were approximately forty so called students, men and women, from all walks of life. There was at least one attorney, a doctor, a policeman, business owners and others. One of the attendees was the ex wife of a very famous Major League baseball catcher. The sessions were run by a man named Jack Watkins. Jack was a very nice and patient elderly man. He always had a smile on his face and a constant attitude of encouragement for everyone. I liked Jack. After introducing himself he asked each of us to stand and introduce ourselves to the rest of the class. He gave us a preview of what the class would be about. We would be learning several methods that would help improve our ability to remember things, names and faces. Most of us laughed when he said that by the second week each of us would be able to stand and recite the names of every other classmate. He also told us that before the course was finished each of us would be expected to stand in front of the class and reveal something personal about ourselves. I shuddered when he said we would have to give two speeches. One was to be an impromptu speech and one a prepared speech. As the classes progressed, somehow through patient encouragement, Jack was able to gradually break down the personal defenses that everyone protects themselves with. Eventually, one by one, most of the class was able to reveal a personal experience, problem or difficulty in front of the whole group. I confess I was not anxious to expose anything about my feelings and held out for several sessions but as I listened to the stories of my fellow classmates a revelation was dawning upon me. All these people who I always thought were, richer, smarter, or in some way better than me, were dealing with the same or even bigger problems than I was. I slowly began to gain more confidence in myself and finally when it came time to relate my personal experience I revealed the following....

"As a child my parents moved more than twenty times and I attended 13 different schools. I was reluctant to make new friends as I never knew how long I would be in the same neighborhood. When I was not in school I would spend long periods of time inside the house or apartment where we lived. I cannot explain why but some of that time alone was spent hiding in a closet. This led to feelings of insecurity and a lack of self confidence. As I grew older I tended to cover up those feelings with excess bravado which sometimes turned off those around me. I am happy to say that being in this class and listening to all of you confess your concerns and difficulties has made me realize I am not alone in my problems. So I thank all of you, and in particular Jack, for helping me to gain a better perspective on life."

When the time came for the impromptu speeches Jack filled a large fishbowl with slips of paper upon which he had written a topic. A person's name was called and they would pull a slip of paper from the bowl and give a five minute speech on that topic. When my turn came I walked slowly up to the front of the class, withdrew a slip unfolded it and read the subject I was to speak on. On the paper was written one word.... SUBWAY! My mind went totally blank. For a moment I was back at Cooley High in speech class embarrassed and unable to think. I struggled to come up with something to say but could not. A minute or so passed that seemed like an eternity and I finally turned to Jack and feebly said ….

"I am sorry. I don't know anything about subways." There are no subways where I live. I've never even been anywhere there are subways"

Jack, seeing my distress, quickly began clapping his hands saying....

"Alright everyone let's show Julian our appreciation for trying."

With that everyone began clapping for me. I went back to my seat embarrassed but amazed as well at the response from Jack and the rest of my classmates. Their kindness alleviated the humiliation I was feeling. Subsequently I resolved to try and be more understanding of others in the future. The next speaking challenge was scheduled to be held two weeks later. After my inability to perform during the impromptu speech I determined to be ready to give the "prepared" speech.

Chapter 15

AN EPIPHANY IN WAITING

Dick Britain was back in town to discuss "Jewel's" plan to consolidate the two divisions. I was often unaware and sometimes confused by upper management's ways and methods. Ever since the apparent opportunity arose, for me to advance up the management ladder, I had tried hard to be cooperative and work diligently toward any goals the company set. When Ron Degenz invited Gail and I to dinner at one of the city's finer restaurants I wondered what was up but accepted without questioning the reasons. We arrived to find Ron's wife was there along with Dick Britain and his wife. After a brief introduction we ordered our dinners and engaged in the usual small talk. The evening seemed to be progressing along normal lines until Ron mentioned to Dick Britain that I was taking a Dale Carnegie course. Britain looked squarely at me with just a hint of a smirk and said....

"You don't really think that's going to solve your problem, Do you King?"

I could not respond or even think. I did not know what, but I knew something had gone severely wrong. A rush of extreme warmth encompassed my entire body and my mind went completely blank. I sat there stunned and embarrassed in the presence of Gail and the other wives, unable to speak. The humiliation I was feeling was so overwhelming that I began to feel sick and started to inwardly shake. I cannot remember another thing that was said the rest of that night. I simply nodded in acquiescence when anyone else made a comment. Somehow I got through the dinner and as soon as it was convenient we left. At home alone with Gail, I asked....

"What just happened?"

"I don't know."

"What did he mean by that comment?"

"Skip, I just don't know."

I sat up alone thinking for the remainder of the night ....

"What have I done to inspire such a degrading remark? That had to be a put down. Why? What chance do I have for promotion with this guy in charge when the divisions merge?" After giving up my comfortable life in Detroit , leaving all my friends, and all the family time that was sacrificed in my efforts to succeed, is my hope for becoming a Division Manager over?

I was devastated but there was nothing I could do? I had nearly twenty years with this company. "Jewel" was my security blanket, my retirement plan, the life and health insurance that protected my family. At the end of every year I had watched "Jewel's" contribution to J.R.E. grow my retirement account to almost thirty thousand dollars. At thirty-seven years of age I had nearly thirty more years to watch that fund grow. If I quit I would lose all the security that originally motivated me to start working for The Jewel Tea Company in 1955. All those considerations pushed me to soldier on. I had to believe I still had a chance. Perhaps I overreacted to Britain's comment. For a week or so after the incident with Britain I remained doubtful about my future with "Jewel". It was evident Britain did not view me favorably. Upon reflection I discerned my little joke of "waving bye bye" had not been received in the good humor that I intended. I was still wondering how I might repair relations with Britain when Degenz summoned me to the office. There were some changes Ron wanted to update me on. "Jewel" had abandoned the plan to merge the two divisions. Oklahoma City Division would remain with Ron in charge. This was good news for me (I thought). My concern regarding working for Dick Britain was gone. I left the office that day relieved from a large mental burden.

The sessions with "Dale Carnegie" were drawing to a close. I was still working on the "prepared" speech I was required to give when the phone rang. It was Ron. This time it was not good news. He told me there was a big problem and I had to get down to Duncan immediately. Schulman had been arrested. Someone had observed him walking up the street carrying the Jewel display basket, completely naked. Later, I learned Schulman had spent time in some sort of California mental institution. He apparently had a relapse. I wondered how he had managed to cover that up when Ron checked his references. Regardless of that, I was back living in a Duncan hotel, to try to hire and train again. My evenings were spent thinking seriously about all the recent events. It seemed to me that a lot of things were not exactly right. Doubts again resurfaced in my mind....

"Was Oklahoma the right decision, Would I have been happier back in Detroit? I miss my old friends. I actually miss my mother. Is all this hard work worth it? Do I really have a future here?"

These thoughts and others kept running through my head. Listening to others at "Dale Carnegie" expose the personal problems they had to deal with caused me to rethink my own experience and my unrelenting negative attitude regarding my mother. I was starting to realize that despite all her faults I wanted her to be part of my life. I began to think it was time to tell her how I felt so I wrote a long and heartfelt letter to my mother expressing how I missed her and that I thought we both had made many mistakes over the years but I loved her and wanted her in my life. I apologized for the occasional times I had spoken harshly. I told her I was still learning the lessons of life and was realizing how difficult her life must have been. I closed the letter with .... "I love you"

My stay in Duncan was welcomely interrupted by a regional conference for District Managers, in Dallas, hosted by John Ellen Several instructional workshops were held, one of which was regarding the control of bad debt. Due to continual monitoring of my salesmen route books I did not find it necessary to keep exact figures written down on paper. I always had an innate awareness of anything to do with financial matters. I attended that workshop feeling confident in the knowledge that the routes I managed had the lowest total bad debt as well as the most significant reduction of bad debt in the region. In front of all the district managers at that gathering John Eleff asked me to report the previous months total bad debt on all my routes. I could not quote the exact figure but with a feeling of pride I gave him an approximate estimate that I knew to be very close to the actual figures. Ellen replied....

"I an not interested in estimates! I want facts! If I were you, King, I'd have that exact figure tattooed on my underwear!"

There I stood, at the very moment I expected to be lauded for my accomplishment, humiliated in front of my peers. I thought....

"He very well knows the facts from corporate audit statistics show that my group's bad debt is by far the lowest in the region Why is he deliberately trying to embarrass me? How could this be happening again? Where am I going wrong? What in the world do they want from me?"

At the banquet that was held at the end of the conference John Ellen announced the Division Manager of Dallas was retiring and he introduced the new Division Manager. It was the same fellow I observed him with many times on the tennis courts. The same guy who had flat sales and very poor bad debt results from his group of salesmen. The wind came out of my sails. I thought my opportunity was in Dallas. It was not. Ron saw I was let down and attempted to "buck me up" saying....

"Don't let it get you down. There will be other openings coming up for you."

"Yeah, yeah, yeah! And whose ass will I have to kiss first?" ....
I thought.

If that wasn't enough of a message for me I was to get anther one shortly. It was raining hard one afternoon as I made the return drive from Duncan. I entered the exit ramp and softly touched the brake pedal to slow down as I approached a small curve in the ramp. The 1970 Ford Falcon suddenly began to slide. I hit the brakes hard. *Nothing!* Into a barrier went the car. I was not hurt but the car sustained a lot of damage to the front end. It was undriveable and had to be towed. The Falcon was sent to be repaired and Jewel supplied me with a new car. That accident is how I discovered the dangers of driving on wet roads in Oklahoma. Rain runs the red clay soil down on to the roadway and the clay makes the surface of the roads slick. Hitting the brakes on wet roads in Oklahoma produces the same result as hitting the brakes on an icy road in Michigan. The car slides and you lose control.

A few weeks later I was in back in the office with Ron and John Ellen Ellen laughed as he remarked on my driving skills then said....

"Look's like you made another mistake, <u>King</u>, on that Schulman character." I waited for Degenz to say something but he remained silent. I thought a moment then decided I was in an untenable position and remained quiet.

"Exposing that Schulman was recruited by Ron and I hired him based on Ron's recommendation might get me off the hook but also create a rift between Degenz and myself."

No more was said on the matter and we went on to other business.

Someone was needed to run the route in Ardmore, Oklahoma. The route man was going on vacation and I was assigned to run the route. I left the office disappointed in Ron's failure to take responsibility for the Schulman fiasco. During the two hour drive to Ardmore, the following Sunday, my thought process was in turmoil. Try though I might I could not understand or make sense of all the recent happenings. Still, I thought....

"I must resolve to produce the best results possible on the Ardmore route. I will analyze the books and assist the route salesman to make a bonus at his next audit. I will continue to do my very best in every endeavor. I will not allow a few setbacks to stop me from my goal of becoming a Division Manager. I will succeed!"

I checked into a motel and prepared to operate the Ardmore route. The first stop on Monday's route was in a Lone Grove, a small town 10 miles east of Ardmore. I loaded the truck that morning and began driving out to call on the first customer. As I drove my thoughts alternated between psyching myself up and worries about my future. Back and forth these two themes competed for dominance in my mind. Approximately halfway to my destination I pulled over to try and resolve my thinking....

"What am I doing?" I'm out here in the middle of nowhere about to begin what I've dreaded for years, calling on customers again. Trying to impress! Who? Why? What's the use? They're using me. It's a waste of time! I can't take any more of this! Denied a raise! Insulted by Britain! Put down by Ellen! Ron using me to cover his ass! I've worked my fanny off and got them the results they needed only to be overlooked in favor of Ellef's fair haired college boy. I'm done!"

I turned around and headed back to the motel . A few miles from the motel I stopped again....

"I can't do this. I cannot give up. I've put too much effort into this. My family is depending on me. I've got to keep trying. What else am I going to do. Jewel has been my life. Without "Jewel" I have nothing!"

I turned around and again headed out to call on the first customer but after driving a few minutes I gave up and began driving back to the motel once more. Three times I convinced myself to drive out that highway to begin calling on customers.

Three times I could not bring myself to make that first call. Up and down the highway I went for at least three hours until finally I gave up. Dejected I entered my hotel room and flopped on the bed exhausted. There I laid confused and numb with the inability to make sense of what I was doing. I stared blankly at the ceiling for hours and tried not to think. Later that evening I left the motel and began the long drive home. When I walked through the front door Gail, surprised to see me, asked....

"What are you doing home?"

Without answering I collapsed onto the couch.

"What's going on?'

"I couldn't do it."

" What do you mean?"

"I can't go on anymore. I think I'll have to quit before they fire me.

Without going into details I quietly explained that I had found it impossible to operate the route in Ardmore. Once said, I went into a depressed state and couldn't say any more about it for a day or two. Gail saw my distress and comforted me without pressing me for answers. The next day she called the office to tell Ron I had returned home "sick". I called Ron a few days later to tell him I was quitting. Ron asked me to reconsider.... "Don't make a hasty decision. Take the rest of the week off and think about it."

The rest of the week was spent in deep contemplation of my situation. Weighing what I might gain or lose by the action or inaction I decided upon. What will become of us? How can I do this to Gail and the kids? I sat in a chair immobilized, unable to decide what to do and the indecision only depressed me further. Gail suggested a psychiatrist might help me but I refused. When my condition did not improve she made an appointment anyway and I relented. During the hour I spent with the psychiatrist I explained my predicament. He listened carefully to my story then offered the following....

"Mr. King,you have been working quite a while for your company and even though you have received various promotions you are still earning less than many of your friends that work in factories or major auto companies. Do you think that after such a long period of feeling you are underpaid and under appreciated that could be the cause of your frustration and disenchantment?"

"Maybe."

He continued.... "Also these promotions you accept all seem to require quite a bit of travel taking you away from home. Is it possible you no longer love your wife and that you accept these positions because they get you out of the house and you are looking for ways to be away from your wife and family?"

"Absolutely not. I love my wife very much"

"Well, I suggest you think about these suggestions. If you wish to schedule a new appointment please see my receptionist. Thank you for coming."

I left the office with a quick step. I was a changed man. Gail was waiting and asked....

" How did it go?

" Well I know one thing for sure. I am not crazy! He is!"

" Who?

" The shrink!"

" What are you talking about?"

" He suggested I might not love you. That's why I think he's the crazy one."

We both laughed. I cannot say for sure that the visit with the psychiatrist solved my problem but for whatever reason I left there with an upbeat attitude. Perhaps, the questions he posed helped clarify my thinking. The Dale Carnegie sessions along with a better understanding of what was or was not my problem brought me to conclude it was time for *me* to emerge from the bubble of naivete I had been living in and take charge of my situation. I needed to make some changes. I spent the weekend thinking and formulating a plan for leaving "Jewel". I thought....

"If I give up my career with "Jewel" I may as well return to Michigan. My family is there and I really miss Michigan's big trees and overall "greenness". But Detroit is in a mess so I can't go back there or to any other big city. I would really like to live in northern Michigan but how would I earn a living? Maybe we could buy and run some kind of business?"

I discussed these thoughts with Gail as they began to make some sense to me. We were both full of apprehension but agreed we would look into the idea of owning our own business. Problem number one was ... we did not own a car. The car I drove was a company car. We needed a car. Without informing Ron of my plan to quit, I inquired about buying the Ford Falcon that was in the shop being repaired. Ron contacted Jewel's fleet manager and later told me "Jewel" would sell it to me for two hundred dollars. Surprised at the minimum price, I happily agreed to buy it when the repairs were finished. Next I found a news stand that sold out of town papers and started buying newspapers from Traverse City, Cadillac and other Northern Michigan cities. I searched the "Business for Sale" want ads, contacted a few Realtors and set up some tentative appointments. We booked a flight for Gail and myself and flew to Michigan, rented a motel room and spent the weekend looking at businesses. We looked at a motel in Hillsdale, a marina in Traverse City, various restaurants in Grayling and Houghton Lake. Despite my recently found confidence I was concerned about lacking sufficient knowledge to operate a restaurant and I knew nothing about the marina business, Although the real estate salesmen utilized their various selling skills I still could not *"pull the trigger"* on any of the businesses we looked at. We had one last appointment in

Houghton Lake. We were to meet at the Big Boy restaurant. We arrived a little early and sat drinking coffee and mulling over our options. I thought the Hillsdale Motel was a possibility but we were not very excited about that either. Don Hendershott and Warren Teeter from Stark's Real Estate showed up for the meeting. After we talked awhile regarding our plans, a little of our personal history and our finances they invited us to their office across the street. We were introduced to a saleslady who began pitching a listing for a group of tourist cabins. She was very persuasive. I can't say for sure we would have moved on the "cabins" but just as we were showing some interest, one of the salesmen interjected saying emphatically....

" We don't want to sell them those "cabins"! They've got six kids.!"

At the time I didn't quite understand the comment or the reason for it but a few years later, when the poor soul that eventually bought the cabins went broke, I realized that interruption saved us from making a disastrous mistake. Don and Warren took us down the road to show us the Waynorth Motel. The Waynorth was a 14 unit motel located just off the intersection of the US 27 expressway and M-55 highway. Right behind the motel there was a canal, leading out to the lake, where sat four rowboats. Renting out the rowboats provided small additional income for the motel owners. The Waynorth was the second motel to be found by travelers exiting the expressway. There were no large franchised motels in the entire Houghton Lake area, at that time. The first motel off the expressway had only twelve units so the Waynorth appeared to be in a good location.

Their business records showed a yearly occupancy rate of sixty percent with an average room rented at eight dollars. I mentally calculated various financial scenarios and came to the conclusion that even if the occupancy rate dropped to fifty percent, we could survive financially. It seemed odd that the owners wanted to sell when they had acquired the motel only six months ago but the real estate agent explained that the wife was from the city and found she did not like "up north" small town living. That explanation seemed reasonable (or perhaps we simply wanted to believe it). The owners were asking $135,000 on a land contract with a down payment of $35,000. The down payment seemed prohibitive but we said we would think about it. We returned to our motel room to contemplate our next move. We both agreed that, without experience in operating an actual business, running a motel might be the simplest and best option. Of the two motels we looked at, I leaned towards the Waynorth. I had been to Houghton Lake as a young man deer hunting with Kenny and Gail's brother. Perhaps too, I enjoyed fishing and that motel came with boats.

An in depth analysis of our financial situation revealed we were far short of the down payment but by then I was determined to make a change in my life. I had spent so many years afraid of failing and returning to a life of impoverishment, that I continually allowed myself to be at the mercy of others. I had wasted too much time believing I wasn't as good as most other people. In whatever situation I found myself in I always tried to put on the "face" of being a competent, knowledgeable person but I hadn't truly believed it. Deep inside I knew I was a fake. Although I had achieved a modicum of success in my "Jewel" career I still felt inferior, even to plain ordinary people. All my life I believed school teachers, policemen, gas station attendants, waiters, waitresses, local business owners, and even most of my friends were somehow better than me. At "Dale Carnegie" I learned the fallacy of those defeatist thoughts.

"No More!"

I vowed to myself. From that point forward I was going to determine my own future. I would no longer place my hope for success in the hands of others. Somehow I had to find a way. On the night before our return flight to Oklahoma I sat up late formulating a possible plan in my mind....

"Gary informed us he was not attending college so l could redeem the insurance policy for the cash value.... I could take the

records for seven years of un-filed income tax returns to an accountant
for filing. There were refunds due for each year as I never claimed
all our dependents.... I always charged all my travel expenses for
lodging and meals to my credit card then I submitted my expense
report to "Jewel" and received a reimbursement check every month.
If I stopped paying the entire credit card balance and only made the
minimum payment I could put the rest in the bank.... I could apply
at a local bank for a $1200.00 loan to buy the Ford Falcon from
Jewel. When the car became available I could buy it for $200.00
and put $1000.00 in the bank."

After estimating the potential funds that we could raise, if
everything worked according to plan, I realized we still would
not have enough for the down payment. Not ready to give up,
I called the real estate people Monday morning and inquired....

"We can only come up with $25,000.00. Will the sellers
accept a lower amount down?"

"We will check and get back to you Mr. King."

The next day we received the good news. The sellers
agreed to accept our proposal. With Gail's approval I started
implementing all parts of the the plan. I requested a weeks
vacation and in August, 1972 we flew to Michigan to review
the land contract. With little actual business experience we
decided to seek an attorney's opinion. We drove down M-55
and stopped at the first law office we encountered. We explained
we were buying a motel in Houghton Lake and asked the lawyer
to review the "contract". With a slight smile on his face Attorney
Mike Bauchan made a puzzling comment....

"You folks are walking targets."

I didn't ask what he meant. Maybe I didn't really want to
know. We returned the next day to hear his opinion. He told us
the contract looked fine but he advised adding the condition
that the $700.00 a month payments would not start until June.
I doubted they would agree but said....

"Fine with me if you think they'll go for it."

Amazed when they did agree we finalized the paperwork and happily returned to Oklahoma as the soon to be owners of the Waynorth Motel in Houghton Lake, Michigan.

I phoned Ron Degenz to tell him I was leaving "Jewel" effective February 1st, (six month's notice). He seemed surprised and asked me to come to the office. Ron queried me about my reasons for leaving but not wanting to make it personal I simply said I wanted to own my own business. Ron attempted to dissuade me by explaining all the soon to come great opportunities that lay ahead for me but I remained firm. During the following months whenever I was in the office or anyplace with Ron he continually tried to talk me out of leaving. As I looked forward with the anticipation of a new career it became difficult to maintain the regimen of interviewing, hiring and training new salesmen but I was committed to being a responsible person. I did what was required but there was no longer any joy or satisfaction in the doing of it.

I continued attending the Dale Carnegie sessions. It was time for the class to give their prepared speeches. When my turn came I arose trembling and gave my speech. After the entire the class had given their speeches a vote was held to determine the best speech. No one could have been more surprised than me when the class voted mine as the best prepared speech. At first I was delighted but then came the bad news. The winner in the prepared speech category was required to give the same speech in front of all the guests at the graduation ceremony and Ron Degenz would be in attendance. On graduation day I rose to the podium and gave following speech....

"Absence makes the heart grow fonder. In March of nineteen seventy-one I learned what that old saying meant. Up till then I thought I knew how much my family and most especially my wife meant to me. At that time I was asked by my company to accept an assignment here in Oklahoma. I was living in Detroit at the time.

I accepted the assignment which took effect immediately. I made the move to Oklahoma City while my wife remained In Detroit until we could sell our house. We thought it would take six to eight weeks to sell. Instead it took six months. I was authorized to fly home every other weekend. This meant I was away from my wife and kids for two weeks at a time and with my family only four days each month. It was during this time that I learned what my priorities in life really were. I had a lot of time to be alone and think. I thought about how much I missed my wife. How much I depended on her, how much I needed her physically, mentally and emotionally. I reviewed in my mind all the times I had been unfair or unkind or sometimes downright mean. This made me feel ashamed and small. I decided to put my feelings down on paper. I wrote to my wife explaining how I felt and apologized for those bad times. Eventually we sold the house and she joined me here. Since then we have become very close. Closer even than when we were first married. My point is that sometimes you don't recognize a good thing until it is gone. I was fortunate to have the opportunity to learn this before it was too late. I want thank all of you and especially Jack for helping me to realize what is important and find the confidence to make this speech"

Surprisingly Ron congratulated me on the speech but once again reminded me there were more opportunities waiting for me in the future. Not long after I was called to the office for a meeting with John Ellen Mr. Ellen calmly stated he was aware I was leaving and asked what problems I had. I saw no point in explaining and simply said I always wanted to run my own business. He asked what I was going to do after I left "Jewel". He listened as I informed him of my purchase of a motel in Northern Michigan then quietly commented ....

"There's a lot of risk in owning your own business. What if it doesn't work?

"I'll make it work."

"I'm sure you will but think about this, why don't you take a "leave of absence". That way you can keep your health insurance by paying the premiums yourself for three months and your "JRE" account will remain intact. Then if your venture doesn't succeed you can still come back to "Jewel".

At the time I was not allowing any negative thoughts to dominate but I saw no harm in agreeing to a "three month leave of absence". I agreed. We shook hands and I left.

It was a difficult six months until we assumed ownership of the Waynorth Motel. All my enthusiasm for "Jewel was gone, still I had a responsibility to fulfill. I began training a new man to take over my position. I showed him how I made the analysis of the routes. I did whatever was asked of me but not much more. All my thoughts were on our soon to be new life back in Michigan. Several times, whenever I was in the presence of Ron Degenz, he tried to talk me out of leaving "Jewel". I guess I will never understand what was motivating Ron or what he was thinking but on the evening of my last day with "Jewel he requested me to go with him on an interview at the home of a prospective hire. We completed the interview and departed. As we stood on the front sidewalk, shaking hands and saying goodbye, he unbelievably once again attempted to talk me out of leaving. This last minute effort to dissuade me seemed non nonsensical. I simply said....

"Ron, I have U-Haul van parked in my driveway already packed with our furniture. My time with "Jewel" is at an end. I am leaving for Michigan tomorrow morning."

Chapter 16

A NEW START

The next morning, we began the one thousand mile drive back to Michigan. I drove the rental van and my son Gary followed behind in the 1970 Falcon. We stayed a couple days at my mother's house in Dearborn Heights while the last few details of the motel sale were completed. On February 5th 1973 we took possession of the Waynorth Motel. The living quarters were quite sparse. There were only two small bedrooms, one bathroom a living room and kitchen area. The three boys squeezed into one small bedroom. Gail and I took the other small bedroom. There was no bedroom for the three girls. I was aware the living quarters were inadequate when I opted to purchase the motel but there was an unfinished storage room above the laundry room where the three girls could sleep. It was a hardship for the girls as there was no bathroom in the storage room. They had to come down to our small living quarters to use the one bathroom there. A family of eight sharing one bathroom was far from ideal but we had to make it work. After all in my teens I survived living in what was essentially a "garage" with no bathroom.

"When we had enough profits from running the motel we could have a bathroom installed for the girls".... I thought.

It was winter in Houghton Lake but there was not a sign of snow anywhere. All the snow had melted a few days earlier and there was no appreciable snowfall the rest of that winter. We were in for a big surprise. No customers! At least very few. Our motel business depended on tourists. Tourism in Houghton Lake was highly dependent on snow for snowmobilers or skiers traveling north through the area. Without snow we were in trouble. The rental rate then was six dollars for a single room with one bed and eight dollars for a room with two beds. There were three units with modest kitchen facilities that we could rent for twelve dollars a night. At the end of our first week in business we had rented only one room for eight dollars. In order to scrape together the cash for the down payment we had exhausted every possible resource. By the time we arrived in Houghton Lake we had only seven hundred dollars available to buy food and pay our bills. Our land contract payment alone was seven hundred dollars and our bills for natural gas, electric, insurance and others exceeded another thousand dollars each month. A harsh reality was descending upon us. Something had to change quickly or we would not survive. Nothing changed, however, and I realized the importance of the "no payments til June" clause in the land contract. That lawyer may just have saved our fannies. Our total revenues for the first month were less than one hundred dollars. We delayed paying whatever bills we could and paid only the bills that threatened having to close the motel. Remembering that I had survived times of extreme deprivation in the past Gail and I dedicated ourselves to finding every possible way to conserve our meager finances. For a time we could keep the thermostat low, suspend buying new clothes, avoid driving the car and purchase only the least expensive groceries. We learned to make a can of coffee stretch by roasting grains of barley In the oven and mixing them half and half with ground coffee. We substituted powdered milk for whole milk. Whatever we could do to conserve money was utilized. Survival was uppermost in our minds.

At one point it seemed necessary, at least to me, to venture into what now seems ridiculous. I saw a notice that beaver meat was for sale. Other Houghton Lakers told me beaver was good to eat. We were running very low on money and I knew not when business would pick up so for a very low price I purchased a whole skinned and dressed beaver. I decided not to tell Gail or the kids what I was doing. While Gail was busy in the motel laundry room I washed the beaver, seasoned it and placed it in oven to cook for that evening's dinner. Perhaps it was fate but about the time the beaver was ready to come out of the oven, a customer came to the door. Gail was busy doing laundry so

I waited on the customer. He wanted to see a room before he decided so I walked him to a room where he started asking about places to eat and so on. All this took some time and by the time I finished with the customer and returned to the kitchen smoke was emanating from the oven. Alas the beaver was overcooked, In fact the outside of the meat was nearly black. I was in despair. I wasted our scarce money on that beaver and then burnt it. Racking my brain to find a way to salvage this folly, I searched the cupboard where stood a bottle of barbecue sauce. I spread it generously over the burnt beaver hoping to disguise both the burning and the source of the meat. My next brilliant idea was to tell everyone we were having barbecue "beav" for dinner. It seemed to work as everyone thought I said barbecue beef. I thought I was getting away with this deception, however as they began to eat, frowns appeared on their faces accompanied with several ughs. I apologized for overcooking the dinner and pleaded with them to finish eating but it was no use. They wouldn't eat the barbecue "beav". I was depressed and disgusted with myself. It was truly a disaster at the time, but over the years recalling the barbecue "beav" story has provided our family with happy memories and much laughter.

February and March passed with little improvement in room rentals. I began to doubt the wisdom of my decision to give up my career of nearly twenty years with "Jewel". With little to no money left and debts accumulating rapidly it was starting to look like we would default on the land contract and lose the motel. I had no alternative but to call John Ellen and inform him I wanted to come back to work part time. I knew even before I contacted Ellen that the only part time job available was one I had vowed over and over that I could not and would not do. With a family and my own survival dependent on me I had no choice. I simply had to succeed as a "direct salesman". Ellen was receptive to the idea and offered to have me trained in the job by his best "Direct salesman". As a condition of that training he wanted me to spend four weeks verifying a route that was nearby Houghton Lake. The offer of a two hundred dollars a week paycheck for the four weeks was a Godsend. I desperately needed and accepted his offer without hesitation. Verifying a route meant to ride along with a route salesman and check to see if the balances that showed on the company "books" matched every customers records. I arranged to meet the route salesman at his home on Monday morning but when I got there he handed me the route books and told me he was quitting. He told me to take out all of the "Jewel" inventory he had stored in his garage. I spent half a day moving the inventory and placed it in a storage room at our motel. I spent the next four weeks verifying the route on my own. I reported several discrepancies between the customer records and the balances shown on the company books resulting in significant missing dollars but I never heard what was done about it.

When the verification was done I traveled to Grand Rapids to meet Jim Halper, the fellow that would train me for direct selling. We hit the territory we were assigned around ten am. Without going into the details all I can say is Jim had a unique and very successful approach. When a housewife answered the door he held up the "Jewel" catalog and quickly flashed through the pages while asking....

"Did you receive your new catalog yet?

This quick view of the glossy images portrayed in the catalog sparked enough interest to cause the prospect to pause just long enough for Jim to launch into his spiel. I knew from past experience that most direct salesmen struggled to write up more than six orders in a day. The weekly production of a direct salesman averaged less than twenty new customers a week. I was in awe as I watched him be invited into houses over and over and was further amazed at his high degree of success after presenting his sales pitch. At 2 pm Jim looked at me and said....

"We are done."

"Done? It's only two o'clock!"

"I know but I've written up sixteen new customers. That enough for the day."

He had signed up, in only 4 hours, as many new customers as many other salesmen did in a week. I was impressed. The next day he had me try writing orders using his approach. It worked. Within a few hours I was finding success similar to his. I could hardly believe I was actually able to do the job I had vowed many times I could never do and long dreaded. Once again at 2 pm Jim informed we we were done. In fact he said....

"Your training is over."

"Over? I was supposed to spend a week with you."

"I know but I have shown you how it's done and you are doing it, so go home and don't tell anyone from "Jewel". We will both get paid for a week of training and no one's the wiser."

Jim further explained that whenever he had written twenty or more new customers he took the rest of the week off. He said he really only worked two or three days a week but simply changed the date the orders were written and claimed expenses for the whole week. So I heeded his advice and drove home satisfied with the result of my training but wondering....

"Will I be able to repeat my one day success writing new customers for "Jewel" or was it just a fluke?"

With the five paychecks I received for the week of training and the verification of that route I was able catch up on some bills and fend off the creditors. The month of May arrived and with it came an improvement in tourist visits to Houghton Lake. When a few mushroom hunters and fishermen stopped and rented rooms at our motel it helped a bit but realizing our financial situation was still tentative I made the call to tell John Eleff I was ready to start writing new customer orders. I was first assigned to work in Grand Rapids where I met Ken Kristoff (the division manager). He gave me a map indicating the territory I was to work. Prepared to utilize the techniques I had learned and with some apprehension I knocked on the first door. The approach worked and I was inside the house making my presentation. The lady of the house happily signed up as a new customer and I was on my way down the street to knock on another door. My second attempt was successful as well. I was gaining confidence. There were times, of course, when I was rebuffed or even cursed at but by the end of the day I had written up twelve new customers. I contemplated my success. I was paid four dollars for each new customer so I earned forty-eight dollars that day. I thought....

"Writing an average of 12 orders for five days would result in more than $200.00 a week."

I started the second day full of an enthusiasm that resulted in 16 signed orders. Aware that the 28 total orders were much more than the company expected me to produce in a week I drove home and contemplated what Jim had told me. Early in life, by necessity, I learned how to manipulate circumstances to my advantage. This was a time for such skills. I said to myself....

"If I can write about 24 new customers in a couple days and make it look like I spent a week doing it, I can claim mileage reimbursement from "Jewel" for 4 or 5 days and put a few extra dollars in my pocket"

I knew it wasn't completely honest but I justified it by telling myself....

"I'm not really cheating "Jewel". I am actually reducing their costs when I produce more new customers in my "fabricated week" than other salesmen do in an actual week."

As the spring season progressed more travelers stopped at the motel, easing, somewhat, our financial concerns. My success at writing at writing new customers for 'Jewel" further alleviated my concerns and I began to think ....

"I will have to travel throughout the state to write orders and Gail will be alone so maybe it is time to buy a new car."

in 1974 we purchased a new Chevy station wagon and for the very first time we became a two car family. During the years we operated the motel Gail's mother and my mother and Tony came to visit at various times. We always put them in one of the motel rooms without charge. One evening that first year we took Gail's mother for a drive in the woods to look for deer. We drove quite a long way down winding two track trails that I had not yet explored. We were not seeing any deer so I kept driving and changing from one trail to another. It was nearing sunset and dusk was settling when the trail I was on ended at some sort of a huge construction site. There was a bank of dirt at least 20 feet high. I could not see what was on the other side. Curious, I exited the car and climbed up that large bank of dirt. At the top I saw what appeared to be a highway under construction. I had no idea what it was. We returned home that night wondering what we had seen. The next day I queried some of the locals about the highway construction I had stumbled upon. I was told it was a new extension of the I-75 expressway. It was to be completed that year and provide a direct route from south to north. Travelers from Detroit, Flint, Saginaw etc would no longer have to use the US 27 expressway to make the journey to various northbound destinations. It began to "sink in" then....

"How naive I was to believe the story about the previous owners wife being disenchanted with life up north. They probably realized that when the last part of the I-75 expressway was completed, travel on US 27 would diminish dramatically and along with it a sharp decline in number of cars exiting at Houghton Lake to look for a motel.

That turned out to be quite true. Still, as spring advanced into summer the tourist traffic did improve. All fourteen rooms were rented almost every weekend and many rooms were rented on weekdays also. On days when all our rooms were rented I observed that occasionally a customer departed their room early. It was usually around midnight when that happened so I watched to see if they returned later that night. Often they did. Occasionally they did not. One time I walked by the room of an early departure who had left the drapes partially open. I saw no luggage or a sign of anything they left behind. I concluded this was most likely a "one night stand". After I waited a while to be sure they didn't return I went quickly back to that room, changed the bedding, cleaned the bathroom, and prepared for the possibility of renting the room a second time. Shortly thereafter a car pulled into our driveway with a couple looking for a room to rent. Bingo! From then on whenever all the rooms were filled I stayed up late hoping to see a customer leave. Whenever a customer left I went to see if there were any belongings left behind. If I found the room was deserted I got it ready to rent again to a late traveler or another one night stand couple. For all the years we owned the motel I sat up late, sometimes til 3 a.m., hoping to make that extra rental. We needed every dollar we could get.

We were able to start making the land contract payments when the first payment came due. Unsure of how long the good motel business would last I continued writing new customers for "Jewel". During the summer when our motel was very busy or when various maintenance needed doing, I took time off from writing customers. Room rentals declined to a moderate pace when summer ended. We soon became aware of the seasonal vagaries of the tourism business. Room rentals soared in summer then plunged when summer was over, soared again during deer hunting season then slowed once more until snowmobilers showed up for Christmas week. The third weekend in January brought Tip Up Town U.S.A., one of the nation's largest winter festivals followed by the Grand Prix snowmobile race on the next weekend. These events attracted thousands of tourists that spent millions of dollars in the Houghton Lake area. Rooms for Tip Up Town (TUT) were booked a year in advance. After TUT was over we saw only an occasional customer until the spring and summer seasons returned.

After a year in business an analysis indicated our occupancy rate hovered around 35 per cent. We considered trying to survive on just the motel income, provided we lived "close to the belt", but then decided it would be wise for me to continue working for "Jewel". With the combined motel revenue and the Jewel paychecks we were able to stay current on our utility bills, pay off the huge credit card balance I had incurred to help fund the motel down payment, pay for our health insurance and even begin putting some money in the bank. Experiencing such dramatic ups and downs during our first year in business, taught us a valuable lesson.

"Don't spend all your money when times are good because bad times may be just around the corner."

Writing orders for "Jewel" took me to large and small town and cities all over the state. A trip to Flint led to some quite interesting experiences. I arrived in Flint about ten in the morning and began knocking on doors. I wrote up four new customers in the first hour and it was feeling like a good day. Around the eleven o'clock hour my knock was answered by an attractive young lady dressed in see through, baby doll pajamas. I nervously diverted my eyes but could not help but notice her breasts through the sheer fabric of her skimpy attire. I was trying not to look when surprisingly she said come in. I cautiously entered. She went to an easy chair, sat down and invited me to sit as well. She listened and seemed interested while, with great difficulty, I stuttered through my sales spiel. I was pleased when she signed up as a new customer and agreed to accept the introductory trial products. I had a smile on my face as I left her house to fetch the package of introductory products that I kept in my station wagon. Two thoughts were on my mind. Not only had I signed up five new customers by noon but I was going to get another look at that scantily dressed pretty young woman. I knew nothing would come of it but was still thinking ....

"Yes I am married and I love my wife but I am still a man after all and there's no harm in looking."

Returning to her front door I knocked again. Immediate disappointment! The door opened. It was a man. Presumably her husband. He motioned for me to enter. The young lady was sitting in the same chair but totally covered by a large flannel bathrobe. My enthusiasm somewhat deflated, I completed the transaction, thanked the couple and left.

Once I had signed up twenty new customers I decided to head home. On my way back I stopped at "Meijer's Thrifty Acres" super store. We had been looking for some empty whiskey barrels that I could cut in half to use as flower planters. I bought six whiskey barrels, stuffed them into my station wagon and started for home. During the two hour drive back to Houghton Lake I began feeling a small pain in my abdomen. As I drove the pain kept getting stronger. I perceived it to be due to excess stomach gas. Arriving back at the motel the severe pain made me unable to straighten up as I exited the vehicle. Seeing me doubled over as I walked in the door Gail asked....

"Whats wrong?"

"I think I'm having gas pains. I'm gonna lay down."

The pain became increasingly intense as I laid in bed. An hour or so later I could not stand it any longer and decided I needed to see a doctor. My daughter, Terri drove me to the doctors office. After being examined and a lot of pressing on several areas of my abdomen Doctor DaVito asked....

"Do you think you might have appendicitis?"

By then the pain was so excruciating I was barely able to impatiently utter....

"How on earth would I know! You're the doctor!"

"I think it's likely your appendix. You need to go to the hospital."

"I don't think I can even walk with this pain. Is there something I can take for it?"

"I'll give you something for the pain but it will be a mild dose. It wont last long because they need to be able to analyze your condition at the hospital."

He gave me a shot of some kind which dulled the pain and my daughter drove me to Grayling Mercy Hospital. At the hospital additional tests were performed. During the next several hours various doctors came to my room to push and prod the area of my abdomen. All the doctors seemed puzzled. I overheard them discussing a possible diagnosis of appendicitis but apparently I was not showing the response to their prodding that would confirm their suspicions. Around midnight (I later learned) the doctors confronted my daughter in the hallway and asked if she knew whether or not I was an alcoholic. When she said she did not think I was. They pushed her on the subject saying I reeked of the smell of alcohol. Terri called home to ask her mother if she knew I was an alcoholic or could I have hidden bottles of whiskey around the house. When Gail told her "no way" Terri then told the doctors that she had no knowledge of any alcoholism. Meanwhile the pain had gradually increased to an unbearable level. Sometime after midnight they decided to operate. Dr. Blaha removed my forty year old appendix and a few days later I was back home. When I heard the doctors had questioned my sobriety I was totally dumbfounded. My first thought was they must be crazy but after thinking for awhile I nearly broke out laughing as the reason for their consternation dawned on me....

I had driven home from Flint with six whiskey barrels in my "wagon". They were old but they were real whiskey barrels from a distillery. Although they were drained before leaving the distillery, due to their roundish shape a few ounces of whiskey often remained in the concave bottom of the barrels. During the two hour drive home the barrels had been bouncing and shifting in my vehicle causing the few ounces of whiskey to slosh around. The barrels had emanated the whiskey odor, permeating my clothes. It was gradual and unnoticeable by me but the doctors obviously could detect the smell of alcohol, leading them to a logical suspicion. Reflecting on the circumstances surrounding the loss of my appendix caused much laughter in our house. What a hoot!

Shortly after our move to Houghton Lake we were visited by a representative from the Chamber of Commerce who convinced us to become a member. I attended a few meetings and that fall I was asked to run for election to the Chamber Board. Hesitant to believe I could gather even one vote I agreed to let them put my name on the ballot. A feather could have knocked me over when learned I was elected to the "Board". I attended monthly meetings and got to know some fellow businessmen and women. I also learned a lot about the Tip Up Town Festival. How it was financed, what the philosophy was, and it's impact on the business community.

Writing new customer orders for "Jewel" continued for about three years. The extra money boosted my confidence. We made improvements to our motel. We had a swimming pool built, added telephone service and purchased Color TVs for the motel rooms. We had 14 rooms but I bought 17 Color TVs. I was aware that my mother and Gail's mother had never owned a Color TV so I gave each of them a Color TV. The third extra TV was for our living quarters.

It appeared my decision to abandon a management career with "Jewel" had worked out. Of course my surprising success at writing new customer orders was highly contributory to our financial stability. However after my initial enthusiasm for writing up new customers wore off, boredom once again began slowly setting in. Over the next two years the boredom morphed into dread. It was becoming harder and harder for me to start the workday. Maybe I was the most productive salesman "Jewel" had, albeit with the fewest hours expended, but I did not enjoy what I was doing. All the time I spent traveling all over Michigan to write up new customers meant time I was not at home, leaving Gail with the burden of raising our children. All but our youngest were in their teenage years and some were caught up with the prevailing problems of the 1970's, drugs, alcohol and rebellion. I began wondering if I should leave that semi-career and the money that I earned. The income from the motel was definitely not enough to support our family so before I could quit the "Jewel" job I needed to find some kind of local job to supplement our modest motel income. Unless I wanted to work as a gas station attendant or a waiter there were almost no other jobs available in the Houghton Lake area. The other possibility was to find another business for me to run. We thought that if Gail could pretty much operate the motel by herself and I could find another small business to run that produced a profit of three or four thousand dollars a year, we could get by. For more than a year we toyed with the idea of finding some sort of local business that I could run.

Chapter 17

MORE RESPONSIBILITY

The business climate in Houghton Lake was slowly changing. Three years had passed since the I-75 expressway was completed and northbound traffic on US 27 had declined considerably. Many small business owners were experiencing a drop in business. Tip Up Town was one of the exceptions. Many thousands of people traveled to Houghton Lake to experience the excitement of Tip Up Town (TUT). The festival brought much needed revenue to the area. It was known that motels and hotels in surrounding towns for miles around were being filled by Tip Up Town visitors. The Grand Prix snowmobile race, which was held the weekend after Tip Up Town, gave another moderate boost to the local economy but in 1976 officials announced the race would no longer be held in Houghton Lake. Soon after the 1976 Tip Up Town festival was over an idea began circulating among a few business owners, including me. I kept thinking....

"Tip Up Town is so popular that many tourists stay in other nearby towns simply because there are not enough restaurants, resorts and motel rooms in Houghton Lake, to accommodate all the folks that come for the festival. Now that the Grand Prix race is canceled what if we expand TUT to two weekends? Wouldn't some people decide to come on one weekend and others decide on the other weekend? Allowing people to choose between two weekends would lessen the extreme demand and provide an avenue for more customers to find accommodations in Houghton Lake instead of having to stay in other towns. If more Tip Up Towners stay in Houghton Lake it would provide more tourism dollars for our community."

This idea was growing more prevalent within the business community. A small contingent of business people held a meeting where a discussion of this idea took place. Most were in favor of a "two weekend Tip Up Town". A few were not. Being the only person at the meeting who was a member of the Chamber Board of Directors I volunteered to present the idea of two weekends to the "Board".

At the next "Chamber" meeting I presented the concept of having a second Tip Up Town weekend to off set the loss of the Gran Prix race as well as the following....

"The Chamber invests a tremendous amount of money promoting, organizing and preparing to put on the event. Think about the financial impact on the Chamber if there is a large snowstorm or some other catastrophic event that occurs on the exact dates of Tip Up Town preventing travel to Houghton Lake. If we have two weekends we spread that risk. Should one weekend have to be canceled the losses would be mitigated by second weekend."

This idea swayed some "Chamber" directors but there were a few adamant holdouts. The opposition centered on the fear that a second weekend would dilute the drawing power of events that the original weekend was famous for. Although I believed their concern was unwarranted I knew it had to be addressed or the idea of two weekends might be voted down. An idea popped into my head at the very last minute. I asked....

"What if we agree to feature all new events on the second weekend and not hold or duplicate any first weekend events?"

That proposal mollified most of the objectors but a few doubters remained. Cliff Roberts a well known businessman and big supporter of Tip Up Town stood up and asked if I was willing to take the job of Director for the second weekend of TUT. When I accepted, he made a motion that the idea be approved based on all new events for the second weekend. The motion was seconded and approved. I had a new and big responsibility. One I knew I had to meet. Cliff Roberts turned out to be a big help to me. He possessed past knowledge of the functioning and organization of Tip Up Town that I did not have. I often drew on his experience and advice to help with problems I encountered along the way. My first priority was to design a set of activities and demonstrations hat would entertain TUT visitors for the two day festival without repeating any of the "sacrosanct" events of the first weekend.

The Tip Up Town festival originated in 1951 primarily as an ice fishing contest. Badges were sold to raise funds that were used to finance the next years event. Eventually a Tip Up Town committee was formed to oversee the finances and money raised from selling badges was put into a separate Tip Up Town account only to be used for the purpose of promoting and putting on Tip Up Town. As the festival grew in popularity there were more and more attendees and badge sales increased dramatically. More money from badge sales prompted the TUT committee to add entertaining demonstrations that would appeal to the whole family. When I attended my first TUT in January 1974, there were helicopter rides, an aerial show featuring various aerobatic airplane stunts, a Hot Air Balloon, professional "Sky Divers" that jumped from a flying airplane. Various contests were held. The Grand Parade down M-55 kicked off the event on Saturday mornings with a noted celebrity as Grand Marshall. I recall country singer Jim Ed Brown was Grand Marshall one year. On another year I found myself drinking beer with the Grand Marshall who played the iconic "Marlborro Man" on television. I was faced with structuring a new second TUT weekend without the advantage of any of the tried and true events used previously. I devoted many hours that summer considering the best approach to use. I finally decided TUT's second weekend should focus on snowmobiling and cross country skiing. With help from Gail and Cliff Roberts I came up with plans for several snowmobile style events, a treasure Hunt, poker run, drag races on the ice, cross country ski race, a snow sculpture contest, several demonstrations and more. We were not supposed to repeat the Grand Parade on M-55 so we planned a decorated snowmobile parade on the lake. The next step was to find chairmen for each of the 78 committees required to put on the second TUT weekend. I called a special meeting for the general public where

I found several local business men and women, anxious to see a second weekend succeed. Many volunteered to serve. My wife accepted the job of publicity chairperson. Once the planning was underway I felt comfortable returning to writing "orders" and helping with the motel.

While we continued toying with the idea of my running another small business. the problems with our teenagers were growing more serious. Raising a family of six children by it's very nature required us to establish some rules we considered important and the discipline to enforce them. Rebellious teens are not fond of rules or discipline. The culture of the1970's enhanced the popularity of marijuana and other drugs which exacerbated the normal teenage problems. Our family was no exception. There were problems with runaways, teen pregnancy, alcohol, drug use and so forth but names are not necessary. These were a few but not all the challenges we faced. A feeling of helplessness plagued me. Back then and even now, as I write this story, the same thoughts continue to dog me.

"Why couldn't I have been a better father. Why do I make so many foolish mistakes. I should know how to handle these situations. So what if I had no father to show or train me? I am still responsible. Maybe if circumstances had not forced me to be constantly intent on our survival I might have done better."

Despite the many problems at home I had to stay focused on two simultaneous goals. It wasn't fair but Gail had to deal with the majority of the teenage problems. Most of my time was divided between working for "Jewel" to earn the money we needed and building an organization for the second weekend of Tip Up Town. Within a few months I came to the conclusion that so much of my time was needed to meet the increasing demands of the "second weekend" project that I had to limit writing new customers for Jewel to one day a week. I made up various excuses when questioned by "Jewel" management regarding the decline in my production of "orders". The following six months were devoted to holding organizational meetings, seeking volunteers, obtaining necessary permits, negotiating contracts with various vendors and solving a myriad of naturally occurring problems. The most difficult part I had to deal with was my own doubt. Constantly in the back of my mind was the possibility of failure. I had staked whatever reputation I had on the success of the second weekend....

"What if nobody came?"

Of course I knew that some people would come. The question was....

"How many? Would the numbers of people that came be enough. Would the sale of T.U.T Badges increase enough to justify the added expense and extreme effort that the hundreds of local volunteers had put in to holding this questionable expansion of our vital festival."

Worrying would accomplish nothing. There was no choice but to proceed. The support, enthusiasm and all out effort of the majority of the business community kept me going. Word of our T.U.T expansion began to appear in downstate newspapers and I was booked on some local television news shows to promote the event. When our motel phone began to ring with people wanting to make reservations for the second weekend I started to relax a little. They say "time flies when your busy". That was true for me. The third weekend of January 1977 was upon us and Tip Up Town was here. By then, exhaustion overtook me and a visit to the doctor resulted in a diagnosis of walking pneumonia. I was unable to attend the first T.U.T. Weekend. By the second weekend I was able to mosey down to the Tip Up Town site. Arriving to the site I was delighted to see throngs of happy people and families swarming over the ice and nearby shore of Houghton Lake. Later that week the financial report revealed that more badges were sold on the second weekend than on the first weekend. It turned out the weather was extremely cold on the first weekend keeping the crowds down. By the second weekend the weather was sunny and much warmer resulting in a much larger turnout. The second weekend was a success. In the next few years I would be tasked with co-directing the entire festival. Once the concept of two weekends was established many objections were dropped and both weekend activities that began with separate themes were morphed together. The concept of two T.U.T. weekends has continued for forty years bringing tens of millions of tourism dollars to the Houghton Lake area.

Chapter 18

THE TWISTS of FORTUNE

The decision to end my "Jewel" career was quite fortuitous because a few years later I learned that "Jewel Companies Incorporated" had decided to discontinue the "Home Shopping" division. The route salesmen were given the option of purchasing their individual routes and forming a cooperative organization of their own, completely separate from their former parent company. A few salesmen opted to join the cooperative while the majority of them chose to retire or seek other means of employment.

Now that my years with "Jewel were over it was back to looking for a some sort of little business for me to run. Sometime previously I read or heard advice regarding going into business. The advice was to find out what the area was lacking instead of going into a business because it involves something you like to do. Considering that advice led me to realize that the only pizza restaurant in town was located ten miles from my motel in Prudenville. They did not deliver so when I wanted to buy a pizza I had a round trip drive of twenty miles. As did other residents on the west side of this huge lake I live on. I thought....

"Maybe a pizza restaurant is needed closer to my end of town."

I began looking into pizza and other style restaurants. Gail reminded me that we used to buy Little Caesars pizza when we lived in Detroit so we wrote to them. We received some literature from Little Caesars and decided to pursue it further. After submitting financial information and my employment history we were invited to come to Detroit for an interview with Vice President Charles Jones. I was on pins and needles during the interview hoping Little Caesars would find my years with "Jewel", along with a good reference, enough to grant me a franchise. We returned home after the interview and waited for a decision from Little Caesars. A phone call the following week notified us we had been approved for the Houghton Lake franchise. When our Little Caesars unit opened in Houghton Lake it would be Little Caesar's fifty-third store. Note: *Years into the future Little Caesars would have more than five thousand units.* Little Caesars Enterprises was extremely helpful with showing us what was required to get started. They introduced us to an equipment supplier who showed us how to obtain the needed financing. They sent a representative that assisted us in finding a location. Mr. Randall who owned Pinky's Plaza took a huge chance on me when he agreed to new construct a new building to house our Little Caesars Pizza restaurant. We signed a ten year lease and everything was underway in 1977 for a planned opening the following year. Once I was sure we were definitively going forward with a Little Caesar's franchise I contacted "Jewel" with my final termination notice and requested the distribution of my J.R.E. retirement fund.

The following several months were filled with anxious anticipation. I grew impatient as we waited for all the licenses and permits that had to be approved before construction could begin. Aware of the significant impact the summer season had on Houghton Lake business we set a my goal to be open by Memorial Day. Weeks went slowly by while the trees were cleared from the site. More weeks passed as the foundation was poured. It seemed an eternity until I saw the cinder block walls slowly taking shape. Filled with extreme pride and anticipation I was dropping by the site daily to see how much progress was being made. Before long I discerned my constant inquiries were irritating the builders so I decided not to bother them as often.

Part of the agreement with Little Caesars Corporation was to receive the proper training to run a Little Caesars Pizza franchise. I requested the training be in the Detroit area. My mother and Tony had bought a house in nearby Dearborn Heights and she offered to let me stay with them during the two weeks of training. Prior to leaving home to start the training period I received the J.R.E retirement check from "Jewel"for $36,000.00. During my twenty plus years with "Jewel" I had contributed $11,000.00 to the fund and "Jewel" contributed approximately $25.000.00 which was eligible to put in an I.R.A. rollover account. Researching my options I found that First Federal Savings Bank in Detroit offered 15% interest on a five year I.R.A. Certificate of Deposit. I took that check with me to Detroit to open said account while I was there for training. At 15% interest it would double in five years

My training took place at a Little Caesars Pizza Parlor on Grand River Ave. The manager was Peggy Bailey. She was all business and didn't seem all that anxious to train me but she wasted no time putting me "through the ropes". I learned how to crush tomatoes, roll dough, toss pizza crusts in the air and to distribute the toppings according to specifications. Determined to learn as much as possible while at this training store, I bombarded Peggy with all sort of questions. She answered all my queries but did so quite perfunctorily. Peggy seemed surprised when at closing time I stayed to observe her close out the cash registers and complete the nightly paperwork. She asked....

"Don't you want to go home?"

"No! I need to see how the closing paperwork is done."

"Okay, but I won't say anything if you would rather leave."

"I'd like to stay."

When I arrived for work the next day Peggy smiled slightly and said, questioningly....

"Oh! You're back?"

Not sure what she meant by her remark, I ignored it. She was a little friendlier that day and as I returned each day her attitude seemed to improve. After a few days went by she asked me how long I intended to stay. When I said I would be there every day for the whole two weeks of scheduled training she seemed surprised. As I reported for training each day her demeanor improved and we began having real conversations. She revealed that the reason for her standoffish attitude was due to her experience with the only other franchisee she tried to train. According to Peggy after spending only one day being trained, that franchisee abruptly left saying he saw how everything worked and needed to see nothing more. Peggy had assumed all franchisees were like him. By the time I completed the full two weeks of training I grew to like and respect Peggy. I believe she felt the same.

The two week training period that I stayed at my mothers was the most time I had spent with her since Gail and I had moved to the flat on Stoepel more than twenty years ago. The time I was there became an opportunity to reconnect with my mother. We enjoyed talking about old times and as our conversations progressed I gained a better understanding of her as a real person. As I previously related, lavish displays of emotion were not the norm in our family so I was taken by surprise one night when out of the blue she came up behind me, wrapped her arms around me and hugged me tightly. I quickly wiped away my tears while she was still behind me. No words were spoken be either of us. My slight embarrassment was overwhelmed by great relief. It became possible for me to accept that despite all of the perceived wrongs, I harbored in my mind for so long, she loved me, at least a little. I would later learn how fortunate it was for me to be able to spend those weeks with her.

My concern was mounting as spring arrived and a Memorial Day opening for our Little Caesars looked doubtful. Memorial Day came and went and a new goal was set. To open for business by the Fourth of July. That did not happen either but on July 5th 1978 at the age of forty-three I opened our Little Caesars door to the public. During the weeks leading up to our opening I had planned and set up newspaper ads and Grand Opening "fliers" to be released as soon as the Health Department granted us approval to open. The newly hired inexperienced crew was to be trained on the spot by two representatives from Little Caesars

Corporation and myself. One of the "Reps" was quite helpful in pointing out a specific way to maximize my income. I awaited as the hands on the clock progressed ever so slowly to the 11 A.M. opening hour.

"Will the customers come? Will there be enough to justify the time and money we invested. Can this inexperience group of teenage employees perform the jobs they've been assigned to? Will I be able to earn a profit of three or four thousand dollars to supplement the income from the motel?"

These and many more thoughts were racing through my mind as I saw the first car pull into the parking lot. In less than a wink a second car appeared then a third. I looked at the clock it was 10:45 A.M., still fifteen minutes till opening. At 11 A.M. the lot was filled. The doors were opened and throngs of customers poured into the lobby. We were in business *"and how!"* I was elated. This was far more than I expected. The throngs of customers continued almost continually all day and all evening long. Somehow we pulled together and got through it without too many mistakes. The following day was the same, as was the rest of the week. I was walking on air. This was beyond my wildest dreams. At the time I thought Michael Ilitch (Little Caesars founder) was at least a genius if not God himself. I could not be more grateful than I was at the time.

After the first two weeks of business the Little Caesars Corporate representatives left and I was on my own. Business slowed somewhat but was still robust. By the end of the first month my books reflected a profit exceeding the minimum goal I hoped to achieve for an entire year. Having learned from the motel experience the extreme affect the seasons had on business I did not get carried away with our initial success. Instead I saved every possible dollar in preparation for a downturn in business that winter might bring. After a very strong August, business began to slow down as the summer residents departed the area. Weekends were busy during the fall season with color tourists and deer hunters but weekdays were quite slow. Winter weekends were busy when there was enough snow for snowmobilers but very quiet without snow. Christmas week and Tip Up Town weekends gave us a welcome surge in business which carried us through to Spring and Summer. After we closed the books on the first year in business our Little Caesars Houghton Lake store had produced a profit exceeding by tenfold my minimum goal of three thousand dollars. This was triple the highest annual income I had ever experienced. Most of that profit remained in our savings account at the bank.

For the next few years I continued to run my Little Caesars restaurant and help out at the motel as needed. Gail hired people to assist with cleaning motel rooms but it was hard to find good help. Often her help did not show for work and she had to clean all the rooms herself as well as do the motel laundry. The summer season, with all rooms filled, was extremely difficult for her and she was often exhausted at the end of the day. With our newfound prosperity the motel assumed far less importance and Gail was tiring of the daily grind. Additionally a new Holiday Inn Hotel was erected just off the U.S. 27 expressway and we were no longer the second motel from the expressway exit. Then another mom and pop style motel went up on the corner of Old 27 and M-55 and that made us the fourth motel from the exit. Our pizza restaurant was still producing lots of income and we thought it might be wise to sell the motel. We contacted Stark Realty and listed with the same two guys that sold us the Waynorth. Over the next several months they brought a few interested parties but we received no offers.

I continued as a Director of Tip Up Town one more year and then as Co-director with Bill Buckrop and Tom Janise for a few more years. Tip Up Town continued to flourish on both weekends. My term on the Chamber of Commerce expired in late 1976. Busy with Tip Up Town planning, I paid little attention to "Chamber" goings on until two good friends approached me about running for the "Chamber Board" again .I was reluctant but Dick Fuller and Randy Stuck said the "Chamber" was in financial trouble. They suggested the three of us should run for election to the the "Board" and attempt to get the "Chamber" solvent again.. Apparently a few so called "big shot" businessmen had talked the then present board members into paying for the placement of several downstate billboards promoting Houghton Lake as a tourism destination. That may have been a worthwhile goal however the cost was more than the Chamber could afford and they sank tens of thousands of dollars in debt. The plan was for the three of us to get on the board and see if we could alleviate the problem. We submitted our names and all three of us were elected. The new "Board" elected me as treasurer. The billboards were canceled and during the three years I served as treasurer we paid off all the outstanding debt. My secret weapon was to simply say no to spending money we did not have. This strategy made a few "Chamber" members and the manager unhappy but it worked and by the end of my three year term the "Chamber" was "out of the red".

CHAPTER 19

COMING APART

In 1980 on the last day of March the phone rang. It was my brother Jerry calling to tell me....

"Mom's in the hospital."

"What happened?"

"They think she had a stroke."

"My God! I'll be right there."

I threw a few things together and headed for Detroit. I arrived at the hospital to find Jerry and Tony extremely distraught and in a state of semi shock. When I asked how my mother was they seemed unsure of her condition. I could get no information from anyone at the nurses station. All I heard was ….

"You'll have to ask the doctor."

"Where do I find him?"

"He's gone home for the day."

After repeated strong insistence I obtained his number. Down the hall I found a phone and called. A woman answered and I asked to speak to the doctor I heard her abruptly respond....

"He is eating dinner."

"This is an emergency. I have to know about my mother, Mildred Gryzezinski!"

The doctor came to the phone. He responded quite tersely....

"You are interrupting my dinner. I already told your people. Your mother suffered a stroke and is brain dead. She is still alive but there is nothing more we can do. She will not recover. I will see you at the hospital tomorrow. Goodbye!"

I was stunned. Until I heard the doctor utter those words I had not allowed myself to consider such an outcome. Even though I heard the doctor's medical opinion it was hard to accept. Struggling to remain strong and in control of my emotions I found Tony and Jerry who seemed equally stunned when I told them what the doctor said.

The doctor met with us the following day at the hospital. His attitude was more amenable. He calmly explained that her brain was completely nonfunctional and she was only being kept alive by artificial means. He said there was no hope for her recovery and suggested it would be humane to disconnect the various machines attached to her. None of us wanted to do it but after much crying and heartfelt discussion Tony finally agreed to discontinue the life support. We were allowed to go in, one at a time, to make our final goodbyes. I went in her room, sat down next to her bed and took her hand in mine. I felt the warmth of her hand. I could see her chest rise and fall with each artificial breath. It was hard to accept that this woman was really only alive because of the machines she was connected to. A sadness from deep in my being encompassed me. Through a flood of tears, not sure if she could hear me, I spoke to my mother....

"Hi, mom. I hope you can hear what I am saying. I love you so much. I am so sorry this is happening to you. I wish there was something I could do to help you. I know I haven't been a very good son. I know you had a very tough life and you tried your best under the circumstances. I wish I could have been more understanding. Please forgive all the harsh things I said over the years. I am just a stupid kid. I truly hope you find peace. I love you. Please forgive me."

Tears flowed profusely as I kissed her forehead and said a final goodbye. When the three of us had spent the time needed to say goodbye the doctor then entered my mother's room to do what had to be done. Several minutes later he emerged and said we could visit her one last time. I entered the room sat down again and once more took her hand in mine. It was cold! I was struck by the extreme contrast. Only a few minutes earlier I had felt the warmth of her hand and saw the color in her face. Now her hand was cold as ice and her face was a dull gray. Her life was finally gone and a significant part of mine was gone as well.

For the next few days many tears were shed but somehow the three of us got through the funeral arrangements. My mother had requested cremation. I had called Gail with the sad information and she and my children headed south to meet me. I had girded myself for the coming funeral with thoughts that I had made peace with my mother but my rationalization was futile. I sat in the front row with my wife, my brother, and Tony as some sort of eulogy was pronounced. I could hear the words being uttered but nothing was registering. I could think only of the tremendous loss. Not the loss of a life but instead, of all the missed opportunities to share love between a son and his mother. Many years previous, after seeing Leonard break down when his mother died, I had vowed that would not happen to me. No! I would take steps to avoid such a scene. I tried. I wrote to her what I thought was, a nice letter. I felt good that during the two weeks of Little Caesars training we talked over old times and reconnected to some extent. I poured my heart out to her a few days ago as she laid in the hospital, yet, when the time came to take her away in the casket I completely lost it. I broke down unable to contain myself, sobbing over and over. I could not control my grief. I was on the verge of collapse as a river of tears from my eyes mixed with volumes of mucus pouring from my nose covering my chin then dripping on my clothes. I was a mess. My wife and my Uncle Red held me up and kept me from falling over. I was so distraught that even now I cannot remember what happened afterward. I cannot remember anything about the gathering that occurred somewhere. All that was lost in my extreme grief.

Before being hit with this tragic unexpected news we had planned a trip to Virginia. It was to visit with our son,Gary, on the occasion of the Christening of his first child, Aaron. Unfortunately the funeral was on the very day we were scheduled to fly out. Gail took charge. She arranged for us to be put on standby status and the day after the funeral we left for Virginia. I can't relate much of what took place the week we were there. I know we made a trip to Washington D.C. with Gary, his wife Linda and her parents. We visited many historic sites and museums but it is all a blur. Memories of my mother, and my childhood with her completely dominated my thoughts for the entire trip. I cannot even recall returning home.

Chapter 20

ENDINGS OR BEGINNINGS ?

We had tried listing our motel with a few real estate companies but there were only a few "lookers" and no offers. After several months passed without any offers we gave up on listing with any realtors. In 1981 on somewhat of a lark I ran a small advertisement in the real estate section of the local newspaper. It seemed futile at the time but nothing else had worked. The ad ran for a few months with no response. To our surprise one morning we received a phone call from a lady who owned a small resort on Houghton Lake. She claimed a relative of hers who lived in New York wanted to move to Houghton Lake and buy a business. She wanted a few details such as the number of rooms and the actual location. I answered her questions and she said she would have her relative call us if they were interested. I thought....

"This will never happen." and forgot about it.

A few weeks later I received a call from New York. It was the folks that lady had talked about. They were coming to Michigan and wanted to make an appointment to see the Waynorth. I could hardly believe it! All those real estate companies were a waste of time. I received a response from a little two inch ad in the Houghton Lake Resorter. The interested parties came on schedule, made a tour of the motel, asked a few questions and asked the selling price and down payment. They said they would think it over and left. Property values had increased since we purchased the motel in 1973 and we set a sale price somewhat higher than we had paid. I knew if we sold the motel at the proposed higher price along with the increased equity that came from eight years of payments when all was said and done we would come out with a decent profit.

The following day they were back with their offer. They would accept the asking price without any haggling if we would accept a lower down payment. We agreed and the sale was completed. We needed a place to move to so Gail began a search for a house. She found a house located on a canal that lead directly to Houghton Lake. I took time out from managing the pizza store and went to look at the house she was interested in. Considering the variety of previous "dumps" I had lived in, a brick house located on the corner of a canal where I could look out the window directly at the lake was a dream come true. We bought that house. After the details of the motel sale and the purchase of the house were finalized we moved into our new home.

Shortly after we moved I received a call from the owner of the Little Caesars store in Grayling, Michigan. He informed me he wanted to sell his store and wondered if I was interested. When I responded in the affirmative he also informed me that the sale included the building his store occupied. This dampened my early enthusiasm for buying the Grayling Little Caesars. We were leasing the building for the Houghton Lake store. Purchasing the actual real estate required a much bigger investment and a bit more risk. My initial instinct was negative but Gail had the opinion that buying the real estate was a good idea. After reviewing the previous years records of the Grayling store we decided to go ahead. We purchased the the building and business on a land contract. During the ownership transition there were few problems, mostly centered around the different management style. When I informed the Grayling employees they could not smoke in the restaurant while they were working, there was a mass rebellion and all but one crew member walked out. I immediately asked for volunteers from the Houghton Lake crew to help run the Grayling store. Several responded and helped keep the store running until I could recruit and train a new staff. My youngest daughter, Cynthia, was promoted to manager of the Graying store. She turned out to be a good manager. It was a good decision. The Grayling location produced a bigger profit than the store in Houghton Lake and continued to do so for many years.

With two successful stores my confidence level was growing. At the same time Little Caesars Corporate was on a big push to expand and was pushing current franchisees to open more stores. I began thinking about being part of the expansion. During the years I worked as a new customer salesman I had traveled all over Michigan writing orders. I remembered working in Ludington. It was a pretty big town. Maybe it could support a Little Caesars Pizza. A quick look at the demographics revealed it was much bigger than Houghton Lake or Grayling. I applied for the Ludington franchise and it was granted. We opened Ludington in 1983. It was another success story. We were growing fast. In 1985 we opened our fourth store in Manistee, Michigan.

Every year we went to Little Caesars annual conventions. The entertainment was tremendous. At different conventions we were entertained by Dolly Patton, the Oakridge Boys. Lou Rawls, Mellisa Manchester, Bob Hope, Tim Conway and many others. I was a blast but it was also work. We attended every workshop offered, digesting and learning every thing we could about operating multiple franchises. We loved Little Caesars. We were making more money than we ever dreamed possible but no matter our business profits we continued to maintain our conservative lifestyle. Always conscious of where we started in life, instead of driving a Cadillac or even a Mercedes we were content with a "Chevy" or a Ford. We could have a house on Mackinaw Island but our priority was the security of knowing we had the money in the bank. Rather than staying in the luxurious hotels that hosted the Little Caesar conventions we opted to rent a motel room down the street at half the cost. As I progressed down the road of life I determined that having money empowered decision making. Phony status symbols did not. The main themes at the conventions was "Family" and future expansion of the brand. Little Caesar stores were opening along the I-75 corridor all the way to down to Florida. Franchisees were "pumped up" and anxious to take part in the proliferation of Little Caesar stores. We were caught up in the excitement as well. I was constantly looking for new locations to build another store. The small city of Clare, Michigan looked like a possibility also Cadillac was a location I really wanted. There was an existing (out of favor) franchisee already located there. When I heard the scuttlebutt that, "Corporate" would like him out, I let it be known I would like to have the Cadillac franchise. Everything was going so well I even started thinking about the possibility of expanding outside of Michigan. After I let it be known we were interested in expanding out of Michigan the "Corporate" office informed us that new store locations were no longer available on a single store basis. Instead you had to commit to open multiple locations and pay the franchise fee for more than one store in advance. To complicate things I learned there were only a few territories that were not already spoken for. Some areas not spoken for were in Louisiana. We made a trip to review some of the available territories. We looked at Shreveport, Baton Rouge and the West Bank of New Orleans (Jefferson Paris). We decided on the "New Orleans" area. The option for that area required a commitment to open six stores. Our enthusiasm could not have been higher. All our stores in Michigan were in cities or towns with population of ten thousand or less. Our successful store in Grayling had only two thousand residents. There were literally hundreds of thousands of people living in Jefferson Parish. I thought....

"How could we possibly fail?"

We applied for and received the franchise for Clare and the option for six stores in Jefferson Parish. For the next ten years both Gail and I worked day and night managing the affairs of our expanding business. Locations had to be decided on, leases had to negotiated, contractors hired, advertising planned, management trained and financing obtained. I was constantly driving to Detroit Metro Airport to fly back and forth to New Orleans. By 1986 the cost of equipment and remodeling necessary to open a Little Caesars Pizza store had risen substantially. We paid little attention to the eighteen percent interest rates on financing through National Bank of Detroit. Our past success had us on a mental "high". We were sure our venture into the New Orleans area would bring even bigger rewards but we were unaware of events that were conspiring to have a significant impact on our plans.

The oil industry was very important to the economy of the New Orleans area. The OPEC inspired oil crisis caused a rise in the price of oil, bringing boom times to the New Orleans area. In December of 1985, about the time we were working on the New Orleans project, a barrel of oil was $23.00 dollars. As we were planning and implementing the development of the New Orleans area stores the price of oil was declining dramatically. By the time we opened our first store oil prices collapsed to less than $10.00 a barrel. The West Bank area was hit the hardest as tens of thousands of workers lost their jobs and moved out of the area. It almost seems unreal as I recall it now but unbeknownst to us, two rival pizza chains were in the process of opening multiple units in our same market area at the same time. A new outfit called "DePizza Delivery" as well as a new concept from "Pizza Hut" of delivery only units, opened several new stores and began selling pizza in that area before we could open our first Little Caesars store for business.

Despite thousands of dollars spent on advertising to promote the opening of our first Little Caesars store, it met with moderate response from the public. I attributed the slow opening to the suddenly increased competition combined with the dramatic decline in population. Our early enthusiasm faded somewhat. Disappointed but still optimistic we continued with the opening of a second store which also failed to meet our expectations. Year end accounting results showed we were losing money in New Orleans. We turned to Little Caesars Corporate for advice and were told it would take time and more stores to impact such a large metropolitan area. We pursued and obtained approval for another location. In 1987 we opened our third store. It was an improvement over the first two but still far short of the openings of our Michigan stores. Our New Orleans stores lost even more money the second year. For the next few years we continued to open more Little Caesar units in Jefferson Parish with little success. When we turned to various Little Caesars so called experts for advice we were repeatedly told the answer was "more stores".

I was busy planning an advertising campaign for New Orleans one afternoon in early October 1987 when the phone rang. I answered to hear a quiet voice on the other end say....

"Hello Skip... It's Frank, your half brother. I have some sad news. Our father died yesterday."

I remained silent a moment as I attempted to digest this unexpected news. Frank continued to inform me of the location of the funeral home and the time of the burial adding he hoped I could come. I responded weakly....

"I will try to get there."

After hanging up the phone I sat for quite a while trying to process all the thoughts running through my mind. I felt sad, not despondent, but sadness mixed with regret. I was never able to feel close to my father. I met him too late in my life and there was too little contact. I felt sorry for not meeting him that time when I was eighteen years old and we were supposed to go fishing. At that time I was still an immature teenager and so much in love with Gail I could think of nothing else. Had I ever seen him again I would have apologized. Now he was gone. I found myself thinking of all that was lost....

"He would never experience the joy of meeting six of his grandchildren and two great grandchildren and they too would never know him. The possibility of developing a positive relationship with his first born son was also gone. Why didn't he care enough to simply pick up the phone and call me? Did he really hate me that much for becoming Catholic or is there something else wrong with me? Now and forever I will never know"

Although somewhat dejected I decided to make the trip south hoping to achieve some sort of finalization and try to pull the cover closed over the deep hole in my psyche. Two of my children, Cindy and Jeff, accompanied me on the journey. We arrived at the funeral home and as I exited the car I observed several others walking toward the entrance. I was struck by the fact that I was instantly aware of which attendees walking to the entrance were my relatives. They had that "look". Never having the opportunity to interact with my relatives on my fathers side I wasn't aware of the "King look" but there it was on full display. I re-met my brothers and my sister. The last time I had seen them Richard was six years old, Frank was four, Joyce two and Bob was a tiny baby still in his crib. Richard was the spitting image of my father. The long curly hair Frank sported as a four year old was gone. He was now bald. Joyce still had the same twinkle in her eyes. All except Bob were very friendly and seemed anxious to see me. Joyce took my arm and walked me over to meet Bob who seemed quite uninterested to meet me. I attributed his seeming indifference to the sadness he must have been feeling. I accompanied the family to West Mound Cemetery where our father was laid to rest. It seemed strange to observe so many younger people, at the grave site, sobbing and referring to my father as Grandpa. At least (I thought) he had experienced the joy of interacting with some of his grandchildren. I found myself crying quietly to myself still contemplating what we both had missed out on. After the funeral there was a gathering at Frank's house. I was reintroduced to my fathers second wife Anna and my fathers brother, Uncle Frank. I was probably no more than three years old when I last saw Uncle Frank and could only vaguely remember him. As I was about to depart for home my sister Joyce approached to hand me what appeared to be a small well worn envelope and said....

"This is something your father left for you. It isn't much but apparently he wanted you to have it."

On the outside of the envelope the following was written....
For Skippy if alive."

An immediate, indescribable pang went through my body and mind....

"If alive? If alive? If alive? What the fuck! What the fuck! How on earth could he possibly write that? Did he not know my name? Did he not have a phone book? Was he incapable of looking in one to find my phone number? Who was he trying to fool by scrawling that ridiculous statement on an envelope? Me? His other children? I give up! This is the final insult"

Aware of the feelings of my newly reunited siblings I tried to conceal the total confusion, anger, and disappointment simultaneously traversing my mind. I could not then and even as I write this story I cannot understand why or how a man can live his life isolated from one of his children. Adding to my already extreme state of confusion I opened the envelope to find savings bonds in the amount of five hundred dollars issued in the name of Julian Withrow King Junior. I was in a state of unbelief as I bade my goodbyes and left for home. For a few weeks I retreated, as much as possible, from my company responsibilities and spent a lot of time in contemplation. I experienced a great sadness that lasted for several days. Yes my father was gone but I was also perplexed by the savings bonds....

"Why would he write "if alive" on the envelope? He had to know I was alive. I was continually listed in the phone book since 1955. If he decided to purchase those bonds in my name he most certainly would have done something similar for his other children. After all wasn't he was much closer to them? I wonder how much he left them? Even if he left them the same amount, how and when did he come up with so much extra cash? He's gone now, forever, and I have nothing to remember him by but these lousy bonds. What a waste!"

Adding to my depressed state was the recollection of losing the man I called Daddy, when I was ten years old. He, just like my father, never made an effort to look for me or contact me. I had no knowledge of what ever became of him. Rationally I knew it was they who were responsible for abandoning me but the same old doubt resurfaced....

"What's wrong with me? Why didn't they care enough to find me?"

During this very short time away from my hectic life I found myself forgetting the many current problems and reflecting instead on the past. There were even times when, in a funk, I just stared in space thinking of nothing. It was at one of these moments when that suppressed "memory" that had lurked somewhere in the recesses of my mind made another attempt at entering my consciousness. It had laid dormant during the years I faced the challenges of supporting my family, pursuing a "Jewel" career and building my franchise business but it was always there waiting to emerge only to be pushed back. Who knows why? Maybe I had to attain enough years or experience enough of life to be able to consciously process it. I have no explanation for why this remote memory resides in my mind. Apparently it will not go away. I wrote early in this story that I would reveal it later. Some may find it strange (as do I) and some may be disgusted. Much of it remains vague but here it is as much, but not all, came back to me....

"I seem to be a baby, maybe one or two, maybe younger maybe older, and I am lying on a narrow bed next to a woman. It is not clear if she is awake or asleep. The bed is pressed up against a window. I crawl between her legs exploring the area there. A thick sticky substance is on my fingers. I am unsure what I am doing there. Maybe just playing or who knows? Immediately a door opens and my grandmother, Aunt Rie and several others appear in the doorway with an astonished look on there faces!"

This short and fast memory is all that comes back to me. I am unsure of the identity of the woman but I feel it is someone I know. It could be my mother or Aunt Doris but its someone I must have been comfortable with. The puzzle remains. What is this about? Why do I have this distant memory? Is this a real happening? Is it possible I am remembering my birth or is there a darker reason? Why was my conscious mind so determined to repress this revelation for so many years and why was at least this small bit able to fight its way out now? As of this writing this is all I know. I may never know more. I allowed myself to wallow in self pity for a few days but realizing I had many responsibilities before me I snapped myself back to reality and resumed working.

In 1989 one of our stores won a Little Caesars Corporate contest for the largest increase in sales. First prize was an all expense paid trip to watch one of that years World Series games. That October, excited and full of anticipation, we flew to San Francisco to watch game two of "The Battle of the Bays" world series. We stood with hands across our hearts as "The Whispers", an R & B group I never heard of before, sang the National Anthem. The the game itself was not that exciting. It seemed to be over in a blink of the eye and I can't even remember who won. The thrill of it was just to be there and be part of the huge crowds of people in attendance. All expenses were on "corporate" dime so we stayed at an expensive hotel and splurged for dinner at a Ben Ni Ha Ha Has restaurant. We marveled at the magnificent view of the surrounding city as we enjoyed watching the dramatic performance of the chef preparing our dinners. Our flight home was late in the evening on October 16th so we spent the following day taking in the sights of the city in our rental car unaware of what was transpiring far below. We flew back to Detroit, arriving late that night, and drove north to Houghton Lake safe and sound but somewhat tired from the travel and excitement. The next day, a little past 5pm as we watched the news in horror as we saw what had taken place in California's bay area. There were images on the television showing a portion of Nimitz freeway, that we had driven on just hours earlier, had collapsed. Gas lines were broken, fires broke out, buildings we had driven by the day before were severely damaged. Without our knowledge the slow continual grinding of the Pacific Plate and the North American Plate against one another finally resulted in the 6.9 magnitude earthquake that took place less than twelve hours after we left. I sat stunned for a while and reflected on all the close calls that I survived throughout my life and thought....

"In geological time twelve hours is probably less than a hundredth of a second. I have been spared again.... Why?"

Earlier that year we were granted the Cadillac, Michigan franchise. I planned an extensive advertising campaign for the Grand Opening which was fabulously successful. At that years Little Caesars convention we were given an award for that years second highest Grand Opening dollar sales of the year. The only store that had a higher opening was a Little Caesars store in Hawaii. We concluded the Hawaii store could probably sell a lot fewer pizzas at prices substantially higher than ours. Still we were thankful for the success of the Michigan stores that enabled us to cover the New Orleans losses. We continued to explain our problems to Little Caesars Corporate. Representatives from real estate, advertising, and many others all sang the same tune....

"You need more units. With enough units you can form an advertising cooperative and afford television commercials to increase exposure. Other franchisee are coming to your area so you will be able to combine resources."

It sounded reasonable and we continued to open additional stores all of which either lost money or produced minimal results at best. Other franchisees opened units nearby and a "co-op" was formed. All units contributed funds to the co-op, an advertising agency was hired, and a television campaign was launched. We had high hopes that the increased exposure from television advertising would be the answer but the small improvement in sales was not enough to eliminate the yearly losses we incurred. Still we held on believing the answer was "more stores". We eventually had six stores operating there. All of which were unprofitable.

My cousin Bill called me in 1994 to let me know his father (my beloved Uncle Red) had passed away in his sleep. Note: Aunt Polly died a few years earlier. Uncle Red had remarried and was living in Florida. Gail and I attended the funeral and I got up to speak to my cousins regarding what a great positive influence their father was in my life. I think of Uncle Red often. Together with my grandmother he provided me with the view that a normal life was attainable.

In September 1995 while having a drink with friends in the club house after a round of golf I noticed the beer I sipped on had a funny taste. I sat thinking for a minute then feeling slightly off, announced I was going home. Surprised to see me come home a few hours earlier than usual Gail asked....

"Whats wrong?"

"Don't know. Not feeling right."

She took a closer look and said....

"You don't look right. Your face is looks gray. You need to go to the hospital."

"I'll be okay. I just need to rest awhile."

"No! You need to see a doctor. I'm taking you to the hospital."

When I wouldn't get up from the chair I was sitting in she called my son, Jeff. He arrived several minutes later. They each took me by an arm and walked me out to our car. At the hospital they took my blood pressure. The emergency room doctor said,,,,

"Your blood pressure is 238 over 120. That's stroke range!"

"When can I go home?"

"You are not going home tonight. You're being admitted."

I spent three days in Cadillac Mercy Hospital. I was tended to by the doctor on staff During my time there several tests were performed. My blood pressure returned to normal and I was feeling better. About the time I was to be released I asked one of the nurses what the various tests revealed. She told me I would have to ask the doctor. Then added....

"Ask him about your PSA test. It was eight."

I was discharged the following day and instructed to see my family doctor within seven days. I had no family doctor so I arranged an appointment with the doctor that saw me in the hospital. At the doctor's office, a week later, my blood pressure was normal. When I inquired about the PSA test he told me not to worry about it. He asked to see me again in two weeks. After the second office visit he informed me he would not be seeing me again as he was retiring. I asked if I should be seeing another doctor. He said I should and recommended I see Dr. Nair (a cardiologist). An appointment was made and I visited Dr. Nair a month later.

Dr. Nair checked me over completely, reviewed my complete medical history with me then suggested I have a heart catherization to determine any possible problems with my heart. I made an appointment for the heart "cath". Then just as I was leaving Dr. Nair said firmly....

"You need to see a urologist right away."

"Why?"

" Your PSA is too high!"

Dr. Nair was just what I needed. A doctor that was direct and to the point. Hearing him speak left me with no room for vacillation. I did as he instructed. The urologist (Dr. Rez.) reviewed the results of the hospital tests and decided I needed a biopsy of my prostate. I endured the embarrassment of watching the procedure on a television screen with a female nurse in attendance. An appointment to receive the result of the biopsy was scheduled on the same day my heart "cath" was to be done. In late September, at noon, Dr. Nair performed a catherization of my heart. When the the procedure was over I had to lay on my back without moving for three hours after which Dr. Nair informed me I had four blockages in my arteries. Three of them were in excess of 90 per cent. He recommended I have open heart surgery. I was unpleasantly, surprised, thinking....

"How can this be? I feel good almost all the time. It was just once that I felt bad."

My first inclination was to refuse but Dr Nair was confident in his diagnosis and though disappointed in his recommendation I said I would think it over. My next appointment, that same day, was with the urologist to get the results of the biopsy. Dr. Rez. was sitting at his desk looking at a report. I stood holding Gail's hand anxious to hear what he had to say. He turned in his swivel chair looked up at me and said.....

"You have an aggressive form of prostate cancer."

According to Gail, my face went completely gray. Stunned for a moment I said....

"I've heard that often the cancer grows so slow that you die of something else first."

"You have an advanced stage. If you do nothing you could be dead in six months."

I was shaking inside. All this bad news in just a few hours. I could barely compose myself and weakly asked....

"What are my options?"

"You can try radiation or you can have it surgically removed."

"What are my chances for survival?"

"Radiation about eighty-five per cent. Removal about ninety-five per cent."

At that point Gail asked for time for us to discuss the situation. Unable to process all this at once I just stood there not sure what to do. Gail said....

"What do you think"

" I don't know."

"Your chances are a lot better if you have it out."

"I might not be able to have sex anymore."

"I don't care about that. I didn't marry you for your penis."

"Are you sure it would be alright?"

"I'm very sure. I want you with me."

We went back to the doctors office and told him I wanted to have the surgery. We also informed him of the heart "cath" results whereupon Dr. Rez. told us it would be too dangerous to undergo surgery until the heart bypass was done. That settled my decision on the bypass. Dr. Rez told us he could slow the progress of the cancer by inserting, what turned out to be a quite large pill, female hormones, directly into my abdomen once a week until I could have the operation.

The heart bypass was done in Traverse City on November fifteenth 1995. Seven weeks later I underwent the prostatectomy in Cadillac. The two operations left me with a "zipper", only an elite few have seen, from my groin to my neck. Gail and the supervisors handled the Little Caesars business as best they could during my recuperation of several weeks.

Never letting an opportunity pass them by, while I was out of commission, certain of my employees in Cadillac and Manistee conspired to embezzle an amount exceeding more than ten thousand dollars from each of those stores. Recalling the often quoted saying …."What goes around comes around" I remembered my days as a sixteen year old usher and all those late sales I copped at the Tower theater.

My recuperation allowed time for reflection on my health problems, and our lack of success in New Orleans. It caused us to take a more realistic look at our situation. We were only able to stay afloat there by funding the New Orleans bank account with the profits from our Michigan stores but after ten years we had transferred over one million dollars. (Thank God for the Michigan stores). Coincidental with our problems in New Orleans the Little Caesars Pizza "chain" which had grown to over 5000 units in almost fifty states was experiencing a small slump in sales at the same time. Our Michigan stores, while still profitable, were experiencing this same slump and a decline in sales and profits. During the years of struggle to keep New Orleans afloat Gail and I worked long hours without taking a salary. We did everything we could think of to conserve capital. To handle the administration of four stores and more than one hundred employees in two different states we had to hire extra office personnel but instead of renting some office space to accommodate four people we converted one of our bedrooms into a makeshift office. Even so, the loan payments we were still making on the failing New Orleans stores were fast depleting our Michigan bank accounts. Something had to be done. We decided to contact other franchisees and "Corporate" to notify them we wanted to sell our stores in New Orleans. Months passed without any sign of an interested buyer. When we realized there were no buyers for those failing stores we finally decided we could bear no more. I contacted "Corporate" and Michigan National Bank and informed them of our decision to hold an auction for the equipment and close the six New Orleans stores. Arrangements were made with a New Orleans auction house. I signed a contract with the bank guaranteeing all proceeds from the auction would go to partially settle the outstanding balances on the various loans they had granted us.

Finally in December 1996 I flew south to meet the auctioneer. One by one I went to each of the six stores to observe the equipment being auctioned off. I watched in dismay as each piece of equipment was sold for a tiny fraction of the original cost. I stood trembling as pizza ovens that cost us thirty-five thousand dollars went at auction for as little as five hundred dollars. Heartbroken, I struggled to maintain composure as I watched my dreams crumble before me. We had obtained equipment and remodeling loans in excess of one hundred ten thousand dollars for each one of the six stores. The combined total raised at the auction for all six stores was only thirty-six thousand dollars. That was less than half of a single loan for just one store. As required by a prearranged agreement the auction company sent the proceeds from the auction directly to the "Bank". There it was. It was over. Nothing more to do but return to Michigan, get back to work and continue using the Michigan profits to pay off the substantial balances that were still owed on the New Orleans stores. However the Michigan business was also suffering. I had devoted too much time to the New Orleans situation and serious problems with some of the management in Michigan had developed, causing profits there to decline as well. Two of the six stores were losing money. Our financial situation was nip and tuck for the next three years. My confidence was slipping away. For a while we were riding high. It seemed nothing could stop our success. Now dark clouds were gathering overhead and the threatening the forty plus years we had spent building some financial security. Adding to my concerns was the motel we sold on a land contract. A few years after the sale the buyers missed a payment. The following year they missed another. As time passed the Waynorth continued to lose customers as more franchised chain motels located in Houghton Lake. During the period that I was building my little so called "pizza empire" they continued to miss more payments. They were in trouble but I had been too busy to do anything about it. Finally they were more than a year behind in payments. I was worried that we might have to assume ownership of the Waynorth Motel again. Our financial problems continued to escalate.

Many things happened during the ten years we attempted to make a go of it in the New Orleans area. Various franchisees became unhappy with certain "Corporate" actions. I was one of them. A franchisee association was formed to try and resolve some of the differences. I was elected vice president. The inability to come to a mutual agreement on a solution to the grievances of some franchisees evolved into complicated legal entanglements. Attorneys were hired and the resulting battles went on for years. Unhappily, on more than one occasion I had serious disputes face to face with the founder who I once idolized. I wondered....

"How do I get myself into these situations? I am having volatile disagreements with this organization that I was once so happy and grateful to be a part of. "

A welcome respite from our present day problems arrived in early summer 1999. It came in the form of an invitation to attend the 100 year anniversary party for the Jewel Tea Company in Barrington, Illinois. That August we flew to Chicago, rented a car and drove to Barrington. I had been to Barrington twice before when I was still working for Jewel in Detroit. Back then it was the headquarters for the Jewel Home Shopping Service division. It was also the central distribution center and a thriving manufacturing plant where many Jewel products were made and packaged and shipped. The vast grounds had been mowed, hedges were trimmed and a huge tent filled with folding chairs was set up in preparation for the gathering but my heart sank when I saw the deteriorated condition of the headquarters and office buildings. All the doors were locked the huge complex was totally abandoned and in disarray, It was being whispered that the entire complex was soon to be demolished. The Jewel Home Shopping Service where I worked nearly twenty years was no longer. Changing demographics spelled it's demise. Women were no longer content to remain at home and wait for milkman, the Jewel Tea man or other delivery men to call. Many of those one time housewives now had jobs or careers to pursue and were not home to accept deliveries or place orders.

Later we listened to a speech by Bob Woodsome whose hair was now completely white. He looked old and somewhat drawn. As we strolled the grounds with some old Jewel friends from Detroit we encountered my old Detroit boss and mentor, Cliff Anthon. We exchanged pleasantries and small talk. Cliff had retired to Florida. I thanked him the help he provided in my early career. When one of my companions mentioned to Cliff that I was the owner of several Little Caesar stores. Cliff said....

"I'm not surprised. I always knew Skip was going somewhere!"

Feeling humbled and embarrassed, I smiled and remained quiet. A short time later we ran into John Ellen He seemed to be in a hurry to go somewhere I attempted to have a short conversation but he seemed nervous and anxious to get away.

"Nothing lost".... I thought.

Gail was sitting on one of the benches while I was busy talking with another acquaintance from Detroit when out of the corner of my eye I saw a man talking to Gail. Next, he the walked over to me and held out his hand. It took a moment and then I recognized him. It was one of the McCook brothers from Oklahoma. We shook hands and spent a few minutes recalling some of the events from "back then". He informed me that after "Jewel" closed down the routes division some of the old salesman had formed a cooperative and were still running their routes under the name of J. T. Barringtons He told me the cooperative was having a separate meeting that he had to attend but when he saw me he wanted to be sure to say hello. I wished him well and he left for his meeting. I asked Gail what he had said to her. She said ….

"He wanted to know if you were "Skip King' that used to work in Oklahoma City. When I told him yes. He told me that all the guys from his group were sad to see you leave. He said you personally taught him more than anyone he ever worked with and that he really appreciated having you as his supervisor."

I knew I had done a good job during my Oklahoma assignment but I guess I wasn't necessarily sure of how the salesmen felt. It was nice to hear some one said it.

Chapter 21

An Awakening

In 1999 we were growing weary from the stress of several years spent building a successful Michigan business followed by ten more years of our failure in New Orleans. In addition my involvement with the newly formed franchisee association had caused our relationship with the founder of Little Caesars to deteriorate significantly. The excitement and challenge of being in business was losing it's appeal. Confronted with the what seemed to be an unending array of problems we came to the decision to sell the Michigan stores and retire. Accomplishing this sale proved to be more difficult than we imagined. We soon realized that with two of the Michigan stores losing money there would not be a buyer for all six stores. We began approaching individual potential buyers and after many months of negotiations and difficult concessions on our part we were only able to secure buyers for four of the stores. It looked like we would have to "bite the bullet" and shut the doors of the other two stores if we wanted to retire. We would need "Corporate" approval for selling the four stores and approval to close the two stores. Aware I no longer enjoyed any sort of "favored status" with the "Corporate Office" due to my participation in the franchisee association. I wondered if they would grant the required approval or find reasons to withhold or delay the approval. I began to worry over our financial situation. Profits from some of the Michigan stores had declined significantly over the last few years. We had lost a million dollars on the New Orleans venture. Additionally it looked like we would not be getting any more payments on the motel and might have to foreclose. We were too old to start running a motel again and the business climate for Mom & Pop motels had "Gone down the tubes." After forty five years of struggling and planning to secure a worry free retirement I began to wonder....

"Will we have any thing left? Maybe a lifetime of saving money instead of spending it on more and better things for myself and my family was a foolish waste of time. In the end we may wind up with nothing anyway. Maybe I should I have done things differently but I would rather die than return to a life of poverty."

The fear of losing everything was ever present in my thoughts and had been my prime motivator as long as I can remember. I was not going to let that happen.

One afternoon in the late fall of 1999 while still fretting over all the things that seemed to be going wrong in my life the phone rang. It was a call regarding the sale and closure of our Little Caesars Stores in Michigan. I listened apprehensively as the details slowly became clear. The sale of the four stores were approved and we could close the two that we did not have buyers for. A sigh of relief emanated from my being. While I was relating this good news to Gail the phone rang again. I answered. It was a call from the local bank. I heard the bank manager say....

"Mr. King I have the owners of the Waynorth Motel here in my office. The bank has approved them for a mortgage on the motel and I want to know if you are willing to accept a bank's check for payment in full of the balance they owe you on the land contract?"

"Yes."

"There are some documents both you and your wife have to sign. I'll have the check ready for you whenever it is convenient for you to drop by."

"We will be right there."

Neither Gail or I could believe what just happened. We thought we were approaching the brink of tremendous financial difficulties and suddenly in a matter of minutes our two most immediate problems ceased to exist. Back at home, after signing the documents at the bank, we held each close for several seconds envisioning our life soon to be relieved from the demands of customers, employees, government and "corporate" regulations.

Over the twenty years we were in business in Michigan we had leased the buildings for three stores and negotiated to purchase the buildings in the other three cities we operated in. We owned all three buildings free and clear and property values had increased substantially. We found buyers for four of the Michigan businesses and closed the other two. Two of the three buildings we owned were leased to buyers of our Little Caesars franchise businesses and we sold the third one. We had several happy and prosperous years as Little Caesar franchisees but near the end both Gail and I were tired from the years working long hours and happy for it to be over. We finalized the sale of the last store in December of 1999.

As a young man I had hoped to live long enough to see the year 2000 and there it was only a few weeks away. I was prepared to greet the millennium as a "free" man. Free from the whims of anyone else seeking to manipulate or control my decisions. Power over my own life was a goal I set for myself. Discovering the power of compounding interest, in my "teens", allowed me to achieve one of my dreams....

"To accumulate the amount of money needed to earn enough interest to allow me to live without financial worry and not have to work for the rest of my life."

A lifetime, together with Gail, conserving every dollar possible had helped us to attain that goal. At the age of sixty five we were retired with much more than I would have had with "Jewel" if .I had stayed there. Still, we were and still are quite satisfied with living a moderate lifestyle. I never felt it necessary to live in a fabulously luxurious house or to drive the fanciest car available. The security of knowing I would not have to go to sleep in a cold apartment on winter nights, to be confident I would not have to push my car to get it started each time, to know that I could travel on vacation anytime and anywhere, to be able to pay cash for anything I decided I wanted was enough for me. My youthful dream to have enough interest income to live comfortably without working was now a reality.

When I was a very young child I had another dream....

"To have a nice family and a beautiful wife who would love me and live with me in a nice loving home and never leave me alone."

My greatest luck was to have found Gail in my life to make that dream come true. I made many mistakes along the way and there were more to come but I faced the future confident we could survive whatever life sent our way.

While pursuing the expansion of our franchise business the upkeep of our home had been severely neglected. I spent a few years repairing and remodeling our home. After that Gail and I began traveling. We flew to Vegas several times. We took several cruises to Mexico, and the Caribbean. In Alaska we were lucky to get a view of Mt. McKinley on a clear day. We hired a pilot to fly us up in his four seater plane and land on a glacier where we threw snowballs at each other. It was wonderful to be able to spend all that time and share the benefits, we both worked so hard for, with my beautiful life partner. A twenty-one day cruise around the tip of South America from Santiago to Buenos Aires was the best of them all. We cruised around Cape Horn and through the Drake Passage that connects the Atlantic and Pacific oceans. We stopped at the Falkland Islands where we were delighted by the myriad of little penguins hopping to and from the sea.

While on this cruise I experienced another unexplainable experience relating to one of my very good friends. Dick Fuller was one of the first people I met after moving to Houghton Lake. He was a gregarious and friendly fellow with a welcoming attitude toward almost everyone he met. Dick was a heavy smoker and drinker. Wherever you might encounter Dick he had a cigarette and a beer close at hand. I liked Dick... a lot! For more than twenty years we played golf together. We joined the same bowling and pool leagues. For more than thirty years Dick, myself, and several friends spent the first week of November Pheasant hunting in South Dakota. In early 2000 apparently the smoking caught up with him and Dick became ill. He was diagnosed with cancer. He underwent a series of chemotherapy treatments. Family and friends held out hope for his recovery but at the time we departed for this cruise it did not look good. While asleep on the cruise ship early one Tuesday I had a strange dream.... I dreamt I had just walked into the house that Gail grew up in on Sorrento Ave. There on the dining room table lay her father Earl Starr. He was dead. The room was full of mourners. Without a word her dead father arose from the table, walked to me and wrapped me in his arms. Then the dream immediately began to repeat exactly the same with one exception, the man on the table changed, the dead man was now Dick Fuller. He too arose walked to me and put his arms around me. I awoke in a start. I thought it strange to have such a dream and took note of the day and date. When Gail arose later I told her about the dream. Due to earlier experiences with dreams I was concerned for my friend. When we returned from the cruise approximately a week later I immediately searched through the pile of mail and newspapers that accumulated during the several days we were gone. I found the Houghton Lake Resorter that corresponded to the date of my dream and sadly read the obituary for my longtime friend Richard Fuller.

> He died on November 22, 2005.....The exact day of that
> unusual dream! There are things in this universe that
> are not yet understandable. Perhaps never!

One of our vacations was in Gulf Shores, Alabama. We spent a month in a rented house on the Gulf of Mexico. The white sand beaches and beautiful blue water of the Gulf was enticing. We really enjoyed the area. We returned to Gulf Shores a few more times. We began thinking about buying a condo. We thought we could spend our winters in Gulf Shores and rent the condo to Floridians escaping the heat in the summer. Home prices were surging. Everyone was making money on real estate. Why not us (we thought.) We began a month long search and settled on a two bedroom condo five minutes north of the Gulf Beaches. The price was $189,000.00. We had a permanent place to go to every winter. It seemed like a good plan. We were jolted back to reality with the collapse of the housing market soon after. Within the next few years the company developing our condo complex went bust and maintenance became non existent. The previously beautiful pool was covered over with a greenish scum. The spa was non functional. The office doors were locked, The landscaping was overgrown with weeds. The entire complex deteriorated to the point most buyers would not consider a purchase there. The price of some units in that complex fell to a low of $29,000. *"Unbelievable!"*.... I thought.... *"Another big mistake! How do I keep doing this?"*

We could not control what was happening. We had to make the best of it and hope the real estate market would comeback. For the next four years we spent the winter months at that condo then Gail's health began deteriorating. On an early January morning we had our Nissan Minivan completely packed and ready to make the drive south. I filled my thermos with coffee and sat at the kitchen table waiting for Gail. She came out of her bedroom and informed me she was too ill to make the trip. I was disappointed but more concerned with my wife's health. I reluctantly unpacked the van and we did not go to Gulf Shores that year. The following year Gail was again not able to make the trip. After another four years passed without being able to journey to Gulf Shores I concluding Gail would no longer be able to endure the long drive. We listed the condo for sale. It sold for $90,000. Considering the purchase price and the cost of furnishings we lost over $100,000 on our Gulf Shores folly. Looking back on all the major financial mistakes I made, I often wonder why am I not broke. It seems, at times, hard to believe but In fact I am not! As I conclude this story, the habits of a lifetime persist. Conserving money still remains a priority. On any Sunday afternoon you can still find me clipping coupons from the newspaper inserts. We cook most our meals at home instead dining at restaurants. On our occasional visits to a restaurant I always look for and order the least expensive dinner on the menu. We do not throw out leftovers, we eat them the next day or two. As an octogenarian I still mow my yard, clear snow from the driveway and do most maintenance on my home. I intend to keep doing so as long as I am able.

Chapter 22

STILL NOT READY TO GO

On a 2015 Fourth of July family gathering I observed my three year old great grandson, Joey, running excitedly around the house wearing a superman cape. As I watched smilingly I had a sudden impulse to surprise him. I went into the bathroom retrieved a large bath towel from the rack and tied it around my neck to imitate a cape. I had to pull very hard to get the two ends of the towel together around the thickness of my neck. I left the bathroom, ran into the living room intending to surprise and play with little Joey. I saw him laughing and leaping around and I thought I would imitate his actions. I remember laughing and attempting a little jump in the air. I remember feeling woozy and falling. Then all is blank. The next thing I remember is waking up and weakly saying....

"Why are you pushing on me? Stop pushing on me!"

I opened my eyes to see Dave (a local volunteer fireman) bending over me. I can see my granddaughter and the rest of the family all standing around me. Dave and another volunteer fireman are trying to get me on a stretcher. I hollered....

"What are you doing?"

"You're going to the hospital."

"No! I'm Okay. I don't want to go to the hospital"

"Yes, you are going."

I protested as they carried me to the ambulance and continued my objections as they drove the twenty-five miles to the hospital in Grayling, Michigan. I remember being very unhappy in the emergency room as various personnel looked at me and then someone began cutting off my shirt, pants and underwear. Then I felt someone tugging at the towel, still tied around my neck, that was laying underneath me. I yelled out....

"Don't cut the towel! I want that towel!"

By then my family had arrived at the hospital and I heard someone telling me to stay calm. But I repeated angrily....

"I want that towel!"

I heard the emergency room doctor that apparently was in charge of my case say to Gail....

"It's a good sign that he is confrontational. I worry more when they're docile."

I was admitted to the hospital and completely embarrassed when a male nurse cleaned me up and wiped the defecation from my behind. Until then I had not realized I had completely eliminated myself.

The following day when Gail and my daughter Terri visited me in the hospital I learned I had apparently died. For three minutes. I was not breathing and had no pulse. My son in law tried to revive me using mouth to mouth and chest compression, with no response. As a last resort my granddaughter, who is a doctor. gave me a cardiac thump which apparently brought me back. Even after being told those facts I said I did not believe I had died. My son in-law informed me....

"You were definitely gone. Your eyes were fixed!"

If what they told me is true I guess once more I miraculously escaped that ultimate destination. Who knows why? A visit with my cardiologist and further testing revealed the electric signals that tell my heart to beat did not work on one part of my heart. Now I wear a pacemaker.

Once again in 2020 I tested positive for the dreaded Covid 19 virus. With known heart problems, diabetes, thirty pounds overweight and approaching eighty six years of age I had all the high risk factors. For five days I sustained a slight fever, weakness and total loss of taste followed by complete recovery.

I have eluded the so called "grim reaper" many many times during my long life. I wonder how long my good fortune will continue.

CONCLUSIONS

As I complete this story I have attained the age of eighty-seven. The years have brought me the joy of six children, 14 grandchildren and 9 great grandchildren. My oldest great granddaughter is twenty-one so I entertain the possibility of becoming a great great grandfather some day. Looking back, regardless of some of the early unfortunate circumstances of my upbringing it has been a good life. During my long voyage through life I encountered many problems. It is true that several were the result of my own missteps, yet others were thrust upon me, still somehow knew I just had to keep going. A shy little boy that spent his childhood moving more than twenty times to different neighborhoods, afraid to make friends never knowing when another move was due, now sits secure in the same house he has owned for forty years. He can look out the window at a beautiful lake knowing he will never have to move or be alone again. With absolutely no financial assistance from government and only a modest education, determination alone allowed me to attain a financially secure life. A thoughtful reading of this story reveals my constant concern regarding the saving of money. The accumulation of money provides one with power and oh! how I wanted power. Power not over any one else but simply power over my own life.

I titled this book "A Place of Truth" so a reader might expect to find that here. This story is the truth as I recall it. I have attempted to include both the negative and the positive events of my life but not all is told here. I would like to say I have no regrets but that would not be true. I don't believe anyone can spend eighty plus years on this earth without some regrets. I suppose everyone has things in their life that they wish had not happened or that they had not done. Most are probably minor events that one recalls occasionally. But for me not a day passes without being haunted by my significant blunders. I think to myself....

"Why did I put that thorn in my grandmothers heart? Why did I lose my temper and break the leg of that sweet, helpless little doggie? Why would I ever drunkenly strike the face of the woman I love more than life itself? Why couldn't I realize that my mother was an alcoholic and try to understand while she was still alive. Why? Why? Why?"

A few of those closest to me will know of other significant transgressions, not revealed in this story. Those too, never cease to weigh on my conscience. They are left out, not to spare myself, rather to spare the feelings of others who are important to me. To everyone I have caused pain, those still on this earth or those gone to a better world, I truly apologize. Looking back I am most assuredly puzzled by some of the things I have done. Late and alone almost every night in tears of remorse I ask myself....

"What compels me, a man who normally thinks things logically through, to respond to an irresistible inner force motivating or driving me to undertake certain actions without first contemplating the consequences".

So there it is, for good or ill, the story of one man. I started with next to nothing. Many may say I have been lucky and in some ways that is true. Certainly I was fortunate to be born in a country where, through determination and willingness to do whatever necessary, one can rise above any circumstances they find themselves in. I was also very lucky to have lived in an era where a myriad of government welfare agencies standing by ready to provide food stamps, health care, housing assistance and counseling was non existent. Instead I faced the future knowing it was up to me do do whatever was necessary to survive. No one else was going to do it for me. It is unfortunate that so many people today are being deprived of that important motivation. Many years passed by before good luck happened my way but then consider this .... Suppose I had not spent decade after decade conserving every dollar. Suppose instead I had opted for the immediate thrill or gratification offered by simply spending those extra dollars I had available in my pocket or in the bank.

Suppose I had not built a reputation of constant responsibility. Would I have been able to take advantage of that so called luck when it presented itself. I leave it for the reader to decide. The true luck in my life was finding a young girl who truly loved me and would continue to love me, despite all my faults, and share in the struggles of a long and mostly happy life.

In the course of eighty seven years I have made mistakes some of which caused hurt for others and for which I am constantly remorseful but other paths I chose not to follow might have brought them even more pain. (I am not my father!) In the end I can only hope to be judged on the totality of my life. As the few years left for me pass I am assuredly and with great anticipation hurriedly approaching that final....

"Place of Truth."

The End.